The New Italian Republic

Since the fall of the Berlin Wall in 1989 and following the subsequent *Tangentopoli* (Kickback City) scandals, Italian political life has been transformed by the dissolution of the Italian Communist Party and the demise of the Christian Democrats, the Socialists and their government allies.

The New Italian Republic charts the collapse of the old party system and examines the changed political climate that allowed new protagonists such as the Northern League and Silvio Berlusconi to rise to political prominence. The first part of the book sets the crisis in historical context and explores the political changes that resulted from electoral reforms. In the second part, the old party system is analysed with chapters on the main political parties including the Christian Democrats, the Socialists, the Communists and the lay Centre parties. The third section is concerned with the new party organisations and includes chapters on Forza Italia, the far Right, the Democratic Party of the Left (PDS), Communist Refoundation and La Rete. The fourth and fifth sections deal respectively with the wider social and economic aspects of these political changes, with separate chapters on political corruption, the role of the judges, organised crime, the South, the mass media, the labour movement, public-sector reform and economic elites. A final chapter considers recent political changes in Italy within a European perspective.

Stephen Gundle is Lecturer in Italian History at Royal Holloway, University of London. **Simon Parker** is Lecturer in Politics at the University of York.

The New Italian Republic

From the Fall of the Berlin Wall to Berlusconi

Edited by
Stephen Gundle and Simon Parker

London and New York

First published 1996
by Routledge
11 New Fetter Lane, London EC4P 4EE

Simultaneously published in the USA and Canada
by Routledge
29 West 35th Street, New York, NY 10001

Reprinted 1997

Phototypeset in Times by Intype, London
Printed and bound in Great Britain by
Clays Ltd, St Ives plc

British Library Cataloguing in Publication Data
A catalogue record for this book is available from the British Library

Library of Congress Cataloguing in Publication Data
A catalogue record for this book has been requested

ISBN 0–415–12161–2 (hbk)
ISBN 0–415–12162–0 (pbk)

Contents

Contributors

Felia Allum is a Graduate Teaching Assistant in Government at Brunel University.

Percy Allum is a Professor of Politics at the University of Reading.

Martin J. Bull is a Senior Lecturer in Politics and Contemporary History at the University of Salford.

Mimmo Carrieri is Coordinator of Industrial Relations Research at IRES, Rome.

Donatella della Porta is Associate Professor of Local Government at the University of Florence.

Ilvo Diamanti teaches Sociology at the Universities of Padua and Urbino.

Mark Donovan is a Lecturer in European Studies at the University of Wales, Cardiff.

John M. Foot is a Junior Research Fellow at Churchill College, Cambridge.

Alan Friedman is International Economics Correspondent of the *International Herald Tribune* and a regular columnist for *Panorama*.

Paul Furlong is a Senior Lecturer in Politics at the University of Birmingham.

Paul Ginsborg is Professor of Contemporary European History at the University of Florence.

Stephen Gundle is Lecturer in Italian History at Royal Holloway, University of London.

Stephen Hellman is a Professor of Political Science at York University, Toronto.

David Hine is Official Student (Tutorial Fellow) in Politics at Christ Church, Oxford.

Salvatore Lupo is a Professor of History at the University of Naples.

Patrick McCarthy is Professor of European Studies at the Johns Hopkins University Bologna Center.

David Nelken is Professor of Sociology and Head of the Department of Social Change, Legal Institutions, and Communication at the University of Macerata.

Noëlleanne O'Sullivan is researching the Italian media at Gonville and Caius College, Cambridge.

Fiorella Padoa Schioppa Kostoris is a Professor of Economics at the University of Rome.

Simon Parker is a Lecturer in Politics at the University of York.

Carlo Ruzza is a Lecturer in Sociology at the University of Essex.

Oliver Schmidtke is a Researcher at the European University Institute, Florence.

Abbreviations

AC	Catholic Action
ACLI	Catholic Association of Italian Workers
AD	Democratic Alliance
AN	National Alliance
BR	Red Brigades
CCD	Christian Democratic Centre
CEI	Conference of Italian Bishops
CGIL	General Confederation of Italian Labour
CISL	Italian Confederation of Workers' Unions
CLN	National Liberation Committee
CSM	Supreme Council of Judges
DC	Christian Democracy
ENI	State Energy Company
FI	Forza Italia
IRI	State Industrial Holding Company
MSI-DN	Italian Social Movement – National Right
NAP	Autonomous Proletarian Nuclei
NCO	New Organised Camorra
NF	New Family (Camorra)
PCI	Italian Communist Party
PDS	Democratic Party of the Left
PLI	Italian Liberal Party
PPI	Italian People's Party
PRI	Italian Republican Party
PSDI	Italian Social Democratic Party
PSI	Italian Socialist Party
RAI	Italian Radio and Television
RC	Communist Refoundation
UDC	Union of the Democratic Centre
UIL	Union of Italian Labour
USIGRAI	Union of RAI Journalists
STET	State Telecommunications Holding Company
SVP	South Tyrol People's Party

Introduction: the new Italian Republic

Stephen Gundle and Simon Parker

It would not be an exaggeration to describe the events which took place in Italy between 1992 and 1994 as a political earthquake. First a political elite dominated by a party, the Christian Democrats, that had been in power without interruption since 1945, was brought down by grave allegations of extensive corruption and connivance with organised crime, burgeoning demands for reform and the near bankruptcy of the state. With it fell an electoral system that was seen to have guaranteed the irremovable character of this elite. Then the widely expected rise to power of the Left, headed by the former Communist Party, the Democratic Party of the Left, was thwarted by a loose alliance of right-wing parties which won a resounding victory in the March 1994 election. The most remarkable feature of this development was the emergence as a political leader of the media mogul Silvio Berlusconi, whose own Forza Italia movement was founded only two months prior to the poll – using the skills and resources of his Fininvest empire and in particular its advertising arm, Publitalia. Scarcely less striking and ostensibly more disturbing was the success of another component of the Right alliance, Alleanza Nazionale. For the first time since World War II a party with roots in the fascist regimes of the inter-war period broke through the legitimacy barrier and achieved a place in government. The brief duration of the Berlusconi government (May to December 1994) did not lessen the broad significance of these events. Although faith in traditional parties of government and opposition was in decline everywhere in the advanced industrial world, and modern media techniques tended in the 1980s to displace traditional forms and vehicles of political mobilisation, the complete meltdown of a long-established and apparently immovable party system was without parallel in an established democracy. The only approximate equivalent, the fall of the Fourth French Republic, occurred in the context of a colonial crisis and potential civil war.

The purpose of this book is to examine the events and circumstances which contributed to this watershed in the history of post-war Italy. Our aim is not to provide a total account or a complete explanation of a crisis that continued to evolve even as we were assembling the volume and which may well not have run its full course for several years. Rather it is to offer material for reflection and some keys to interpretation. The book is divided into five sections. In the first, the origins, forms and trajectory of the crisis are explored. The second and third sections focus respectively on the parties that dominated politics from 1945 and the new forces that have replaced them. In the fourth and fifth sections changes in the party system are examined from the point of view of civil society and of the economy. Finally, the Conclusion considers the crisis and its outcomes in relation to other political transitions and wider trends in comparative politics.

The essays presented here do not focus exclusively on recent events. In particular the chapters in the second section range widely over the history of the Republic. However, the main thrust of the discussion, as the subtitle indicates, is concerned with the period between the fall of the Berlin Wall in November 1989 and the downfall of the Berlusconi-led government in December 1994. This reflects our belief that, although the Italian state and political system long exhibited numerous defects, the collapse of the parties and the proportional system was due to a specific set of developments. We take 1989 as the starting-point because the end of the Cold War in Europe undermined the anti-communist cleavage around which much of the political system had been organised, and caused various irregularities and forms of gross maladministration to be exposed to empirical scrutiny and political sanction on the part of an electorate that had long seemed impervious to them.

Both Paul Ginsborg, in the opening chapter, and David Hine in the concluding one, offer their own interpretations of the crisis in its broader context, the former focusing in particular on the social, economic and cultural dimensions of the crisis, the latter reflecting on the constitutional significance of these changes through a comparison with other European political systems. Our intention in this introduction is to provide a brief account of the political process between 1989 and 1994, a survey of the reasons why the right-wing alliance won the March 1994 election and some considerations of the implications of this victory.

THE MAKING OF THE CRISIS

The first sign that public opinion in the country as a whole was moving decisively away from the established parties came in June 1991. Although little coverage was given by officially controlled media to the referendum to end the system of multi-preference voting, and though leading politicians clearly hoped that a low turnout would render the result invalid, in fact 62.5 per cent voted and 95.6 per cent endorsed the proposal. This dealt a blow to the political elite, as Simon Parker shows in Chapter 2, and was a major triumph for those who sought to promote reform by

modifying procedures that had facilitated the rise of irresponsible government and corrupt electioneering.

The result of the general election of April 1992 may be seen as a direct
outgrowth of the 1991 referendum. For the first time since 1948 the four-
party coalition failed to poll a majority of votes cast. The Christian
Democrats' share of the vote fell below 30 per cent, while the Socialists
saw the slow but steady expansion in their electoral fortunes come to an
end. Although the parties conserved a slender parliamentary majority,
their leaderships were no longer in a position to control the political
game and allocate positions within the state at their pleasure. Following
the resignation of President Francesco Cossiga, one month ahead of the
end of his seven-year mandate, no official candidate succeeded in winning
majority backing from the electoral college. Only after the country's top
anti-Mafia investigator, Giovanni Falcone, was murdered near Palermo
on 24 May was the stalemate overcome. The new President, Oscar Luigi
Scalfaro, was a fervent Catholic and former DC interior minister, regarded
as a man of transparent honesty and renowned independence of the
factions within his party.

It had been expected that President Scalfaro would offer the post of
Prime Minister to the PSI leader Bettino Craxi. But in April and May
the anti-corruption investigations in Milan which had yielded their first
victim, the Socialist administrator Mario Chiesa, in February, developed
into a major scandal which took the name of *Tangentopoli* (Kickback
City). With Chiesa's collaboration, the prosecuting magistrates, whose
role is examined by David Nelken in Chapter 12, exposed a network of
corruption that had assumed the character of a well-organised system.
Current and former legislators in the city belonging to the PSI, the DC,
the PRI and even the post-communist PDS were arrested on charges of
taking bribes and rake-offs on public works contracts and illegal financing
of political parties. As Donatella della Porta shows, these practices became
widespread in local government in the 1980s. When the judges sought
Parliament's permission to start proceedings against two Socialist deputies
who were former mayors of Milan, Craxi was forced to remove his own
son from the post of PSI secretary in the city. These events fatally damaged the Socialist leader's prospects of becoming Prime Minister and
brought an end to a political career that is assessed by Stephen Gundle
in Chapter 5. Instead, another Socialist, the law professor turned politician
Giuliano Amato, formed a government that included a number of
respected experts in place of controversial former ministers.

Subsequent events showed that the Amato government constituted the
last chance for the parties to redeem themselves and restore their rapidly
ebbing credibility. The Prime Minister began purposefully. He listed his
priorities as institutional reform, the public sector deficit, anti-corruption
legislation and the campaign against organised crime. It was the last of
these that provided Amato with his first test. In July the Mafia struck

again in Palermo, killing Falcone's close associate, the judge Paolo Borsellino. In response the government issued an anti-Mafia decree that was rapidly turned into law with the support of the main opposition parties. Amato also moved decisively in tackling Italy's impending financial crisis. Throughout the 1980s the national debt had been allowed to rise, until it reached 10.5 per cent of Gross Domestic Product in 1992 – nearly three times the European Community average. Interest charges alone for the year amounted to the equivalent of the entire budget deficit, which by October was projected at 160,000,000 million lire. In order to meet an imminent revenue shortfall in the second half of the year, an emergency package of measures was forced through while plans were formulated for reducing the public sector, partly through privatisation, and removing it from the sphere of political patronage. Amato also responded swiftly in September when speculation on foreign exchange markets first forced a devaluation of the lira by 15 per cent and then compelled the government to withdraw the plummeting national currency from the Exchange Rate Mechanism (ERM) of the European Monetary System. Sweeping cuts to public spending and an emergency budget were introduced, while a rigorous austerity package for 1993 was approved that entailed reforms in the health service, pensions, the civil service, local administration and the system of revenue collection. Steps were also taken towards privatising state holdings in banking, foods, engineering, insurance and energy. According to Fiorella Padoa Schioppa Kostoris (Chapter 19), such steps were long overdue.

The result was a restoration of international confidence that permitted the Bank of Italy to lower the discount rate by steps to 12 per cent, easing the high interest rates charged to industry by the banks. For a government that had not been expected to survive for long, it was a notable achievement. Yet Amato was unable to restore confidence in the parties, which saw their standing decline markedly in local elections in June, September and December 1992. Nor was he able to head off the referenda sponsored by Mario Segni's movement for political reform that eventually sounded the death knell for the DC, the PSI and their system of power in April 1993. Amato increasingly took on the character of a technical rather than a party political Prime Minister and, following the referenda, he was replaced by a genuine technician, the governor of the Bank of Italy, Carlo Azeglio Ciampi, who was the first non-deputy to become Prime Minister in the twentieth century. The Ciampi administration carried on the work of its predecessor in the economic field, but otherwise it was a transitional government whose principal task was to ensure the passage of a new majoritarian electoral law to replace the proportional one partially abrogated by the April referenda, and prepare the way to fresh elections.

There are three main reasons why it proved impossible to arrest the decline of the established parties of government. In the first place, many of the measures adopted by Amato were unpopular: they involved extra taxes, including in July 1992 a special one-off tax on property and savings, and a brusque reduction in the flow of public funds which weakened links to traditional clienteles. Second, while the parties allowed Amato to tackle economic matters with relatively little interference, they retained control of political reform. A 60-member bicameral commission was established by Parliament to work on proposals for electoral reform that needed to produce a new law by the end of 1992 if the referendum (which eventually took place the following April) was to be avoided. But it failed to reach any agreed conclusions, with the result that Italians were called upon to formulate a decision that, in the context in which the referendum took place, took on the characteristics of a judgement on the party system as a whole. The third and ultimately most important reason was the continuing anti-corruption investigations which led to the arrest of numerous businessmen as well as politicians on the orders of Milan magistrates – prompting similar inquiries in Rome, Naples, Reggio Calabria and other cities. By the end of 1992 nearly one hundred members of Parliament were under investigation for corruption. The highest echelons of the parties were soon reached. In December 1992 Craxi received the first of a series of notices that he was under investigation, and in February 1993 he finally resigned as secretary of the PSI. He was later followed by the leaders of the Republican, Liberal and Social Democratic parties, whose fate is discussed by Mark Donovan in Chapter 6. Although Parliament on occasion blocked requests to proceed against politicians, the exposure of systematic corruption continued apace, and cast discredit on all established parties, although not in equal measure. Amato remained in office throughout this time, but no fewer than five of his ministers were obliged to resign between February and March 1993 and, by defending Craxi's political reputation, the Prime Minister tied himself to the old system in the public mind. This linkage was confirmed when he sponsored a highly unpopular measure to decriminalise retrospectively the offence of illegally financing political parties: a measure which following widespread protests had to be withdrawn, and which President Scalfaro in any event refused to sign.

Support for the Christian Democrats and the Socialists held up in the South well into 1993 even as it crumbled rapidly in the North. But even this area, which as Salvatore Lupo shows was not as immune to change as some believed, began to waver when magistrates moved on to the offensive. Far from being intimidated by the murders of Falcone and Borsellino, Sicilian magistrates redoubled their efforts to combat the Mafia. Thanks to the collaboration of repentant *mafiosi* (the so-called *pentiti*), several crime bosses were arrested including Salvatore Riina, the alleged chief of the Mafia who was captured in January 1993 after twenty-three years in hiding. As part of these successes new light was shed on the complicity of politicians. Connections between the DC and the Mafia had been highlighted in March 1992 when Salvo Lima, a prominent Sicilian Christian Democrat, was assassinated. This was widely interpreted as a 'message' from the Mafia to the head of Lima's faction, Giulio Andreotti, that 'debts had to be paid'. From the revelations of the *pentiti* it became apparent that Lima was the point of contact between the Mafia and the DC's Rome leadership. He was killed because he failed to deliver the acquittal by Italy's supreme court of the *mafiosi* convicted in the maxi-trials of the late 1980s. Thanks to these testimonies precise links were uncovered between the Mafia and Andreotti, whose faction drew much of its support from Sicily. The *pentiti* asserted that Andreotti had met with Riina and other bosses and that he had urged the murder of the right-wing journalist Mino Pecorelli in 1979 and of the anti-Mafia prefect Carlo Alberto Dalla Chiesa in 1982 because they were in possession of sensitive information concerning the 1978 kidnap and murder of the then President of the DC Aldo Moro. Andreotti vigorously protested his innocence and called for an early trial when Parliament voted to lift his immunity from prosecution in May 1993. But enough damage had been done to end the most remarkable and enduring political career of the Republic. Revelations of this sort were not confined to Sicily. In their chapter Percy Allum and Felia Allum explore how the careers of Antonio Gava and other Neapolitan Christian Democrats also came to an abrupt end when their connections with the Camorra (the Neapolitan Mafia) were exposed.

That the restoration of legality in public life should have heralded the downfall of an elite that had prospered in a climate of systematic illegality was, if not inevitable, then a strong likelihood. What requires explanation is why the investigations were not blocked or suppressed as had so often occurred in the past. To deal with this issue it is necessary to consider the broader context. The explosion of *Tangentopoli* was certainly the moment when the crisis broke through the surface of the political system – with such force that no television bulletin or news headline could report anything else for months after. However we interpret *Tangentopoli* not as the causal moment in the eruption of the 'revolution', but as part of a conjunctural crisis in Italian democracy which resulted from major shocks to a political system that found it increasingly difficult to reestablish a point of equilibrium after several of its traditional supports were removed or weakened.

From the late 1980s onwards, Italy's power elite was undermined by certain foreign and domestic trends which were to a large extent related. Since the advent of Mikhail Gorbachev in 1986, the Soviet Union had been moving towards a 'post-communist' society which in just a few years demolished many of the assumptions on which East–West relations and Western domestic politics had been based. The crisis of 'really existing socialism' in the East inevitably had major repercussions for the few remaining mass communist parties in the West. The secretary of the Italian

Communist Party, Achille Occhetto, reacted to the fall of the Berlin Wall in November 1989 by proclaiming that the party should cast off its Communist identity and transform itself into a thoroughly Western, reformist force belonging to the Socialist International. The fall of the regimes of Eastern Europe – which even in the 1970s the PCI had held up as an example of a superior type of social organisation – and the protracted and divisive process of transition both weakened the party electorally. The background to these events is examined by Stephen Hellman in his chapter on the PCI, while Martin Bull and John Foot focus on the two parties which were born after its demise. The mistake the PCI's opponents made was to believe that the collapse of Eastern Europe would only have negative consequences for the Left. In fact one of the first consequences of the end of the Cold War and the collapse of the Soviet Union was the discovery of the existence of a 'stay-behind' network (*Gladio*) set up by the Americans in the 1940s. The purpose of this amateur para-military organisation was to carry out sabotage and guerilla warfare in the event of a Communist invasion. As such its patriotic role was sternly defended by President Cossiga and others. Yet it soon became clear that it had been manipulated for internal purposes, and that its structures had been used by those plotting military coups in the 1960s and 1970s. This in turn led to questions about the involvement of the security services in the neo-fascist bombing campaigns of the period and to the role of successive Interior Ministers. In consequence a shadow was cast even over some senior DC members who boasted unblemished reputations. Despite all this the parties of government, and especially the DC and the PSI, continued complacently to assume that the 'triumph of capitalism' was an endorsement of the rather peculiar form it had assumed in the context of post-war Italy. With the United States – the Christian Democrats' long-standing 'friendly uncle' – now no longer keen to protect an increasingly discredited government in the interests of anti-communism, the old guard found themselves struggling to conserve power.

In the local elections of 1990, the Lombard League won 18 per cent of the valid vote in the provinces of the North which had traditionally been a bedrock of DC support. Suddenly a new political actor had entered the scene, and the Italian political landscape began to undergo a dramatic transformation. Umberto Bossi's party had broken the spell of the Cold War years that in the veteran journalist Indro Montanelli's famous phrase had induced many of those who feared Communism 'to hold [their] noses and vote for the DC'. With the official proclamation of the death of world Communism, there was now no need to choose the lesser of two evils. As Ilvo Diamanti shows, the League presented itself as a non-leftist force which eschewed the insider language and official values of the old party system. Bossi and his acolytes said the unsayable and said it with great relish: 'there are too many immigrants spoiling our pleasant northern towns and villages'; 'the government in Rome is run by thieves and *mafiosi*'; 'your taxes are used to support feckless DC-voting southern families', and 'all the traditional parties care about are big business and the union barons'. It was not subtle, but – especially in a climate of deepening recession – it was effective, and for a long time the established political elite was unable to come up with an appropriate response.

As the League succeeded in placing the issue of federalism firmly on the Italian political agenda, the Treaty on European Union was signed at Maastricht in December 1991 – seen by many as a decisive move towards a federal European political and economic system. Verbally at least, virtually all Italy's political parties subscribed to an ardent European outlook, even though Italy had one of the worst records in the Community for implementing Commission directives. However the Maastricht Treaty opened a new phase in which the room for divergences between word and deed was sharply curtailed. Under pressure from business to ensure that Italy remained on the fast track of Economic and Monetary Union, and convinced that the Treaty provisions would constitute a useful disciplining mechanism, the then Prime Minister, Giulio Andreotti, signed up to a set of convergence criteria that could not possibly be met in the short or even the medium term. In this way the government unwittingly paved the way to the lira's ignominious exit from the ERM, which was likened in the press to Italy's historic defeat in the World War I battle of Caporetto.

The reasons for the weakness of the lira were different from those which led to the simultaneous withdrawal of sterling from the ERM. In the Italian case the weight of the massive public sector debt was a key factor. This was itself the legacy of ten irresponsible years in which economic growth had been allowed to fuel spiralling public spending without any measures being adopted to render the public administration or the state industrial sector more efficient and cost-effective. In the competition between the Socialists and the Christian Democrats for clienteles, questions of the public interest simply did not figure. To tackle these problems was all the more difficult when the phase of expansion of the mid-1980s came to an end, and it proved beyond the capacity of conventional political leadership to deal with the economic consequences.

WHY BERLUSCONI WON

Although the parties of government conserved some institutional power up until the 1994 election, they were decimated by the corruption investigations and weakened by the loss of much of their support. Their eclipse was confirmed in council elections which took place in June and November 1993 in a range of important cities, and under a new system which allowed citizens to choose their mayor directly in two rounds of voting. In no case did any member of the DC, the PSI or any other government party reach the second round. Instead in virtually every case candidates backed by the Left duelled with the Right, the League in the North, the MSI in the South. Although the League conquered Milan in June, it was the Left that won in Turin, Genoa, Rome, Naples, Venice, Palermo, Trieste and other cities. The scene seemed set for the Left, for so long excluded from office at the national level, to win power once a new electoral law was approved.

Several chapters in this volume offer insights into why, instead, it was the rightist coalition headed by Berlusconi that swept to power in the elections of March 1994. To say simply that Berlusconi won because he deployed the immense media resources at his disposal is insufficient, although these undoubtedly constituted a formidable launch-pad and a source of advantage over his adversaries – especially given the role they played in Italian modernisation in the 1980s. However it is also necessary to consider the context in which the elections occurred, the impact of the new electoral law, and the strengths and weaknesses of the two alliances. First of all it should be borne in mind, as Ginsborg argues, that the downfall of the parties did not occur as the result of any great popular protest or mobilisation. Although the revival of a civic spirit in the South was important, most people simply watched as the judges proceeded pitilessly and the financial crisis unfolded. Moderate voters in particular were disoriented by the removal of their traditional political reference points, and in some cases voted for the Left in the local elections because there was no other acceptable alternative. The DC's attempts to put its house in order and relaunch itself as the Partito Popolare Italiano, as Paul Furlong shows, came too late to be credible or to prevent the Catholic party from splitting. Berlusconi perceived that whereas the League and the National Alliance could appeal to sectional and regionally specific electorates, a new national force was needed if the moderate social bloc that had sustained Italian governments for more than four decades was to remain intact and conserve its dominant position. When it became clear that the existing parties of the Centre and Right failed to respond to the alarming local victories of the Left by submerging their differences, he gave the go-ahead for Forza Italia clubs to be formed and entered the fray himself. Berlusconi appealed not only because he was 'new' to politics, although this was important, but also because he was reassuring and populist. In the public mind he represented prosperity and consumerism, television and football. Patrick McCarthy draws attention to Berlusconi's special appeal as a self-made man to Italy's vast commercial lower middle class, while Alan Friedman sheds further light on his outsider status with respect to the traditional economic elite.

Berlusconi proved to be an able mediator and a formidable campaigner. Forza Italia bridged the gap between the two incompatible forces of the Right by forming separate alliances with the League in the North and Alleanza Nazionale in the Centre and the South. It also made great play of the fact that it was the newest force on the scene at a time when everything associated with the old order was discredited. Despite Berlusconi's notorious connections with Craxi's Socialist Party, he appeared to many to be just the national saviour he perceived himself to be. Essential to his attraction was the priority he gave to economic issues. There was much adverse comment in the serious press about his rash pledges of a 'second economic miracle' and a million new jobs. But these ideas caught the imagination both of those engaged in productive or commercial activity and of those, especially young people, who were excluded from the labour market. Fifteen years after the Reagan and Thatcher revolutions, Italians were offered a similar ideology of deregulation and self-interest. Berlusconi's criticisms of the judges, which were echoed in ferocious terms by various allies and subordinates, should also be seen in this light. Few Italians were displeased to see corrupt politicians knocked off their pedestals, but the proliferation of inquiries and arrests in the business sector had adverse economic effects and spread fear among the many who operated in situations of semi-legality. To such people the whole process of moralisation seemed to be going too far. To these groups must be added a range of other clienteles and established interests, some of whom had not turned their backs on the old parties, who were profoundly disturbed by the implacable rationalisation enacted by Ciampi's technocratic ministers, who paid little or no attention to the need to build political support. Continuity with the old was most evident in the way the Right played on the fear of communism. It appeared bizarre, to say the least, that, after the demise of the Soviet Union, judges, television journalists, the foreign press and anyone else who opposed the Right should have been labelled as communists. But in fact this was a skilful mobilisation of a rallying call that conserved a certain cultural appeal and corresponded to the collective mentalities of moderate voters even after its decline as a political fact.

It is likely that Berlusconi and his allies would have won even if the Left had fought a flawless campaign, but in fact it made a number of errors, as Ginsborg, Bull, Foot and Parker point out. The Progressive Alliance grouped together no fewer than seven left-wing forces, including both the PDS and the left-wing splinter party Rifondazione Comunista (which lent grist to the Right's mill), the remnants of the PSI, La Rete and Alleanza Democratica as well as some left-wing ex-Christian Democrats. There was a lack of clear leadership as no Prime Minister designate was indicated; there were damaging disagreements over policy; and there was an absence of any suggestive vision that might have caught the popular imagination. Instead of seeking to win over the interests that had abandoned the DC and its allies, the alliance focused on winning the backing of domestic and foreign economic elites. Berlusconi was not challenged but rather demonised. Occhetto for example attacked him as a potential Latin American style dictator – but this had the effect of personalising the contest, which was precisely the objective of Berlusconi's campaign team. In addition, there were tactical errors. The left-wing vote suffered from a dispersal in the proportional section as no common candidates were put forward, and all but the PDS and RC failed to reach the minimum 4 per cent required to achieve a share of the 25 per cent of seats in Parliament that continued to be allocated on a proportional basis.

THE BERLUSCONI GOVERNMENT

The accession to power of the Right, with Berlusconi himself assuming the office of Prime Minister, provoked widespread controversy abroad. This was not mirrored on the whole in Italy, for the result of the election was unequivocal and undisputed by the defeated parties. But the statements of ministers and the actions of the new government soon gave rise to negative reactions.

Broadly speaking, there were three areas of concern. In the first place the presence in government of members of the MSI – albeit in the guise of National Alliance – was disturbing. Although its leader Gianfranco Fini was born after World War II and did much to modernise the appeal of his party – as Carlo Ruzza and Oliver Schmidtke show – its roots were Fascist. Indeed the party had been founded in 1946 by Mussolini's surviving henchmen from the Republic of Salò. Fini was careful to define his revamped party as 'post-fascist', but he refused to embrace Italy's post-war tradition of anti-fascism and even let slip a remark about Mussolini being the country's greatest statesman in the twentieth century. Second, there was concern about the extraordinary concentration of power in Berlusconi's hands. If one of the components of democracy is the separation of powers, it was at the very least irregular that one man should control such economic resources, including a substantial slice of the broadcast and print media, and also hold the most important political office. The absence of rules to deal with this eventuality, and Berlusconi's reluctance to divest himself in any meaningful way of his holdings, created a great number of potential conflicts of interest and introduced a grave element of distortion into the functioning of Italian public life. It is true, as Ginsborg and Hine point out, that Italy's transition is one that has taken place within a consolidated democracy, but the questionable democratic credentials of one component of the government coalition, the unequal resources of another and the incomplete nature of the legal system of checks and balances, created a situation in which a deterioration in the quality of democracy was a distinct probability – as Adrian Lyttelton argued forcefully in the *New York Review of Books* (1994).

The economy constituted the third area of concern. Under Amato and Ciampi stern measures were undertaken to tackle the recurring budget deficit and the public sector debt. Remarkably, cutbacks were achieved without destroying the social peace: as Mimmo Carrieri shows, these relatively neutral governments were in fact more successful than their predecessors in securing compromises between capital and labour. There were fears that the Berlusconi government would both fail to continue the work of correcting past abuses and that it would penalise the less well-off, giving rise to a new season of social conflict. The first fear derived from the nature of Berlusconi's electoral programme – promising wealth and rewards without sacrifices or tax increases. As an entrepreneur more concerned with advertising and retailing than production, his recipe for a relaunch of the economy was to fuel a consumer-led boom. The second fear sprang from the nature of the social bloc which sustained the electoral victory of the Right. Although housewives, young people and even a significant number of workers voted for the Right, the bulk of its support came from a commercial and self-employed middle class that was predominantly northern and urban. No component of the organised labour movement was included.

From the start the right-wing government found itself on shaky ground. The great length of time it took to form the government and the extreme wrangling that was involved set the scene for a period of instability and disputes over policy and position that were even worse than those that characterised the five-party coalition in the 1980s, when competition between the Socialists and the Christian Democrats was at its height. Especially turbulent was the Northern League. As the force which acted as the political catalyst of the crisis, it was angry to see itself supplanted and a large part of its electorate seduced by Forza Italia. It was also disturbed by the number of recycled Christian Democrats and Liberals that occupied government posts. Its unease was compounded when Forza Italia and National Alliance formed a close working alliance and began to implement a struggle for power within the institutions – broadly excluding the League from the share-out of posts.

The assault on positions within the para-state sphere began with RAI. As Stephen Gundle and Noëlleanne O'Sullivan show in Chapter 13, there was deep hostility to the transitional board appointed under Ciampi as it was keen to render RAI more competitive and also because there had been a swing to the Left in news coverage. There was a desire to grasp all positions and render RAI tame and limited in scope. However the process did not stop here. In IRI, STET and a whole host of other agencies there were moves to consolidate the Right's influence. Even the long independent Bank of Italy came into the firing line. In a series of editorials in *La Repubblica*, Ciampi's Minister of Public Administration Sabino Cassese sounded the alarm about this new and virulent form of political control, which, unlike the old practice of *lottizzazione*, systematically excluded the opposition (Cassese 1994a, 1994b).

There were other ways in which the process was simply one of normalisation. A halt was called to Cassese's reforms to the civil service and also to reforms to the system of public contracts – which had barred companies guilty of having been involved in corruption from submitting tenders. The first measure was designed to appease civil servants, who voted *en masse* for National Alliance and Forza Italia. In the second case, the ostensible aim was to remove restrictions on business and ease up the economic recovery. But it also meant a reduction of vigilance on corruption. Graver still was the attempt in July 1994 to downgrade the crime of bribery – echoing Amato's earlier moves. The difference was that whereas Amato had acted to try to save his political mentor (Craxi) from ignominy, the new government was concerned to pre-empt any move by the prosecuting magistrates to extend their inquiries to Fininvest. The threat of the *mani pulite* pool to resign, and widespread public anger following approval by the cabinet of a decree designed to impede the preventive detention of alleged bribers and corrupt politicians forced the government to retreat. The decree was dropped, and instead a campaign of intimidation and vilification was waged against the Milan investigating team. This reached fever pitch in November when Berlusconi himself fell under judicial investigation in connection with bribes paid by Fininvest to Milan's financial police.

In economic policy, the government fulfilled fears by failing to carry forward the austerity policies of Amato and Ciampi. While Berlusconi was zealous in defending his private interests, he failed to tackle the national debt, neglected to defend the lira and presided over an extraordinary flight of capital. The government broke with the unions and concentrated its efforts to reduce spending on cuts to the health service and pensions. In this way it penalised salaried workers and provoked accusations that it was pursuing a class-oriented policy. A one-day general strike on 14 October 1994, and a demonstration on an unprecedented scale in Rome in mid-November in protest against these provisions of the Finance Bill highlighted growing public hostility to an economic policy which Berlusconi had attempted to portray as being without victims.

Overall the right-wing government displayed a marked lack of statecraft. There were examples of practical incompetence, gaffes, public disputes and an absence of stability and direction, two essential ingredients for sound government. In addition there was a disturbing lack of respect for constitutional propriety. But despite this the administration proceeded in a way that broadly met the expectations of the main components of the social bloc that sustained it. In this sense it may be said that it acted strategically and that it began the process of consolidating its position at all levels. For this reason the Right maintained a very high level of support, despite the Prime Minister's difficulties with the magistrature and the withdrawal of the League from the majority, which precipitated Berlusconi's resignation in December 1994. Under President Scalfaro's direction, a stop-gap technocratic administration was formed the following January, headed by the former Director General of the

Bank of Italy and Berlusconi's Finance Minister Lamberto Dini. This was charged with undertaking emergency measures to deal with the financial crisis, tackle pensions reform and establish new rules of fair play governing the use of the mass media in election campaigns. Although the ousting of Berlusconi from office was a major setback for the Forza Italia and Alleanza Nazionale, which lambasted as 'traitors' the League, Parliament, Scalfaro and Dini, the strenuous efforts of Berlusconi and Fini to convene new elections at the earliest opportunity rested on the belief that they could easily win a fresh mandate.

In the light of the apparent stability of the support base of the Right, if not, in the short term, of the political forces and governments it expressed, it is legitimate to ask what sort of political change was marked by the 1994 election. Italy has never had a normal change of government and 1994 could hardly be regarded as normal. Although some sort of alternation occurred it was an anomalous one that was internal to the Centre Right. What perhaps needs to be clarified is whether the Right alliance represented merely a new incarnation of the old social bloc, or whether rather it created a new bloc. In essence, it may be said that it continued to represent the old bloc with four important differences. First there was a removal of autonomous mediation by the political: the new political class was predominantly the direct expression of a vital component of the old bloc that, latterly, the DC had fatally neglected, that is, small- and medium-scale business. Second, while the lower-class element was still there (necessary to every popular conservative force of government), there was no pretence at including even a part of organised labour. Third, the support base was not mainly southern, as the DC system had increasingly become, but mainly northern, despite the contribution of Alleanza Nazionale in the South and the success of Forza Italia in Sicily. Fourth, the keys to the DC's long-term hold on power had been Catholicism, anti-communism and clientelism. For the rightist bloc, anti-communism retained all its appeal and validity. Catholicism too remained important – for example both Berlusconi and Fini endeavoured to appear as good Catholics and family men – but the link was not as organic as it had been with the DC. The integrative role of clientelism, however, was usurped by television and consumerism, as the most universal expressions of contemporary Italian society. The limited nature of these shifts gives an indication of the extent to which the 'new Italian Republic' is both the direct heir of the *partitocrazia* and its practice of absorbing and neutralising a wide variety of interests, and of the extent to which its future will be shaped by a range of territorial, class and interest group conflicts that can no longer easily be reconciled. Together with the issues of probity in politics and business, and the application of clear rules governing all possible interactions between the two spheres, the question of conflict-resolution in a situation of cleavage redefinition is likely to be one of the key terrains on which Italians and foreign observers will judge the new order that began, uncertainly and haltingly, to take shape in 1994. Whatever the solutions that are adopted, by the end of 1994 it was clear that the optimism that marked the early stages of the process of political reform had been excessive. The fall of an old political system that was bankrupt in every sense did not lead to a democratic rebirth, but rather to a protracted struggle for power in which most of the running was made by powerful vested interests that had much to lose from any redefinition of rules and procedures.

REFERENCES

Lyttelton, A. (1994) 'Italy: the triumph of TV', *New York Review of Books*, 25–29: 29.
Cassese, S. (1994a) 'Le mani sulle nomine', *La Repubblica*, 20 July.
—— (1994b) 'È arrivato il governo pigliatutto', *La Repubblica*, 19 September.

Part I
Context

1 Explaining Italy's crisis

Paul Ginsborg

At the end of 1991 Christian Democrat and Socialist leaders were comfortably engaged in setting the pattern of Italian politics for the new decade. *La Repubblica* (17 November 1991) reported that Craxi and Andreotti had stored away an agreement on governing together for another five years. On the same day and from the columns of the same newspaper, Antonio Gava, former Minister of the Interior and Neapolitan city boss, proclaimed unwisely that 'from now on we will get votes for who we are, and not simply for our anti-communism'. Nobody could have been more wrong, but at the time few if any commentators would have dared to predict a radically different scenario. The shortcomings of the Italian state and its political system had long been studied and denounced, but year after year the stability of the Italian electorate and the durability of its political elite were confirmed.

Instead, the years from 1992 to 1994 were amongst the most dramatic in the history of the Italian Republic. In the course of one year, 1993, the five ruling parties of the post-war period were wiped off the political map. A group of magistrates attacked corruption in a way that was unprecedented in the history of the unified state. Unyielding war was waged against the Mafia, receiving for the first time widespread popular support in Sicily, and especially in Palermo. The old political elite, seemingly as immortal as its Japanese counterpart, fell, not only from power but into ignominious disrepute. Finally, in the elections of March 1994, the political climax to the crisis, an extraordinary coalition which included the neo-fascists and was headed by the entrepreneur Silvio Berlusconi, won a resounding victory.

Even from this bare list of the crisis's major elements and principal political outcome, it is possible immediately to grasp its complexity and contradictory nature. The crisis of 1992–94 is not a historical process which has a homogeneity and inner cohesion, such as the events of 1968–69 had for all of Europe. Rather it is constituted of very disparate elements, more than one of which is in open contradiction with another. It does not have at its heart a political party or strategy, or a single class or social force which causes it, pushes it forward and reaps its benefits.

Viewed from differing vantage points, it presents quite diverse faces: from the Palace of Justice in Milan, it is a battle against corruption and for the restoration of the rule of law; from the Bank of Italy it is a crisis of debt and of international confidence; from Lombardy and the Veneto it is about devolution, a new social bloc, the triumph of the self-made man; at Montecitorio its focus is on electoral laws and the demise of the old elite; in the fragile civil society of Palermo it is a desperate fight against Mafia power.

The purpose of this chapter is to attempt an explanation of the causes of this extraordinary crisis, and of the form it has taken. Before starting though, it is perhaps worth signalling a number of methodological points. First, it is not at all helpful to adopt what may be called a Cassandrian view of recent Italian history, according to which the Italian Republic has been in permanent crisis since its inception, and that riven by its many contradictions, its demise was inevitable and merely a matter of time. Eugenio Scalfari has always been one of the most lucid exponents of this scheme, from his *Autunno della repubblica* (1969) onwards. While only the most fervent of apologists for the Christian Democrats would attempt to deny the many and deep fault lines of the Republic, to concentrate exclusively on them impedes us from explaining both the timing of the crisis and its specific shape. The account which follows suggests rather that the crisis of 1992–94 owes much to the virtues of Italian democracy as well as its vices, and is indeed incomprehensible without considering both.

Second, my explanation attempts to avoid a mono-causal interpretation of events. Massimo Salvadori (1994) has recently argued powerfully for an interpretation which ascribes the failures of successive Italian political regimes (liberal, fascist, republican) to the perennial absence of political alternation such as that found in most other twentieth-century Western democracies. There is an obvious kernel of truth here, but also a real danger of reductionism. The 'regimes' of the last 130 years of Italian history were profoundly different one from another, and the crises at their ends (if 1992 is an end) bear little relation to each other. It is only natural to seek patterns in historical explanation, but perhaps dangerous to make them over-dependent on a single, political causal factor.[1]

By contrast, I have tried to build an account which takes into consideration a number of different spheres – economic, political, social and cultural – and to apply to them diverse levels of explanation – long and short term, external and internal, structural and subjective.[2] To establish a hierarchy of causation is always a hazardous operation, as Marxists (but not only they) have discovered to their cost. Hopefully, the relationship between the various elements of my explanation and its ordering of priorities will become clear as the argument unfolds.

PUBLIC DEBT AND INTERNATIONAL CONFIDENCE

After the major economic crisis of 1974–75, in which 'the authorities all but lost control of the situation' (Giavazzi and Spaventa 1988: 10), the Italian economy could boast of a considerable number of positive indicators in the following years. Italy's GDP grew by almost 50 per cent between 1976 and 1990, six percentage points above the average of the EC (Padoa Schioppa Kostoris 1993: 225, note 1). Her percentage share of world exports was 4.6 in 1970, fell to 4.4 in 1982, but rose again to 5.0 in 1987 (Zamagni 1994: 365, table 12.4). Her internal market was extremely buoyant throughout the period (consumption being 13 points higher than the EC average), and her inhabitants' propensity to save – as well as to consume – amongst the highest in the West. Michael Porter, in his comparative study of the competitive economic advantage of ten nations, acknowledged Italian industry's 'remarkable ability' to innovate in products as well as to incorporate state-of-the-art manufacturing and other technologies in relatively small and medium-sized firms. He also paid tribute to 'sophisticated and advanced home buyers and the development of world-class Italian supplier industries' (Porter 1989: 691).

However, the downside of Italy's economic performance in this period was also considerable. It took the form of a failure to invest in research and technology, a lack of major international companies in a period of accelerated global concentration (Baldassari 1994: 15), and the marked weakening of international standing between 1979 and 1993 in the key sector of goods produced on a high economy of scale – cars, consumer durables such as washing machines, electronic office equipment, organic and inorganic chemical products, etc. (Guerrieri 1994: 384, table 1).

Above all, Italy's economic performance was viewed with growing concern at an international level because of the unchecked increase of public debt. This had not been a historic problem of the Italian Republic: in 1960 for instance, Italy had a primary surplus, a very low borrowing requirement and a low debt ratio (Giavazzi and Spaventa 1988: 5). The situation deteriorated slowly in the 1970s and dramatically in the 1980s and early 1990s. At the heart of the problem lay high spending on pensions, high but inefficient spending on health provision, and very low levels of fiscal income from the self-employed – especially shopkeepers and the small business sector.

At the time of the European-wide discussions of the Maastricht Treaty, with their strong thrust to greater economic unity and a single European currency, public debt in Italy became a question of national emergency. Historically, Italy's standing in the Community had been a modest one, her presence characterised by passivity and absenteeism, by strong verbal enthusiasm but a failure second to none to enforce EC regulations or even to spend its money (Giuliani 1992).

These long-term failings were compounded sharply in 1991 by the realisation that the country came nowhere near meeting any of the three main requirements for European Monetary Union. Her public debt stood at 103 per cent of GDP, in the face of a European requirement of not more than 60 per cent; her budget deficit at 9.9 per cent, against a requirement of 4 per cent; inflation was at 6.9 per cent – well above the three best performing countries. Overall, only Greece did worse (Menet-Genty 1992: 261–268). The result was a sort of national panic, with unprecedented coverage in the mass media of the country's economic plight, and of her imminent relegation from the premier league of European nations to the second division. 'Enterprise Italy, overwhelmed by debt, will miss the European train' (*La Repubblica* 22 December 1991), was only one of many such headlines of the time.

Worse was to follow. In January 1990 Giulio Andreotti had moved the Italian lira into the narrow band of EMS currencies, hoping that its new position would reap rewards in terms of discipline and competitiveness. In the event, so exalted a position could not be sustained. Just two years later the lira came under heavy attack and the government of Giuliano Amato was forced to intervene heavily in order to save it. Then, in September 1992 international confidence in the exchange rate of the lira (and simultaneously of the pound sterling) gave way completely. Devaluation and exit from the EMS followed immediately.

Debt crisis and waning international confidence cannot, therefore, be treated as simple constants in recent Italian history. The present crisis should be seen rather as the conflict between two very different forces: on the one hand, the refusal of successive Italian governments to take seriously the growing debt mountain, choosing to buy consent at home at the cost of compromising Italy's standing abroad. The responsibility of the governments of the second half of the 1980s – a time of economic boom – was very considerable in this respect (for a good view from the inside see Amato 1990).

On the other hand, we find a concerted push, from the most advanced and successful of the European capitalist economies, towards greater economic unity, to a single currency as well as a single market. Again, this is not a constant in the history of the European Community, but a specific sequence of events in the late 1980s and early 1990s (Tsoukalis 1991).

These two tendencies, the one of international capital, the other of national mismanagement, enter into direct conflict in September 1992. Initially, it is the wider European project, which retreats with a bloody nose. But the conflict of interests and perspectives will certainly not go away, and in the long run it is a very uneven contest. In this part of the explanation of Italy's crisis, external, structural and long-term elements play a predominant role and their power of constraint is considerable. Public debt and international confidence are the *contrôleurs* of the crisis, the measuring rods by which all political projects for its solution will be judged.

VICE AND VIRTUE IN ITALIAN DEMOCRACY

The failures of Italian democracy have been so often rehearsed, albeit with different tonalities (e.g. Ginsborg 1990; Scoppola 1991; Lanaro 1992; Hine 1993; Lepre 1993), that only the briefest summary will be presented here. The electoral system of proportional representation, with its concomitant weak government, the dominance of one party and its allies for so many decades, their occupation of the state, and the absence of a feasible alternative, have all had grave but as yet non-fatal consequences for Italian democracy. The development of 'party-ocracy' (*partitocrazia*) not only affected all the state's inner workings, but coloured with brutal tints its intervention in society. The need for a party card, the politicisation (in the worst sense) of all public appointments (from hospital managers to opera administrators), the division of the spoils of state radio and television between the major political parties, both of government and opposition, have been amongst the worst features of Italian democracy. They are real insults to any reasonable concept of political citizenship.

A similar story must be told for the civil service. Sabino Cassese, the enlightened and reforming minister for the public administration at the height of the crisis (April 1993 to March 1994), has calculated that each Italian citizen loses between 15 and 20 working days each year trying to cope with the country's lethal bureaucracy (Presidenza del Consiglio dei Ministri, Dipartimento per la Funzione Pubblica 1993: 13). A deeply deformed relationship between state and citizen developed over time, based on the inefficiency of the civil service and its consequent discretionary power. The speed and efficacy of a bureaucratic act depended to a great extent upon the pressures that a citizen could exert upon the administrator. Naturally, not all the citizens were equal or could exert equal pressure. Inducements to bureaucratic action varied, from the relatively innocuous use of contacts to outright corruption (Ginsborg 1990: 149).

These vices of Italian democracy, both in its formal and informal workings, were historical growths, not immutable features of a Republican landscape. As with the question of public debt, so in this area, the 1980s was a grim period: as Gian Carlo Caselli, the chief prosecuting magistrate at Palermo, has said, these were 'years of political arrogance which threatened the balance of the Constitution ... years of shameless idiocy on the part of certain power centres of the state' (Caselli 1993: 15–16). Along with the Christian Democrats, and often exceeding them, the Socialist Party of Bettino Craxi played a leading role in the systemisation and theorisation of corrupt practice. This was the period when kickbacks on public contracts became a highly organised affair, when party and personal financing flourished directly from the illegal use of political prerogative.

At stake was something more than the European-wide decline of interest in politics, noted by many commentators and made manifest in the rising levels of absenteeism at national elections (Flickinger and Studlar 1992). Rather, the pattern of misgovernment seemed part of the failure of Latin Socialism, and many of the same features of state plunder were (and are) to be found in the Spanish, Greek and even French parties. Rather than trying to reinvent political agency (Dunn 1993: 265), the southern European Socialists were content to maximise their own advantages.[3]

However, the political explanation for the crisis does not lie simply in the long-term failures of the system, aggravated by Socialist arrogance. The virtues of the Republic have also played a crucial causal role. In the long term, one of the most important of these elements has been the official morality of the Republic created in the years 1943–48. Italy's post-war settlement in many ways lagged far behind its counterparts in France, West Germany and Great Britain. Italy failed to overhaul its state apparatus or to provide the bases for social citizenship. However, the founding fathers of the Republic were much more successful in translating the Resistance origins of the Republic into the institutional settlement, and the Constitution in particular. In the post-war years we find the creation of an official morality – democratic, anti-fascist, constitutional, European – which is frequently abused rhetorically but never replaced. The Resistance generation finished for the most part on the fringes of politics, but they remain powerful witnesses – Norberto Bobbio, Leo Valiani, Vittorio Foa, Sandro Galante Garrone and, above all, because he actually held power and became the most popular President of the Republic, Sandro Pertini. The comparison with Japan is illuminating in this respect, precisely because no such Resistance generation served as the conscience of the new democracy (Samuels 1994). In Italy, a certain idea of what the Republic should be, even if it was not, was never lost.

The rule of law, similarly, was flouted in innumerable cases but was never entirely discredited. The post-war period was not propitious: it is enough to read Calamandrei's denunciation of what remained of the Fascist Codes twelve years after the end of Fascism to understand how slow was the pace of change (Calamandrei 1955). But the rule of law, repeatedly battered and submerged, always obstinately bobbed back to the surface.

In the history of the Republic, therefore, there is a considerable tension between everyday political practice – frequently based upon favours, placemen, corruption and so on – and an official morality to which, in the last analysis, everyday morality remains subordinate. At a symbolic level, nothing illustrates this better than Mario Chiesa's curtain. Mario Chiesa, the director of the Pio Albergo Trivulzio, an old people's home in Milan, was the first Socialist to be caught in the act of collecting his kickbacks. His arrest on 17 February 1992 marks the beginning of *Tangentopoli*, and is most often adopted as the official starting-point of the crisis. He later told the magistrate Di Pietro that when local contractors came to pay him, he pulled a curtain so that no-one could see what was happening (della Porta 1993). He could not operate in the full light of day: a strong sense of impropriety was still attached to what he was doing.

This tension between everyday practice and official morality proved the undoing of the Italian political class – their most vulnerable spot, the mechanism that left the king without any clothes on. The political class did not collapse because of the strength of the opposition, because of mass demonstrations, because of enduring social movements. It collapsed rather because it had no answer to accusations which were couched in terms of the revenge of public morality. In a country where honour still counts for a great deal, discrediting of this sort weighed very heavily indeed.

Another, more recent virtue of the Republic was the political mechanism of the abrogative referendum (such referenda could not propose legislation, but only exercise the negative power of repealing an existing law). Originally included in the Constitution, the right to hold referenda became law in May 1970. The right to initiate the procedure may be exercised by 500,000 citizens or five regional councils or one-fifth of either House of Parliament. The debate on the democratic value of referenda is an open one, and it is clear that there will always exist the real danger of ruling parties using the mechanism in a plebiscitary fashion, as a populist support for their wider ambitions.

However, this has not to date been the predominant role of the referendum in the history of the Republic. If Craxi used it to good effect to attack the judiciary (see below), more often than not referenda campaigns have been the occasion for large-scale movements in civil society to protect progressive legislation. This was the case in the famous divorce referendum of 1974 and again with that on abortion in 1979 – both called as the result of clerical mobilisation and both decisively defeated.

The referendum mechanism was used again in a novel and dramatic fashion by Mario Segni on 9 June 1991. Segni, an honest if limited Christian Democrat politician and son of a former President of the Republic, was disliked by many leading members of his own party and was in bad odour with the Socialists. He launched a brave, relatively isolated referendum campaign, with some support from the PDS, for the abolition of the multiple-choice preference vote, one of the essential mechanisms of political clientelism. In spite of a barrage of hostile media coverage, in spite of Bettino Craxi's advice to the electorate not to bother to vote but to spend the day by the seaside, 26 million Italians voted overwhelmingly in Segni's favour. This was the first major blow to the ruling parties, and the first detonator of the crisis.

THE ROLE OF THE JUDGES

The Italian state has been likened to an archipelago (Donolo 1980), and in this it represents an extreme version of the physiognomy of any modern state – not a cohesive unit with a clear line of command, but an aggregation of different power centres often in conflict with one another. In the Italian case the control of the political parties over the many islands of the state archipelago had become pervasive with the passage of time. However (and this is the crucial point), it had not become all-pervasive. Within the state there remained what can best be called 'virtuous minorities' who were resistant to party pressure and not solely dependent upon it. The structures and officials of the Bank of Italy are the most famous example.

Another influential minority, central to any explanation of the crisis, is the judiciary. As their role is analysed at length elsewhere in this volume (see Nelken, Chapter 12), I shall confine my remarks to the essential linkages for my general argument. Once again the post-war settlement was crucial, for it decreed the establishment of the Consiglio Superiore della Magistratura and established the potential for independent action by prosecuting magistrates. As Neppi Modona has written, 'for the first time in Italian history, the Constitution asserted the full and total independence of the judges and the *pubblico ministero* (prosecuting magistrate) from control by the executive' (1994: 477). Judges and magistrates, henceforth, were beholden only to the law.

This judicial autonomy is in stark contrast with the situation in many other European democracies. In France and Spain, government control of judicial enquiries is commonplace, resulting in the constant burying of delicate investigations involving politicians and the margination of over-zealous prosecuting magistrates (Jean-Pierre 1993, and the interview with him in the *Observer*, 17 July 1994). In Britain control is more subtle, for the very nature of recruitment to the judiciary results in the creation, as Nelken writes (Chapter 12), 'of a small group of middle-aged and middle-minded members of the establishment'.

Judicial autonomy was not obtained easily in Italy. The Consiglio Superiore della Magistratura (CSM) only began to function from 1959 onwards, and it was only in the late 1960s, with the formation of separate associations which reflected the plurality of political positions in society as a whole, that the struggle for an independent judiciary really took off. In the wake of 1968–69 many idealistic young law graduates entered the profession (see Dalla Chiesa 1992), and the fight against the Mafia and the hidden powers of Italian society began in earnest. The reforming magistrates remained a minority, and there were others who aimed at much less deserving targets, such as the Bank of Italy. Nonetheless, the judiciary had ceased to be simply a closed conservative caste.

All this, naturally, was bound to provoke a reaction, both from official and unofficial power centres in Italy. The late 1980s were a critical period, when it seemed as if the judiciary's room for independent manoeuvre would be eliminated. In 1987 the Socialists, as has been mentioned, used the referendum mechanism to try to make judges financially responsible for their mistakes: they gained a crushing victory for this populist proposal. Then Francesco Cossiga, in the latter part of his Presidency of the Republic (1990–92), launched a series of blistering attacks on the CSM. *Tangentopoli* came at a critical time, just when it seemed as if the President and the executive were about to take the judiciary by the neck. The revelations of Mario Chiesa, another major detonator of the crisis, opened up a vital line of counter-attack, ably exploited by some of the most independent-minded, responsible and courageous magistrates in the country – the very epitome of a virtuous minority. However, they would never have made any progress if their actions had not coincided with the other parts of the structural crisis of the political elite.

SOCIAL TRANSFORMATION AND POLITICAL PREFERENCE

So far, the structure of explanation would seem fairly straightforward, and almost to contain elements of a morality play: the disfunction of Italian politics (with especial reference to the unsavoury agents in charge of it in the 1980s) are ruthlessly exposed by external factors (especially the move to European unity), and are convincingly routed by internal ones (the survival and revenge of the virtuous minorities). However, if the focus of attention shifts from the state to society, the explanatory image becomes less clear, and the crisis acquires its full complexity.

The virtuous minorities, in order to make the crisis *their* crisis, and bring it to a successful conclusion, had to form alliances within the State and society. By themselves, they were much too isolated to hope to win. Some elements of the situation, especially in 1993, seemed to comfort them in this endeavour. Within the state, the new President of the Republic, Scalfaro, gave them cautious support, in marked contrast to his predecessor. The Ciampi government (April 1993 to March 1994) did the same, avoiding the sort of attempt at a whitewash job which had done so much to discredit its predecessor, headed by Giuliano Amato. In society, public opinion remained firmly on the magistrates' side, opposing any attempt to let the perpetrators of *Tangentopoli* off the hook.

The public's support, however, did not translate into the sort of cultural revolution that had rocked Italy in 1968–69. *Tangentopoli* remained very much a spectator sport, far removed from the realities of everyday life. There was a crucial failure, or refusal, to connect the themes raised by the magistrates with the power structure and culture of Italian society.

Its many corporations – of lawyers and notaries, of accountants and hospital consultants, university professors and journalists – emerged almost unscathed from the crisis. The long-standing political anthropology of *parentela* and *clientela*, the *basso profondo* of *Tangentopoli*, was not called into question. Ordinary Italians were never forced to ask uncomfortable questions about their own behaviour – of how much the dominant culture of *Tangentopoli* – (clientelism, corruption, nepotism, tax evasion, etc.) – was in fact their own.

In order to understand why this was so, it is worth trying to trace, if only in the broadest outline, how far Italian society had been transformed from the mid-1970s onwards, and in what direction. The answer is by no means a linear one. Here I shall concentrate briefly on diverse social and political patterns in North and South, with special reference to Lombardy and Sicily.

The Italian version of the social change that has characterised advanced capitalist nations in the last 20 years is a fascinating one. In Italy the consequences of post-Fordism for the organised working class have been particularly dramatic, because they contrast so sharply with the role that that class was accustomed to play for much of the post-war period. From being considered the protagonist of a transformative vision of Italian society – 'the social force which is today the principal motor of history' (Berlinguer 1977: 11–12) – workers have seen their numbers diminished, their ideology debunked, and their centres of aggregation decimated. The result has been massive political and cultural disorientation, especially in the north of the country.

Coincident with this profound change has been the explosion of what Ulrich Beck has called the long-term process of 'individualisation' (Beck 1992: 87ff). The individual is increasingly forced to confront the risks and choices of a society where large-group aggregations and solidarities are on the decline, where family cohesion is very much under threat, where gender roles are being radically redefined. 'Community', writes Beck, is 'dissolved in the acid bath of competition' (1992: 94).

In order to enjoy the choice of an ever-wider range of consumer goods, the individual, ever more alone, has to confront the risks, both global and personal, of an unprotected society. By fighting for educational qualifications, by being ready to accept unlimited mobility and flexibility in the dominant tertiary sector of the labour market, the individual hopes to construct a constant pattern of employment in a world where work is increasingly scarce. The alternative is to slip into the growing underclass of under- and un-employed, without savings or security in old age.

The translation of Beck's scenario into northern Italian society is a complicated process, with zones both of resonance and dissonance. Northern Italian society is certainly marked by the severe decline of both Catholic and Communist sub-cultures (Cartocci 1994), by ever smaller families, with very low fertility rates in most regions (Ginsborg 1994c), and by an increase in the autonomy of women and their presence in the labour market. However, it is also marked by very strong family loyalties (the 'long' family if not the large one (Rosci 1994)), by relatively high standards of health and social services, by the ethos of *mettersi in proprio*, of setting up small family businesses.

The balance of risk and choice has therefore been quite heavily tilted over the last twenty years towards choice – houses, holidays, cars, colour televisions, videos, portable telephones, fashion, the full hedonism and romanticism of late twentieth century consumption (Campbell 1987). Risks, on the other hand, have been held in check by a number of protective mechanisms – family above all, but also employment opportunities in dynamic industrial districts and reasonably efficient local government (Trigilia 1986).

This is a society characterised by strong localisms, scarce respect for regulations governing working conditions, contributions and taxation, growing intolerance of the inefficiencies and arbitrariness of central government; a society with more than a vein of racism (towards Southerners and immigrants), and a culture of hard work, self-enrichment and the ostentation of new-found opulence. It is a long way removed from the austerity, ethical rectitude and idea of service to the state embodied in the figure of Francesco Saverio Borrelli, the chief prosecuting magistrate of Milan. Such men and their struggles may be respected and supported, but from afar.

Of course it would be foolish to identify the whole of northern Italian society with these socio-economic and cultural traits. There are sections of the population and geographical areas (urban peripheries, zones of deindustrialisation, etc.) where risks far outweigh the real possibility of choice. There are others where associationism (a phenomenon which grew nationally by 2 per cent in the decade prior to 1993) gives the lie to the end of aggregation and solidarity. The organised working class has certainly not disappeared, nor have its *consigli di fabbrica* (factory councils). But these elements are far from dominant – and the tide of modern society seems to be flowing away from them.

The *political* expression of the majority of northern society was influenced by the dramatic events centring around the fall of the Berlin Wall and the final discrediting of the communist regimes in the East. This is a point that enters almost every explanation of the Italian crisis, and it is worth reiterating briefly here. The ties of electoral stability in Italy were significantly loosened, though how exactly the crisis of world communism contributed to this process and whether it would have happened anyway are questions that are worth posing. The main effect seems to have been more one of 'liberating' the traditional Christian Democrat vote than flight from the Communist one. In the 'white' areas of Lombardy-Veneto, with traditional Catholic culture in decline and dissatisfaction with local politicians rife (Diamant 1993), the terrain was ripe for new political forces which reflected the societal changes described above.

The Northern League, with its combination of strong regionalism and invented ethnicity, with its loathing of the central state and exaltation of local interests, with its espousal of individualism, hard work and free market values, made very rapid progress in the electoral consultations of the early 1990s. Its strongholds were precisely the Catholic zones of dynamic small businesses, but its influence was not limited to them. At the height of its expansion in 1993, its candidate for mayor of Milan, Marco Formentini, was able to defeat with ease the vast and variegated front of the educated middle classes, Catholic volunteers, and traditional left-wing forces which had gathered around Nando Dalla Chiesa (Stajano 1993).

It is essential to understand that the Northern League was not the political expression of many of the new social trends in the North, but had a continuity with longer-standing traditions. For all its rhetoric, there is little evidence to show that the League ever had any intention of breaking with the clientelist, familial and party-dominated ethos of the old regime. Quite the opposite seems to be true. Here one example will have to suffice: on 23 April 1994, the *Corriere della Sera* reported that Marco Vitale, a powerful, non-League member of Formentini's local government team in Milan, had written to his colleagues in the following terms: 'I have to ask every single one of you, regardless of your position or responsibilities, to stop exerting pressure on me to obtain offices, garages, private lodgings for your personal use or that of your relatives, cousins, blood relations, domestic servants, boy or girl friends, or other persons or organisations bound to you by ties of loyalty and affection'. The League was a revolt against the old regime, but its political culture was more dependent on that regime than it would care to admit.

The success of the League, above all in the national elections of 1992, broke the stranglehold which the Craxian Socialists had for some time exercised on Milanese politics. Borrelli's pool of magistrates now had political space in which to move. In turn, other elements of the crisis fostered the League's cause. In response to the debt crisis, the Amato and Ciampi governments attempted to claw back income, imposed a minimum tax on the self-employed and cut services; all this at a time of relative economic depression. Small businesses were faced with tax controls, often for the first time, and householders with a bewildering variety of taxes. Northern fury with Roman government found its outlets in calls for autonomy, privatisation, the free market – and further votes for the League. The crisis thus acquired a circular dynamic of great force, but without any unity of objectives.

Later on, though this lies outside the scope of this chapter, Silvio Berlusconi emerged as the dominant figure in the North, eating up the League's votes and driving it back to its provincial strongholds. Berlusconi, too, represented that mix of the very new and the very old which characterised the League, but the component elements of his appeal differed from those of his ally and rival in the North. He offered a more respectable and reassuring image for the middle classes than did the crude and histrionic Bossi. He was the expression of Milan, not of its hinterland. Above all, his concept of politics was profoundly different, based not on local, grass-roots mobilisation, but on national appeal via the mass media which he controlled. Politics had increasingly been trans-formed in the 1970s and 1980s from the piazza and the local party section to the television, and from the television, in Berlusconi's scheme, would emanate back out to the nation. Much more than Bossi, Berlusconi was the incarnation of a variety of consumer dreams, the self-made man who would safeguard individuality against collectivism within a familist, sporting and national framework.

CIVIL SOCIETY IN THE SOUTH

Southern Italian society in the last 20 years has been subject to many of the same long-term changes as the North, especially that of home-based consumption, but presents some radical differences. In the South, the balance between choice and risk is much more heavily tilted towards the latter. If we concentrate only on Sicily because of its crucial role in the wider structure of the Italian crisis, certain key characteristics become visible immediately. Possibilities of employment are very much more limited than in Lombardy-Veneto, with very high levels of youth and female unemployment. A certain number of dynamic small industries exist in the east of the island, but the structure of the island's economy remains weak and dependent on state funding (Balistreri 1994). Social services are grossly inadequate, with state aid often taking the form of individual handouts rather than collective provision (Boccella 1982). Local government has been uniquely corrupt and based on clientelist principles (Chubb 1981). Class solidarities have, historically, been very limited, and distrust is the dominant element of interpersonal relations (Gambetta 1988); civil society has consisted more of isolated outposts than a complex and consolidated network.

In this context, families have sought to maximise their chances by maintaining a relatively high birth-rate, by maintaining strong and tra-ditional patron–client relations, and by adopting strategies that are relent-lessly individualist – as symbolised by the massive wave of unauthorised house building in the 1980s, buildings constructed anywhere and every-where, and often left unfinished. As Balistreri has written, 'the *tufo giallo* – the poorest building material that can be used – is everywhere dominant, and from afar it is as if a huge sandstorm has taken pleasure in creating senseless forms in the urban desert' (1990: 170).

A society without civic trust or responsibility finds its classic outlet in the high-risk choice of working for the Mafia. On the one hand the Mafia offers the possibility of rapid enrichment and consumer fulfilment, of a strong sense of belonging, of prestige and honour. On the other hand there are the recurrent dangers of lethal, internecine warfare between the different bands, of intrafamilial conflict (loyalty to one's own family and to a Mafia 'family' do not always coincide), and of growing state reprisals.

In the period under consideration, the Mafia was an industry in dynamic expansion, but increasingly in conflict with elements of State power, especially after the assassination of General Alberto Dalla Chiesa in 1982. Sicily makes its contribution to the crisis fundamentally through this state–Mafia conflict. The generation of magistrates formed in the 1970s found some of its ablest and most courageous exponents in Sicily. The pool of magistrates in Palermo who in 1987 organised the maxi-trial of 456 mafiosi, of whom 19 were sentenced to life imprisonment, paid the highest possible price for their actions. With the assassinations of Giovanni Falcone and Paolo Borsellino in May and July of 1992, terrible detonators of the crisis in the literal sense, the collaboration of the old political class with criminal activities could no longer be hidden. Less than a year later (27 March 1993), Gian Carlo Caselli, the new chief prosecutor in Palermo, informed Giulio Andreotti, the longest-serving politician of the Republic and six times Prime Minister, that he was under investigation for collusion with the Mafia.

The fight against the Mafia in Sicily was not carried forward by the magistrates alone. Here, and here alone, the judiciary was able to forge an alliance with significant sections of society – an active alliance rather than the passive one that characterised the North. The murder of Falcone and Borsellino provoked, at least amongst a significant minority, an ethical, social and spiritual revolt. It was as if the distrust, violence and individualism of Sicilian society had reached such a point as to provoke a mass movement in reaction.

Temporarily at least, Robert Putnam's geographical and historical location of Italian civic virtue (Putnam 1993) seemed to have been turned upside down. While the League reaped the reward of essentially individualist, secessionist and even racist politics, Sicily in 1992–93 was a beehive of civic and anti-Mafia initiatives, of student mobilisation, of new associations of shopkeepers and entrepreneurs, of the famous sheet protest, whereby on a given day every household which wished to demonstrate its anti-Mafia sentiments hung out a white sheet on its balcony (Abate 1993; Schneider and Schneider 1994).

The principal political expression of this movement, unique in post-war Sicilian history, was Leoluca Orlando's La Rete (analysed at greater length by John Foot in Chapter 11). In analysing the Rete's success (and also its rapid demise), it is essential to contrast its social base with that of the League in the North. If the League was the expression of the

Lombard popular classes, the Rete was dominated by the highly educated youth of the new Sicilian middle classes. A survey published in *Iter* (no. 4, 1992: 27–28) revealed that of the 487 members of the movement in the sample, 30.4 per cent had degrees and 52.8 per cent upper secondary school diplomas. Their previous experience of civic organisation came from cultural associations, parish circles, pacifist groups, etc. White-collar workers, students, professionals and teachers accounted for 71 per cent of membership; 55.5 per cent were below 35 years old, and another 24.4 per cent between 35 and 45.

This youthful and idealistic middle-class elite succeeded only fitfully in linking with a wider popular base. Lacking a strong material element in their programme to complement the ethical one, they were always going to have great difficulty in creating a stable political majority in the island. Subjective errors, especially of their charismatic but primadonna-ish leader, Leoluca Orlando, made the task even more daunting. In November 1993 the political disorientation of the Right and the absten-tion of the Mafia considerably assisted Orlando's triumphant victory as Mayor of Palermo. However, when Berlusconi moved into the political field in January 1994, he found fertile ground in this part of the South as well as in the North. His promise of the creation of a million new jobs had a particular resonance on the island. His familist and consumerist dreams were as evocative here as elsewhere, reaching mass audiences through his television channels. Above all, the Mafia vote swung behind him. It was not that Berlusconi deliberately chose the Mafia, but certainly it chose him. One of his own members of Parliament, Tiziana Parenti, was amongst the first to denounce Mafia infiltrations in Forza Italia.

THE UNCERTAINTIES OF THE PDS

The last element of explanation concerns an absence more than a pres-ence. With the violent discrediting of the dominant political parties, especially the DC and PSI, it would have been reasonable to expect the opposition to have taken their place in governing the country. That this has not happened is another particularity of the Italian crisis and merits a brief reflection.

In 1989 Achille Occhetto showed considerable prescience in changing the name of the Italian Communist Party to the Democratic Party of the Left. For some months his action seemed the portent of a new strategy and a new appeal. However, within the party, the change of name pro-voked great dissent and eventual schism. Occhetto did his best to mediate, but the overall result was paralysis. It is from this period that the first, crippling weakness of the PDS dates: a degree of internal dissent which consumed the major share of its energy and prevented it from relating with sufficient force and clarity to the outside world. The atmosphere within the party on the eve of the crisis can best be summed up by the title of an editorial by Michele Salvati in *L'Unità* of 9 July 1991: 'If the PDS could unite, perhaps it might be able to have a political line'.

The crisis, as must now be clear, was not initiated by the Left. Its heroes (dead and alive) were Falcone and Borsellino, Segni and Di Pietro. None the less the PDS could well have profited from the turmoil of the crisis, as Silvio Berlusconi was eventually to do. The reasons that it did not would seem to be threefold (Ginsborg 1994e).

The first was that the PDS itself felt menaced by the judicial offensive. From the first weeks of *Tangentopoli*, it became clear that elements of the party had in the past been involved in the malpractices of the system. Occhetto made a speech asking the pardon of the nation for the short-comings of his former party, but it was not accompanied by any clear indications that the PDS really intended to come clean and that it was not afraid to reveal the skeletons in the Communist cupboard. The party seemed rather to choose a defensive strategy – waiting for the magistrates to find out what they could, and hoping that this did not amount to much.

To ask the PDS to have acted differently was a tall order (if there had been too many skeletons the young party would have been crushed by a mass of old bones). It was, though, the only way to demonstrate the undoubted difference between the PDS and the old ruling parties. To have come clean in the spring of 1992 would have been traumatic and disruptive, but it would have put the whole of the Left in a much better position for the crucial elections of two years later. As it was – and this is testimony to a failed strategy – the PDS seemed at the key moment to be a more compromised element of the old system than it actually was.

Second, the PDS failed almost completely to launch initiatives that would have taken the crisis away from the courts and the television screens and into everyday life. Here there reemerged an old failing of the PCI: a certain immobility and lack of imagination with respect to modern social movements. To have challenged the many closed and corrupt corporations in society, a revolt was necessary; strangely enough, such revolt was alien to the political culture of the PCI/PDS.

Finally, the Left as a whole was unable to read correctly the trajectory of the crisis. This was a task of extraordinary difficulty, requiring a special political talent. With the advantage of hindsight, it is clear that the height of the crisis was in the spring of 1993. Practically every day in the month of March, another important figure of the establishment was discredited by the magistrates' scrutiny. This was the moment, with the political class falling apart in front of everyone's eyes, to have pressed for a greater leadership role. Not only did the PDS not do this, but it pulled out the left-wing ministers – Barbera, Berlinguer, Rutelli and Visco – who had joined Ciampi's government. Every effort should have been made to go to the polls at an early date. Every week that passed was a week in which the Right regrouped, the crisis slackened, the moment slipped away. The Left still did well in the local elections in November to December 1993, but that was before Berlusconi had launched his campaign. Once he did, the PDS responded with a truly lacklustre performance in the national elections of March 1994. The Right successfully presented itself as a dynamic new force in Italian politics, while the Left seemed old, static, defensive and short of ideas.

DRAWING THE STRINGS TOGETHER

The first and fundamental point on which to insist in any conclusion is that the events of 1992–94 were a crisis within a democracy. Comparisons with recent events in Eastern Europe are, for the most part, wide of the mark. They fail to make the distinction between crisis in a one party state and crisis in a state based for nearly 50 years on free elections and universal suffrage. They also fail to distinguish between a country with an exceptionally turbulent and vivacious civil society, and those countries in which civil society was denied any existence at all.

It is also important to insist that events in Italy to date have not been a revolution, in any meaningful sense of the word. As Theda Skocpol has painstakingly taught us (1979), revolutions are about mass action, state-breaking and state-making. They are about the destruction of an *ancien régime* and not just the disgrace of leading figures in politics, about mass mobilisation, about the attempted construction of profoundly different political and often social systems. None of these characteristics apply to Italy. Indeed, one of the elements which emerges ever more strongly, day by day, is the continuity with past political practice, and the attempt to absorb and exorcise the innovations and consequent traumas of 1992–94.

Precisely because Italy has, so far, been a democracy, it makes sense to look for the origins of the crisis, not just in its failings as a 'regime', but in the pluralism that democracy alone permits. The emergence of an independent judiciary and the role of courageous and public-minded prosecuting magistrates within it, the existence of a highly specific official morality dating back to the Resistance, the slow (too slow, as Parker (1994) has pointed out) development of secondary education, the possibility of recourse, both from below and above, to referenda – these are all essential elements in the explanation of the contesting of Italy's time-serving politicians.

The external connections of Italian democracy have also played a crucial role in the causation of the crisis. Two elements stand out – the one liberating, the other of necessary constraint. The fall of the Berlin Wall meant fundamental changes in the politics of the West as well as of the East. In Italy the end of the Eastern bloc seems to have played an important role in encouraging voters, for the first time since 1948, to choose parties without reference, however vague, to a Cold War context.

Even more importantly, at the time of the Maastricht Treaty Italy's

long-standing membership of the EC forced into every home an awareness of the mismanagement of her public economy. The rescue operation
attempted by the anomalous governments of Amato and Ciampi, dominated more by technical experts than party politics, inevitably produced
cuts in services and higher taxation. These served further to alienate
families at a time of economic downturn, and caused them to respond
positively to more extreme, as well as illusory electoral appeals.

These mutations of international circumstance need not necessarily
have spelt death for Italy's ruling political elites. However, in spite of all
socialist claims to 'modernity', the decade of the 1980s had signified a
further decline in what was already a most undistinguished conduct of
public affairs. Systemised corrupt practice, major offensives against the
independence of the judiciary, grave irresponsibility over the public debt,
were only the principal expressions of the inglorious era of Bettino Craxi.

Turning to the immediate causes of the crisis, it is perhaps worth
recomposing in chronological terms the prevalently thematic analysis of
the previous pages. The major catalysts of the crisis – each representing
a different aspect – are situated in an arc of time that runs from the
summer of 1991 to the summer of 1992. Early warnings came with
the referendum of June 1991 and the national panic over Maastricht; the
crisis took off in earnest with the arrest of Mario Chiesa in February
1992, and the League's victory at the national elections of April. That
summer the killings of Falcone and Borsellino marked the dramatic entry
of the South into the crisis; in September 1992, the lira was devalued and
Italy abandoned the EMS.

From then on, the country reeled under an endless stream of judicial
investigations, arrests, suicides, and the demise of political parties. For a
number of months its history acquired an extraordinary fluidity. The crisis,
though, was multi-directional. It appeared to be dominated by the judges,
but their powers were only punitive, not creative. There was no proper
connection, with the partial exception of Sicily, between political opposition, civil society and the prosecuting magistrates. The attempt at 'democratic restoration', the return to legality and the Constitution, the ethical
revolt against the excesses of the 1980s, never broke through into mass
politics and cultural revolution.

Instead, a majority of the country's electorate fought shy of radical
change and responded to quite different sorts of appeal, launched to
great effect first by Umberto Bossi and then by Silvio Berlusconi. Behind
their choice lay many of the long-term social and economic changes, as
well as cultural continuities, which the dramatic surface of the crisis had
in some way masked: the tendency towards individualisation, the decline
of working-class solidarities, the vision of the family as a limited company
(De Rita 1988), the resonance of the consumer revolution, the suspicion
of the State and the tendency to defraud it, the survival of a strong
patron–client culture. To put it simply, a far greater synchrony existed

between the real nature of society and its northern political expression than between the 'virtuous minorities' and any wider public.

Such a conclusion, espoused with great and pessimistic vigour by Marco Revelli (1994), brings us back full circle to one of our points of departure, the relationship between structure and agency. If we are to accept the argument that the structural transformations of the last twenty years led inevitably to the triumph of Berlusconi's right-wing coalition, then little or no room is left for agency, either individual or collective.

Determinist explanations of this sort rest on a double fallacy, the one sociological, the other methodological. First, social and economic change is not uni-directional and its consequences are not easily predictable (who foresaw the League, or for that matter the events of 1968?). In the case under consideration, rising educational standards, the growing independence of women, the growth of associationism can all be seen as possible countervailing elements to predominant trends.

Second, an over-emphasis on structure at the expense of agency debilitates historical explanation, which is based on the essential interdependence of the two. Once agency conquers its proper space, specific failures and successes, the uncertainties of the PDS, the exceptional war of manoeuvre of Silvio Berlusconi, can be allowed their just weight. The complexity of the origins of the crisis, the multiplicity of its sectors and actors, can then be complemented by an acknowledgement of the variety of its possible outcomes.

NOTES

1 A similar explanatory shape accompanies Alessandro Pizzorno's interesting article (Pizzorno 1993) on the categories of the crisis. According to his argument, it is the long-standing consociational pact between the government parties and the Communist opposition that is the dominant factor of the crisis.
2 For an illuminating discussion of structure and subject in historical context see Perry Anderson's work of the early 1980s (Anderson 1980, 1983).
3 For some comments on a shared southern European political culture, see Ginsborg 1994d.

REFERENCES

Abate, F. (1993) *Capo d'Orlando. Un sogno fatto in Sicilia*, Lignari: Rome and Naples.
Amato, G. (1990) *Due anni al tesoro*, Bologna: Il Mulino.
Anderson, P. (1980) 'Agency' in *Idem Arguments Within English Marxism*, London: Verso: 16–58.
—— (1983) 'Structure and subject' in *Idem In the Tracks of Historical Materialism*, London: Verso: 32–55.
Baldassari, M. (ed.) (1994) *The Italian Economy: Heaven or Hell?*, New York: St Martin's Press.
Balistreri, G. (1994) 'Sicilia: la ricerca di una nuova identità', in P. Ginsborg (ed.), *Stato dell'Italia*, Milan: Il Saggiatore.

Balistreri, P. (1990) 'La società mafiosa', *Micro Mega*, 5: 169–83.

Beck, U. (1992) *Risk Society*, London: Sage.

Berlinguer, E. (1977) *Austerità, occasione per trasformare l'Italia*, Rome: Riuniti.

Boccella, N. (1982) *Il Mezzogiorno sussidiato*, Milan: Einaudi.

Calamandrei, P. (1955) 'La Costituzione e le leggi per attuarla', in L. Valiani *et al. Dieci anni dopo, 1945–55*, Bari: Laterza: 209–316.

Campbell, C. (1987) *The Romantic Ethic and the Spirit of Modern Consumerism*, Oxford: Blackwell.

Cartocci, R. (1994) *Fra Lega e Chiesa*, Bologna: Il Mulino.

Caselli, G. C. (1993) 'La cultura della giurisdizione', *Micro Mega*, 5: 15–18.

Chubb, J. (1982) *Patronage, Power and Poverty in Southern Italy*, Cambridge: Cambridge University Press.

Dalla Chiesa, N. (1992) *Il giudice ragazzino*, Turin: Einaudi.

della Porta, D. (1992) *Lo scambio occulto*, Bologna: Il Mulino.

—— (1993) 'Milan: immortal capital', in S. Hellman and G. Pasquino (eds) *Italian Politics: A Review*, London: Pinter.

De Rita, G. (1988) 'L'impresa-famiglia', in P. Melograni and L. Scaraffia (eds), *La famiglia italiana dall'Ottocento a oggi*, Bari: Laterza.

Diamanti, I. (1993) *La Lega*, Rome: Donzelli.

Donolo, C. (1980) 'Social change and transformation of the State in Italy', in R. Scase (ed.) *The State in Western Europe*, London: Croom Helm.

Dunn, J. (ed.) (1992) *Democracy, the Unfinished Journey*, Oxford: Blackwell.

Ferrara, M. (ed.) (1991) *Le dodici Europe*, Bologna: Il Mulino.

Flickinger, R. and Studlar, D. (1992) 'The disappearing voters? Exploring declining turnout in Western European elections', *Western European Politics*, 15 (2): 1–16.

Gambetta, D. (1988) 'Mafia: the price of distrust' in D. Gambetta (ed.), *Trust: Making and Breaking Cooperative Relations*, Oxford: Basil Blackwell: 158–75.

Giavazzi, F. and Spaventa, L. (eds) (1988) *High Public Debt: the Italian Experience*, Cambridge: Cambridge University Press.

Ginsborg, P. (1990) *A History of Contemporary Italy*, London: Penguin.

—— (ed.) (1994a) *Le virtù della Repubblica*, Milan: Il Saggiatore.

—— (ed.) (1994b) *Stato dell'Italia*, Milan: Il Saggiatore.

—— (1994c) 'La famiglia italiana oltre il privato per superare l'isolamento', in *Stato dell'Italia*, Milan: Il Saggiatore.

—— (1994d) 'L'Italia, L'Europa, il Mediterraneo', in *Stato dell'Italia*, Milan: Il Saggiatore.

—— (1994e) 'La sinistra, la crisi, la sconfitta', in *Stato dell'Italia*, Milan: Il Saggiatore.

Giuliani, M. (1992) 'Il processo decisionale italiano e le politiche comunitarie', *Polis*, 2: 307–342.

Guerrieri, P. (1994) 'La collocazione internazionale dell'economia italiana', in P. Ginsborg (ed.) *Stato dell'Italia*, Milan: Il Saggiatore.

Hine, D. (1993) *Governing Italy*, Oxford: Oxford University Press.

Jean-Pierre, T. (1993) 'Come si manipolano i giudici in Francia', *Micro Mega*, 5: 69–72.

Lanaro, S. (1992) *Storia dell'Italia repubblicana*, Venice: Marsilio.

Lepre, A. (1993) *Storia della prima Repubblica*, Bologna: Il Mulino.

Menet-Genty, J. (1992) *L'Economie italienne*, Paris: La documentation française.

Neppi Modona, G. (1994) 'Giustizia e potere politico', in P. Ginsborg (ed.) *Stato dell'Italia*, Milan: Il Saggiatore.

Padoa Schioppa Kostoris, F. (1993) *Italy: the Sheltered Economy*, Oxford: Oxford University Press.

Parker, S. (1994) 'Review of P. Ginsborg (ed.), Le virtù della Repubblica', *ASMI Newsletter*, 25: 41–44.

Pizzorno, A. (1993) 'Categorie per una crisi', *Micro Mega*, 3: 81–96.

Porter, M. (1989) *The Competitive Advantage of Nations*, London: Collier Macmillan.

Presidenza del Consiglio dei Ministri, Dipartimento per la Funzione Pubblica (1993) *Rapporto sulle condizioni delle pubbliche amministrazioni*, Rome.

Putnam, R. (1993) *Making Democracy Work. Civic Traditions in Modern Italy*, Princeton: Princeton University Press.

Revelli, M. (1994) 'Forza Italia: l'anomalia italiana non è finita', in P. Ginsborg (ed.) *Stato dell'Italia*, Milan: Il Saggiatore.

Rosci, E. (1994) 'Le lunghe adolescenze dell'Italia d'oggi', in P. Ginsborg (ed.) *Stato dell'Italia*, Milan: Il Saggiatore.

Salvadori, M. (1994) *Storia d'Italia e crisi di regime*, Bologna: Il Mulino.

Samuels, R. (1994) Unpublished comparative paper on Japan and Italy, presented at the Centre for European Studies, Harvard University at the conference 'Reconstructing Italy: sources of pathology and forces for reform', February.

Scalfari, E. (1969) *L'autunno della Repubblica*, Milan: Einaudi.

Schneider, J. and Schneider, P. (1994) 'Mafia, antimafia and the question of Sicilian culture', *Politics and Society*, 22 (2): 237–58.

Scoppola, P. (1991) *La Repubblica dei partiti*, Bologna: Il Mulino.

Skocpol, T. (1979) *States and Social Revolutions*, Cambridge: Cambridge University Press.

Stajano, C. (1993) *Il disordine*, Turin: Einaudi.

Trigilia, C. (1986) *Grandi partiti e piccole imprese*, Bologna: Il Mulino.

Tsoukalis, L. (1991) *The New European Economy*, Oxford: Oxford University Press.

Zamagni, V. (1994) *The Economic History of Italy, 1860–1990*, Oxford: Clarendon Press.

2 Electoral reform and political change in Italy, 1991–1994

Simon Parker

FIRST TREMORS: THE LAST POLITICAL BATTLES OF THE FIRST REPUBLIC

The Italian party system has for most of the post-war period represented something of a paradox in its combination of governmental instability and seemingly static electoral behaviour (Farneti 1985; La Palombara 1987; Mannheimer and Sani 1994). The swings in the fortunes of the major parties so familiar to political analysts in other industrial democracies were alien to Italy's political culture where change was incremental and halting. To take Gramsci's famous military allegory, throughout most of the history of the Republic, electoral competition in Italy had been a war of position fought over a thin, treacherous and unyielding no-man's land of the non-partisan.

Any disruption to the pattern of Christian Democrat dominance was hailed as an earth-shattering event. Thus the near 'overtaking' of the DC by the Italian Communist Party (PCI) in 1976 was described as an 'earthquake' (Ghini 1976), but the foundations of political Catholicism were able to withstand the Left's assault, and the walls of Jericho remained standing. The seeming impossibility of electoral realignment in Italy prompted many political scientists and sociologists to speculate on the reasons for the country's apparent political under-development, a charge that had originally been made by Almond and Verba in their influential study of political culture in the 1960s (Almond and Verba 1963).

The reasons advanced focused on the persistence of strong regional sub-cultures, the continuing importance of pre-modern ties of kinship and group loyalty, the reluctance of the major parties to become genuinely 'catch-all', and the lack of a popular belief in the possibility of change through electoral choice. Moreover the 'civic culture' considered essential to the proper functioning of a modern democracy, it was argued, was only to be found in a limited number of central and northern regions (Putnam 1993). However, an important study published in 1987 questioned some of the assumptions on which political analysis had hitherto been based (Mannheimer and Sani 1987). The authors argued that although sub-cultures continued to play a determining role in electoral politics, important signs of change could be discerned which pointed to a steady erosion of the cleavage patterns that had underpinned the 'polarised pluralism' described by Giovanni Sartori a decade before (Sartori 1976).

In the wake of the 1992 parliamentary elections, the authors of *Il mercato elettorale* were even more certain that this trend had now become a political reality and they argued that 'the results of 5 April 1992 signalled the presence of elements of rupture which entailed a partial destructuring of the party system' (Sani in Mannheimer and Sani 1994: 45). In order to understand the significance of the vote of 5 April and what had contributed to this partial destructuring of the party system, we first need to consider the referendum on the electoral system that took place the previous summer.

The 1991 referendum on preference voting

On 9 June 1991, Mario Segni moved to the centre of the political stage as the chief promoter of the referendum on the abolition of the multiple preference vote. The preference system had allowed a corrupt market in vote trading to develop among the leaders of the main party factions and their local representatives (the 'exchange vote'). The aim of the reformers was to deliver a large part of the electorate from the clutches of the vote traders by allowing only one preference to be expressed on the ballot paper. The reform would have resulted in a concentration of votes for the nationally important names of the party factions, but it would have made it virtually impossible for their subordinates to be guaranteed 'sponsorship'. Thus the faction leaders risked becoming generals with no armies to command.

The PDS, Segni's reformist Catholics and most of the leftist parties backed the change. Fearing a political backlash for supporting an unpopular system, Forlani's Christian Democrats took an agnostic position (at least in public) but hoped that their supporters would desert the polling booths so that the measure would fail to reach the necessary 50 per cent quota. The Socialist Party secretary, Bettino Craxi, had no such scruples and he urged voters to follow his example and 'go to the seaside' on the day of the referendum. Craxi even threatened to provoke a constitutional crisis if the referendum was approved, and by doing so he raised the stakes of the referendum by insisting that no negative verdict should be allowed on the system that had brought the Craxi–Andreotti–Forlani triumvirate (the so-called CAF) to power.

Two weeks before the vote the satirical weekly *Cuore* had dedicated its front page to an appeal which read 'Don't be a grafter's lackey, Vote Yes' (Bellu and Bonsanti 1993: 85–86). On the day, 27 million Italians, or

62.5 per cent of those eligible to vote, cast their ballots overwhelmingly in favour of ending the multiple preference vote (by 95.6 per cent to 4.4 per cent). The consequences of the abolition of the preference system were to exceed even Mario Segni's highest expectations. The whole exchange vote system was in jeopardy – and with it the basis of factional power in the ruling party coalition.[1] As Furlong argues in the following chapter, the change encouraged reformers in the DC to press for greater democracy and accountability inside their own party, and it encouraged pretenders to the leadership of the PSI, such as Martelli, to talk about political renewal and an opening to the PDS. But the Christian Democrat secretary Arnaldo Forlani's warning that the choice for supporters of the government was either business as usual or chaos proved to be a prescient interpretation of the impending crisis (Wertman 1993: 18).

The April 1992 elections: the barbarians at the gates

Less than a year after the referendum victory, Italy was again called to the polls to elect a new Parliament. The outcome was once again compared to an 'electoral earthquake', but for once the analogy appears to have been justified (Mannheimer 1993: 85). A fault-line had opened up in the Italian party system, and for the first time the four parties of the government coalition (the *quadripartito*) failed to win a majority of votes cast. Also for the first time since 1948 there was no Italian Communist Party, instead Occhetto's PDS appeared on the ballot in competition with the breakaway minority of the former PCI, now called Rifondazione Comunista. Like their Russian predecessors it was the (minority/bolshevik) Rifondazione that claimed to carry the banner of communism, while the PDS struggled to assert itself as a new-look European social democratic party. However, the old PCI proved to be more than the sum of its post-1990 components since the PDS and Rifondazione's combined vote in 1992 was nearly 6 per cent less than the PCI's vote in 1987. It was not the collapse that many of the PDS and Rifondazione's opponents gleefully predicted, but it meant that Occhetto's attempts to present the PDS as a new party of government would require more than a name change and a different symbol.

But the most significant outcome of these elections was undoubtedly the rise of a relatively new political force that was decidedly 'anti-system'. Umberto Bossi's Lega Lombarda led the coalition of regional autonomist *leghe* that had been struggling without success at the margins of northern Italian political life for more than a decade. Bossi's movement had taken the mass media and the other political parties by surprise by leaping from 0.5 per cent to 8.7 per cent of the national vote in 1992, and accounting for nearly 3.4 million votes for the Chamber of Deputies (see Table 2.2 and Diamanti, Chapter 7). The most striking aspect of the League's success, however, was that these millions of 'new political subjects' were overwhelmingly concentrated in the towns and villages of Lombardy, the Veneto and the alpine North (Mannheimer 1993: 87–88).

A new regional, indeed regionalist sub-culture had been born, but unlike that of the 'red belt' which could be harmlessly insulated from the centres of national power, the League threatened the hegemony of the DC and PSI in their heartland regions of Lombardy, Piedmont and the Veneto. Having won hundreds of seats on the councils of the smaller northern towns in the local elections of May 1990, the League took 21 per cent of the vote in the province of Milan in the 1992 parliamentary elections. With their 55 deputies, the Lega Nord represented a compact bloc of constitutional revisionists who were only too willing to challenge the system of 'bargained pluralism' of the post-war Republic (Hine 1993).

Umberto Bossi's boast that his party had liquidated the CAF was not without foundation. The usual behind the scenes fixing that went on between the party faction leaders and the President was no longer so straightforward after the reform of the preference system had made the *manuale Cencelli*[2] if not redundant, then certainly badly in need of revision. Within a matter of weeks President Cossiga resigned without appointing a new successor, and it took 16 successive ballots and the assassination of Judge Giovanni Falcone to elect Oscar Luigi Scalfaro as his successor (Allum 1993). The end of Cossiga's presidency and the eclipse of the CAF could perhaps be seen as the swan song of the old Republic, although the real deluge was yet to come.

PANDORA'S BALLOT BOX: THE CAMPAIGN FOR ELECTORAL REFORM AND THE MAKING OF THE 'MATTARELLUM'

After the success of the 1991 referendum on preference voting, the stage was set for a more thorough-going reform of the electoral system which the sponsors hoped would bring about the end of the proportional system which many considered to be the cause of Italy's political malaise. The Segni initiative should however be seen as but the latest in a series of manoeuvres dating back to the early years of the Republic to tackle the problem of Italy's political immobilism. The Christian Democrats attempted to break the log-jam by passing what the Communists success-fully labelled the *legge truffa* (swindle law) in 1953. The law sought to create a *premio di maggioranza* (a majoritarian prize) of reserved seats that would guarantee a working parliamentary majority if the combined votes of a 'linked list' of parties amounted to a majority of votes cast. The law was met by a campaign of civil resistance on the Left, and no serious attempt to reorganise the electoral system was made for more than three decades (Ginsborg 1990: 142–143). In the mid-1980s the Bozzi Commission was established in order to develop an alternative to the current electoral impasse which could win cross-party consensus. But while the Commission's deliberations were often learned and imaginative, the logic of the party system meant that any genuine reform proposals that emerged would be frustrated because even the opposition had a stake in maintaining the status quo (Hine 1993: 302).

The proportional system suited the PCI very well, as Warner and Gambetta have argued, because under a majoritarian system, the DC would have become the unique party of government without any need to resort to the 'opening to the Left' which brought the PSI into power in the 1960s and the rapprochement with the Communists that heralded the 'historic compromise' of the 1970s (Warner and Gambetta 1994). For the PCI there were many consociational advantages to being the largest opposition party which a 'winner takes all' majoritarian system would almost certainly have denied them. But the metamorphosis of the PCI into the PDS allowed the party's leadership (now free from its hard-left core) to rethink its political strategy and to remodel itself as the moderate left alternative to Christian Democracy. It also allowed it to seriously contemplate the reform of the electoral system in a majoritarian direction that left-wing constitutionalists such as Augusto Barbera and Gianfranco Pasquino had been promoting for many years (Ruffilli 1987; Messina 1992).

This new thinking on the Left coincided with Segni's vision for the complete renewal of the Italian political system, which the success of the June 1991 referendum had done much to encourage. Segni's role was to be a determinate one because of his ability to link together such unlikely personalities as the leader of the Italian Greens, Francesco Rutelli, the veteran Liberal Alfredo Biondi, the PDS secretary Achille Occhetto and the Catholic historian and constitutionalist Pietro Scoppola. A new referendum committee was established and the necessary signatures were collected to put the proposal to the public. By deleting a small number of clauses in the existing electoral law, the 65 per cent threshold for winning in a 'first-past-the-post' fashion for the regional senatorial seats would no longer apply. In total, 238 senatorial seats would be assigned in this way, while the remaining 77 seats not assigned to regional electoral districts would be decided on the basis of a national ballot decided on a proportional basis.[3] Those candidates who won constituency seats would have their votes subtracted from their party's national list in the proportional contest.

The Constitutional Court, having refused to allow similar questions to be put to the nation a few years before (Sentence no. 47, 1991), this time decided to permit both the referendum for new procedures for electing the Senate and for the introduction of a majoritarian system also for the election of councils with populations greater than 5,000 inhabitants (Sentence no. 32, 1993 see Ambrosini 1993: 142). The greater flexibility of the court suggested that even this supposedly Olympian institution was attentive to the popular revolt against the *partitocrazia*.

After the April 1992 elections, Parliament was forced to acknowledge the changed political environment by establishing a bicameral Commission on Electoral Reform. However, consensus was no easier to find in the XIth legislature, and when the Commission's President Ciriaco De Mita (until the advent of Segni, long considered the best hope for a reform-oriented DC) fell from grace after his brother's implication in the Irpinia earthquake relief funds scandal, the Commission became of only marginal importance to the electoral reform debate (Abse 1993: 17). The initiative was with the referendum committee and their supporters, and despite the Constitutional Court's aspiration that a political solution should still be arrived at, the momentum for change was clearly coming from outside Parliament, and by now it had become unstoppable.

The campaign and the outcome of the referendum

From the outset the 'Yes' camp had the advantage of an almost entirely sympathetic mass media which gave considerable exposure to Segni as the 'new man' of Italian politics, capable of building a consensus for change across the political spectrum. Only the scale of the victory for the 'Yes' campaign was at issue when voters were called to decide on 18 and 19 April. Of the voters who turned out (75 per cent of the electorate), 82.7 per cent cast their ballots for change, making the case for reform constitutionally and morally unanswerable. Many of the other referendum issues such as the abolition of three government ministries, the decriminalisation of drug possession for personal use, and the abolition of state funding for political parties were completely overshadowed by the electoral reform question. But in the case of party funding the consensus against the *partitocrazia* was even greater, with less than one in ten voting to retain the subsidy.

The *Corriere della Sera* heralded the result as the start of a new Italy, while *Il Giornale* announced the birth of a Second Republic. Even the PSI daily *Avanti!* had to confess that the result was a landslide in support of a measure that its recently resigned secretary had implacably opposed. One of the few dissenting voices was Luigi Pintor who in his editorial for *Il Manifesto* claimed that the whole reform initiative was a sham designed by the old regime and supported by a naive or deceitful PDS to save it from political oblivion.[4] The sour grapes at seeing the 'vote for change, vote for no change' campaign overwhelmingly rejected by the electorate did not detract from Pintor's point that what was now effectively a rump Parliament was to be charged with the task of its own unmaking. This rather uncomfortable fact, as the *avvisi di garanzia* (notices of criminal investigation) rained down on as many as a third of Montecitorio's deputies, was overlooked in the euphoria of the victory celebrations. But the hand that broke the mould of Italian parliamentary representation would not be the one to shape its less than elegant replacement.

The Mattarellum

The electoral reform promoted by the Christian Democrat Mattarella was approved in the first days of August 1993 (hence Sartori's epithet of the 'Mattarellum' – a compound of its parliamentary sponsor and the referendum of 18 April that had forced a change in the law). The bill was approved by 55.4 per cent of those present – which meant that only 45.5 per cent of deputies actively supported the measure (Warner and Gambetta 1994: 67). This was a fitting peroration to a legislature that had voted four times in succession to protect the parliamentary immunity of Bettino Craxi, and which even in its death agonies was incapable of responding to the popular will for change in a concerted and dignified manner.

However, it was the Christian Democrat majority in Parliament – the very political class against which the referendum had been directed – that finally decided the content of the law. Mattarella argued that all of the (13) bills put forward in committee aimed at reducing the fragmentation of political representation and the intermediation of the parties as well as providing a more direct connection between the choice of the voter and the formation of the government. According to Mattarella there were broadly two approaches (if one ignores the PDS double ballot proposal which had dropped out of contention): (i) the maintenance of some kind of proportional system (RC, MSI), and (ii) the adoption of a 'first-past-the-post' English model (Lega, Pannella). In true Christian Democrat style, Mattarella suggested a compromise solution which would 'reconcile elements of the majoritarian system with elements of the proportional system' (Camera dei deputati 1993: 151).

The final law was therefore a hybrid which provided for the election of three-quarters of the Senate and Camera on a simple majority constituency basis, and one-quarter on a proportional basis. For the Senate there would be only one vote which would elect both the constituency senators and the proportional Senate seats elected on a regional basis. There would be two votes for the Chamber of Deputies, one for the constituency seat and another for the proportional seats which would be elected on a national basis. In order to compensate the losing parties in the constituency contests in both Chambers, a 'proportional recuperation quotient' (*scorporo*) was instituted for the Senate where votes were to be deducted on a one-for-one basis from the proportional list of the winning candidate's party in the constituency ballots. For the Chamber of Deputies a partial *scorporo* was to be applied to winning constituency candidates' lists in the proportional ballot. This partial deduction was based on the number of votes (plus one) of the second-placed candidate, or 25 per cent of the total constituency vote – whichever was the higher. These votes were then to be nationally summed for each list or lists that appeared on the winning constituency candidates' ballot paper. Winning candidates supporting more than one list would have their votes deducted pro-portionately (Parker 1994).

The reform of the local electoral system

Unlike the system proposed for the Senate and the Chamber of Deputies, the new electoral law for the election of municipal administrations was based on the direct election of the mayor according to a second ballot system, where if a candidate failed to obtain a majority of votes in the first round, a second ballot would take place between the two candidates with the highest share of the vote (Senato della Repubblica 1993). The two-vote system certainly contributed towards the bi-polarisation of the local electorate. In the big city elections in November 1993, the PDS had been shrewd enough to realize that a pre-electoral pact with the other parties of the 'Left area' was vital if progressive candidates were to have any chance of forming majorities.

The Christian Democrats were too preoccupied with their own leader-ship crisis in the wake of *Tangentopoli* to organise such an alliance, which meant that voters in the Centre, if they wanted to avoid wasting their vote, were forced to align with a Left that still included members of the hard-line Rifondazione Comunista or with a newly resurgent neo-fascist right (MSI-DN) in the South, or with a Northern League that had failed to impress the majority of Catholic voters in the previous parliamentary elections. For the moderate voter it was an unenviable choice, but mar-ginally more of them chose the Left than the Right, giving the Left control of Palermo, Catania, Naples, Rome, Genoa, Turin, Venice, and Trieste.

The electoral triumph of the municipal Left was the clearest sign that the Centre could no longer hold. Having failed to persuade Segni and Martinazzoli to sink their differences and join forces with Fini's renascent MSI, Berlusconi decided that he alone had the resources and ability to rally the forces of the Centre-Right to 'save Italy from communism'. On 26 January 1994 Berlusconi threw his hat into the ring and his entry into politics signified, in Mannheimer's phrase, 'a profound and perhaps irreversible change in the ... logic of [political] competition beginning with the way that the electoral campaign is conducted' (Mannheimer 1994: 29).

THE 1994 ELECTION CAMPAIGN

The 1994 parliamentary election campaign was extensively trailed as the first election of the Second Italian Republic, but the historical significance of the vote did not inject the contest with the passion and enthusiasm of other landmark elections of the post-war period – despite the controver-sies over media manipulation and 'dirty tricks'. *Tangentopoli* and the abolition of public financial support to the parties, together with the new rules on the limitation of election expenditure may help to explain the lack of the usual party jamborees (Parker 1994). Campaign rallies took on a rather ritual demeanour – it was obvious to anyone who attended that the public were there to provide an enthusiastic back-drop for the party leaders' platform speeches, which were timed and tailored for the news bulletins. Of course there was nothing new in this, but undoubtedly Berlusconi's determination to fight the campaign over the television networks (half of which were owned by his companies) rather than on the streets made the town square rallies seem more like the anachronistic pageants of the old party system than an affirmation of popular democracy.

The *progressisti* campaign was aimed at promoting the PDS as the linch pin of responsible government. Occhetto was received by the City of London and New York financiers, and while his programme won plaudits from *The Economist* and the *The Financial Times* for its moderation, it could hardly be described as inspiring (PDS 1994). Berlusconi's promise to found 'a new economic miracle', to cut taxes and to create one million new jobs were dismissed as fantasies by the Left, but many Italians seemed ready to be convinced that what Berlusconi had done for Fininvest he could do for Italy (Forza Italia 1994). The *progressisti* team, which included the centrist Alleanza Democratica and Bertinotti's Rifondazione Comunista, was hardly a convincing government coalition in the making. Indeed Occhetto felt the need to exclude the participation of RC in any future *progressisti* government if Bertinotti refused to accept what was effectively a 'social market' programme (see Foot, Chapter 11).

Possibly another of Occhetto's mistakes was to talk in terms of the continuity of 'institutional government' by proposing Carlo Azeglio Ciampi or some other similarly worthy neutral to head a reforming coalition government.[5] Although Ciampi's brief administration set about the process of reform with a greater dedication than virtually any post-war government, to the average Italian, institutional government had merely meant more taxes and a more serious approach to tax collection (which amounted to the same thing). By reducing the budget deficit Ciampi's administration had also posed a threat to the state subsidies on which so many poorer families were dependent (many of them in the South). Alleanza Nazionale were able to seize on this fear and clothed themselves in the apparel of *garantismo* (the guaranteeing of existing privileges) which had previously been monopolised by the Christian Democrats and the Socialists. It was the exact opposite of the neo-liberal rhetoric of Bossi and Berlusconi in the North, but it was shrewd product differentiation given the very different demands of the centre-right electorate in other parts of Italy.

The Catholic centre was perhaps the least prepared for an election campaign because the newly formed Partito Popolare had to cope with unresolved factional struggles over its leadership and programme, while leading figures defected to form rival Catholic parties on the Right (the Centro Cristiano Democratico) and on the Left (the Cristiani Sociali) (see Furlong, Chapter 3). By insisting on keeping his campaign separate (if united on the ballot paper for the constituency seats), Segni split the Catholic centre vote and contributed to the fragmentation of the Catholic electorate. Despite Segni and Martinazzoli's protestations, the media presented the election as a head to head between Berlusconi and Occhetto, making it difficult for the two Catholic leaders to assert themselves in such a polarised contest. Martinazzoli had more or less conceded that he was fighting for the political survival of Christian Democracy and promptly resigned after the PPI were humiliatingly defeated. Segni might have received the endorsement of either side as a potential President of the Council of Ministers at certain points in the campaign, but ended by becoming the most famous casualty of the system he had campaigned for by losing to Alleanza Nazionale in his home-town constituency of Sassari.

THE POLITICAL LANDSCAPE OF THE NEW ITALIAN REPUBLIC

Had the 1992 vote been held under the new majoritarian system the outcome would have still given the Christian Democrats the greater share of the parliamentary seats. This was the basis of Libertini's claim on behalf of Rifondazione Comunista that the new electoral law would consolidate rather than eliminate the power of the old governmental parties (Libertini 1992; see also Abse 1993). For example, in Milan Central, based on their previous vote the Christian Democrats would have won the seat from the League albeit on the tiniest of margins (17.2 per cent to 16.57 per cent), closely followed by the Republicans (14.28 per cent) and the PDS (11.19 per cent) (Camera dei deputati 1994: 23). In the event, the League leader Umberto Bossi won by a comfortable margin, taking 48.7 per cent of the vote compared to 25.4 per cent for the *progressisti* and 11.9 per cent for Patto Italia. In the vast majority of Senatorial and Chamber constituency contests the race followed a similar pattern, with the Polo della Libertà in the North and the Polo del Buon Governo in the South battling against the *progressisti* for first and second place while the PPI and Segni candidates limped home a poor third.

In just under a third of the Camera constituencies (31.2 per cent) the winning candidate obtained a majority of votes cast, and in 71.7 per cent of these contests the victors took over 40 per cent of the vote. If the 1992 elections had been contested according to the new majoritarian system, approximately a third of all candidates would have been returned with less than 30 per cent of the vote, whereas only 4.4 per cent of candidates were elected with less than this share of the ballot in the 1994 contest (Camera dei deputati 1994; Agosta 1994: 22–23). Of course the two

Table 2.1 Results of the elections to the Senate 27 and 28 March 1994 and voting share (proportional results) for 1994 and 1992

Party/coalition	Seats			Percentage of vote (P)	
	C*	P**	Total	1994	1992
Polo Lib.	74	8	82	19.9	–
Polo BG	54	10	64	13.7	–
Progr.	96	26	122	32.9	23.5[a]
Patto It.	3	28	31	16.7	27.3[b]
AN		8	8	6.3	6.5[c]
Pannella		1	1	2.3	0.5
Lega N.				–	8.2
Other L.				1.0	–
Lega A.		1	1	0.7	–
SVP	3		3	0.7	–
L. auton.	1		1	0.6	–
FI-CCD		1	1	0.5	–
PSI				0.3	13.6
PRI				–	4.7
PLI				–	2.8
Verdi F.				0.3	3.1
Socdem				0.2	2.6
La Rete				–	0.7
Others	1		1	3.9	6.5
Total	232	83	315	100	100

Source: RaiTelevideo/La Repubblica, 30 March 1994

Notes: C*=constituency; P**=proportional; Polo Lib.=Freedom Pole (Forza Italia, the Northern League, Christian Democratic Centre, Union of the Centre, Pannella List); Polo BG=Pole of Good Government (Forza Italia, National Alliance, Christian Democratic Centre, Union of the Centre); Progr.=Progressives (Democratic Party of the Left, Socialist Party CSI), Rinascita Socialista, Communist Refoundation, Greens, Democratic Alliance, the Network, Christian Social); Patto It.=Pact for Italy (Segni, Italian People's Party); AN=National Alliance (ex-MSI); Pannella=Panella List (ex-Radical Party); Lega N.=Northern League; Other L.=Other Leagues; L. auton=Autonomist League; SVP=South Tyrol People's Party; FI=Forza Italia; CCD=Christian Democratic Centre; PDS=Democratic Party of the Left; RC=Communist Refoundation; AD=Democratic Alliance; PPI=Italian People's Party; PSI=Italian Socialist Party; PRI=Italian Republican Party; PLI=Italian Liberal Party; Verdi F.=Federation of Greens; Socdem=Social Democratic Party; La Rete=The Network. a=Democratic Party of the Left + Communist Refoundation; b=Christian Democracy; c=Italian Social Movement–National Right (Neofascists)

elections were fought under very different conditions and with a very different array of parties and candidates, meaning that any comparison should be made with caution. However, if the PSI and DC had been able to maintain their 1992 vote it is interesting to note that the biggest 'fragmentation regions' would have been in the North, while the Centre and the South and Islands (with the exception of metropolitan Rome) would have produced solid majorities for the former Communists and Christian Democrats respectively.

The 1992 results and the subsequent local elections led many observers

Table 2.2 Results of the elections to the Chamber of Deputies 27 and 28 March 1994 and voting share (proportional results) for 1994 and 1992

Party/coalition	Seats			Percentage of vote (P)	
	C*	P**	Total	1994	1992
Polo Lib.	164		164		
Polo BG	137		137		
Progr.	164		164		
Patto It.	4		4		
AN	1	23	24	13.4	5.4ᶜ
FI		30	30	21.0	–
PDS		38	38	20.4	16.1
RC		11	11	6.0	5.6
AD				1.2	–
Pannella				3.5	1.2
Lega N.		11	11	8.4	8.7
PPI/DC		29	29	11.1	31.7
Segni		13	13	4.6	–
SVP				0.6	0.5
PSI				2.2	14.5
PRI				–	4.7
PLI				–	3.0
Verdi F.				2.7	3.0
Socdem				0.5	2.9
La Rete				1.9	2.0
Others†	5		5	2.5	0.7
Total	475	155	630	100	100

Source: RaiTelevideo/La Repubblica

Notes: See Table 2.1; †=includes Aosta Valley constituency

to predict that Italy would continue to polarise geographically, and that the new electoral law would result in a more homogeneous and concentrated voting pattern. The actual results produced an even more complicated political map – that Natale has divided into six geographically distinct categories (Natale 1994). With the exception of the 'red belt' which still presents a strong degree of continuity with the parliamentary elections of the post-war period, the new political boundaries are not self-contained and show considerable discontinuity with respect to the past. In addition to the 'red zone', the ecological types that Natale identifies include a 'strong Right', a *'leghista'*, an 'autonomist', a 'southern rightist', and a 'Left–Right equilibrium' area. The Italian electorate is shown to align with one of the three poles (Left, Right and Centre) and it is the degree of 'mix' with alternative political formations that gives each category its special character. For example, because of the significant presence of Centre and Left voters (leaving aside the ideological differences within the Right), the 'rightist South' differs from the 'strong Right' that can be identified in many northern provinces. Similarly, the near irrelevance of other political parties in the few provinces dominated by the South Tyrol People's Party and the Union Valdotaine confirms these areas as solidly and exclusively autonomist (Natale 1994).

The movement of the vote

The question that most frequently occurred in the post-election analysis of the results was 'has Italy moved to the Right?'. The Polo della Libertà/ Polo del Buon Governo alliance comprised parties as diverse as Marco Pannella's pseudo-libertarian Radicals, Gianfranco Fini's 'post-fascist' Alleanza Nazionale, Umberto Bossi's 'anti-fascist' League, Berlusconi's 'anti-communist' Forza Italia and an assortment of Catholic fundamentalists and old style Liberal conservatives. From previous studies we know that MSI voters consistently located themselves at the far right of the political spectrum, whereas the League voter occupied a more central position (Mannheimer 1993: 93). Forza Italia held a more ambiguous position since Berlusconi's supporters did not diverge significantly from the positions taken by other Italians on subjects such as immigration, trade unions, and faith in the institutions (Mannheimer 1994: 37). But while there may be no strong Forza 'animus', Berlusconi's message did not convince those who considered themselves to be on the political Left. By default then, the Forza Italia electorate was essentially restricted to the Centre and Right of the political spectrum.

Again it is perilous to talk of a national trend since there were great regional and even intra-regional variations in voting patterns which confirmed the relevance of political sub-cultures particularly in the 'red belt' which stayed mostly loyal to the *progressisti*. In Sicily however, the Rete's hopes of consolidating its victory in the municipal elections of the previous year were dashed as their voters deserted them in droves in favour of the AN/Forza Italia bloc. Former Socialist voters were the most 'transversal' in that they tended to vote for the *progressisti* in the red belt, for the League and Forza Italia in the North and in nearly equal measure for the Left and the Right in the South (Natale 1994: 92). The vast reservoir of former Christian Democrat voters (over 11.6 million in the last Chamber of Deputies elections) was crucial to the outcome of this election since barely half of them supported the remnant PPI and Segni. They backed Forza Italia and AN in large numbers in the South, stayed predominantly loyal to the PPI and Segni in the Centre and supported Forza Italia (and to a much lesser extent the League in the proportional ballot) in the North (Natale 1994: 93). Thus while one in ten of ex-Christian Democrats voted with the *progressisti*, four out of ten defected to one of the two Berlusconi poles.

The ex-lay parties voted overwhelmingly for the Polo del Buon Governo in the South and for the Polo della Libertà in the North. Berlusconi was also popular with League voters (63 per cent wanted to see him as

Prime Minister) and as many as a half of previous League voters chose Forza Italia in the proportional ballot – confirming the view that the League electorate was more concerned with neo-liberal values than federalism or 'ethno-regionalism'.

FROM CULTURE SHIFT TO POST-MODERN POLITICS?

Ronald Inglehart defined the new cleavages of the 1970s (and 1980s) in Western society in terms of a fundamental change in values, away from corporatist or sectional identities (be they class, religion, language, or ethnicity) towards a more fluid and subjective relationship to politics (Inglehart 1977, 1990). Although we can agree that a movement away from traditional political identities was in progress throughout Western European democracies in this period, it would appear that the identification with a 'post-materialist' politics, in the case of Italy at least, has been a minority interest. The success of Berlusconism points to the persistance and entrenchment of materialist and consumerist values in a civil society that has become progressively less attached to Communist or Catholic sub-cultures, but which has been unable or possibly unwilling to seek a replacement political ethic.[6]

Authors such as Giacomo Sani have demonstrated that the 'politically literate' – those who follow politics closely or take part in any political activity – are a dwindling minority in Italy (Sani 1994: 31). The recent collapse in membership of the former Christian Democratic and Communist Parties and their affiliated organisations exacerbated a trend that had already been established by the late 1970s. While this is a pattern that can be found in many other European societies, because the mass party was such an essential feature of Italian politics for most of the postwar period, its disappearance has left a much greater chasm in the post-Cold War landscape than is the case with its European neighbours. This decline in political awareness or interest is progressively more pronounced the younger the age-range, and it would appear that sub-cultural identification has less importance for the current generation of Italians than it has for their parents' generation (Censis 1992). It is significant that the youngest electors voted in greater numbers for Forza Italia and tended to reject the traditional parties whatever their new campaign colours.

Women also voted for Berlusconi in proportionately greater numbers than men (see McCarthy, Chapter 8), and although it is difficult to isolate the precise factors which contributed to this greater responsiveness, it is significant that the values Forza Italia sought to promote were precisely those domestic, familial, and consumer-oriented images that Berlusconi's advertising companies had successfully targeted at Italian women throughout the 1980s (see Gundle and O'Sullivan, Chapter 13). Thus although Forza Italia attracted many former Christian Democrats and Centre voters, it did particularly well at attracting support from those who had not previously held strong political views, and in this sense Berlusconi was uniquely able to create his own 'political market'.

By presenting himself as the conciliator and unifier of sectional interests, Berlusconi portrayed himself as an 'outsider', reluctantly called to the political vocation in the national interest and at the service of the Italian people – much as another business tycoon turned politician, J. Ross Perot, had portrayed his candidature to a different audience in the 1992 US Presidential elections. These brokering skills were made manifest in the forging of the seemingly improbable alliance between *leghisti*, neo-fascists, and neo-liberals, which was presented as the political equivalent of a soccer manager marshalling a team of rogue talents. The *squadra* had been built, and as Berlusconi famously admitted, whenever his team walked onto the park he expected them to win (Fracassi and Gambino 1994: 38). By contrast Occhetto, Bossi, Martinazzoli and even Fini would have been quite happy with a draw. Here was the essential difference in approach between a group of enterprising politicians and a political entrepreneur.

However, the representation and the reality of Berlusconi's achieve-ment should not be conflated. Although Forza Italia's electoral perform-ance was impressive, Berlusconi's candidates obtained only 0.6 per cent more of the national vote than the PDS, and none of the other compo-nents of the Polo della Libertà/Polo del Buon Governo could claim to be more popular than the PSI at the zenith of Craxism. It was a landslide for the 'Rights', as we ought properly to call them, but not for any one party. Although Forza Italia consolidated and strengthened its position in the European elections of June, no party of the Second Republic has yet come close to winning the consensus once enjoyed by the DC (see McCar-thy, Chapter 8).

The elections of March 1994 certainly confirmed the demise of the old party system and the emergence of new and newly rehabilitated political forces, but what the elections also produced was a sense of uncertainty and instability which derived partly from tensions within the governing coalition itself, though also from a heightened sensibility among all the parties to the greater volatility of the electorate and the continued vulner-ability of political leaders to the 'judicial revolution' – which showed no sign of abating after the elections despite the continuing search for a 'political solution' to the corruption problem by some leading magistrates (see Nelken, Chapter 12). The new Italian Republic has therefore an indistinct but complex shape, and it seems unlikely that its form will fully emerge until the broader constitutional ideals which for most of the post-war period have been subordinated to the exigencies of party rule, are genuinely and purposively applied throughout Italian political and civil society.

NOTES

I would like to thank the Nuffield Foundation for supporting the research on which this chapter is based.

1 For a detailed analysis of voting behaviour before and after the preference vote reform see Sani and Radaelli 1993.
2 The system by which ministerial portfolios and other more junior government posts were allocated according to the relative parliamentary strength of each party and party faction.
3 Law number 276 of 4 August 1993 actually attributed 232 senatorial seats to the constituencies and 83 to those elected in the party lists for the proportional vote.
4 It should be said that some veteran left-wingers inside the PDS such as Pietro Ingrao publicly opposed the party's 'Yes' stance, but Ingrao's position was an increasingly maverick one within a party that had become unashamedly social democratic in its philosophy and political strategy. See Martin Bull (Chapter 10) for a fuller discussion of this point.
5 For a more detailed discussion of the PDS's 'errors' before and during the election campaign see the preceding chapter by Paul Ginsborg.
6 It is worth remarking that the term 'postmodernism' came into use in the same year that Berlusconi's first television station TeleMilano was launched in his 'private city' Milano2 in 1978.

REFERENCES

Abse, T. (1993) 'The triumph of the leopard', *New Left Review*, 199, May–June: 3–28.
Agosta, A. (1994) 'Maggioritario e proporzionale', in I. Diamanti and R. Mannheimer (eds) *Milano a Roma. Guida all'Italia elettorale del 1994*, Rome: Donzelli.
Allum, P. (1993) 'Chronicle of a death foretold: the first Italian Republic', *Reading Papers in Politics*, Occasional Paper No. 12.
Almond, G. and Verba, S. (1963) *The Civic Culture. Political Attitudes and Democracy in Five Nations*, Princeton: Princeton University Press.
Ambrosini, G. (1993) *Referendum*, Turin: Bollati Boringhieri.
Bellu, G. and Bonsanti, S. (1993) *Il crollo. Andreotti, Craxi e il loro regime*, Bari and Rome: Laterza.
Camera dei deputati (1993) *Nuove norme per l'elezione della Camera e del Senato. Schede di sintesi n.128/I. XI legislatura – settembre 1993*. Rome: Camera dei deputati Servizio Studi.
— (1994) *Riaggregazione dei dati elettorali 1992 secondo i nuovi collegi uninominali costituito con il decreto legislativo n.536 del 1993*, Rome: Camera dei deputati Servizi Studi.
Censis (1992) *La situazione sociale del Paese. Speciale 26° Rapporto.* (10–11–12, Oct-Nov-Dec), Milan: Franco Angeli.
Diamanti, I. and Mannheimer, R. (eds) (1994) *Milano a Roma. Guida all'Italia elettorale del 1994*, Rome: Donzelli.
Farneti, P. (1985) *The Italian Party System (1945–1980)*, London: Pinter.
Forza Italia (1994) *Programma*, Caltignaga (No): Forza Italia.
Fracassi, C. and Gambino, M. (1994) *Berlusconi. Una biografia non autorizzata*, Rome: Avvenimenti.
Ghini, C. (1976) *Il terremoto elettorale*, Milan: Feltrinelli.
Ginsborg, P. (1990) *A History of Contemporary Italy: Society and Politics 1943–1988* London: Penguin.

Hine, D. (1993) *Governing Italy. The Politics of Bargained Pluralism*, Oxford: Oxford University Press.

Inglehart, R. (1977) *The Silent Revolution: Changing Values and Political Styles Among Western Publics*, Princeton: Princeton University Press.

—— (1990) *Culture Shift in Advanced Industrial Society*, Princeton: Princeton University Press.

La Palombara, J. (1987) *Democracy Italian Style*, New Haven, Conn.: Yale University Press.

Libertini, L. (1992) *La truffa svelata. Riforma e controriforma nelle istituzioni*. Rome: Napoleone.

Mannheimer, R. (1993) 'The Electorate of the Lega Nord', in G. Pasquino and P. McCarthy (eds) *The End of Post-War Politics in Italy. The Landmark 1992 Elections*, Boulder, Col.: Westview Press.

—— (1994) 'Forza Italia', in I. Diamanti and R. Mannheimer (eds) *Milano a Roma. Guida all'Italia elettorate del 1994*, Rome: Douzelli.

Mannheimer, R. and Sani, G. (1987) *Il mercato elettorale. Identikit dell'elettore italiano*, Bologna: Il Mulino.

—— (1994) *La rivoluzione elettorale. L'Italia tra la prima e la seconda repubblica*, Milan: Anabasi.

Messina, S. (1992) *La grande riforma. Uomini e progetti per una nuova repubblica*, Rome and Bari: Laterza.

Natale, P. (1994) 'La nuova mappa geopolitica', in I. Diamanti and R. Mannheimer (eds) *Milano a Roma. Guida all'Italia elettorale del 1994*, Rome: Donzelli.

Parker, S. (1994) 'The March 1994 parliamentary elections: an overview' *ASMI Newsletter*, 25: 28–35.

Pasquino, G. and McCarthy, P. (eds) (1993) *The End of Post-War Politics in Italy. The Landmark 1992 Elections*, Boulder, Col.: Westview Press.

Partito Democratico della Sinistra (1994) *Programma di governo del PDS. Per ricostruire un'Italia più giusta, più unita, più moderna*, Rome: Editrice L'Unità.

Putnam, R. (1993) *Making Democracy Work. Civic Traditions in Modern Italy*, Princeton: Princeton University Press.

Ruffilli, R. (1987) *Materiali per la riforma elettorale*, Bologna: Il Mulino.

Sani, G. and Radaelli, C. (1993) 'Preference voting: before and after the 1991 referendum' *Italian Politics and Society* no. 38.

Sani, G. (1994) 'Modelli di cittadino e comportamenti di massa', in R. Mannheimer and G. Sani (eds) *La rivoluzione elettorale. L'Italia tra la prima e la seconda repubblica*, Milan: Anabasi.

Sartori, G. (1976) *Parties and Party Systems*, Cambridge: Cambridge University Press.

Senato della Repubblica (1993) *Dossier provvedimenti. La riforma del sistema elettorale locale elezione diretta del sindaco (A.C. 72 e abb. – B). Sintesi dell'iter parlamentare al Senato. n.154 XI legislatura – marzo 1993*, Rome: Camera dei deputati Servizi Studi.

Warner, S. and Gambetta, D. (1994) *La retorica della riforma. Fine del sistema proporzionale in Italia*, Turin: Einaudi.

Wertman, D.A. (1993) 'The Christian Democrats: a party in crisis', in G. Pasquino and P. McCarthy (eds) *The End of Post-War Politics in Italy. The Landmark 1992 Elections*, Boulder, Col.: Westview Press.

Part II
The old party system

3 Political Catholicism and the strange death of the Christian Democrats

Paul Furlong

The decline of a governing party from dominance to near extinction is a phenomenon less rare than it used to be. But outside the old Soviet bloc, in stable liberal democracies, such events are still remarkable. The decline of the DC has been spectacular in its rapidity and completeness. The Christian Democrats were Italy's dominant party in the first four decades of the post-war Republic. Their national vote never dropped below 34 per cent from 1948 to 1987. They provided every Prime Minister from December 1945 to June 1981, and several thereafter. Their ministers occupied influential posts in every government of the post-war period up to April 1993, their elected local councillors controlled most of the major cities in coalition, and their appointees managed the largest proportion of Italy's public sector finance and industry. Even in the parliamentary elections of 1992, they were the largest single party, with 29.7 per cent of the national vote and 207 seats in the Chamber of Deputies. Their power was such that Italian politics was categorised by some as a dominant party system, one in which there was no real alternative to the main party of government. But by the 1994 elections they had ceased to exist as a party. Their main successor, the Partito Popolare Italiano (PPI), won 11.7 per cent of the proportional vote and (with a splinter group) 46 seats in the Chamber of Deputies. Another splinter group, the Christian Democratic Centre, won seats within the new dominant grouping led by Forza Italia and were rewarded with two ministerial posts. Other than these two ministers, political Catholicism has lost all its formal trappings of power. More importantly, it has lost its capacity to make the informal rules by which public money and public sector jobs of all kinds were allocated. No longer are the banal speculations of minor DC back-benchers subjected to reverential analysis by journalists in case they might imply subtle shifts in the balance of power between factions. The much-vaunted apparent permanence of their role has been proved illusory. Their leaders, the old names of one of Europe's most long-lasting ruling groups, have disappeared from the front pages. An entire political elite has been replaced.

This chapter concentrates on the Christian Democrats and on the process of their decline. The object is to describe how the DC worked the political system for their own purposes, and what their responses were when this role was threatened by the changes outside its previously unchallengeable control.

POLITICAL CATHOLICISM AND THE DC BEFORE 1992

The emergence of the DC as the dominant party after the war was relatively rapid. The bases of its power developed but did not alter radically once the initial pattern had been established. One of the reasons why it was able to assert its predominance very quickly was the close relationship it enjoyed with the Vatican and the Catholic bishops. The DC also had the overt support of the Allies, particularly the United States, which was also concerned about the potential for disruption by the Communists. However, the long-term success of the Christian Democrats rested on a third pillar, which only emerged at a later stage. The main instruments for this were the state participation system led by the state holding companies IRI and ENI, the Fund for Southern Development (*Cassa per il Mezzogiorno*) and the uncontrolled extension of state-supported occupational pension schemes. With the enormous resources of the state at their disposal, the DC and the other governing parties were able to develop mass patronage as an independent instrument of electoral mobilisation, and thus to create the organisational basis for long-term survival in power. With this development, the party severed its direct link with the Catholic hierarchy – the beginning of a process of separation which economic growth and the secularisation of the electorate reinforced without ever quite completing it.

There is not space here to describe in detail how this system changed over the nearly five decades of uninterrupted DC predominance. For the purposes of this study, it is important to note that one condition of DC power remained unchanged, and this was the exclusion from power of the Communists. Since the PCI remained the second-largest party by a considerable margin, the refusal to countenance them as coalition partners meant that there was no alternative to the DC as the main party of government. In the long term, their performance in government had little electoral impact.

They could claim for some time a record of success – with rapid economic growth and unprecedented improvement in standards of living throughout the country. When growth became more difficult and the regional and class imbalances more obvious, the DC responded by shifting the balance of power both internally and among its various coalition partners. The modern mass DC was a party based on factionalism, in which the leaders of the factions drew their support from increasingly vague ideological identifications and increasingly sharp disputes about control of ministerial, local government and public sector appointments.

The difficulty of maintaining a minimum of party coherence in such circumstances resulted in 1969 in an internal agreement among the factional leaders, the Pact of San Ginesio. This began life as a party document drawn up by one of the emerging younger politicians, Arnaldo Forlani, and was eventually formalised by adoption at a party congress as the 'Forlani preamble'. The Pact of San Ginesio – a text in typical DC coded language – said in effect that internal shifts in the balance of power within the DC would result from time to time in changes in the choice of coalition partner, but would not be allowed to affect the external unity of the DC. The pact enabled the party to separate internal power struggles from the business of running the government.

This had several important results. One consequence was to give the party great flexibility in the choice of coalition partners, always excluding the Communists. This meant that ideally the party ought to be able to maintain its dominant position by playing off potential and actual allies against one another, and for some time in the 1970s the system did function in this way. A further result was to standardise the distribution of rewards for occupation of power through the share system known as *lottizzazione*. In particular, ministerial posts in incoming governments were allocated on the basis of the balance of power among the various factions, in accordance with stable values attached to the individual ministries. The values – the 'worth' of each ministry – were set down in a famous (or notorious) document drawn up by a DC official, the document being known as the Cencelli Manual after its author. Third, the regularisation of the procedures encouraged factional leaders to regard their internal battles as not having serious consequences for their electoral standing, and led to increasingly unconstrained feuding between factions, thus exacerbating government instability and the propensity for short-term policy-making.

In 1989 one might have been forgiven for believing that the DC faced no fundamental threats to its position. Indeed, the conduct of its leaders seemed to reflect this view, since they continued to observe the same general rules of behaviour, and had carried the same generation of party leaders intact for two decades without major change. The only serious party-political challenge to their position came from the Socialist leader Bettino Craxi. Since the Socialists are discussed elsewhere in this book, the detail of this relationship can be omitted here. What is significant is that Craxi's successful and assertive occupation of the Prime Ministership (from August 1983 to April 1987, including the longest single period in office since the war) threatened the San Ginesio principle by preventing the DC from controlling coalition strategy. Craxi's leadership implied in the long term the weakening of the DC's pivotal role in government, and thus the disruption of the internal organization of the party. During the same period, there was increasing public concern over the ineffectiveness of Italy's policy-making procedures, including government instability and the alleged irresponsibility of Parliament. This resulted in a major report on institutional reform and continuing public debate, without however producing any substantial results.

DECLINE AND FALL

The trajectory of the DC through the three years from the referendum on electoral reform in June 1991 to the March 1994 elections requires a detailed and complex analysis for which there is not the space here. However, in synthesis, the argument may be stated briefly. The Christian Democrats in June 1991 were embattled and divided. The pressures for institutional reform were more intense than ever, but found no coherent echo within the party leadership. Despite repeated promises, the DC itself remained unreformed, apparently ever more unrepresentative and distant from its natural constituencies, its factional disputes increasingly obscure and inexplicable. Weaknesses in economic and industrial policy threatened the party's standing with an increasingly sophisticated electorate: particular problems were persistent unemployment, uncontrolled public sector deficit, and the patent difficulties in implementing the European Single Market programme. In Sicily, judicial activism was achieving unprecedented successes against the Mafia, and in the process coming perilously close to demonstrating long-term links between the Mafia and the local DC. Elsewhere, public concern over law and order found immediate issues in drugs, the alleged influence of immigrants from North Africa, frequent financial scandals involving state-owned industry and banking, and the spread of organised crime. Revelations about secret 'stay behind' military groups organised by NATO implicated DC-led governments and DC ministers in, at the least, deception of Parliament, and at worst, complicity in subversive and possibly terrorist organisations (the Gladio affair). The President of the Republic, Francesco Cossiga, a Christian Democrat, and one of those directly involved in Gladio, was increasingly critical of his own party's performance in government and seemed to be moving towards support for a directly elected Presidency. The issue of control of the mass media – particularly of the spread of the Berlusconi empire – found the government unable to pass effective legislation through Parliament. These and other policy issues divided the party without finding clear expression through the traditional groupings. Tax reform, public expenditure cuts, educational reform were not new to the agenda, but remained unresolved.

But for the Christian Democrat leadership, none of this necessarily threatened the overall stability of the tried and tested methods, which were based, as we have seen, on the priority of internal DC organisation, the pivotal role of the DC in determining coalition developments, and the apparently infinite capacity of the DC to buy the consent of all but the most intractable adversaries. The DC believed itself, in the phrase of

Giulio Andreotti, 'condemned to govern', irreplaceable and immovable, a governing party to which there was no alternative. Even the Communists seemed to have acknowledged this with the refounding and renaming of their party at Rimini in March 1991.

The problem faced by the DC therefore was that despite all the difficulties, they persisted in believing that the fundamentals of the system remained intact – more complex negotiations perhaps, more allies to win over, more external pressures for economic competence, but essentially the same methods applied. The DC continued to apply the old rules, in the face of major institutional changes which undermined both their organisation and their legitimacy as a party. New political forces, particularly the League, were disrupting the electoral stability on which the five-party government carousel had relied. By the time the Christian Democrats had grasped that the party needed to recast both its entire internal structure and its coalition strategy (the spring of 1993, broadly speaking), its leadership had been discredited and its electoral predominance destroyed.

Within the DC itself however there were movements for reform. Some of these were led by academic technocrats such as Massimo Severo Giannini, a former minister for administrative reform, whose concern was mainly with effectiveness and integrity in government. Others, particularly that led by Mario Segni, son of the first-generation DC leader, had directly political concerns as well. The reformers within the DC identified electoral reform as the key to other institutional reforms. The direct election of the mayors of large cities would impose the logic of numbers on the Socialists, while the changes in the preference voting system for parliamentary elections (introduced by a referendum held in June 1991) would improve internal party discipline. After the success of the referendum, Segni proposed a bill in Parliament to introduce the single-seat simple majority system for both Chambers of Parliament. Segni and Giannini lacked the influence within the party to push through such ideas however, and were compelled to pursue their proposals outside the party and through further referenda. In the DC, power continued to reside with those who controlled the votes at party congresses and on the party's National Council.

Changes were also occurring in the political stance of the Italian Catholic Church, visible in particular through the activities of the CEI, the Italian Bishops' Conference. These were to have a significant impact on the way the DC responded to the crises. In general, the shift in the Church's approach was towards closer attention to Italian political developments, more frequent comment and criticism, and more direct control over the lay organisations. In part the new activism of the CEI was prompted by its status after the new Concordat of 1984 with the Italian state, which gave the CEI juridical existence in Italian law.

In general terms, as the disintegration of the DC gathered pace, the CEI through the newspaper *Avvenire* and through its subsidiary organisations, followed a relatively coherent line. The Church gave it to be understood that its priority was national unity, and that it regarded a single Catholic party for all Catholics as the best way of expressing the Christian values on which such a unity had to be based. The CEI encouraged closer involvement of its lay organisations in political activity, arguing that political commitment was a duty of all Catholics. While the link between unity of values and unity of organisation was recognised as important, it was clearly the first of these two which had priority. In this way the Church faced again the tension between the unitary nature of its religious authority, and the pluralism of developed societies. Unlike the period after the war, at no point during this crisis did the CEI or the Pope try to impose political unity on all Catholics.[1] The Church made it clear that it was not 'binding the consciences of the faithful'. CEI statements and the debates within the hierarchy recognised the pluralism of political opinion. The main qualification to this, repeatedly made, was that Catholics were bound in this matter not by a direct injunction from the Church but by their own consciences, formed of course by the Church's teaching. This important distinction was backed up by references to the need for coherence between belief and action. As the fragmentation continued, the Church clearly preferred the PPI, which was the main successor to the DC – not least because this party was characterised by a much greater involvement of Catholic lay associations than the DC had been for many years. But the door was never closed on the other identifiable offshoots of the old DC (mainly the CCD and the Movimento dei Cristiani Sociali), and after the March 1994 elections, the relative success of the CCD was welcomed.

In response to the referendum result and the rise of the Northern League, the DC held a special national conference at Assago near Milan in November 1991. This revealed a perhaps surprising degree of agreement within the party about the need for institutional reform, including calls for a 'constituent legislature' after the next elections, opposition to Cossiga's Presidentialist ambitions, support for electoral reform but opposition to the majoritarian system; there were also high-sounding appeals for national unity and a return to morality in public life. On internal organisation, the Assago conference proposed a three-term maximum for Deputies and Senators.

The Assago conference was followed by a meeting of the DC's National Council on 18 January 1992, which approved several reforms to the party's structure, including incompatibility of ministerial office with membership of either Chamber of Parliament. This was supported strongly by Forlani, party secretary, amid some scepticism as to whether it would actually be applied. Troubles continued to accumulate. The week after this meeting, Cossiga announced his resignation from the party, with barbed references to its desertion of its traditional values and its responsibility for the problem of weak government. On 6 February 1992, the President of the European Commission Jacques Delors publicly criticised Italy for its failure properly to implement the Single Market Directives of the European Community. On 17 February, magistrates in Milan arrested a minor Socialist politician on charges of corruption, and further arrests and revelations implicating the local DC followed quickly. In March, the Sicilian MEP and former minister Salvatore Lima was assassinated by the Mafia in Palermo. Since Lima was notoriously rumoured to have close connections with the Mafia, the murder was interpreted as a warning to the Christian Democrats about the activities of Sicilian magistrates and the Mafia's expectations that it would be protected.

Despite these difficulties, the results of the parliamentary elections of April 1992 actually appear to have encouraged some elements in the DC to seek to postpone long-term changes. Despite the rise of the League and the loss of 5 per cent of the vote, the Christian Democrats remained the largest single party, with nearly twice as many votes as the next largest, the ex-Communists. In the difficult negotiations for the next government, the DC was able to prevent Craxi regaining the position of Prime Minister. His substitute as Prime Minister, the Socialist Giuliano Amato, was clearly in a weak position and dependent on the Christian Democrats. After the surprise resignation of Cossiga in April, the DC were eventually able to secure the Presidency for another Christian Democrat, Oscar Luigi Scalfaro. In September they were also able to get their former party secretary Ciriaco De Mita elected as chairman of the intra-parliamentary commission on institutional reform. In conventional terms, therefore, the DC successfully reasserted its control over the political institutions in the spring and summer of 1992.

These institutional successes could be described as the dying throes of the old San Ginesio system, in which the manipulation of external levers of power masked almost complete internal immobilism. Forlani attempted to resign as party secretary twice, and twice had his resignation rejected. The obvious successor was a left-wing Senator from Brescia, Mino Martinazzoli, whose programme appeared too radical for the factional leaders. But Forlani agreed to stay on only on condition that he was given full powers to reform the party, and these were denied him. In June 1992, a senior DC deputy, the former minister of public works Giovanni Prandini, became the first figure of such seniority to receive formal notification from the magistrates that he was under investigation. In the same investigation was the party's national administrative secretary Severino Citaristi. Throughout the summer of 1992, the activities of the magistrates gathered pace, and the Segni reform movement became ever more cross-party and less Christian Democrat. External pressures mounted: *mani pulite* (the 'clean hands' investigation) even reached the influential Catholic gingergroup Comunione e Liberazione. Their traditional August meeting at Rimini was marked by acrimonious debate about whether the involvement of CL local councillors in corruption charges was the result of excessive identification with the DC or an unfortunate side-effect of CL's crusading activism.

The point at which the DC began to respond can be clearly identified. At the end of September 1992, the League made big gains in local elections in Mantua, replacing the DC as the largest single party – with over 30 per cent of the vote. The day after, the National Secretariat called an emergency meeting of the National Council for October. At this meeting the factional disputes cleared, and Martinazzoli was elected party secretary by acclamation.

Martinazzoli's declared programme was to refound the party, to renew its Catholic values and to make its internal structure genuinely democratic and representative. He wished to do so in order to retain the party's pivotal role at the centre of Italian politics, the determinant of co-alitions and the arbiter of the balance of power within the party system. As the reform effort proceeded the inadequacy of this project became clear.

First, there was no consensus within the DC about internal reform. All previous efforts by reforming secretaries had foundered on the inability of the national party to control the local factional organisations. Martinazzoli had one instrument which had been denied his predecessors, namely the renewed enthusiasm of the Catholic left and of the Catholic associations. The most vocal expression of this group was the new regional secretary of the Veneto, Rosy Bindi. Bindi was a member of the European Parliament with a previous career in the official Catholic lay organisation Azione Cattolica. Her high-profile approach was to renew the party organisation with a regional constituent assembly, from which all party members who were under judicial investigation were excluded. In Sicily, a deputy national secretary of the party, Sergio Mattarella, had already been appointed as regional commissioner, and under Martinazzoli he extended his activities with a mandate to refound the regional party. This he did by nominating a group of 25 independents without previous office to draw up a new regional constitution and new organisational structure for the party. In some regions, particularly in the South, neither of these two strategies could be applied because of a lack of appropriate personnel. As Martinazzoli discovered, the regions where the party structures were best able to reform themselves were also the regions most under threat from the Lega, particularly the northern regions of Lombardy and the Veneto. Elsewhere, especially in the South, the need for reform was at least as great, but the perception of threat much weaker and the resistance to Martinazzoli much greater. Nationally, the centre-right of the party quickly objected to what they correctly identified as a take-over of party structures by the left. This was partly a dispute about balance within the party, but it brought to the foreground serious ideological divisions between the left and right of the party which the broad pluralism of the party had masked. What therefore emerged from the reform process was not a refounding of the DC but a party of a different kind, which lacked the DC's apparently infinite embrace, which had a relatively sharp ideological identity, and whose national coverage was significantly weakened by the reform.

Second, the party's attitude to institutional reform was also ambiguous. Martinazzoli initially opposed the majoritarian electoral reform and continued to oppose the use of referenda, even though the alternative parliamentary reform route was both unpopular with the public and uncertain as to outcome. In March 1993, in what may have been a crucial tactical error, Martinazzoli rejected a possible local election alliance with Segni, including a common action programme on electoral reform. Even at this stage, DC Parliamentarians could be found arguing that despite the rise of the League the DC could retain its pivotal role. In brief, the belief was that granted modest success throughout the rest of the country the DC would always be able to pick up sufficient votes in the South to ensure its position as largest single party. It would then either form a coalition with the PDS or force the League to take responsibility for a weak minority government. This appears to be the reason why the DC group on the intra-parliamentary commission on institutional reform persistently objected to the two-ballot proposal for single seat constituencies, similar to the French electoral system, which was favoured by the PDS. On the anti-corruption drive, Martinazzoli initially supported Craxi, whose response to the magistrates' *avviso di garanzia* (notification of investigation) was to complain of conspiracy against him. This gave the unfortunate and no doubt incorrect impression that Martinazzoli was not wholeheartedly behind the drive against corruption.

It followed that his relationship with reform-minded centrists in all the government parties was difficult, and that despite the successes of Bindi in the Veneto and some others, the internal reform narrowed rather than broadened the party's base. On 10 October 1992, two days before Martinazzoli's election as secretary, Segni left the DC, declaring that his aim was to create a new Catholic party outside the DC. Segni correctly observed that the new secretary was internally dependent on the new Catholic left, and unreliable in his commitment to institutional reform. The world of political Catholicism was indeed wider than Martinazzoli's new troops seemed to believe. But Segni also had no obvious winning strategy. As de facto leader of the referendum movement he had mass backing from the electorate across the political spectrum, but he was unable to translate this into a cohesive political movement, or to establish a seat-winning organisation. His electoral base was made up of reform-minded lay and Catholic conservatives, a relatively small group, who furthermore were unlikely to follow him into an alliance with the much larger progressive wing of the reformers. Apart from the appearance of chronic indecisiveness produced by his strategic shifts, his cross-party referendum movement lacked the organisational strength to win seats in local and national elections on its own. This was demonstrated clearly in the local elections in June and November 1993, when his Popular Reform Movement failed to win seats wherever it stood separately from the larger alliances. He initially worked closely with Alleanza Democratica, a progressive group of mainly non-PDS reformers, but left this in October 1993, and fought the March 1994 elections in alliance with the PPI. The electoral reform of August 1993 had removed the main source of argument between Segni and his former colleagues. Segni's circuitous route around Italy's political families thus brought him back to his starting point. From back-bencher in Italy's largest national party he became Prime-Minister-designate of one of its smallest.

The reform of the party gathered pace from December 1992 to June 1993, and with it the divisions between the centre-right and the new left. The disastrous local election results of June 1993 – the first fought under the new system of direct election – in which the DC won 11 mayorships out of 143, produced bitter recriminations. The centre-right attacked ACLI and AC for not supporting DC candidates, while the left argued that the results demonstrated that the reform had not been sufficiently thorough. On 22 June, Pierluigi Castagnetti, Martinazzoli's aide, declared that the party would dissolve itself at the next meeting of the national executive. It was not clear whether this was intended to be a self-fulfilling prophecy or was actually a premature leak of a decision already made by the party's inner circles. Against the background of calls for unity by the CEI secretary Mgr. Tettamanzi, the executive duly met on 25 June and announced that the party would hold a national constituent assembly in July to refound itself. When the July meeting actually took place, some centre-right deputies had already left, most notably the Rome deputy Publio Fiori, formerly a member of the Andreotti faction, who threatened to set up a *Rifondazione Democratica*, parodying the ex-Communist splinter group Rifondazione Comunista. It was not only the centre-right who objected. Some of the traditional left such as Paolo Cabras complained that they had been excluded from the old oligarchy led by Andreotti and Forlani and were being excluded from the new one. A relatively compact group of former right-of-centre backbenchers emerged, led by two backbench deputies, Pier Ferdinando Casini from Bologna and Clemente Mastella from Benevento. Though they remained inside the party, their emphasis on traditional conservative themes suggested genuine policy differences with the new leadership which could not easily be resolved. Strong support for the new party was visible from the lay associations, including ACLI, AC, and the intellectual ginger group *Carta 93* sponsored by the Jesuit periodical *Civiltà Cattolica*. The new party would formally exclude from full membership all DC members under judicial investigation, and imposed a maximum two terms for Parliamentarians.

Further bad election results followed in November 1993. In December

Martinazzoli announced that the party membership had approved the new name and constitution by referendum, and marked out the party's change of direction with a series of speeches recalling the origins of Italian Christian Democracy in the ideas of Sturzo and De Gasperi. One of these speeches came on the 75th anniversary of Sturzo's famous anti-fascist declaration *Ai liberi e ai forti* ('To the Free and the Strong'); at the same time the centre-right announced their formal break with the PPI, and the establishment of a new group calling itself the Christian Democratic Centre.

The old DC therefore presented itself at the parliamentary elections of March 1994 in at least four different guises: the Partito Popolare Italiano led by Martinazzoli; Patto Segni in alliance under the title Patto per l'Italia; the Centro Cristiano Democratico led by Casini and Mastella in alliance with Berlusconi, and finally a left Catholic group, the Cristiano-Sociali led by the former trade union leader Pierre Carniti, which was in alliance with the Progressives. For the PPI/Segni alliance, the results were disastrous. They were reduced from the 207 deputies of the old DC to 46 in the new Chamber of Deputies, and perhaps most disturbingly, only three of these were won in the single-member constituency section. The three constituencies returning PPI/Segni deputies were Baldo Garda in northern Lombardy, Avellino in the southern hinterland, and Olbia in Sardinia. All the remaining seats were won under the proportional list system. Even Mariotto Segni was defeated by Alleanza Nazionale in his home town of Sassari. Martinazzoli did not stand. All the old guard, the senior factional leaders, were excluded from standing for the PPI because of the judicial investigations, and chose not to stand for the CCD. There was no Forlani, no Andreotti, no Antonio Gava and no De Mita (who however threatened to return and resume). Among those elected for the PPI were Bindi, the former Treasury minister Beniamino Andreatta, and Rocco Buttiglione, who took over as party secretary following the resignation of Martinazzoli – only to be defeated within his own party in March 1995 on the issue of an electoral pact with Forza Italia and Alleanza Nazionale. Buttiglione strongly favoured this line, whereas the centre and left opposed such an alliance and favoured instead a centre-left coalition under the leadership of the former President of IRI, Romano Prodi.

CONCLUSION

It is difficult to avoid the conclusion that the DC suffered from a serious lack of leadership, with both Martinazzoli and Segni making major strategic errors, particularly in their relations with one another. To this, the obvious reply is that the DC had flourished for over four decades on a highly collegial style of leadership which rewarded compromise and which punished charisma. It was therefore ill-suited to the demands made on it. Furthermore, the difficulties faced by the Christian Democrats during the crisis should not be under-estimated. They were beset on three fronts simultaneously: judicial investigation, institutional reform and shifts in the electorate. There was nothing in their previous period of dominance which could have prepared them, and the pace of change left many others flat-footed also.

One should however resist the argument that the results were in some sense inevitable, that the DC was doomed to defeat in March 1994. Even in October 1993, it might have been possible for them to argue that the logic of the new electoral system would work in their favour, that elections of mayors are not true tests of how the electorate would behave in parliamentary elections. As most of their traditional supports crumbled, their remaining advantage was very simple and had previously been very effective: the absence of a viable alternative which could aggregate sufficient votes among Catholics and conservatives. The critical change therefore, which undermined the strategy of their reform, was the emergence of Forza Italia. Electoral surveys in March 1994 showed that Berlusconi's party won 30 per cent of those who defined themselves as practising Catholics, and his right-wing alliance including AN and the League amounted to nearly half of all practising Catholics (49 per cent). According to the same survey, the PPI/Segni alliance won 23.5 per cent of the votes of practising Catholics. The term 'practising Catholic' in this context refers to about 34 per cent of the entire electorate.[2] A winning party would need a wider base than this, but if the new PPI with its clear Catholic organisational basis and programme cannot win a larger proportion of what should be its natural constituency, its electoral future appears bleak.

The obvious parallel here is with the career of the MRP in the French Fourth Republic and its subsequent decline in the Fifth Republic. In both cases, we have a party which was a permanent part of government, winning a significant proportion of the Catholic vote and others besides. A serious difference between the DC and the MRP is that the electoral base of the DC was always much broader than that of the MRP. The MRP eventually succumbed to identification with the excesses of the discredited previous regime, combined with a loss of much of its Catholic support to a new lay party of the Centre-Right led by De Gaulle, in an electoral system which moulded the parties into Left–Right confrontation. Despite the differences between Italy in 1994 and France in 1958, it is not absurd to read from the comparison a very difficult path ahead for political Catholicism in Italy.

NOTES

1 There were provocative suggestions to the contrary by Catholic far-left groups which had been opposing the DC in splendid isolation since the 1960s, and

who evidently sought from the authorities a more complete renunciation of their past (*Confronti*, 2, February 1994, 2).
2 See Carradi 1994: 5.

REFERENCES

Carradi, M. (1994) 'Cattolici, il fascino della destar', *Avvenire*, 30 March, p. 5.
Furlong, P. (1987) 'The Vatican in Italian politics', in L. Quartermaine and J. Pollard (eds) *Italy Today – patterns of life and politics*, Exeter: Exeter University Press.
—— (1988) 'Authority, change and conflict in Italian Catholicism', in T. Gannon (ed.) *World Catholicism in transition*, London: Macmillan.
—— (1994) *Modern Italy: Representation and Reform*, London: Routledge.
Leonardi, R. and Wertman, D. (1989) *Italian Christian Democracy: the Politics of Dominance*, London: Macmillan.
Scoppola, P. (1977) *La proposta politica di De Gasperi*, Bologna: Il Mulino.
Wertman, D. (1982) 'The Catholic church and Italian politics: the impact of secularisation', *West European Politics*, 5:2, 87–107.

4 Italian Communism in the First Republic

Stephen Hellman

Throughout most of the post-war period, the Italian Communist Party (PCI) was the largest communist party in Western Europe, and from the 1960s on, it was the largest non-ruling communist party in the world. It hegemonised the opposition in Italy during this time span: after 1963, its electoral support never fell below 25 per cent of the vote, and it rose above 30 per cent in the mid- and-late 1970s. When its organisation went into deep crisis after the announcement that a new, post-communist party was to rise out of the ashes of the PCI, its membership of 1.3 million was still far greater than all other Italian parties: for most of the post-war period, membership never fell below 1.5 million. Nor is this a complete picture of the party's influence in Italy, which included, among other things, its massive presence in the trade union and cooperative movements, as well as its domination of society and government in the 'red zones' of central Italy.

These facts are a necessary starting-point for any assessment of the PCI's role in what is increasingly being referred to as the First Italian Republic. They remind us of the party's formidable strength, and its influence in Italian society. But they also remain the vital statistics of a party that never gained full legitimacy as a governing force, despite considerable efforts to do so.

The primary purpose of this chapter will be to illuminate the strategy and politics of one of the key actors in the Italian Republic. In the course of this discussion, I will examine some of the more contentious debates concerning the nature of the PCI. An essay of this length can neither cover all the issues nor treat them in the detail they deserve, but it can indicate the major sign-posts along a hotly contested trail. To anticipate the narrative, I will treat the party's trajectory as the history of an ambiguous but initially quite successful concept – the 'new party', or *partito nuovo*, that represented a radical departure when it first appeared towards the end of World War II. Its distinctive combination of characteristics enabled the PCI to carry out quite well the functions for which it was designed, but as its environment changed, the party's adaptations were uneven. The apotheosis of the *partito nuovo* came in the 1970s, when its greatest successes also created the most severe stresses on both the organisational forms and the strategic assumptions that had underpinned it throughout the post-war period. The exhaustion of the organisation and strategic model became increasingly evident from the end of the 1970s onward, but this was a drawn-out process. It is in this last phase that the 'degeneration', which critics now wish to attribute to the party's entire history, became most evident.

THE EMERGENCE AND CONSOLIDATION OF THE *PARTITO NUOVO* (1944–56)

When Secretary-General Palmiro Togliatti returned from Moscow in 1944 and announced that the Communists would subjugate everything to the unity of the anti-fascist struggle, he was setting a pattern that would frequently anger others on the Left, as well as many of his own comrades. In this instance, he collaborated with a discredited monarchy, putting off the resolution of the 'institutional question' until the war's end. More significantly, collaboration broke the impasse that had paralysed the anti-fascist parties. Later, and notoriously, the PCI supported Article 7 of the Constitution, which accepted without revision the 1929 Lateran Pacts granting Roman Catholicism the status of state religion, among other privileges.

Togliatti was no spur of the moment improviser. It quickly became clear that the *partito nuovo*, in its behaviour as well as its structure, really did represent a departure for a communist party. The 'Italian Road to Socialism' was like the 'national' lines being elaborated by all communist parties in the immediate post-war period, but Togliatti's repetition of the same themes until his death in 1964 shows the depth of his commitment to them (Togliatti 1972).

The PCI was a hybrid, organisationally and strategically. Its leadership consciously and successfully shaped it in a fashion that blended the vanguard principles of the Communist Third International with the mass-party structures and practices of the Socialist Second International. This blend was fraught with tensions, and indeed contradictions, from the outset. The PCI often benefited from what was best in both traditions, but at times it seemed to exhibit the worst tendencies of its mixed heritage.

Broadly speaking, this hybrid turned out to be well-suited to the conditions of the immediate post-war period, and to the intense polarisation of the Cold War that immediately followed. The party never managed to sink deep roots in the inhospitable social and political structure of the South. But elsewhere, it rapidly displaced the Socialists as heir to Italy's revolutionary traditions: the PCI was soon the dominant force in both the central 'red zones', where agrarian Socialism had flourished, and in northern industrial centres. The injunction to extend the party's presence into every crease and fold of Italian society was never fully successful, but by the early 1950s the PCI commanded a formidable organisation of over 2 million members (Sivini 1967). In 1950, one out of three industrial workers was enrolled in its ranks; even when it lost ground as the decade progressed, it still organised a fifth of the industrial workforce (Centro Francovich 1969: 9).

The reasons for the party's commitment to broad alliances and a *mass* organisational structure in the post-war period are easy to trace. Although founded in 1921, the PCI's key formative moment was Fascism. The isolation and destruction of the workers' movement in the 1920s, and the generation-long ordeal of clandestinity and exile that followed, irrevocably marked those who built and led the post-war PCI. At the same time, the PCI remained a *communist* party and its Leninist and Third International heritage marked its organisation. The most rigorous strictures of democratic centralism only began to be loosened toward the end of the 1950s, and even then factionalism continued to be banned and debates were usually couched in coded, opaque terminology. And while the highest ranks of the PCI hierarchy may have embraced the precepts of the Italian Road to Socialism, and increasingly viewed the Soviet Union in critical fashion, this was decidedly not the case for the lower ranks of the organisation.

The leadership's toleration of these attitudes led to charges that the PCI practised duplicity (*doppiezza*) throughout the post-war period. In its most hostile form, this reproach is akin to an accusation of original sin: it sees the rank-and-file's views as evidence of the party's lack of democratic credentials – or even as proof that the PCI wanted to carry out a Soviet-style revolution. More moderate criticisms of *doppiezza* agree that the PCI's ambiguities made it impossible to address this issue, especially during the Cold War. (De-Stalinisation of even the full-time apparatus only began on the local level at the end of the 1950s.) The best of these interpretations put the emphasis where it more properly belongs: not on sinister motivations, but on (admittedly hypocritical) organisational imperatives.[1] A huge corps – at its peak over 150,000 – of militant volunteers set the PCI apart from other parties, enabling it to practise mass politics in a context in which it was badly disadvantaged. Activists gave generously of their time to perform routine, seemingly dead-end tasks because they were motivated by the party's ideology and symbolic identity, and other non-material incentives (Lange 1977; Panebianco 1979). A reflexive, polarised set of views was tolerated because this kept the party machinery running. *Doppiezza* may have been functional to the party's day-to-day operations, but it did exact a toll. It conditioned the party's evolution, and nourished a deep commitment to a strong, radically diverse identity that in the 1980s would lead a sizeable minority of the party to refuse to abandon the 'communist' label.

One of the reasons why the PCI's presumed duplicity – and thus its intentions – is the focus of so much attention is that its actions provide little evidence of subversive behaviour. Through the worst of the Cold War, only twice did the PCI try to paralyse Parliament: in the 1949 debate over the ratification of NATO, and in the debate over the 1953 'Swindle Law', when a proposed alteration to the electoral system would have guaranteed a lop-sided permanent majority to the winning coalition. Most of the time the Communists were more than willing to work with, and compromise with, the ruling parties in the legislature (Di Palma 1977). This may have produced myriad special-interest laws instead of coherent legislative packages, but it hardly comprises evidence of 'anti-system' behaviour. In reality the PCI leadership was absolutely terrified of isolation. This fear was, in the first instance, born of the Fascist experience, but it also reflected a limit that the party imposed on its opposition status. It might be excluded from power, but it would not accept permanent marginal status, either politically or in society. Its actions – in the 1980s as well as the 1950s – show that the PCI was always most intransigent when it felt the balance of power was changing at its expense.

FROM 1956 TO THE *AUTUNNO CALDO*

Nowhere was this pattern more evident than in the case of the DC's 'opening to the Left', which eventually resulted in the PSI joining the governing majority in the early 1960s. As the country showed signs of dramatic economic growth and the political balance of power began to shift, the PCI evolved in ways that distinguished it from other communist parties. Yet at the same time that it began to take its distance from the Soviet Union and resuscitate and elaborate the post-war 'Italian Road to Socialism' as its guiding strategy, its strategic and tactical confusion was very much in evidence.

Although the PCI had emerged after World War II with distinctive traits, these only flourished following Stalin's death in 1953, and in particular, following Khrushchev's denunciations of Stalin's excesses at the XX Congress of the Soviet Communists (1956). Togliatti's critique of the limits of the Soviet analysis of Stalinism is widely, and correctly, acknowledged as a watershed in the (re)emergence of the PCI's autonomous brand of Communism. It would take until 1968 and the invasion of Czechoslovakia for the PCI to openly break ranks and criticise the 'socialist fatherland', but it clearly reasserted its autonomy from the mid-1950s onward. One should not exaggerate Togliatti's innovations in 1956, however: he never pushed his analysis as far as hagiographers claim (Franchi 1990: 64), and his fundamental belief in the Soviet system was reiterated when he endorsed the crushing of Hungarian resistance in 1956.

The PCI's organisation evolved and adapted to changing Italian conditions in the post-Stalinist period, but it was seriously frayed around the edges by the end of the 1960s, despite a steadily rising share of the vote.[2]

The party machine stagnated as grass-roots participation decreased throughout the 1960s. The Resistance generation and those mobilised immediately following the war finally rose to positions of power, but the consolidation of this new elite slowed the recruitment of even younger leaders in the provinces (Hellman 1975). The Communist Youth Federation's plight was especially disturbing: its membership dropped drastically in the course of the 1960s, and the organisation collapsed in the wake of the student movement's surge at the end of the decade.

Had this decline continued, the PCI might have been forced to confront the inherent shortcomings of its organisational model in the 1970s, rather than a decade later. But the rise in militancy that began in the late 1960s reversed the organisation's crisis; indeed, the much-needed infusion of fresh blood (and huge electoral gains) seemed to reconfirm the *partito nuovo*'s basic assumptions.

Events in the 1960s made it even easier for the PCI to assume an uncompromising oppositional stance. As student and then worker militancy exploded toward the end of the decade, pent-up demand for reforms increasingly spilled into the streets. These waves of social mobilisation were neither planned nor instigated by the Communists – on the contrary, new movements often left them flat-footed and uncomprehending. But no political force was better situated to benefit from the new upsurge in collective action. At the same time, the PCI's actions revealed, from the start, that the party had no intention of simply riding the tiger of social protest, as its own left wing and the militant New Left groups hoped. During the 1950s, the PCI had moved from hegemonising to largely monopolising social as well as political opposition in Italy. Although it dominated the Left at the end of the 1960s, it now often found itself attacked by a variety of forces as insufficiently militant and revolutionary.[3]

The party's reaction to these criticisms was far less harsh and dogmatic than that of other Western Communists (the French immediately come to mind), and this relative openness paid off both electorally and organisationally. But the course of events, and the instincts of the party leadership, produced a quintessentially political, and primarily defensive, response to the crisis into which Italy was plunged. A generation after the war ended, in the wake of tremendous social change and mass mobilisation, the PCI's response to the Italian crisis was to offer up something very similar to its post-war strategy of collaboration. This was the famous 'historic compromise' proposed by the PCI's new secretary, Enrico Berlinguer.

BERLINGUER AND THE HISTORIC COMPROMISE

Berlinguer would push (or drag) the PCI into clarifying many of its long-standing ambiguities, making it the leader of the 'Eurocommunist' phenomenon, but his frame of reference always remained the *partito nuovo*. This is not to minimise his very significant achievements, but rather to contextualise them. Under his aegis, the party increasingly distanced itself from the Soviets, and became openly critical of the entire system of 'really existing socialism'. It dropped anti-democratic vestiges like the 'dictatorship of the proletariat', and explicitly embraced Western democratic values. And while Berlinguer retained some traditional autocratic, top-down methods of leadership – some of the most dramatic shifts in party policy and strategy took place with little, if any, consultation – all aspects of party life, including internal debate, opened up considerably during his tenure. But for all this, his vision was Togliattian: the parties, especially the large mass parties, were the most authentic repositories and interpreters of popular aspirations; Italian society continued to be seen as divided into great ideological 'families', and institutionally mediated cooperation between these party-families was the only way to guarantee progress (and stability).

These assumptions informed the *compromesso storico* (Historic Compromise) proposed by Berlinguer in the early 1970s as the solution to Italy's crisis. The idea of long-term cooperation between the major political forces (and above all the DC and PCI) responded to one very significant part of the difficult political situation at the time – but at the end of the day it revealed a blindness to some of the most dramatic changes the country had experienced in the course of the 1960s. As the party edged closer to national power, it became increasingly clear that it lacked any coherent programme of reforms. Had the compromise been proposed as a transitional phase to accustom the country to the PCI in power (akin to the German Grand Coalition of 1966), these shortcomings would be more understandable, and the historic compromise would have been less problematic. The course of events between 1972 and 1979 revealed, however, that this was not a tactic, but a strategy; and it was a strategy to which Berlinguer was deeply committed.

Berlinguer first broached the subject of Communist participation in government in 1972; he fully spelled out the *compromesso* in the wake of the 1973 coup against Chile's left-wing government. From then on, despite signs of a sea-change in Italian society and public opinion (the resounding victory in 1974 for divorce; the massive losses of the DC in the 1975 local elections), Berlinguer continued to pose Italy's biggest challenge as the threat from the extreme Right.

When the PCI jumped to over 34 per cent of the vote in the 1976 general elections, a genuine stalemate ensued. The DC had held its own, but only by plundering the votes of its smaller coalition partners. Nor could the ruling party count on continuing Socialist support. Bloodied by the unrelenting attacks it had suffered for its participation in the Centre Left, the PSI pledged not to join a government that excluded the Communists. Within the ideologically divided trade union movement, a younger, more militant generation of workers was less wedded to Cold

War schemes that had prevented united action (and greater benefits) in the past. By the mid-1970s, as union efforts to wrench reforms directly out of the government were constantly frustrated, even those who distrusted the Communists realised that serious change could not occur without the inclusion of the workers' major representative in government.

Under these circumstances, which were by no means uniformly negative, the PCI lent its (essential) support to two 'National Solidarity' governments between 1976 and 1979. Although informed by the historic compromise strategy, this was a restrained, limited version of Berlinguer's long-term vision. But it immediately created problems for the Communists. By 1977, pressure from workers, intellectuals and his own left wing forced Berlinguer to frame PCI support for austerity programmes in terms of a radical transformation of society. But this was years after the *compromesso* was first enunciated, and many months after the PCI had fully committed itself to supporting DC-led governments.

PARTY AND MASSES IN THE 1970S

Between 1969 and 1977, PCI membership soared to 1.8 million, and party structures sprang up or were revitalised in work-places and residential areas throughout the country. With more than 100,000 new members joining every year, the turnover was extraordinary: by the end of the 1970s, more than half of all Italian Communists had joined the party since 1969. Nearly a third were in their 20s or even younger. This dizzying expansion of the party organisation would create numerous problems for the PCI. But it unquestionably reversed what had appeared to be an inevitable decline, and contributed to a much-needed rejuvenation of an ageing party structure. Moreover, the flood of new members supplied a fresh generation of young leaders and militants who would prove essential to the ambitious and radical changes of the late 1980s.

The growth of the party organisation raises interesting questions about the PCI's relationship to the social movements of the late 1960s and early 1970s. Some analysts argue that the PCI was never as successful in drawing the core of the movements into the party as was commonly assumed at the time (Barbagli and Corbetta 1978). Others, in a more explicit criticism of the PCI from the Left, say that the movements were never 'captured' by the PCI, which, dominated by its apparatus throughout the 1970s, remained hostile to them. As a result, the PCI was only able to attract peripheral elements (Flores and Gallerano 1992). This may be a bit forced, but it represents an understandable reaction against interpretations which argued that the PCI 'absorbed' these movements in the course of the decade. My own position is that while the party may not have 'captured' the most militant activists, a restrictive definition of 'core' and 'periphery' over-simplifies the complexity of the social movements, and misses the most important impact they had on the PCI. The party *did*, after all, recruit large numbers of workers and young people precisely where the movements were strongest. This had significant consequences, with implications exactly the reverse of claims made by those who argue that the party was characteristically closed and bureaucratic. In fact, all manner of new constituencies, voices, and tensions were now *inside* the party, which had great difficulties in sorting them out. These new forces may have rejuvenated the PCI, but they also starkly exposed its weaknesses – from its vision of society to the inadequacy of its organisational schemes and practices.[4]

I have emphasised this period for in my opinion it was the crucial turning-point in the post-1968 evolution of the party. The *compromesso* was the last gasp of the Togliattian vision of a system organised in and by mass parties, which exhaust the 'space' of civil society. When it was abandoned, little more than *partito nuovo* reflexes remained. In a memorable turn of phrase, Piero Ignazi argues that the PCI may have had a 'Eurocommunist facelift' in the 1970s, but its profile remained distinctively that of the Third International until the late 1980s (Ignazi 1992: 44). But while it is true that a definitive break with the past would not come until the end of the 1980s, the die was clearly cast a decade earlier. The PCI's contradictions were obvious by the end of the 1970s; by the 1980s they had become intolerable. Berlinguer dropped the *compromesso* in 1979 and committed the PCI to a 'democratic alternative', but it was evident until his premature death in 1984 that he had only abandoned the strategy with the greatest reluctance. And if the Communists were confused and floundering in the early 1980s, they at least had Berlinguer's uncontested leadership to provide continuity. Later in the decade, their floundering became even more apparent.

THE PCI IN THE 1980S

The PCI would evolve significantly in the 1980s, but the problems it would have to face would not, until the tumultuous events of 1989, be qualitatively different from those that were raised, and not resolved, in the 1970s. The PCI's plight in the 1980s was not made easier by the Socialists' behaviour. PSI secretary Bettino Craxi had his own agenda, and had deeply resented the dismissive contempt in which Berlinguer held his party (see Gundle, Chapter 5). Like many of his party comrades, Berlinguer believed that the once-glorious PSI, having lost its mass base and working-class support, was a relic of the past, subordinate to the DC. For his part, Craxi, despite paying lip-service to the future unity of the Left, led the Socialists back into power, where he set about maximising his party's leverage, and its share of the spoils. This strategy committed Craxi to fierce competition with the DC inside the coalition, but making the PSI the fulcrum of governability also meant he had to do everything possible to underscore the PCI's obsolescence and irrelevancy. Since the

Communists' new 'alternative' strategy required good relations with the PSI to be even remotely plausible, its dilemma in the 1980s is hardly surprising.

Nor, in retrospect, is its behaviour surprising. Excluded from power and threatened with political isolation, the Communists reacted with a degree of militancy that had not been seen for some time. This is not to suggest that the PCI simply took a workerist turn and practised a reflexive opposition (as the French Communists were doing precisely at this time). There was some of that, but there was also constant institutional manoeuvring, and trying to play the DC and PSI off against one another, which led to considerable confusion within the party as to the leadership's ultimate goals. Moreover, having achieved a significant degree of legitimation – and a share of real power – during the 1976–79 period when it offered its support to governments of 'National Solidarity', the PCI was not inclined passively to give up its limited leverage within the system.

Here was the most damaging legacy of the 1970s. If there is such a thing as the PCI's *systematic* participation in the proportional division of spoils (*lottizzazione*), that was always a hallmark of the Italian system but came to dominate it in the 1980s, it is traceable to the solidarity period. There is certainly nothing shameful (especially in a political system built on the exclusion of the major opposition party from the very possibility of participating in a share of governmental power) about obtaining whatever power was available, and even about fighting hard to increase one's share of the pie. But the question remains as to what, if anything, a party intends to do with these 'pieces of power'. The most telling criticism of the historic compromise is that it evolved into something that eventually stood for nothing other than the 'presence' of the PCI. Never – not in 1976 when its support was vital, nor later in the 1970s – had the party extracted a substantive 'quid pro quo' for its votes. Participation in power-sharing had become an end in itself, so great was its complex about legitimation. Thus, 'legitimation often became *lottizzazione*, and participation became an obstacle to control and denunciation' (Flores and Gallerano 1992: 244). Another observer noted that the PCI underwent 'unequal, subaltern, and ruinous consociation' because it lost its alternative and antagonistic thrust during this period (Vacca 1987: 226). It had obtained legitimation, but it seemed oblivious to the fact that it had done so when there was growing disgust with the whole party system. It moved back into the opposition, but it had lost the distinctiveness that used to distinguish it from other parties.

It is from this point that we can date the slide of the PCI into the corrupt practices revealed by the *Tangentopoli* scandals. At the centre of the system, the DC and PSI jostled each other in what increasingly became a pure power struggle. On the periphery, the PCI was drawn into the division of illicit spoils that was becoming routine in Italy. To be sure, the *degree* of corruption of the PCI was minuscule compared to the two pillars of the system, since, by definition, it was not a full partner in power. Moreover, it retained to the end powerful vestiges of communist morality in the best sense, that is moral commitment and abnegation that discouraged illicit behaviour – or channelled it to party and not personal ends when it did occur. But other factors also increasingly pushed the PCI toward a dependency on all the funding, illegal or otherwise, that it could obtain – and in this regard it truly had become more like the other parties. From the mid-1970s on, the expansion of private broadcasting and the explosion of mass communications in Italy reinforced the Communists' sense that they were not 'connecting' with significant portions of society. This made them spend heavily on modern communications and advertising techniques,[5] as well as continue their commitment to publishing (at all cultural levels, from the daily *l'Unità* to highbrow journals). And these enterprises generated significant losses. Modern politics was very expensive, and traditional mass party techniques were increasingly inadequate. The need for increasingly large sums of money was, in short, a powerful incentive to take money wherever it could be found.[6]

THE COUNTDOWN TO DISSOLUTION

In these conditions, the PCI's internal divisions crystallised as the last remnants of democratic centralism eroded. Hardliners never forgave Berlinguer for denouncing the crushing of Solidarity in Poland in 1981: he declared the 'propulsive force' of the October Revolution to be exhausted. From then on, led by Armando Cossutta (and aided by the Soviets), the Leninist Left practised outright factionalism. The Right wing, meanwhile, was distraught over what it saw as the party's irresponsible militancy and its fierce anti-PSI intransigence. They pressed as hard as they could for a full embrace of European social democracy and rapprochement with Craxi. The less dogmatic Left clung strongly to the PCI's historical identity, and the increasingly fluid 'centre' tried, as always, to mediate between the wings.

The time for endless balancing acts was drawing to a close: the different wings shared less and less common ground, and their willingness to break ranks (in Parliament or inside the party) grew. Profound changes were now required to save the PCI from a downward spiral into oblivion. In the wake of the electoral defeat of 1987, party secretary Alessandro Natta was eased out of office. Natta was an elder statesman who had been named secretary in the shock that followed Berlinguer's sudden death. He was replaced by Achille Occhetto, who quickly set about bringing like-minded leaders to Rome.

Over the course of the next two years, nearly every established principle and practice of the PCI would be called into question, often by Occhetto himself. 'Copernican Revolution' was a term frequently used to describe the post-1987 changes. The PCI decided to keep its 'communist' label, but it now acknowledged the need to break with the past. It no longer claimed to be the vanguard of a single class, and adopted a discourse of citizens' rights within democracy as the primary value informing the party's struggle. The French Revolution became a fundamental reference point, and 'the politics of sexual difference' – a separatist variant of radical feminism – was given the status of a founding value in the renewed PCI. By the XVIII Congress of March 1989, these renovations were formally sanctioned (Ignazi 1992: 67–68). It was not clear whether this 'new' PCI would have proved attractive to Italian society, but it enjoyed broad internal centre-left support. Not surprisingly, the right wing was deeply unhappy with Occhetto's eclecticism and his tendency to veer away from the social-democratic tradition (and Bettino Craxi's Socialists).

The collapse of Communism a few months after the XVIII Congress set in motion the dissolution of the PCI and the birth of the PDS (see Bull, Chapter 10). For our purposes, two points are worth remembering. First, the PCI initiated radical changes *before* the Berlin Wall and the Soviet empire collapsed. Second, change accelerated in 1987 under Occhetto's leadership for two fundamental reasons. One is that the party's crisis continued – the fall-off in electoral support to 1968 levels was particularly traumatic, for veterans and newcomers alike. The second is that the extensive recruitment and growth enjoyed by the PCI in the 1970s provided Occhetto with a membership and a cadre of leaders, in the 1980s, who were not products of old schemes and mores, and who were thus more prepared to break with the past. To use a term that gained currency by the end of the 1970s, this group believed that the entire political culture of the party had to be renewed. Events would soon prove how much resistance still existed within the PCI to the final symbolic break with its old identity. But without the dramatic turnover of the 1970s, the internal struggle at the end of the 1980s would have been far more lacerating.

The trauma of the PCI's final years also revealed the weakness of some of the categories that had always been used to explain what had made the party distinctive. Since it did not easily fit received notions of what a communist party *should* resemble, or what the more orthodox communist parties actually *did* resemble, people used to argue that the PCI was 'not really' a communist party, or that it was simply the 'functional equivalent' of social democracy. These assessments were as often made in admiration as criticism. And they undoubtedly captured a basic truth about the PCI, which is that it behaved in a fashion that was precisely the opposite of what those who excluded it from power claimed (and, indeed, served as an alibi for excluding it). That is, far from demonstrating that it was 'anti-system', the PCI carried on an opposition that, in its everyday manifestations, and especially at critical junctures, actually stabilised Italian democracy. But these assessments of its nature were, in the final analysis, a rather simplistic short-hand, for the PCI did all this as a *Communist* party – as the internal struggles of 1989–91 demonstrated. And the course of the 1980s shows that by the 1989 XVIII Congress, it probably had gone as far as it could as a communist party.

CONCLUSION

By the end of the 1980s, the PCI was undergoing two simultaneous and crushing crises. One was the crisis of Communism, which resulted in the definitive end, in Europe, of a discredited but still potent tradition. The other was the general crisis of the Left, and in particular of those elements of the Left most identified with the workers' movement. It might be fruitless to attempt to apportion the party's difficulties under one or the other rubric, but we cannot ignore that these are separate, if ultimately related, phenomena.

It is fashionable, and accurate, to blame the ideological legacy and regressive structures of the Communist tradition for missing many changes in society, as well as for slowing down the party's evolution. Anyone who doubts this need only look at the PCI's performance by the end of the 1970s. But what, precisely, was the PCI supposed to become? We should remember that no other left-wing party or movement, of whatever ideological provenance, can boast of success, however defined, since the 1980s. Whatever its limits, it would be imposing a far heavier burden on the PCI than it deserves to argue that it would have come up with a new synthesis for the Left had it only dropped its baggage earlier. At most, we can say that its many distinctive qualities offered opportunities that might have been promising, but were never pursued.

But even had it somehow resolved all the problems of its historical legacy, it still would have had to confront the dilemma facing all parties of the Left at the end of the twentieth century. Which social groups does it represent, and whose interests will it be willing to attack? In the name of which project for society – assuming that it is still possible to speak of projects (many post-modernists, and pragmatists, insist it is not). Is it possible to be other than a cacophonous gathering of multiple voices, a congeries of dissonant and conflicting claims out of which little more than a lowest common denominator could emerge? On this issue, the present evidence is no more encouraging than that of the past.

NOTES

1 A good scholarly discussion can be found in Panebianco (1979); it is picked up and elaborated in Ignazi (1992). It should be noted that while they did not use the language of organisation theory, many PCI leaders made precisely the same arguments from the 1960s on.
2 The PCI obtained 22.7 per cent in the 1958 general elections, 25.3 in 1963, and 27 in 1968.

3 Respected intellectuals, as well as militant fringe groups, had long been denouncing the PCI's revolutionary inadequacies and 'revisionism'. The difference is that from the late 1960s on, these critical voices had notable – if not truly mass – constituencies.

4 For an elaboration of this argument, see Hellman (1980); for detailed evidence of the PCI organisation's difficulties in the period under discussion, see Hellman (1988).

5 In Turin in the late 1970s, the local party organisation had already undertaken various initiatives in areas that represented radical departures for a Communist party: radio and rock concerts (Hellman 1988).

6 The availability of additional funding did not prevent the PCI (or the DC and PSI) from running up monstrous debts.

REFERENCES

Barbagli, M. and Corbetta, P. (1978) 'Partito e movimento: aspetti e rinnovamento del PCI', *Inchiesta*, 8: 3–46.

Centro Giovanni Francovich (1969) *Documenti delle lotte operaie I. I comunisti in fabbrica*, Milan: Feltrinelli.

Di Palma, G. (1977) *Surviving Without Governing: The Italian Parties in Parliament*, Berkeley, Cal: University of California Press.

Flores, M. and Gallerano, N. (1992) *Sul Pci: una interpretazione storica*, Bologna: Il Mulino.

Franchi, P. (1990) 'Quella strana voglia di cancellar la storia', *Micro Mega*, 5: 60–66.

Hellman, S. (1975) 'Generational differences in the bureaucratic elite of Italian Communist Party provincial federations', *Canadian Journal of Political Science*, VIII: 82–106.

—— (1980), 'Il Pci e l'ambigua eredità dell'autunno caldo a Torino', *Il Mulino*, 29: 246–295.

—— (1988), *Italian Communism in Transition: The Rise and Fall of the Historic Compromise in Turin, 1975–1980*, New York and London: Oxford University Press.

Ignazi, P. (1992) *Dal PCI al PDS*, Bologna: Il Mulino.

Lange, P. (1977) 'La teoria degli incentivi e l'analisi dei partiti politici', *Rassegna italiana di sociologia*, 18: 501–526.

Panebianco, A. (1979) 'Imperativi organizzativi, conflitti interni e ideologia nei partiti comunisti', *Rivista italiana di scienza politica*, 9 (3): 511–536.

Sivini, G. (1967) 'Gli iscritti alla Democrazia cristiana e al Partito comunista italiano', *Rassegna italiana di sociologia* 8: 429–470.

Togliatti, P. (1972) *La via italiana al socialismo* (2nd edn), Rome: Editori Riuniti.

Vacca, G. (1987) *Tra compromesso e solidarietà: La politica del Pci negli anni '70*, Rome: Editori Riuniti.

5 The rise and fall of Craxi's Socialist Party

Stephen Gundle

No party was more dramatically affected by the disintegration of the party system than the PSI and no figure embodied the crisis more completely and tragically than its long-serving leader, Bettino Craxi. Despite a share of the vote that never rose above 15 per cent, the party became the arbiter of political life in the 1980s. It made and unmade governments, to a large degree it set the agenda for political debate, and it held the offices of President (1978–85) and Prime Minister (1983–87). More than any other party, it gave the impression of being in tune with the modern, dynamic Italy that came to the fore with the 'second economic miracle' of the middle years of the decade. Yet within a year of the explosion of the *Tangentopoli* corruption scandal the PSI had virtually collapsed. With many of its leading members at national and local level under investigation and electoral support in vertical decline, all that remained was, in Eugenio Scalfari's picturesque phrase, 'a pile of rubble' (see Natale 1994). In the 1994 elections the rump of the PSI scored just 2.2 per cent. Three months later Craxi (now living in self-imposed exile in Tunisia) and his former deputy, Claudio Martelli, were sentenced, pending appeals, to eight and a half years in gaol for their part in a murky corruption case dating from the early 1980s.

This chapter examines the PSI in the period between 1976 and 1994. It analyses the nature of Craxi's leadership, continuities and discontinuities with respect to the previous history of Italian Socialism and the role of the PSI in the political system. It seeks to explain why the party was so profoundly damaged by the judicial investigations that it was wholly unable to extricate itself from corruption and wrong-doing in the public mind, and conserve a significant, if reduced, electoral following. It will be argued that the PSI was in decline even before the eruption of *Tangentopoli* and that its earlier successes, political and electoral, were in any case modest and fragile. By their actions the magistrates rapidly hastened the party's demise, but the mortal blow was largely self-inflicted. It was the result of errors of strategy and tactics, a failure to read social trends correctly, poor responses to a series of events, and above all, a failure of the leadership to distinguish itself in any way from a system of illegality and corruption that the DC had established – and of which the PSI became an integral part.

THE FALL

Whereas the DC and the small parties of the Centre were drawn into corruption investigations on a significant scale after the clamour over the initial disclosures, and the PDS was affected only marginally and still later, the PSI was a major target from the very beginning. The downfall of an entire political elite was bound up from the outset with the exposure of systematic criminal practices involving the PSI over all other parties. Given that the 'system' which was collapsing had been invented by the DC, and that the PSI had at first reluctantly and then much more willingly been integrated into it, it might be thought that this was unjust. This was certainly the reaction of many Socialists, who cried in vain that there was a conspiracy against them and that their party was being made the scape-goat of evils for which others were at least equally responsible.

In fact there were good reasons why the PSI was the principal victim. First and foremost, it was the dominant party in Milan, the city where the investigations began. The position of mayor was in its pocket regardless of which other parties formed part of the governing coalition, virtually all public institutions in the city were run by Socialist appointees and the party counted on close support from important sections of the business community and civil society. Nothing happened in Milan, it was said, without the Socialists' approval, and above all nothing involving economic activity at the interface of the public and private sectors. To many, it seemed ironic that the Milan investigations sprang from the arrest in March 1992 of the Socialist head of a geriatric home who was caught red-handed having just received a bribe of a mere seven million lire (approximately three thousand pounds) from a cleaning contractor. Yet the very banality of this exchange showed that the system of rake-offs was total – that it operated at every level from the highest to the lowest (see della Porta 1993). For most of the 1980s the system functioned to the satisfaction of all the parties directly involved. The dominant moral climate was conducive to bribery, and business was more than happy to pay in order to eliminate competition and gain a regular share of public resources. Mario Chiesa, the administrator whose arrest and subsequent confession triggered the affair, later revealed that he never had to ask for money. It was always offered to him spontaneously.[1] Two factors broke the back of the system: public exasperation with the wastage, inefficiency and unresponsiveness of the political elite, which created a climate in which the magistrates could proceed, and the recession, which increased pressure both on businesses included in the system and those excluded from it, to the extent that it became intolerable. It was the misfortune of the PSI that its fief, unlike those of such DC bosses as De Mita and

Gaspari which were located in areas of the South where the economy was state-dominated, was the heart of Italy's private economy, and home of an electorate that encountered no obstacles (following the fall of Communism) in giving expression to a protest that found in the Northern League and, for a brief period, La Rete, its most effective mouthpieces.

The second reason that the PSI fell victim first and most completely to the magistrates was that it had discarded virtually all ideological baggage and even principle in the pursuit of power. This change began in the 1960s, when the PSI's access to public office at national and local level increased enormously. But it was completed in the 1980s when the pursuit of illicit finance and of position within the para-state sector ceased to be a means to an end and became the primary goal of party action. In the absence of any ethical basis to its politics, the PSI attracted and encouraged the ruthless, the ambitious and the unscrupulous. A new category of 'business politicians', able at using private resources to build personal support, took over the apparatus at local level. When they were arrested – as the investigations spread, after Milan, to other cities and regions – these officials often expressed astonishment. They were utterly convinced that they would never be caught or held to account. Such was the shock that some, like Sergio Moroni and Renato Amoresi, committed suicide, leaving notes that at once proclaimed innocence and admitted guilt. In most cases though, those arrested very quickly confessed, providing information that enabled inquiries to be extended further. Although theft was claimed to have been carried out in the name of the party, there was little evidence of party loyalty in adversity.[2] This is not to say that there were no honest and principled Socialists. Among the rank and file and even in the higher echelons of the party there were men and women who sought to keep alive the values of reformist Socialism; but such people were systematically excluded from the seats of power.

A further reason lay in the nature of party organisation. Unlike the highly factionalised and decentralised Christian Democrats, the PSI was organised in a quasi-monarchical fashion. Some local 'barons' (notably De Michelis in the Veneto, Formica in Puglia and Lagorio in Tuscany) enjoyed much autonomy, but most local bosses held power because of the backing they received from Craxi. Moreover in the case of Milan, which was Craxi's own power base, there was scarcely any distinction between local action and the national leadership, since the leader personally directed affairs from his substantial offices in Piazza Duomo (rented from the commune for a fraction of the market rate). As a result he was implicated indirectly in *Tangentopoli* from the very first day. Although he held a relatively minor post, Chiesa had run (and financed) the campaign of Craxi's son Bobo for election to the city council, he had procured accommodation for a charitable association headed by the party leader's wife, and he was a peripheral member of the Craxi family circle. In these circumstances it was inevitable that the attempt to blame misdemeanours on a few 'black sheep' (Craxi famously dismissed Chiesa as a *mariuolo* – a rogue – following his arrest, which led the latter, assuming he had been abandoned to his fate, to confess all he knew), would convince neither the public nor the judiciary.

It should also be mentioned that the PSI was much more vulnerable to swings of public opinion than the two larger parties. Although the old organisational structures established by Rodolfo Morandi in the 1950s had not been done away with, they had been left to decline, with the result that the party had no stable social base or sub-culture to fall back on. In contrast to the DC, which could always rely on the support of the Church, the PSI had lost much of its traditional support and instead acquired a following among floating voters, who by definition were fickle (Ercole and Martinotti 1990). The situation was different in the South, but as the recession began to bite and the brake was applied to public expenditure even the exchange voters the party had acquired deserted.

The arrest of Chiesa had little impact on the 1992 election (Hine 1993; Rhodes 1993). But the arrest of many Milanese politicians and the incrimination of two former Socialist mayors, Tognoli and Pillitteri, scotched Craxi's candidature for the office of Prime Minister (his associate Giuliano Amato was appointed instead). The party leader reacted in a typically pugnacious fashion, attacking the Milanese magistrates as a group and seeking to discredit them individually. He also accused the press of participating in the moral lynching of the PSI. In the past intimidatory interventions of this sort had been sufficient to restore 'normality' but this was no longer the case as the DC, content to see its ally take the flak, failed to offer its backing. Combined with these attacks, Craxi launched a defence of his party that amounted in effect to an attempt to distribute blame more evenly across the political elite. In a speech to Parliament in July 1992, he stated that no-one was innocent, that everyone knew about the system of bribes and rake-offs, and that it was common knowledge that the funding of the parties was largely irregular or illegal. By striking this defiant pose, Craxi set himself up as the chief defender of a system of political power and of relations between business and politics that had become utterly discredited. In a clumsy attempt at moral blackmail, he implied that if other party secretaries did not respond to his rallying call, he would reveal all he knew. In this way he identified himself and his party completely with the old order and created a situation in which the PSI could only survive as a significant force if the system did. In fact Craxi's intervention in Parliament only served to worsen his own position, for it convinced the Milanese magistrates that the party leader and his clan stood at the core of the bribery system. When Craxi received the first of a series of notifications that he was under investigation in December 1992, his star had already waned. The man who had led Italy longer than any Prime Minister since De

Gasperi was unable to leave his hotel suite in Rome without being greeted with cries of 'thief' or being pelted with small coins.

If there was at least a sort of warped dignity to Craxi's defence of the old order before Parliament, the same could not be said of his subsequent behaviour. He sought to defend himself by denying all personal connection with the system of kickbacks; the blame was attributed instead to the PSI's former administrative secretary, Vincenzo Balzamo, who had died in November 1992. However this defence was contradicted by Silvano Larini, the chief collector of PSI bribes who turned state's witness following his return from hiding in the Dominican Republic, and by the former party secretary Giacomo Mancini, who told the judges that it was quite impossible that the leader was unaware of specific goings on. His tactical genius seemingly having deserted him, Craxi engaged in a desperate struggle to hold on to power at least in his own party, accusing Martelli of personal betrayal when he advocated a change of line.

Even after his eventual resignation in February 1993, Craxi continued to pull the strings in the party, blocking the efforts at renewal of the two hapless trade unionists, first Giorgio Benvenuto and then Ottaviano Del Turco, who were called in to save the party from disaster. Only after a showdown with the old guard, who made no secret of their sympathy for Berlusconi and who in some cases adhered to Forza Italia, did Del Turco succeed in changing the symbol of the PSI and in joining the Progressive Alliance headed by the PDS. This late shift was insufficient to save the party. In 1994 it failed to reach the 4 per cent necessary to secure a proportional share of parliamentary seats and in the new Chamber it counted just 15 deputies compared to 92 in the previous legislature.

THE RISE OF CRAXI

When Craxi was elected as leader in 1976, the PSI was at its lowest ebb since the war. In the earlier part of the decade it had sought, after ten less than fruitful years in government, to reassert its identity as a party of the Left and of the labour movement – but this failed to produce any improvement in its electoral fortunes. In 1976 it won 9.6 per cent of the vote, the same paltry share as in 1972, while the PCI expanded to an unprecedented 34.4 per cent. Craxi was not initially a powerful leader (his right-wing 'autonomist' faction controlled just 10 per cent of the party) but his election did mark a turning point. It was part of a general turnover which resulted in the old leaders who had governed the party under the Centre Left being replaced by their energetic young lieutenants. Many of these men (Signorile, Manca, Formica, De Michelis), no longer so young, still dominated the PSI in 1992–93.

Although it was not until 1981 that Craxi fully consolidated his position, he wasted little time in giving the PSI a new image. All remaining links with revolutionary theory were severed, and instead pragmatism, the market economy and Western liberal democratic values were embraced. The party sought to cultivate a modern identity that would appeal to the new middle classes that were expanding as the economy moved towards post-industrialism. Its erstwhile partner on the Left, the PCI, was attacked as undemocratic and old-fashioned. A highly competitive attitude was also adopted towards the DC. It was nearly four years before all components of the party were prepared to support him, but from the beginning Craxi's goal was to take the PSI back into government. His intention, however, was not simply to resume the Centre Left. In order to assert the PSI as a major force and ensure that it would not be eroded in office by a manipulative DC (as had occurred in the 1960s), he sought to gain maximum advantage from the pivotal position his party occupied in the political system. This was reinforced after 1979, when the Communists ended their experience on the edge of government and returned to the opposition (see Hellman, Chapter 4). Whereas Nenni had never put DC leadership of the Centre Left in question, Craxi inaugurated a disputatious season in which the PSI continually sought to dislodge the larger party from centres of power.

A new approach was also adopted to patronage. In the 1960s the Socialists had been sucked innocently into the system of party control of the para-state sector. They had nominated trusted men, with the intention of 'conditioning' the DC and checking its policy influence (Padellaro and Tamburrano 1993: 60–61). The new Socialist leadership was much less reticent. It adopted the DC's own practice of procuring backing by spinning a web of relations between institutions and organised interests, public apparatuses and private clienteles (Merkel 1987: 32). It competed on the traditional terrain of *lottizzazione* of the state and the clientelist use of public resources. For example, ENI was entrusted to the PSI in 1979 and immediately became a battleground between left and right within the party.

One of the primary purposes of the struggle for position was to free the PSI of dependence on the DC for funds – 'removing the hand of the DC from the tap and putting its own' (Padellaro and Tamburrano 1993: 63). In this sense as well as a more strictly political one, 'autonomy' was an overriding goal. Yet, paradoxically, being drawn into the world of illicit funds and gigantic kickbacks – while it brought the PSI institutional power and riches beyond those justified by the size of its electoral following – did not emancipate it from the DC. One of the main reasons why it proved completely unable to pursue a more flexible policy after 1989 was its total dependence on sub-governmental power. Despite the disputes that flared up in public – which in any case were usually more concerned with position than with principle – a web of common interests and complicities was spun that rendered the alliance unbreakable. The PSI's efforts to present itself as a modern, lay force would continually be hindered by the commitment it showed to building clienteles. The first in a long series of massive joint deals involving domestic and international business on the one hand and the DC and the PSI on the other, was the ENI-Petromin affair of 1979–80 according to Franco Bassanini, who was expelled from the PSI for inquiring too closely into the matter in the budget commission of the Chamber of Deputies.[3] When the PSI voted in Parliament to absolve politicians of wrong-doing, or when its leaders attacked the judiciary, as Craxi repeatedly did well before 1992, it was no longer out of loyalty to the DC as in the 1960s and 1970s. It was increasingly necessary to protect the PSI's own interests (see, e.g Turone 1984: 270–273; Galli 1991: Chapters 11 and 12).

This change in the nature of the PSI did not go unnoticed. At least two prominent Socialists, the President of the Republic, Sandro Pertini, and the long-serving minister Giorgio Ruffolo, sought to sound the alarm. In 1981 Enrico Berlinguer also denounced the devastating consequences for the country of parties whose internal life was dominated and distorted by warring bands.[4] Political scientists on the whole failed to see corruption as a systematic factor in party life. Instead they spoke of the consequences of a change of perspective that occurred in the PSI, from one oriented towards the good of the country and its institutions as a whole to one dominated by partisan considerations (Pasquino 1986: 129; Merkel 1987: 32). Pasquino noted how the PSI was tending to become a deradicalised and opportunistic party of 'political gamblers', while Ciofi and Ottaviano argued that it was losing its characteristics as a party of government and was acquiring those of a party of power modelled on the substructure of the state (Ciofi and Ottaviano 1988: 65).

This was not something the PSI leadership ever fully accepted either in theory or in practice. There were constant debates on organisational questions and various reforms to the party machine were contemplated to render it more effective as a tool of mass mobilisation. These came to nothing. Instead the PSI developed into an authoritarian-paternalistic Presidential party in which there was near total identification with a charismatic leader. There are four reasons why this occurred. First, personalisation conformed to changes occurring in the formation of public opinion. The Socialists were the first to understand the importance of the mass media in political communication and to seek to supplement declining grass-roots structures with positions of power within the press and broadcasting. They also realised that in a complex society ideas or aspirations needed to be conveyed in a simplified form and that the projection of a single person facilitated identification. Second, Craxi was personally very popular with middle- and lower-ranking PSI officials and elected representatives as well as with the rank and file. He was perceived to have raised the party's profile and to have restored a sense of its pride and dignity. Third, the centralisation of command rendered the PSI flexible and able to react promptly to events. This was important because Craxi's conduct was primarily, and perhaps even exclusively, tactical. He had no strategy or project that went beyond the conquest of advantage. Fourth, Craxi eliminated internal opposition and paid little attention to formal decision-making channels. In this sense the PSI came to resemble the Spanish and Greek Socialist parties, two other deradicalised forces that, probably not coincidentally, also became tainted with corruption. Nevertheless, in the Italian context centralisation had its specific uses – for it was the opposite of what occurred in the DC: the more it had occupied the state, the more factionalised it became. This meant that the PSI leadership was able to challenge the DC effectively over the distribution of posts and resources at all levels as the Catholic party slowly went into decline.

THE SOCIALIST PREMIERSHIP

Although the PSI expanded both at the election of 1979, when it grew to 9.8 per cent, and of 1983, when it obtained 11.4 per cent, the results were on the whole disappointing. What enabled it to seize the political advantage and capture the post of Prime Minister was the sharp drop of the DC, which lost 5.4 per cent in 1983. Craxi was in some ways a typical, weak Italian premier (see Hine and Finocchi 1991), the leader of a factious, multi-party coalition. Yet he managed to remain in office for two years and eight months, and by virtue of this fact alone he achieved a measure of political stability. His two administrations contributed to the lowering of inflation by cutting back the system of automatic wage indexation. There were also achievements in two other areas: a new Concordat was signed with the Vatican to replace the 1929 Lateran accords, and Italy's global standing increased thanks to a slightly more assertive foreign policy than had been the case in the past.

There were a number of areas however in which the government failed. Crucially, nothing was done to address the question of the massive budget deficit and the spiralling public sector debt. In addition, no socio-economic or political reforms were promoted, with the result that in these areas less was achieved than during the Centre Left in the 1960s. Moreover, Socialists did nothing to advance the large-scale institutional reform that they had championed in the preceding period. Finally, no systematic measures were adopted to reverse the massive expansion of organised crime in the South. The reasons for all this were tactical: the Socialists were unwilling to risk taking any action that might have alienated a section of the electorate. Even their interest in constitutional change waned after they took power within the existing institutional framework (Pasquino 1986: 137–138). Craxi himself was seen to embody the firm, executive-led government that Italy needed.

Instead of seeking to lend a meaningful reformist dimension to their slogan of modernisation, at least by tackling wastage and inefficiency within the public sector, the Socialists chose to cultivate a dynamic, modern image by identifying themselves with those who symbolised Italian prosperity and who achieved success during the 'second economic miracle'. An upbeat opulence marked the tenor and scenography of party congresses – which were held more to celebrate the successes of the Socialist premiership than to debate policy. At the Verona congress in 1984 the old decision-making forums were abolished and replaced by a largely ornamental national assembly to which a variety of celebrities was nominated. Socialist gatherings were no longer the mecca of earnest and respectable working-class men; rather they became fashionable social occasions at which participants were guided to their seats by beautiful hostesses dressed in designer uniforms and at which receptions and festivities were as much a part of the event as the deliberations.

In the 1960s, when rake-offs and illicit funding first became customary within the PSI, officials were careful not to draw attention to their ill-gotten rewards. In the 1980s ostentation took the place of reserve. Leading Socialists set the tone with their portable telephones, hotel suites and high living, and lower-level officials followed their example. Just as Craxi counted among his friends super-rich tycoons like Berlusconi and the construction magnate Salvatore Ligresti, so Socialists in the cities cultivated the company of ambitious architects, professionals and business people. It was in this climate of elite interaction (often in corrupt masonic lodges) that the practice of the *tangente* or kickback became routine (see della Porta, Chapter 14). Although the funds served mainly to meet what were termed 'the costs of politics' (rents on offices; staff salaries; publications; the subscriptions of non-existent members to control the party machine; conferences, and above all the election campaigns, that under the system of preference voting combined with private television, became both expensive and personalised), it became accepted within the PSI and other parties that in order to achieve a life-style to which they believed they were entitled, poorly paid administrators would also round out their own incomes.[5]

In such a context the modernity of the PSI could not but be largely illusory. For all the talk of the market, the tertiary sector, the 'rising strata' and post-industrialism, the party did not attract many adherents among the new middle classes or the productive sector. Instead it acted as a magnet for dubious financiers, bogus architects, pop intellectuals, the vulgar fringes of the new rich, place-seekers and time-servers, all of whom were happy to share in the belief that they were on the crest of the wave and that the future as well as the present belonged to them. Far from representing the best of civil society, the national assembly was stuffed with 'dwarves and dancing girls', Rino Formica quipped.

Craxi won plaudits for his statesman-like behaviour as Prime Minister but, far from being a giant in a party of pygmies, he remained in essence a vain and vindictive politician. He allowed himself to be surrounded by a personality cult the like of which had not been seen in Italy since the war. Disturbingly, he also used his position to conduct a continuous struggle against every power in the state and civil society that failed to join the chorus of praise, or which constituted an obstacle to the designs of the PSI and the DC: Parliament, the judiciary, the press, the intellectuals, non-domesticated sectors of the business community. The Craxian doctrine of *decisionismo* (in essence, deciding quickly and without consultation or compromise with the opposition) – which exercised a certain appeal in a political culture that was accustomed to protracted mediation and very slow and often ineffective policy implementation – seemed to rest not on a desire for efficiency but contempt for democratic procedures and representative institutions. Ultimately however this very arrogance, which has been identified as a typical feature of the mercantile or corrupt politician (Pizzorno 1992: 25–26; della Porta, Chapter 14), proved to be Craxi's undoing. A tactical genius in favourable circumstances, he floundered badly when conditions turned and those he had alienated exacted their revenge.

FROM DYNAMISM TO STAGNATION

Socialists pinned great hopes on the outcome of the 1987 election, when they hoped to reap the rewards of the Craxi premiership and the upturn in economic conditions. Their result of 14.3 per cent signalled an increase, but of more modest dimensions than had been expected. The party gained from the PCI in the South and from the Republicans and the DC in the North – where it recovered some of its traditional urban electorate lost in 1983 (Ercole and Martinotti 1990). The principal problem, as Socialists saw it, was that the DC and PCI – which declined to 26.6 per cent – were able to stave off or slow down their inevitable decline by means of extensive structures in civil society. Nevertheless they drew comfort from the fact that the two large parties commanded less than 60 per cent of the vote compared to 72 per cent in 1976, and from the fact that the Communist electorate, which had been three and a half times the size of the PSI in that year, was now less than twice as big. These data confirmed them in their belief that there was an underlying 'long wave' in the PSI's electoral fortunes.

On the basis of this assumption the leadership opted to confirm the governmental alliance with the DC. The principal aim, as Craxi and his associates saw it, was to regain in several years' time the office of Premier, or alternatively conquer that of President for the Socialist leader at the end of Cossiga's mandate in 1992. They took the view that this scenario did not have to be won in the country but rather negotiated with the DC, and in particular the key powerbrokers Forlani and Andreotti. In the light of this the PSI returned to government as a comparatively passive partner in administrations headed by a succession of Christian Democrats. This was a complacent approach that amounted to a renunciation of politics – and contained the risk that the prestige acquired between 1983 and 1987 would turn into a rapidly diminishing asset.

This danger was especially great as the electorate, which had already shown signs of unprecedented mobility, became highly volatile, aided by a series of events which undermined traditional loyalties and introduced new elements into political life. The collapse of 'really existing socialism' in Eastern Europe; the slow and painful transformation of the PCI into the PDS (with relative split); the emergence of the Lombard League, and the rise of Segni's cross-party referendum movement all offered opportunities for the PSI to develop a strategy to enable it to profit from these events, encourage mobility and turn it to its advantage – also to put itself at the head of a movement or alliance for change. Instead it misjudged all of these things and turned itself into a factor of immobility.

There were some attempts to introduce changes of stance and line in the PSI. The vice-secretary Giulio Di Donato and others spoke of the need to rediscover the party's lower-class roots. Others, including Martelli, suggested a more constructive approach to electoral reform. But in practice nothing changed. The period from the late 1980s to the early 1990s was marked not by renewal, *pace* Di Scala (1988), but by signs of degeneration and of increasing distance from the real movement of opinion in society. The party did nothing to distinguish itself from administrations headed by Craxi's long-time ally Andreotti, and it even went into the 1992 election having committed itself in advance to continuity of the alliance, something which had studiously been avoided in 1983 and 1987. Manifestations of arrogance and the abuse of power multiplied rather than diminished. Craxi, for example, installed family members in key positions in the Socialist power structure in Milan, making his brother-in-law mayor and his son party secretary in the city. More gravely, there was no restraint at any level in the demand for funds from businesses tendering for public contracts. As the repentant briber Vincenzo Lodigiani revealed, the 'good coexistence' of the 1980s was suddenly broken as the regular flow of funds was no longer sufficient to satisfy the politicians' appetites. At just the time business was coming under economic pressure, the screws were tightened. It was this that would lead directly to *Tangentopoli*.[6] In so far as the PSI did attempt to interpret public opinion it did so in a way that proved to be counter-productive. It captained a campaign against drug-users that damaged the PSI's libertarian credentials, and even led to an anti-prohibitionist list contesting the 1989 European elections. It sponsored the populist 1987 referendum on the civil responsibilities of judges that gained a massive endorsement but which alienated the judiciary and probably spurred it into action against the parties (see Ginsborg, Chapter 1).

Thus the PSI became identified ever more clearly with the existing politico-institutional system at just the moment when that system was put in question. For a party that had a lower percentage of faithful voters than other parties, and which relied in the North of the country on the favour of a mobile and critical electorate, this was a dangerous position. The decline of the PSI began well before the debacle of 1994. In the European elections of 1989 the party grew overall to 14.8 per cent – but this figure concealed a fall in its electorate of 400,000 since 1987 (Rhodes 1993: 72). The losses were concentrated in the North West and some cities like Palermo. The trend to decline in the North was confirmed in the 1990 local elections. In 1992 the party's support fell by 0.7 per cent, but the decline was more marked in the North (2.8 per cent). It held up better in the South, where its vote was a clientelist one, but even here there were signs that all was not well. In the Sicilian regional elections of 16 June 1991, held just one week after the approval of the referendum, the PSI hoped for revenge: in fact it obtained not the expected 20 per cent but 15 per cent, a decline of 2.2 per cent on the provincial elections of 1990. By late 1993 the PSI had collapsed in the South as well as the North.

It remains to be explained why the PSI found itself in this situation. One factor was poor leadership. Although considered to be a great tactician, Craxi failed when the premises under-pinning his outlook were challenged; he also proved to have no gift for strategy. Faced with a range of unexpected opportunities, he revealed himself to be cautious and lacking courage. Moreover his denunciations of protest as 'anti-democratic', and warnings of chaos if established parties were ousted, showed that he had lost touch with public opinion. This was not perhaps surprising, for the PSI leader was surrounded by yes-men and had grown accustomed to adulation. His only relationship with public opinion was via journalists, with whom he had a highly conflictual rapport. This problem was reinforced by the decay of the PSI. The party had been turned into a series of fiefs managed by local bosses whose only function at national level was to acclaim the leadership. With no internal debate, the party atrophied and ceased completely to act as a meaningful channel of communication with civil society. But there was also a more fundamental reason. Under Craxi the PSI committed itself unequivocally to exploitation of its pivotal role and to the pursuit of power within the Christian Democratic system. Not even as judgement day approached could this 'pact with the devil' be broken.

CONCLUSION

The PSI entered into competition with the DC as the hegemony of the latter began to decline – not with the intention of substituting the policies and methods of government of the former with a new set, but with the aim of substituting the DC within the state and para-state sector and in the mediation of public affairs and private interests. It adopted *en bloc* the methods of the DC, adding only a technocratic and a managerial veneer to long-established practices. At the same time it set aside all reformist aspirations other than those which as propaganda could advantage the party. This abandonment of any sense of the collective good in favour of a conception of the state as a terrain in the battle for resources, position and political advantage had devastating effects for the quality of Italian political life and for the functioning of the country's institutions. In the long run it also failed to bring advantage to the PSI. Despite circumstances that, had the party pursued a quite different course, could have been favourable, it never fulfilled its ambition to lead the Left.

The PSI was penalised more even than the DC for corruption and bad government because it elected itself chief defender of the system – in the expectation that the wave of protest would soon ebb. When it did not, it paid the price. But there were also two other factors. First, the PSI was punished, indeed became the scape-goat of the crisis, because it had, with its talk of reform and modernity, raised hopes that it would offer something new and different. When it was made clear that its sole practical achievement had been to perpetuate a system of power, its support evaporated. Second, the PSI had no sponsoring institution behind it. It was vulnerable because its electorate was fluid and its adaptation to existing socio-economic arrangements had been accompanied by adoption by a lightweight party model, albeit one with clientelist structures and elements of an old mass party. In addition its centralised, quasi-monarchical structure meant that there was no alternative leadership available when the old one was discredited. Whereas the DC could at least produce 'clean' faces in Martinazzoli and Bindi, the PSI was compelled to resort to outsiders like Benvenuto and Del Turco, whose appointments paradoxically confirmed the fact that the party had become unpresentable.

NOTES

1 M. Andreoli, 'Era un sistema bulgaro', *Panorama*, 13 December 1992, p. 46.
2 The speed of many confessions suggests that corrupt politicians always had a sense that what they were doing was wrong (see Ginsborg, Chapter 1). Interviewed later in the press several even expressed relief that their experience in a twilight world of illegality had come to an end.
3 G. Valentini, 'Così il Psi divenne un comitato d'affari', *La Repubblica*, 13 February 1993.
4 E. Scalfari, 'Che cos'è la questione morale', *La Repubblica*, 28 July 1981.
5 The mechanisms of corruption were explained by Vincenzo Lodigiani in P. Colaprico and L. Fazzo, 'Così ho riempito le casse di Dc e Psi', *La Repubblica*, 21 November 1992.
6 Ibid.

REFERENCES

Ciofi, P. and Ottaviano, F. (1988) *Il PSI di Craxi*, Rome: Rinascita.

della Porta, D. (1993) 'Milan: immoral capital', in S. Hellman and G. Pasquino (eds) *Italian Politics*, Vol. 8, London: Pinter.

Di Scala, S. (1988) *Renewing Italian Socialism: Nenni to Craxi*, New York: Oxford University Press.

Ercole, E. and Martinotti, G. (1990) 'Le basi elettorali del neosocialismo italiano', in M. Caciagli and A. Spreafico (eds) *Vent'anni di elezioni in Italia 1968–1987*, Padua: Liviana.

Galli, G. (1991) *Affari di Stato: l'Italia sotterranea 1943–1990*, Milan: Kaos.

Hine, D. and Finocchi, P. (1991) 'The Italian Prime Minister', *West European Politics*, 14(2): 79–96.

Hine, D. (1993) 'The Italian Socialist Party and the 1992 general election', in G. Pasquino and P. McCarthy (eds) *The End of Post-war Politics in Italy: the Landmark 1992 Elections*, Boulder, Col.: Westview.

Merkel, W. (1987) *Prima e dopo Craxi: le trasformazioni del PSI*, Padua: Liviana.

Natale, P. (1994) 'C'era una volta l'elettore socialista', in R. Mannheimer and G. Sani (eds) *La rivoluzione elettorale*, Milan: Anabasi.

Padellaro, A. and Tamburrano, G. (1993) *Processo a Craxi: ascesa e declino di un leader*, Milan: Sperling & Kupfer.

Pasquino, G. (1986) 'Modernity and reforms: the PSI between political entrepreneurs and gamblers', *West European Politics*, 9(1): 120–141.

Pizzorno, A. (1992) 'La corruzione nel sistema politico', introduction to D. della Porta *Lo scambio occulto*, Bologna: Il Mulino.

Rhodes, M. (1993) 'The "long wave" subsides: the PSI and the demise of *Craxismo*', in S. Hellman and G. Pasquino (eds) *Italian Politics: a Review Vol. 8*, London: Pinter.

Turone, S. (1984) *Corrotti e corruttori dall'Unità alla P2*, Bari: Laterza.

6 The fate of the secular Centre
The Liberals, Republicans and Social Democrats

Mark Donovan

During the 'First Republic' the Liberals (PLI), Republicans (PRI) and Social Democrats (PSDI) were known collectively as 'the lay parties'. Though between them they never won as much as 15 per cent of the vote from 1946 to 1992, they were important (see Table 6.1). They were, above all, long-term actual and potential coalition partners to the DC who, with some 40 per cent of the vote, dominated government formation throughout the First Republic (see Furlong, Chapter 3). They also manifested the liberal/lay tradition in Italy, as distinct from the dominant Catholic and Socio-Communist traditions. The end of the First Republic coincided with the demise of these parties, at least as parliamentary formations. They were undone by their identification with the *partitocrazia*, in particular by the 1993 electoral reform (see Parker, Chapter 2) and by the bipolarisation of the electorate between the right-wing Liberty Pole and the Progressive Alliance on the Left.

The strength and nature of Italian liberalism is an immensely complex topic. For one thing, both Catholicism and socialism were deeply influenced by it. Indeed, the DC's 50-year history was partly about Catholicism's *rapprochement* with liberalism. Something similar can be said with regard to Italian socialism, with the PSDI's roots lying in the break-away of liberal socialists from the socialist mainstream. Liberalism, then, was not confined to the lay parties. Furthermore, the consolidation of democracy in post-Fascist Italy went hand-in-hand with a consolidation of liberalism, both politically and economically. At the same time, the ideological origins of the lay parties became less relevant as they became mere power-brokers, representatives of special interests. A reaffirmation of the

Table 6.1 Lay party vote shares, 1946–92

	1946	1948	1953	1958	1963	1968	1972	1976	1979	1983	1987	1992
PSDI	–	7.1	4.5	4.6	6.1	PSU	5.1	3.4	3.8	4.1	3.0	2.7
PRI	4.4	2.5	1.6	1.4	1.4	2.0	2.9	3.1	3.0	5.1	3.7	4.4
PLI	6.8	3.8	3.0	3.5	7.0	5.8	3.9	1.3	1.9	2.9	2.1	2.8
Total	11.2	13.4	9.1	9.5	14.5	–	11.9	7.8	8.7	12.1	8.8	9.9

party-organisational expression of liberalism, or better of Thatcherite neo-liberalism, was witnessed in the 1994 election. But this was expressed by Silvio Berlusconi's brand new Forza Italia (see McCarthy, Chapter 8), and by Umberto Bossi's still evolving Northern League (see Diamanti, Chapter 7).

This chapter outlines the different origins of the lay parties. It then explains how they came to be associated with each other via the creation of a particular party system focused on a bloc of centre parties. Having stressed what the parties had in common, it examines divisions and cleavages within the lay bloc. Next, the apparently revived prospects of these parties in the 1980s is examined. The chapter then emphasises the parties' marginality and passivity during the revolution of 1989–94, a crisis which saw the secretaries of all three parties resign within a month of each other in the spring of 1993. Finally, the conclusion considers the nature of party identities and ideology in the 1990s.

THE LAY PARTIES AND THE POLITICAL SYSTEM

Founded in 1895 with a tradition stretching back to the *Risorgimento* – and in particular to radical democratic Mazzinianism, the Republican Party was the oldest of the lay parties. When parties reemerged in the aftermath of Fascism, the PRI's inheritance was one of radical anti-monarchism, anti-clericalism and uncompromising anti-Fascism. With these leftist features, however, the PRI combined a pro-United States and pro-market stance, though it supported state intervention. It did this for two reasons. First, recognising the difference between the model market economy described in books and the highly imperfect and socially unsatisfactory 'historical capitalism' found in Italy, it concluded that state action was required to break conservative cartels and to spread the benefits of free enterprise. Second, the party believed strongly in public action to assist southern development. Ugo La Malfa, party secretary from 1965 to 1979 and a much admired figure, was himself Sicilian.

The Liberal Party, by contrast, was a more doctrinaire liberal party which moved quickly to link economic liberalism with political authoritarianism. This free market/strong state orientation reflected both true believers' awareness of liberalism's weakness in Italy, and the strength of entrenched economic interests which, out of self-interest, used neo-classical *laissez-faire* ideas to hinder action by the visible hand of the state. Politically the PLI inherited the traditions of the ruling elite which dominated Italy from unification in the early 1860s until the crisis which followed World War I. Formed as a party only in 1922, the PLI was compromised by its relationship with Fascism, supportive of the monarchy, and opposed reforming the quasi-feudal socio-economic structures found in southern Italy. Much thus separated the PRI and PLI. Nevertheless, both were on the same side of several cleavages: state v. Church, market

v. plan, United States v. Soviet Union, and ultimately both parties shared the same lay sub-culture (Pridham 1988).

The Italian Social Democratic Party was born of a historic split in the reborn Socialist Party in January 1947. The schism, led by Giuseppe Saragat, was a crucial moment in the emergence of a bloc of centre parties because it occurred when the CLN (see below) was no longer able to act as the basis for government formation (though it continued to underpin the work of the Constituent Assembly until it completed its task of creating the new republican constitution in December 1947). The establishment of what became the PSDI enabled De Gasperi to provide his post-CLN governments with a not-insignificant reformist socialist dimension. Nearly half the Socialists' national leadership broke away, taking a third of the party's membership, the bulk of the youth organis- ation and the intellectuals. In 1948 the new party captured 7 per cent of the vote. The fact that, with the zeal of the converted, the PSDI sub- sequently became more anti-communist than many whose roots were not in the socialist tradition (for example in the PRI and DC), and thereby became a very conservative party, hostile to change, should not obscure the thoroughly socialist origins of the PSDI. Equally those origins should not obscure the party's political trajectory.

The three small parties were drawn into supporting De Gasperi in 1947–48, and after the watershed election of 1948 they formed a 'lay area' that acted as a counter-weight to the vociferous Catholic Right. This however is not to say that there was much practical agreement between them. At no point in the 1950s and 1960s were they all in government at the same time, and they evolved in quite different ways. The PLI lost all interest in social reform and became a party of the Right – little more than the political arm of Confindustria. The PSDI, despite a short-lived reconciliation come merger with the PSI in 1966–69, turned into a con- servative and clientelistic force concerned mainly with defending pen- sioners' interests. Only the PRI remained politically healthy. It supported the entry of the Socialists into government in 1963 and it championed regional reform and economic planning. In the 1970s it acted as an interlocutor of both the DC and the PCI.

Overall, the liberal centre parties seemed doomed to irrelevancy by the late 1970s. Yet suddenly their fortunes improved. With the DC in decline and the PCI in disarray, it appeared in the early 1980s that a 'lay- socialist' pole might dominate the political system. In the event this did not happen. Despite the increases which all three parties registered in the 1983 election and the successful terms as Prime Minister of the PRI leader Giovanni Spadolini (1981–82) and the Socialist Bettino Craxi (1983–87), the lay-left area failed to become the growth pole of a new alternative to the old system. Change, when it came, came from oppo- sitional movements, not devoid of a radical liberal stamp. Let us explore the reasons for this in detail.

THE FAILURE OF THE 'LAY-SOCIALIST' AREA

The protagonism of the PSI secretary, Bettino Craxi, and his confrontation with De Mita, the DC secretary, dominated the 1983 and 1987 elections and forced the lay parties to choose between Craxi and the DC. The issue split all three small parties. When the decisive moment of confrontation between the DC and PSI came in 1986, only the PSDI backed Craxi (Rhodes 1989). A series of policy issues divided the parties of the putative 'lay-socialist' area, and these exacerbated tensions relating to political style and leadership. Relations between the Republicans and Socialists had never been good, with the former regarding the latter as irresponsible and unreliable. This view reflected the PSI's highly conflictual relationship with the DC. The PLI too was unhappy with the Socialist pretension to lead the lay area, particularly as a strong liberal historiographical tradition blamed Italy's post-war political, economic and ethical inadequacies on the joint hegemony of Catholic and socialist populism.

A tendency to a split between the two nominally socialist parties and the two liberal parties also existed, though neither sub-group even came near unification. Thus, limited PLI/PRI electoral pacts in Senate and European elections were responses only to the difficulties faced by small parties in those contests, and they brought discouraging results. Equally, attempts to integrate the PSI and PSDI lacerated the smaller party which suffered a series of defections, and finally, with the passage of the secretaryship from Rino Nicolazzi to Antonio Cariglia in 1988, saw the party consolidate around a determination to maintain its separate identity until what proved a very bitter end.

Unhappy with Craxi's hegemonic pretensions, the PLI was no more impressed by the PRI's desire to lead a liberal bloc which might come to act as a hinge between a united Left and the DC – rather like the German FDP between the SPD and CDU. The PRI's prominence was clear however, both in the economic world, where its links with *Confindustria* strengthened, and politically. The prestige of the leading republican figures, primarily Giovanni Spadolini and the emerging Giorgio La Malfa, Ugo La Malfa's son, contrasted markedly with the retiring presence of Valerio Zanone, and lacklustre leadership of Renato Altissimo. This difference was recognised institutionally in Spadolini's Premiership and his subsequent election as Speaker of the Senate (1987–92; 1992–94). Unfortunately for the PSDI, its leaders were mostly remarked upon for their involvement in damaging scandals, from Mario Tanassi in the late 1970s, through Pietro Longo and Rino Nicolazzi in the 1980s, to Carlo Vizzini in 1993.

The 1987 election demonstrated the emptiness of the hopes raised. All three parties suffered significant losses. The government-orientated vote showed a tendency to concentrate on the DC and PSI, perhaps encouraged by the media's inevitable focus on those two parties (Gundle 1992).

On the other hand, the entry of the Lombard League into Parliament (and to some extent that of the Greens) plus the continued success of the Radicals, showed the potential of a lay-liberal protest vote which the lay parties in government were unable to capture.

TOWARDS THE 'SECOND REPUBLIC': 1989–94

The dramatic international developments of 1989–91 had great resonance in Italy, focusing attention on the Catholic and Communist sub-cultures and their parties in ways not welcome to them. On the one hand, the unravelling of Communism in Central-Eastern Europe and the Soviet Union challenged both the PCI/PDS and the DC (which lost its *raison d'être* as anti-Communist bulwark). On the other, UN intervention in Kuwait/Iraq brought renewed debate about the power of political Catholicism in Italy, triggered by the large-scale popular manifestations of Catholic fundamentalism in the shape of anti-American pacifism. This debate was reinforced by the way in which Communist mobilisation seemed to echo the more decisive and more prominent Catholic mobilisations. However, neither the lay parties, nor the lay-socialist area proved able to capitalise upon these developments. Rather, it was the new Northern League which went from strength to strength. Whilst the 1989 European elections went badly for the lay parties, the League did well – and went on to do even better, making sweeping gains in the 1990 regional elections.

The lay parties' difficulties were exacerbated by the *pentapartito*'s inability to get to grips with Italy's economic problems – to which renewed salience was given by the fact that from late 1990 Italy was in recession. In these circumstances, the emergent Northern League presented a challenge to more than the *partitocrazia*. It challenged the liberal parties' role of representing northern Italy's middle classes and business interests. The trivialisation of the League prior to 1990, and its vilification thereafter (Diamanti 1993), helped obscure the League's programmatic role (Bull 1993). Giorgio La Malfa's appeals not to isolate the League and even to consider it a potential ally fell on deaf ears.

The swelling campaign for electoral reform led by Mario Segni reasserted the need first identified in the 1970s for institutional change to act as a catalyst for political change. The lay-socialist challenge of the 1980s, such as had existed, had failed and was even made to look ridiculous. As the referendum movement gathered momentum it increasingly became an attack on the *partitocrazia*, of which the lay parties were unequivocally part. With the exception of a few Liberals, all three of the lay parties initially opposed Segni's declaration of his intention to reform the electoral system by referendum, though by June 1991 both the liberal parties supported the single referendum left standing by the Constitutional Court – that on the reduction of voters' preference votes to one.

The PSDI was, with the far-left Proletarian Democracy, alone in urging a 'no' vote (though Bettino Craxi and Umberto Bossi called for the voters to abstain).

In the 1992 election the PLI and PRI made slight electoral gains, whereas the PSDI's slide into irrelevance continued. The novelty was that the PRI entered the election after a year in the opposition. This development provoked great turmoil within the party's parliamentary elite, though it found more favour with the party's extra-parliamentary organisation. The change was led by Giorgio La Malfa. In the spring of 1991 he used an affront to the party in a cabinet reshuffle (Andreotti VI to VII) to leave the coalition. He then turned this ambiguous tactical move into a strategic restyling of the PRI as an opponent of the *partitocrazia*. At the time, the PRI's ostentatious departure for the opposition was dramatic, at least to the narrow range of people interested. It also appeared foolhardy, for it contradicted the party's pro-governmental tradition whilst the government parties' position still appeared solid. Within two years, however, the PRI's manoeuvre was lost in the turmoil of events. It had been too little too late by a party of marginal electoral consequence.

The PRI's 1992 campaign slogan was 'the party of the honest', in favour of technocratic, not party, government. However, the party's local practice contradicted its declared intentions. The 1991 Sicilian regional election had even seen well-supported accusations of trading with the Mafia for votes. The PRI was thus perceived to be involved in the worst of the *partitocrazia*'s crimes. Moreover, the regional party in Lombardy was deeply implicated in the first arrests stemming from *mani pulite* (the 'clean hands' investigation April to May 1992), and in early 1993 Republican involvement in the *partitocrazia*'s systematic abuse of the public sector was revealed by investigations into ENEL, the national electricity agency. At the end of February 1993 La Malfa resigned over undeclared financial support in the previous year's electoral campaign.

The sum involved in La Malfa's resignation was comparatively trivial (about £25,000) and relating as it did to a campaign expenses' gift, rather than to personal profiteering or extortion/embezzlement to fill the party's coffers, many sprang to La Malfa's defence. It was essential, it was argued, to distinguish the wrong-doing of individuals uncovered on the periphery of the *Tangentopoli* investigations – guilty possibly only of the inadvertent non-declaration of items of account – from that of the primary investigations which differed markedly in nature and degree.

The amount of damage done to the PRI by these and further charges is difficult to calculate, but the figures indicating Parliamentarians under investigation in the summer of 1993 damned the lay parties. See Table 6.2.

The PLI was hit as hard as the PRI, if not harder, with the scandal surrounding the Neapolitan Health Minister Francesco De Lorenzo being

Table 6.2 Parliamentarians under investigation, summer 1993

	No.	%
DC	74	23
PSI	49	34
PSDI	9	47
PRI	8	20
PLI	4	18
PDS	5	3
RC	1	2
Lega Nord	1	1

Source: *Corriere della Sera*, 15 July 1993, p. 6

particularly damaging to the party's image. The PRI at least did not have to contend with ministerial resignations.

In March 1993 Renato Altissimo and Carlo Vizzini – the secretaries of the PLI and PSDI respectively – resigned. Within five weeks the secretaries of all three lay parties had stood down. Vizzini formally resigned on the grounds that the party's coffers were empty, rather than because he had received notification that he was under judicial investigation. This soon followed however. Nevertheless, Vizzini's point was good: the abolition of the public funding of parties resulting from the April 1993 referendums, and the climate brought about by the *Tangentopoli* investigations in fact rendered the financial situation of many parties impossible. From the summer of 1993 the lay parties, like the other governing parties, had to lay off party workers and sell off party property, including several prestigious buildings.

In June and December the new local electoral legislation focusing on the direct election of the mayor was put into action for the first time. Whilst all the government parties suffered badly, the small parties suffered particularly. Thus whilst the government parties lost about one-third of the support gained in the same areas in 1992, the lay parties lost four-fifths (Di Franco and Gritti 1994). Whatever caveats are required regarding the non-comparability of national and sub-national election results, this outcome appeared to confirm what had always been assumed – that to move away from proportional representation was ruinous to the smallest parties.

Overwhelmed by scandal, insolvency and the disintegration of the party system the lay parties contemplated dissolution in an attempt to forge new political growth poles. Naturally, such proposals appalled those with jobs to lose or proud of their party traditions. The prospect of building umbrella organisations akin to the French UDF was much preferred.

On the Centre Left the major new proto-party to be born was Democratic Alliance, or AD. This movement, largely born of progressive support for Segni's referendum campaigns, received its first public airing in October 1992. Various members of the PDS, the PSI, the lay parties and the Greens, as well as left Catholics, showed an interest. The key principle underpinning AD was 'alternation'. At the time this meant the need to put together an alternative capable of pushing the DC into the opposition. What was not clear was whether this meant rebuilding the Left, wherein the PDS was bound to play a major role, or whether a distinct bloc could or should be built to operate on the PDS's right flank. Given the heterogeneity of those participating and the fact that what united them was the essentially negative principle of opposition to the DC, the ideology and programme of AD was not, and could not be, clarified.

The disintegration of the DC in the summer of 1993 presented itself less as an opportunity for a new Centre-Left to be created than as a further cause for confusion, for the movement's lack of cohesion was intensified by the uncertainty of the situation. Successive opinion polls indicated three parties each to be gaining about 20 per cent support: the DC, the League and the PDS. It was not clear which of these was the principal foe, which a potential ally. The brief adhesion of Mario Segni with his Popular Reform Movement to AD during the summer of 1993 further confused the picture, since Segni represented a potential centre-right rallying point.

Amidst this turmoil, the PRI and PLI both split in several directions, forming a kaleidoscopic series of linkages with other parties and proto-parties. With the formation of the Centre Union (UDC) in the spring and summer of 1993 by Raffaele Costa, the PLI's new leader, it appeared that the PRI was tending towards the centre-left whilst the PLI favoured a centre-right position (see *Il Giornale*, 27 June 1993, p.3).

Led by La Malfa, the PRI took a close interest in AD's formation and development, and the party's XVIII Congress in November 1992 sanctioned PRI participation in AD. In January 1994 however, La Malfa reasserted his leadership of the party and reversed the party's position, joining instead the centrist electoral pact formed by the PPI (ex-DC) and Segni's Pact for Italy. The justification for this was that the PDS remained too dominant a force within the single left bloc that appeared to be forming. The PDS was, moreover, being pulled to the Left by the decision not to exclude Communist Refoundation and la Rete from the emerging 'Progressive' electoral pact – a decision which also helped justify Berlusconi's embracing of the National Alliance (AN) on the far right. La Malfa's switch to the centre split the PRI profoundly. Fourteen Parliamentarians and several regional secretaries opposed the new course, and La Malfa threatened them with expulsion.

In May 1993 Raffaele Costa was elected secretary of the PLI, having clearly set out to attack the emerging 'pan-leftism' wherein even the conservative Mario Segni was flirting with the Left. Costa proposed the construction of an alternative *rassemblement* of the Centre-Right. The Centre Union was founded in the summer of 1993. Unequivocally hostile to the Left, the development of the UDC implied the PLI's reorientation back to the Right. Such a reorientation had not taken place even in the 1980s despite the international conservative trend of that decade (Ignazi 1993). Several resignations were provoked, including that of Valerio Zanone who had led the party's switch to more social-liberal positions after the 1976 election. Zanone eventually stood as a candidate for the Centre alongside the PRI.

The February 1994 XXXII Congress of the PLI was an impoverished affair which effectively signalled the party's death, though formally a Constituent Assembly was planned for July to establish a Liberal Federation in its stead. Even before the crisis of 1992–93 party membership had collapsed to 19,000 (in 1992). Whilst the UDC all but merged with Forza Italia, other figures in the PLI parliamentary elite variously joined Segni's Pact for Italy, AD, formed independent lists or simply stood down.

For its part, the PSDI had all but ceased to exist by the end of 1993. A half of the party's parliamentary representation had received *avvisi di garanzia* whilst the financial crisis had forced the party to do without any national seat outside the Chamber of Deputies. An MEP, Enrico Ferri, was called in to lead what was left of the party. In March 1994 the PSDI failed to secure the election of a single candidate.

THE 1994 ELECTION AND ITS AFTERMATH

Whilst both the old liberal parties succeeded in getting candidates elected, both depended on electoral pacts to do so and neither was large enough to form an independent group in the new Parliament. La Malfa's switch to form an electoral pact with the PPI and Segni's Pact was particularly damaging. Not only did it split his party very badly, it also rendered the party all but invisible. For most observers the centre bloc was of negligible interest, doomed by the process of bipolarisation and relevant only in regard to the fate of party political Catholicism. In the event, only one Republican was elected as part of the centre alliance. Those Republicans who remained in AD fared better, with five Deputies and three Senators elected. These, however, were awaiting disciplinary hearings and possible expulsion from the party. In the turmoil which followed the election the centre alliance disintegrated. La Malfa looked to the European elections – still fought using proportional representation – to save the party, but his offer of an electoral pact with AD and the PSI was rejected. With a Congress due in the summer, the party's future looked bleak indeed.

Whilst none of the mostly PRI lay candidates in the centre pact won their first-past-the-post seats, all the UDC's FPTP candidates on the Forza Italia slate (four Deputies and three Senators) were elected. Carlo Scognamiglio then pipped Giovanni Spadolini by one vote to become President (Speaker) of the Senate and subsequently Raffaele Costa and Alfredo Biondi became the Ministers of Health and of Justice respectively. The Liberals of the Centre Union at least had backed the winning side.

CONCLUSION

The Liberal, Republican and Social Democratic Parties owed their survival to their coalition role in a highly fragmented, immobile and polarised party system. The consolidation of democracy and social change created the possibility of party system change, and when it came it took catastrophic form: the governing centre parties were swept away. In 1994 the lay parties ceased to exist as parliamentary parties. Their survival as extra-parliamentary parties was unlikely. This was particularly true of the PSDI and PLI. Both the PDS and PSI were members of the Socialist International, whilst Forza Italia and the Lega Nord had substituted themselves for the liberal Right. The proposed Liberal Federation might continue to exist as an intellectual ginger group alongside Forza Italia, not least because the latter looked dangerously dependent on its charismatic leader and his private commercial interests. In many respects the new party system was highly unstable. The new government coalition lacked a majority in the Senate and was deeply internally divided. Equally the Left and Centre were in a state of flux – and it was somewhere here that the PRI had to place itself.

Whilst the independent party organisations were no more, the political traditions underlying them survived – though pessimists cast doubt even on this (see *Corriere della Sera*, 12 May 1994, p. 29). Of course, liberalism, republicanism and social democracy are highly generic terms, and liberalism in particular is a profoundly ambiguous one – as the existence of at least two liberal parties in the First Republic attests. One of the most interesting questions to be raised concerning the new party system of the 1990s was to what extent Italy's Left was now in large part liberal, or radical democratic, rather than social democratic? Finally though, it has to be remembered that parties are collections of interests at least as much as, and perhaps more than, expressions of ideologies – perhaps particularly so in Italy. The degeneration of the *partitocrazia* into a self-interested power bloc, within which a mish-mash of interests and their nominal ideological traditions coexisted, is eloquent testimony to this.

REFERENCES

Bull, A. (1993) 'The politics of industrial districts in Lombardy: replacing Christian Democracy with the Northern League', *The Italianist*, 13: 209–229.

Diamanti, I. (1993) *La Lega. Geografia, storia e sociologia di un nuovo soggetto politico*, Rome: Donzelli.

Di Franco, F. and Gritti, R. (1994) *L'Italia al voto. Analisi delle elezioni amministrative del 1993 e delle prospettive del sistema politico italiano*, Rome: Edizioni Associate.

Gundle, S. (1992) 'Italy', in D. Butler and A. Ranney (eds) *Electioneering*, Oxford: Oxford University Press.

Ignazi, P. (1993) 'Facing the test of the ballot boxes: the PRI, PLI and Greens in the 1992 elections', in G. Pasquino and P. McCarthy (eds) *The End of Post-war Politics in Italy: The Landmark 1992 Elections*, Boulder, Col.: Westview Press.

Padgett, S. and Paterson, P. (1991) *A History of Social Democracy in Post-war Europe*, New York and London: Longman.

Pridham, G. (1988) 'The two roads of Italian liberalism: the *Partito Repubblicano Italiano* and the *Partito Liberale Italiano*', in E. Kirchner (ed.) *Liberal Parties in Western Europe*, London: Croom Helm.

Rhodes, M. (1989) 'Craxi and the lay-socialist area: third force or three forces?', pp. 107–128 in R. Leonardi and P. Corbetta (eds) *Italian Politics: A Review*, London and New York: Pinter.

Ricolfi, L. (1993) 'Politica senza fede: l'estremismo di centro dei piccoli leghisti', *Il Mulino*, 1: 53–69.

Part III
The 'new' parties

7 The Northern League
From regional party to party of government

Ilvo Diamanti

The phenomenon of the autonomist Leagues is the major source of electoral and political change to have emerged in Italy in the post-war period. The most significant novelty lies in their ability to break with the traditional bases of political identity and representation: religion, class, and secularism. The Leagues, and in particular the Northern League, have replaced these with other elements revived from ancient contradictions in Italian society: contrasts between centre and periphery (Rome and the provinces), North and South, public and private, civil society and the traditional parties. Their success has come directly from their ability to present themselves as the expression of these contradictions, devising strategies and making proposals that provoked a disdainful, but totally inadequate response from the other political forces, both new and old. Thus, when we speak of the 'Leagues' (*leghe*) we are referring to a developed and complex phenomenon, of which the Northern League (Lega Nord) is the dominant, but not the exclusive, expression.[1]

Our starting-point is the conception of the League as a 'political actor'. In using this concept, we wish to emphasise that the League's evolution and the consequences of its action reflect not only favourable environmental conditions, but also the League's own capacity to 'act' on them, to modify them or at least to interpret the trends to its own advantage.[2] More specifically, the League as a political actor owes its success to a variety of factors, from which it derived the ability to act as an effective force: a restricted and flexible ideological base, a widespread and flexible organisation, and simple decision-making mechanisms centred on a leader – Umberto Bossi – endowed with charisma, political instinct and an aggressive, anti-conformist but effective language which was able to give the League visibility and specificity.

A BRIEF ELECTORAL HISTORY

Two issues enabled the League successfully to channel social demands and give them expression. The first was 'territory', and the second was a loss of confidence in, and consequent distancing from, the traditional political system. Both these issues in fact represented latent citizen demands and tensions which the League was able to crystallise and express far more successfully than any other political force. This was also because the League, at least in part, created them and stressed their significance, making them into the focus of a specific political identity. In both cases we are dealing with themes that have multiple meanings and mobile boundaries, which are able to take on different significances and adapt to a variety of situations. Hence, the Leagues were able to periodically reconstitute different aspects of these social demands and discontents.[3] At least three conceptions of territory (not necessarily ranked in order of importance) are to be found in Italy, but their articulation should not be solely attributed to the activity of the Leagues.

One view conceives territory as a source of historical and cultural identity which is capable of creating a type of national 'belonging'. Another sees it as a focus for an identity based on interests, that is, on the specificity of the socio-economic context, while a third perceives territory as a negative focus, as a source of an anti-identity, establishing points of communication and cleavage, separating friends from enemies. In Italy this translated into two kinds of tension – that between periphery and the centre (understood in this sense as the state), and that between North and South. Finally, it should be noted that the territorial limits that act as focal points for political and territorial identity can be several – the commune, the region, the North, the state. It is the centrality of one rather than the others that determines the different, and sometimes alternative, theoretical and political models – localism, regional federalism, nationalism and so on.

Even in this detachment from the traditional institutions, there are diverse elements that depend on the different definitions of the 'targets' under attack – parties, the state, mass organisations (trade unions and professional associations), local authorities, public administration. The meaning that this feeling of opposition can take towards the political is various and ambiguous. It is either a sign of the demand for autonomy in the private sphere of the market, or of impatience with the degeneration of the political system at the present time. These two issues – 'territory' in its various connotations, and the anti-party, anti-institutional option – have a different and changing significance for the League's strategy and for its electors in as much as their importance varies over time within the different regions of the North. Thus, in order to reconstruct the 'League phenomenon', it is necessary to analyse all these elements in context, assessing the different ways that they interrelate over time within the principal areas of the North.

In this perspective, the territorial dynamic of the League's vote supplies a particularly useful key, because it helps to highlight certain phases which are generally characterised by a clear 'qualitative' jump in electoral support, and in different areas of electoral strength and weakness. If we

Table 7.1 Percentage share of the vote in local and national elections for the Leagues in six Italian regions, 1983–94

	Year							
	1983	1984	1985	1987	1989	1990	1992	1994
Veneto	4.2	3.4	3.7	3.1	1.7	8.6	25.5	24.8
Lombardy	0	0	0.5	3.0	8.1	18.9	23.6	24.4
Piedmont	0	0	1.1	4.3	3.1	5.1	16.3	16.2
Liguria	0	0	0.9	1.3	1.4	6.1	14.3	11.4
Emilia	0	0	0.4	0.5	0.5	2.9	9.6	6.4
Tuscany	0	0	0.5	0.3	0.2	0.8	3.1	2.2

examine Table 7.1 which records the votes obtained by the Leagues in the 'ordinary regions' where they had established some kind of presence between 1983 and 1992,[4] we can distinguish four phases defined by the various elections that constitute, in terms of the dynamics and localisation of the Leagues' vote, real turning points.

The first phase covers the period from the 1983 parliamentary elections to those of 1987, and corresponds to the 'genetic' phase[5] of the independent Leagues in the Italian political system. It was characterised by the emergence of the Leagues in the Veneto, where the Veneto League (Liga Veneta) won 4 per cent of the votes in the 1983 parliamentary elections. This unexpected success was not repeated in the following elections. The Liga Veneta failed to increase its support, and indeed went into progressive decline, falling to under 2 per cent in 1989. None the less, the 1987 parliamentary elections were a turning point because the Leagues' support spread beyond their original boundaries. In the Veneto, the autonomist Leagues won no more votes than in Lombardy and less than in Piedmont, where the two lists combined obtained just over 4 per cent of the valid votes.

The second phase, already implicit in the 1987 parliamentary election results, covers the period up to the 1990 local government elections. It can be considered a 'developmental' phase. It was characterised by strong growth in the League's electoral support, due in great part to the success of the Lombard League (Lega Lombarda) whose electoral presence in the region rose rapidly from 3 per cent in 1987 to 8 per cent in the 1989 European elections. However, in the 1990 local government elections, with 18 per cent of the vote the Leagues' electoral fortunes finally took off. This occasion was an electoral turning point because Lombardy became the centre of the League phenomenon, which began its progressive expansion beyond its electoral base. The Lega Lombarda's success in the 1990 elections in fact gave impetus to the revival of the Leagues in the other regions of the North, where the 'autonomist' vote exceeded 5 per cent.

The successive phase coincided with the early 1990s and covers the period from the 1990 elections to the 1992 parliamentary elections. It was the period in which the autonomist Leagues enjoyed their maximum expansion, in particular the Northern League, whose electoral importance became dominant in all the northern regions. The Lega Nord won 23 per cent of the vote in Lombardy (almost all of it by the Lega Lombarda); 25.5 per cent in the Veneto (18 per cent by the Liga Veneta and the rest by other autonomist formations); around 15 per cent in Piedmont, Liguria and Friuli, and around 10 per cent in Emilia and Trento-Alto Adige. The League phenomenon extended even as far as Tuscany where it gained almost 3 per cent of the valid votes. With the exception of the Veneto, where more than 7 per cent of votes cast went to other independent formations, virtually all of this electoral support was won by the Northern League.

Finally there is the most recent phase, which covers the last two parliamentary elections, those of 1992 and 1994. This is a contradictory phase which breaks down into two sub-periods separated by two series of local elections. The first, in June 1993, saw the Northern League reach its electoral high-water mark when it won control of some of the most important northern cities, in particular Milan, symbolic capital of the 'Italy of the Leagues'. From then on, and specifically from the subsequent partial local government elections of November 1993, the League's forward march began to slow down, and in the early months of 1994 its vote started to contract. This was a result of the entry onto the political scene of a new political actor that pushed it from centre stage – Forza Italia, the political formation inspired and promoted by Silvio Berlusconi. In the 1994 parliamentary elections, which represented a turning point in the country's long political crisis, although the League's share of the vote was similar in percentage terms to that of 1992, the result had very different implications.

As we can see, its vote stagnated or declined in all regions. More specifically in the Veneto, the League's advance continued (+3 per cent), while the other autonomist *leghe* lost support. The reverse situation occurred in Lombardy and Piedmont where the overall support for the *leghe* held up. In all the other regions where the *leghe*'s development was more recent (in Liguria and above all in Tuscany and Emilia-Romagna), they suffered a decline. As well as a contraction of the vote we can identify a 'return to its roots' in that the League's overall support held up due to an increase in support in its 'areas of genesis'.

This periodisation, derived from an analysis of the Leagues' electoral results in a regional context, provides useful indications for a reading of the Leagues' history in parallel with the country as a whole. It also reminds us that we are dealing with a brief but complex story demarcated by a succession of significant turning points. Indeed so important have these elections been for the Leagues' development that each one has assumed a critical connotation. This signals that instability has become the rule, and that the Leagues more than any other political formation, have become a decisive actor-variable.

FROM THE PROVINCES TO ROME: THE LEAGUE'S SHORT MARCH

The periodisation of the League's electoral performance becomes all the more significant when one examines its political programme, its electors' and activists' social characteristics and attitudes, and its leaders' origins and identities. The evolution and presence of the Leagues in Italy can also be divided into four stages, each of which not only expresses a different level of penetration and localisation of support, but also a different combination of political demand (social and economic trends, electoral characterisations and orientations) and supply (proposals, leadership, language, and organisation). These different combinations give rise to various types of Leagues. In what follows we propose a schematic outline of these developments.

The Liga Veneta: between economic protest and ethno-regionalism (1983–87)

In the first stage, the Leagues had a very limited political and electoral presence, which was initially expressed by the Liga Veneta in 1983, and for several years after by the Lega Lombarda and the independent Piedmontese movements. The League phenomenon was confirmed by the 1983 parliamentary elections in which the Liga Veneta won more than 4 per cent of the regional vote, gaining higher percentages in the central provinces (7 per cent in Vicenza and Treviso and a little less in Belluno, Padua and Verona). Certain important social processes contributed to this initial success. One was the crisis of Christian Democracy in an area which had traditionally been one of its strongholds and which was characterised by the Church's extensive social and organisational presence. Another was the social tensions that invested this area, in which economic growth and the expansion of productive activity had been particularly strong between the 1960s and the 1980s, thanks especially to small business initiative. Connected with this was the dissatisfaction and claims of emerging socio-economic groups (small businessmen and their employees, the self-employed), and the contrast between the capital and the provinces, where social and territorial sectors, considering themselves to be economically central, found themselves to be politically marginal.

The Liga Veneta in this situation 'offered itself' as a channel for the growing dissent that engulfed this section of society, and as a mirror to reflect the decomposition of traditional political solidarities. Thus, its original success was won above all at the expense of the DC, from whose traditional voters it drew considerable support. It catalysed these latent demands and dissent, evoking in a crude but effective form (through slogans, posters and improvised demonstrations) two traditional targets of dissatisfaction and intolerance: the South and the state.

In order to consolidate its political presence, the Liga Veneta developed these objectives within an 'ethno-regional' perspective, claiming, in the name of ethnic specificity, the widest regional administrative autonomy for the nation-region in relation to the centralising nation-state. But this 'political offer' was not really coherent with the demands of the rank and file to whom it was addressed – a rank and file which demanded 'economic centrality' rather than 'economic autonomy'. This greatly restricted the Liga's possibilities for expansion. It was no coincidence therefore that after its initial success the Liga Veneta went into a progressive decline, becoming almost marginal in the 1989 European elections (when it won less than 2 per cent of the regional vote).

The Lega Lombarda: the region as a 'community of interests' (1987–90)

The second stage was characterised by the electoral revival of the Leagues, which occurred above all in Lombardy between the 1987 parliamentary and 1990 local elections. The League's expansion derived from the emergence of the Lega Lombarda and Umberto Bossi's leadership, which was to characterise the successive evolution of the movements. Bossi redefined the conception of territory; in particular he reduced the significance of the historico-cultural references that had previously been attached to it. Instead he presented the territory as a 'community of interests', and he stressed the characteristic lifestyle of the 'Lombard people' – hard-working and productive – in natural opposition to the state and the South which were regarded as centres of dissipation and dependence.

In order to strengthen its regional identity the League manipulated the intolerance towards 'others', especially immigrants who were presented as a social and cultural threat. Abandoning the use of dialect, the 'nation's historic language', Bossi elaborated and used a new political language, crude and direct, borrowed from everyday life. It was very effective: although it enabled him to communicate directly with the public it also conveyed traditional political forms. Since 1989, other factors have contributed to the League's success – the inability of the traditional political forces to understand the phenomenon, and at the international level, the disintegration of the socialist bloc.

If in the initial stage the League's appeal had been above all to the Christian Democrat electorate, in this stage it attracted electors from all the other political parties – at first from the PSI, and then in more limited numbers from the PCI and the minor lay parties. Previously its electorate had a clearly defined social profile – male, middle-aged, with little formal education and with a prevalence of the self-employed and employed workers in the business sector. Now, by contrast, its social profile was much nearer to that of the average voter, particularly in regard to age and education, while the urban middle-class component increased in importance.

The leaders were also changing. In the past they had come from cultural associations interested in research into regional history, tradition and language. But in this subsequent stage they began to be recruited from local associations active in leisure pursuits, sport and social welfare. This group had an experience of associational life that significantly differed from that of the political parties, and yet they were characterised by their strong ties to their locality and civil society.

The Northern League: the opponents of the traditional policies (1990–92)

The League's success in the following years flowed from its decision to reshape its 'political offer', moving from one based on identity to one based on interests. This strategy saw its first positive confirmation in the 1990 local government elections – and it reached unexpected heights in the 1992 parliamentary elections. On this occasion the Northern League won a total of three million votes, 8.9 per cent of the national electorate, and 81 seats in Parliament (Senate and Chamber of Deputies). It was a general success which invested all the northern regions. Indeed, the League gained more than 23 per cent of the valid vote in Lombardy, 18 per cent in the Veneto (where other autonomist parties won a further 8 per cent); it polled around 15 per cent in Piedmont, Liguria and Friuli, and 10 per cent in Trento and Emilia-Romagna.

This result was helped by the intensification of the political crisis of the 1990s which invested the economic and social situation both nationally and internationally. This trend was encouraged by the spreading effects of the political crises of the 'actually existing socialist countries', which accentuated the traditional parties' loss of identity and social legitimacy. It was further aided by the parallel rapid degeneration of relations between politics and civil society in Italy, and was abetted by the country's economic problems, above all its rising public debt which was responsible for increasing fiscal pressures.

Thus the League found itself operating in a particularly favourable climate, but it did not restrict itself to simply exploiting the situation, rather it actively participated in the changes that were underway. It once more redefined its own political agenda and widened its territorial focus from the region to the North as a whole. From a loose grouping of regional movements, it transformed itself in 1990 into a federation of the North – the Northern League. To emphasise its northern identity it proposed an Italy organised into macro-regions – one of which was to be the entire North of the peninsula – each endowed with considerable political autonomy. The proposal was sufficiently radical to raise the question whether the object was in fact secession rather than federation. Moreover, it gave priority to the fight against the traditional political system – against the *partitocrazia*, the political institutions, state centralism and public intervention in both the economy and society.

In extending the focus of its political programme, the Northern League also widened the channels of social demand. Thus its support grew both quantitatively and qualitatively. The social profile of its electors and militants coincided increasingly with that of the population as a whole. It attracted support and votes, particularly from the young and from those who had a secondary education, and won the increasing confidence of the urban bourgeoisie. As far as attitudes and values are concerned, the differences between the League's voters and the rest of the population began to disappear. It appeared as a social group distinguished by attitudes of greater intolerance and lack of confidence in the political institutions – in a society where these attitudes were becoming increasingly widespread.

The League's organisation also evolved and modelled itself on the traditional parties of social integration. It was based on a network of territorial sections – collateral associations aimed at socialising a variety of social and professional groups (workers, businessmen, the self-employed). The new provincial leaders came mostly from the localist associations and from social categories that had been 'marginalised' by the traditional parties: the young, the self-employed middle class (artisans, shopkeepers), liberal professionals, but also workers. The whole enterprise, however, was subject to the centrality of Bossi's leadership and that of his 'faithful' lieutenants. One could describe it as a model based on a form of 'charismatic centralism'.

The party of the North in the conquest of the state (1992–95)

The stage which succeeded the 1992 electoral success saw a further change in the political project and image of the Northern League which was made necessary by rapid and profound developments in the general political situation. The first was the disintegration of the political system and the traditional parties, which became definite as a result of the judicial enquiries into political corruption. The second was connected to the growing instability of the world and European markets, leading to an economic and monetary crisis which hit Italy particularly severely. A third factor was the acceleration in the spiral of violence set off by the various criminal organisations operating in Italy, in particular the Mafia.

All this further weakened the legitimacy of the political parties and the state institutions making a policy of mere opposition rather unproductive for the League. The League, moreover, faced a problem of stabilising and giving expression to a grass-roots that had become both large and segmented. It needed to move its supporters out of the bunker of dissent by providing them with a vision of government. The League therefore abandoned its habit of straight antagonism towards the political system, aiming instead to promote itself as a force for institutional renewal and consolidation. It moderated its territorial proposals, the tone of its anti-political and anti-party polemics, its image and its language. It emphasised the importance of the constitutional and economic aspects of its pro-gramme; it presented itself as the force for the political renewal of the First Republic as well as a distinctly neo-liberal movement. Even this strategic change was successful as the results obtained in the partial local government elections of 1992 and 1993 testify. The final confirmation came in the local government elections of June 1993 when the League won control of many of the northern capitals, including most significantly Milan, symbolic capital of the 'North that produces'.

'SOLITUDE' IS NO LONGER A VIRTUE: TOWARDS THE 1994 PARLIAMENTARY ELECTIONS

Compared to this triumphal ten-year march however, the successive local government elections which were held in several important northern urban areas of Italy in November 1993 marked a very important turning point – when the League embarked on yet another stage of its brief but intense history. On this occasion, for the first time in its history, the League's results were worse than expected. Although it confirmed its position as the largest party in the North, it failed to achieve two key objectives – namely the conquest of the major cities outside Lombardy (its candidates for mayor in Genoa, Trieste and Venice were all defeated), and an increase in its share of the vote in the Centre and South. The cause of this sudden halt can be traced back to three factors which in the past had contributed to its success, but which on this occasion acted as a brake.

The first was its 'language', which was characterised by a provocative tone and content that frightened the moderate electorate and the urban bourgeoisie (skilled white-collar employees, professionals, intellectuals), a group which had previously supported the League – having regarded it as a means of modernisation and/or moralisation of the system rather than an 'anti-system' subject. The second was its 'northern identity' which acted as an unbreachable obstacle to the League's electoral expansion into other areas of the country and, implicitly, its legitimation as a national political force. The third problem was the majority electoral system in which ability to make alliances was decisive, since previously the League had always acted by itself in order to emphasise its difference from all the other political forces. Indeed it had elevated this 'difference' into a virtue. Faced with the alliance-making ability of the Centre-Left, and the PDS in particular, the solitude of the League now became a negative factor.

To legitimate itself nationally, and to overcome the territorial limits of its electoral support while meeting the needs of the new majority electoral system, the League was thus obliged to reconsider its political strategy, and in the first instance, to look for allies. This was not easy for a political force with such a clear-cut identity, strongly distinguished by its opposition to all existing parties. In order to overcome this problem, the League preferred to reach an understanding with 'a party that does not exist' – the movement led by Segni, promoter of the referendum for constitutional reform, and then with the Forza Italia clubs organised by Berlusconi. However an initial agreement was blocked by Bossi himself, who was worried by the thought of the League being involved implicitly in an alliance with the PPI, which as heir to the DC was not only viewed as an implacable enemy but also as a potential reservoir of votes.

The accord with Berlusconi appeared less risky and more advantageous because Forza Italia was a new political force without roots or concrete bases of support, and because Berlusconi could guarantee a presence on the important media networks during the electoral campaign. The conclusion of this accord, however, had unexpected and unfortunate consequences for the League, because far from resolving existing problems it created new and even more serious ones. In fact it gave Forza Italia a real electoral base of support, whereas previously this had merely been inspired by Forza Italia's self-commissioned opinion polls. Moreover, the accord with the League – a 'new' subject 'outside' the traditional political system – transmitted this quality of novelty and difference to Berlusconi, who was a product of the existing political system. As a consequence the League suffered a significant weakening of traditional support. Furthermore, Berlusconi was not simply an ally, he was a political actor who was able to tap into one of the sources of the League's electoral success. Behind the electoral revolt which the various constituencies among the League's voters gave expression to, it was possible to detect a demand for stability – stability of income and the preservation of living standards, economic stability, and the stability of territorial interests. Hidden within the support for the League there also lurked an aspiration to return to the old certainties – to traditionalist values that had long been suppressed, to confidence in the future, and to a desire for security and social cohesion.

Thus behind the 'electoral revolt' provoked by the League we can see the path towards 'social normalisation' which many of the electorate of the former governing coalition (the DC and PSI in particular) followed in the 1990s, particularly after the 1992 parliamentary elections. The League's path was not one that could be pursued for long, however, because it risked generating doubt and uncertainty. In this situation it is understandable that many of these voters began to prefer Berlusconi's smiling and optimistic face to Bossi's rude and aggressive one – the more so since Berlusconi used his own television networks to promise (without a shred of evidence as to how it would be achieved) that the 'Italian miracle' would be repeated. For many of these 'political orphans' Berlusconi represented 'the quiet after the storm' – the opportunity of reconciling themselves with their own past and closing their account with the tensions of the present.

Besides undermining the League's support from the inside, Berlusconi was able to acquire external support, that is, he was able to appeal to social groups who were hostile to the League – above all in the South. Finally he was able to develop an alliance strategy, which was impossible for the League. The political understanding with the most conservative Christian Democrats and Alleanza Nazionale, the formation promoted by the neo-fascist MSI, was the most striking result. In this way, the League found itself indirectly linked to its most hostile political opponents, and this further compromised its image and identity. All this explains how within a few weeks, according to its own polls, Forza Italia's support passed from 8 to 30 per cent, while that for the League went in the opposite direction from 16 to 8 per cent. The League's chosen electoral ally thus became its chief political opponent.

Consequently, Berlusconi became the principal target of the League's electoral campaign, and was defined by Bossi as 'the spare rib of the old regime', 'the old guard's go-between', and 'a recycler of ex-government forces'. The return to the strategy of verbal aggression, contrasting with the style of the previous year, had a predictable result. In fact it drew attention to the internal divisions within the right-wing alliance but nevertheless failed to damage the general support for the two poles (the Lega/Forza Italia 'Polo della Libertà' and the AN/Forza Italia 'Polo del Buon Governo') because the *progressisti* (leftist pole) polemics against Berlusconi maintained a clear distinction between the two electoral alliances. Bossi's strategy was not helped by the fact that the League's electorate was different from a year earlier. The League was no longer the vehicle for all those dissatisfied with the state and the political system, and even if it could present itself as such, it was not the only vehicle. Berlusconi's decision to descend into the political arena changed the available political choices because he appealed to a large part of the League's audience (see Mannheimer 1994). Forza Italia had already weaned the moderates away from the League, but it was able to add other social groups for whom the regional and anti-state demands were less important than those of taxes and law and order. Bossi thus found himself appealing to a smaller audience, but one which was more homogeneous and responsive to the League's traditional themes and language. In this way he was able to reconstruct his original electoral base and restore its identity.

THE ELECTIONS OF 27 MARCH 1994

The electoral results proved Bossi right in so far as the League demonstrated a notable capacity for resistance. While losing votes at the margin, it substantially confirmed the positions it had conquered in 1992 (8.4 per cent of the national vote, or 0.3 per cent less than in 1992). But this resistance, besides marking the end of a cycle of irresistible advance from its origins to late 1993, reflected a further redefinition of its model of territorial and social support.

The substantial stability of the overall result in fact hides a reality of widespread mobility. Of the 211 constituencies in northern Italy, only in 31 (15 per cent) was the League's electoral support effectively stable; in 116 (55 per cent) it fell by at least 1 per cent, and in the remaining 64 constituencies (30 per cent) it actually increased. Hence, it is clear that the League's vote was characterised by a widespread redistribution of support amounting to a concentration in certain well-defined areas. To understand the nature of this change and the processes behind it, it is helpful to examine the group of constituencies where the League made the greatest gains and losses (+ or – 3.5 per cent). Both groups consist of 27 constituencies whose location is clear-cut. Only four are in Lombardy, three in Friuli, five in Piedmont, but 15 are to be found in the Veneto. In this last region the increased support for the League relates almost exclusively to the provinces of Vicenza, Treviso and Belluno – the areas in which the League phenomenon registered its first success. This rooting of the League's most recent electoral success in the areas of its original support also characterises the other regions. In fact, in Lombardy and Piedmont, the League made its strongest gains in the provinces (Bergamo, Sondrio, Cuneo) which appeared as strongholds as far back as 1987.

The 'areas of defeat' (i.e. the constituencies where the League lost more than 3.5 per cent of the vote) offer a mirror image: 14 are in Emilia-Romagna, where the League, although making widespread gains in 1992, had not really put down roots; the same is true for the five constituencies in Liguria where nonetheless its vote had exceeded 15 per cent in earlier elections. But the greatest surprise came from the eight Lombard constituencies where its support fluctuated between 18 and 25 per cent. These Lombard constituencies also have a precise place in the historical geography of the League. Half of them are situated in the province of Milan and half in the provinces of Cremona and Mantua – areas where the League's penetration was much more recent, dating from the 1990s.

The significance of these electoral results is clear. They indicate a sort of 'march back to the past' to the origins of the League's emergence. The League has been prized out of the areas where it was never very strong (the 'red' zones) and those where it had become so only recently (the metropolitan areas – above all Milan, Liguria, the special regions – and in particular Trento). It was strengthened in those areas where it had found favourable conditions for its genesis and development. The League's new political geography, in consequence, is to a large extent a mirror image of its original profile. The constituencies in which its support exceeded 25.5 per cent of the vote are situated in the provinces of Belluno, Treviso, Vicenza, Verona, Bergamo, Como, Varese, non-metropolitan Milan, and Cuneo.

Politically, the League's success developed in areas where, until recently, the DC appeared stronger and the Left (PDS and PSI) weaker. Socio-economically, the League was stronger in the highly industrialised, but small business areas, where the economic crisis in this phase had less impact on employment. All this emphasises that the League is no longer the 'party of the North' – but rather as it was in the 1980s, 'the party of the northern industrial periphery'. The other North, shaped by the role of large-scale urban and industrial concentration, more secular politically, and attracted in the 1980s by the reassuring 'Italian dream' of Craxi's PSI, moved in another direction. It responded strongly to the political offers promoted by the 'political entrepreneur' Silvio Berlusconi and his 'electoral business' Forza Italia, which not incidentally had a territorial and social structure symmetrical to the League's. Its strength was principally in the urban areas, characterised by big business and services, and it appears strongest where the League's base was previously largest (i.e. in the 1992 elections).

THE LEAGUE: FROM THE GOVERNMENT OF BERLUSCONI TO THE ANTI-BERLUSCONI GOVERNMENT

The elections of 27 March 1994 thus saw the emergence of two distinct and differentiated Norths. The League has 'occupied' one, which has a clear socio-economic identity and political background. It is the North of small businesses and Catholic political traditions – the North where the League originally emerged. Today it seems to have returned to its origins, defining boundaries beyond which it will be difficult for it to expand, but within which it will be very difficult for it to be supplanted. It is this social and territorial 'redefinition' that explains, in our view, not only Bossi's opposition to his old adversaries, but also to his new allies. He is obliged to 'defend' the interests and identity of the socio-economic periphery which is under attack not only by old-style capital – the Rome of the 'traditional parties' – but also by that of the Second Republic, the Milan of Berlusconi. More generally, the League found itself challenged on its own electoral territory by competitors who as allies were an even more insidious threat. It experienced the fear of being once more dragged into the orbit of Forza Italia – and seeing its own identity and therefore its own electoral base weakened. After signalling its understanding with Berlusconi to be 'a marriage of convenience', the League began to develop its strategy in three different directions which corresponded to three distinct phases – distinct that is in relation to the position taken towards Berlusconi. These three phases cover the period from the government of the *polo* to the League's new political agreements.[6]

The League in government

Initially the League sought to legitimise itself as a national political force by losing those remnants of an anti-system party that had been associated with its success – to this end it demanded and obtained two key institutional posts, that of the President of the Chamber of Deputies and the Ministry of the Interior, and awarded them to two of the League's most representative leaders (respectively Irene Pivetti the young leader of the Catholic traditionalists, and Roberto Maroni, who was already President of the League's Parliamentary group). However, this line did not produce the intended results but instead saw the image of the League obliterated even more by that of Forza Italia and the Polo della Libertà in general. The result of the European elections in June underlined this development: Forza Italia demonstrated a strong capacity to increase its electoral support and eroded even the bedrock of League support – which fell to 6 per cent of the national vote.

The League: opposition inside government

From the summer of 1994 (in other words subsequent to its 'self-legitimisation' strategy) on the initiative of its leader Umberto Bossi, the League with increasing frequency switched to an alternative strategy which involved the 'delegitimisation of its allies' – the principal target of which was Berlusconi. Having won the coalitional elections with Forza Italia the League could not convincingly represent itself as the 'opposition to the system', but it nevertheless tried to perform the same role 'inside the system' by acting as an opposition 'inside' the government. Thus, some of the most bitter criticisms of the main provisions made by the Berlusconi government came from the League itself. The first important clash came when the Justice Minister Biondi presented a decree aimed at revising the conditions under which it would be possible for magistrates to keep a suspect in preventive detention – thus staunching the flood of investigations into political corruption. However the decree was withdrawn in the face of a storm of criticism which was initiated and sustained by the League. The same conflict occurred in the autumn during the passage of the finance bill, and specifically in relation to the proposed reduction in pension entitlements. Progressively the League moved from being an 'antagonistic ally' to an out and out opponent of Forza Italia and Alleanza Nazionale. This trend saw its confirmation in the partial administrative elections of December, when almost everywhere the League appeared on the ballot paper separately from its government allies. The League joined with other political forces and coalitions, particularly with the parties of the centre: with the Partito Popolare and the Patto Segni predominantly, but also with the PDS. In this way the League succeeded in halting the haemorrhage of its vote and also in electing several of its own candidates as mayors. From being a party that was antagonistic to the traditional parties, the League became the flank of the traditional parties and a reference point for the challenge to the ever more solid axis between Forza Italia and Alleanza Nazionale.

The anti-Berlusconi League

The next phase brought the League to the extreme consequences of these actions. That is, Bossi ended all the League's residual collaboration with the Polo della Libertà: thus opening the government crisis and provoking the fall of the government itself. The League became the principal supporter of the new government of 'technicians', headed by Dini. This was a move which brought to a head the contradictions inside the League which had been building up for months. There were two main reasons for the conflict which overtook the leadership group, and the leadership of the parliamentary group in particular. The first concerned the political line adopted: there was a section of League parliamentarians whose support came from a Centre-Right orientation that saw the League as the federalist wing of the Polo della Libertà. This group was therefore decisively and openly hostile to the rupture with the *polo*. A second reason was more of an organisational problem and had more pragmatic implications. At the elections of March 1994, as we have noted, the League obtained 8 per cent of all votes cast, but thanks to the agreement reached with Forza Italia as the list of candidates was being drawn up, the League succeeded in obtaining 18 per cent of the parliamentary seats. More than half of the League's electorate clearly did not correspond to a distinct base of support however and their political affiliations were closer to Forza Italia than to the League. The departure of the League from the *polo* and from the government thus saw the exit of around a third of the League's Parliamentarians (more than 50 out of 180), including Roberto Maroni himself. However, as Bossi's strict collaborator and Vice-President of the Council of Ministers, Maroni did not join the newly formed group that took up a position within the *polo* (unlike his colleagues). Initially Maroni sustained a critical position towards his leader and remained loyal to the *polo*, but after being defeated at the League Congress held in Milan in February 1995, he left both the League and Parliament – too characterised by his *leghista* history and identity to be able to pass over to (and be accepted by) the *polo*, and too open in his opposition to Bossi to be able to remain with the League.

TOWARDS A FUTURE WITHOUT A CAUSE

It is no easy matter to delineate the possible further prospects for the presence and role of the League in Italian politics. It is certain that at the beginning of 1995 much had changed with respect to the previous 18 months, when the League seemed to be the point of reference for any change that might result from the crisis of Italy's political system. The League not only seemed to have lost its 'propulsive force', but what was worse it even appeared to have lost its bearings – lacking a cause that would help it to find the path which with a different attitude and interest, it had originally started out on. A serious sign of this disorientation is the loss of importance that the notion of 'territory' has had in the Italian political debate, especially the particular connotation that it was given by the League (see Diamanti and Segatti 1994). Paradoxically, the League's highlighting of territoriality seems to have produced the opposite effect to that intended: the North does not have a regional identity, but rather *Italia* (the explicit label of Berlusconi's political enterprise) has become the national identity (in this context it is also worth recalling the denomination of the 'refounded' MSI). In turn federalism appeared to have put an end to environmentalism as the dominant theme of the 1980s – when ecology went from being the slogan of a political subject to a universal watch-word adopted by all political parties. Today it would seem impossible not to describe oneself as a federalist, just as ten years ago it was *de rigueur* to be pro-ecology. But one could have legitimate suspicions that such talk was largely token. On the other hand, recent polls have shown that among the general public the 'disenchantment with federalism' is well in evidence, and that Italy is the territorial referent which has most significance for people. Rather than 'federalism', respondents preferred more reassuring notions of local decentralisation, or even simply favoured a straightforward reworking of the existing system. The same desire to differentiate itself from other political actors – which in the recent past had been a particular feature of the League's identity – would seem to have been translated in an unforeseen way. In the past the League aimed to delegitimate the Right–Left axis, but now it has been forced to acknowledge its new-found significance by seeking refuge in that 'Centre' which it helped to pull apart (was not the League itself the result of the first important schism within the DC?). In the meantime, the identification of Bossi with the League is the main if not the only identifying feature that remains for the friends and enemies of the League alike. This explains why his principal competitors – either on an electoral level or within the leadership group – have already been abandoned by the League and are now parked on the fringes of the *polo* or have been absorbed by it completely. The League therefore presents itself as an organisation at the service of a charismatic leader whose image evokes different sets of references: the relationship with the North, federalism, the representation of the middle class, the anchorage of the 'Centre'. These are important references that are well rooted in the history of the League, but they no longer have the same specific and particular importance they had in the past. Instead they simply provide the background colour on the portrait of the League's leader.

NOTES

This chapter was translated by Percy Allum and Simon Parker.
1 The arguments presented in this chapter are developed in Diamanti 1993. In addition, I have brought the discussion up to date in 'Lega' in Diamanti and Mannheimer (1994).
2 I have defined this approach in Diamanti 1993, Chapter 1, pp. 10–15.
3 On the different meanings that territory can take in relation to political and social action and mobilisation, see Melucci and Diani (1992) and Petrosino (1991).
4 A clear and systematic presentation of the approaches to voting behaviour as an electoral market, in which there is a comparison of demand and supply, is to be found in Dunleavy and Husbands (1985), Part 1.
5 See Panebianco 1988 for the meaning of 'genetic phase'.
6 For an assessment of the League's fortunes in the period 1994–95 see the 1995 edition of I. Diamanti *La Lega*, Rome, Donzelli.

REFERENCES

Diamanti, I. (1993) *La Lega: geografia, storia e sociologia di un nuovo soggetto politico*, Rome: Donzelli.
Diamanti, I. and Mannheimer, R. (eds) (1994) *Milano a Roma: guida all'Italia elettorale del 1994*, Rome: Donzelli.
Diamanti, I. and Segatti, P. (1994) 'Orgogliosi di essere italiani', in *Limes* 4.
Dunleavy, P. and Husbands, C. T. (1985) *British Democracy at the Crossroads*, London: Allen & Unwin.
Mannheimer, R. (1994) 'Forza Italia', in I. Diamanti and R. Mannheimer (eds), *Milan a Roma. Guida all'Italia elettorale del 1994*, Rome: Donzelli.
Melucci, A. and Dianio, M. (1992) *Nazione senza stato*, Milan: Feltrinelli.
Panebianco, A. (1988) *Political Parties: Organisation and Power*, Cambridge: Cambridge University Press.
Petrosino, D. (1991) *Stati, Nazioni, etnie*, Milan: Franco Angeli.

8 Forza Italia

The new politics and old values of a changing Italy

Patrick McCarthy

Forza Italia's victory in the 27–28 March elections appeared to be the stunningly rapid conquest of the Italian electorate by a movement which did not officially exist until Silvio Berlusconi's announcement on 26 January 1994 that he 'was taking the field'. The rapidity was deceptive because Berlusconi had been a political actor since the spring of 1993. Moreover FI offered a solution – which proved at least temporarily convincing – to the underlying issue of the period which began with the elections of April 1992. This issue was the refounding of the Italian state after the crisis of the old regime, which was based on DC-PSI coalitions and on a massive politicisation of the economy and society. To understand what the solution was and why FI was able to offer it, we must glance at the political, but also the economic and social history of the Republic. Since FI is not a party but a populist movement, which a charismatic leader created out of his company, we may begin by considering the roles which Berlusconi and Fininvest had played prior to April 1992.

THE ENTREPRENEUR STRIKES BACK

In Italy the private sector has always looked towards the state. From the Risorgimento industry has been playing catch-up and has needed tariffs, subsidies and public contracts in order to compete with the more advanced countries of Western Europe. The influential Luigi Luzzati (1841–1927) argued that an active state role was necessary not merely in crises but in normal periods. Not that this has instilled into the private sector an affection for the state. The post-World War II reconstruction was carried out in the name of a fierce liberalism. The quest for a correct relationship between state and market is a great theme of modern Italian history.

It has been argued convincingly that the balance between the political power of the DC-led coalitions and the economic power of the lay northern industrialists changed with the nationalisation of the electrical industry in 1964 (Scalfari and Turani 1974). The electrical companies' failure to use the indemnities they received and the emergence of Montedison as a perennially weak chemical giant, which sought success by manipulating politicians rather than by competing in the market, damaged Italian capitalism. It formed a symbiotic relationship with a state which was itself weak, because it was led by a Christian Democrat party that was permanently in power and divided into warring factions. Politico-economic clans emerged, seeking allies in the press, among the magistrates, in the secret services and with segments of organised crime.

Of this regime, which collapsed in 1992 triggering the two years of confusion and debate, Berlusconi was an integral part. His first fortune was made in construction around Milan. Such a business is exquisitely political since it depends on building permits and zoning decisions, as well as on borrowing money from state-owned banks and selling the completed buildings to government organisations. Silvio's brother, Paolo, was arrested in the clean hands investigation (*La Repubblica* 9, 12 February 1994; *La Voce* 19 May 1994). Our aim, however, is not to analyse Fininvest's place in *Tangentopoli*, but rather to set it in the context of the politicised economy, which thrived in the 1970s and 1980s. Berlusconi's membership in the subversive P2 freemasons' lodge fitted this pattern, because the P2, which combined rather vague plans for a right-wing coup with very precise projects for enriching its members, was an organic expression of the manipulation of the market by political power.

Political protection was all the more necessary when Berlusconi turned to commercial television. His alliance with Bettino Craxi, which suited the PSI's image as a modernising party, revealed its value in 1984, when a judge ruled that Fininvest's three networks were infringing the law and should cease to broadcast. Prime Minister Craxi responded with a decree which overruled the judge's decision (Fracassi and Gambino 1994: 59). Berlusconi flaunted his friendship with Craxi, whose son was appointed to the board of AC Milan and whom Berlusconi publicly congratulated in 1993, when Craxi survived an attempt to remove his parliamentary immunity so that he could be prosecuted for corruption.

During the 1992 election campaign DC and PSI indulged in anti-business rhetoric. It was partly a trick to avoid responsibility for the growing economic woes, but it was also a sign of genuine friction between the politicians and the industrialists, who wondered how Italy would be able to compete in the ever more open world economy, when the state was so badly run. However the politicians made an exception for Berlusconi – 'he was on the side of the parties' (Pansa 1994: 158), a member of the Craxi clan.

So it is tempting to see Berlusconi's victory in the 1994 elections as *trasformismo*, and to accept the PDS's attacks on him as a new Craxi: tempting but wrong. There was another, contradictory side to Berlusconi which was apparent to the Italian public: he incarnated the private entrepreneur. He declared that his TV networks 'spread the sane philosophy of the market economy–freedom, individualism and meritocracy' (D'Anna and Moncalvo 1994: 59). He issued diatribes against the state television, the RAI, which soaked up taxpayers' money and could offer cheaper rates for advertising. His own view of his role in Italian society was that he had embarked on commercial TV in the late 1970s, when the PCI was at its peak and Italian capitalism was floundering. While Gianni Agnelli was talking of giving up, he, Silvio Berlusconi, reasserted the values of entrepreneurship (D'Anna and Moncalvo 1994: 212, 234). Later, after Achille Occhetto became secretary in 1988, the PCI ran a campaign (with Federico Fellini's support) to remove commercials from within the films shown on TV. To Berlusconi, whose political allies beat back the campaign, this was an example of state interference in the market.

Although this view of his role is partly a myth, it was plausible enough to enable Berlusconi to appear new in the 1994 elections. With the political parties and the state apparatus discredited by two years of revelations about bribery, an industrialist offered a different set of values. That the private sector had participated lavishly in the corruption, which exemplified the symbiotic relationship, was forgotten. Berlusconi had two special advantages which other businessmen lacked. One was that as the owner of TV networks and of AC Milan, he could engage in politics as spectacle. He was at home on TV, where he appeared surrounded by 'his' newscasters. He was endorsed by 'his' stars like Mike Bongiorno, whose quiz games are a feature of Italian family life. As the owner of AC Milan, Berlusconi could break off campaigning and head for San Siro. His players responded by winning both the Italian championship and the European champions cup. They clinched the national championship three weeks after their owner clinched the elections, allowing him to declare that he would do for Italy what he had done for his team (*La Stampa* 18 April 1994). AC Milan went on to win the European cup the very evening Berlusconi won a close Senate vote.

Italians expect their industrialists to play the role of royalty in Britain and film stars in the United States: Luciano Benetton appears as frequently in the gossip columns as on the economic pages. But no industrialist appears as often as Berlusconi. When the breakdown of the existing political structures increased the importance of politics as spectacle, Berlusconi was bound to fare better than Occhetto or Segni.

His second advantage was that he had created rather than inherited his business empire. Berlusconi, whose father was a bank clerk, did not belong to the economic establishment of the Agnellis and the Pirellis (see Friedman, Chapter 17). His ability to depict himself as a man of the people was crucial in a country where populism, whether left-wing or right-wing, cultural or political, is endemic. The question was not whether the disintegration of the DC and PSI would spark a revival of populism, but rather which brand of populism would win out. Berlusconi had long depicted his TV networks as the voice of the people – 'I think we can be against the TV of the palaces of power ... we can be a positive

TV ... one with which people can feel at home' (quoted in D'Anna and Moncalvo 1994: 229). The Standa department store chain owner had stamped his shops with patriotism by calling it 'the house of the Italians', while the owner of AC Milan had sought to establish a bond with his Fininvest employees by talking to them about Van Basten or Baresi.

Our thesis is that the Berlusconi phenomenon cannot be reduced to a television 'Blitzkrieg', which was a necessary but not sufficient condition for his success. Rather it reflects the response to the crumbling of the state, which one might expect of a country where small business is not just economically but culturally important. Culturally, because the firm has long been based on the family, an institution which has been far more important than the state. Economically, because small business constitutes a greater source of wealth and employment in Italy than in other European countries.

It was, for example, the motor which propelled Italy out of the traumas of the 1970s. Whereas the number of workers in factories with more than 500 employees went down by 13.5 per cent, the number in factories with fewer than 100 employees went up by 11.5 per cent (Salvati 1986: 134). After Italy entered the EMS in 1979 these companies were flexible enough to divert exports from the EC to the United States, where the high dollar gave them a price advantage. The number of self-employed rose from 24 per cent of the non-agricultural working population in 1980, to 29 per cent in 1988. The comparative importance of small firms is evident from a 1986 study which shows that 40.3 per cent of Italian industrial workers are employed in enterprises with fewer than ten employees, whereas the EC average is 26.7 per cent (Sylos Labini 1986: 218).

Politically the thrust of small companies helped propel the Lega Nord to approximately 9 per cent of the vote in the 1992 elections. Unsurprisingly the Lega offered Berlusconi his greatest challenge and his opportunity. His appeal to the Rotary Clubs of Italy was obvious: he personified their dream of success. Moreover he shared their distrust of the Employers' Association – he spoke of the 'rarefied air' which prevailed there (*L'Unità* 11 March 1994) – and their dislike of Roman bureaucrats. He understood their problems – the difficulty they encountered in getting cheap credit from banks – because his own fortune was made advertising their products. Berlusconi told his Publitalia salesmen to see themselves as consultants to the industrialists who bought time on the Fininvest networks (D'Anna and Moncalvo 1994: 229). Now Forza Italia would take up where the Lega had stopped: Bossi had voiced the protest of northern Italian small business people; Berlusconi would bring them to power.

This social group, economically strong but politically under-represented, formed the core of Forza Italia. Meanwhile other strata recognised the cultural attraction of a movement which pitted the values of the family firm against a bankrupt political system. To embrace the rules of the market because the order of the state has collapsed is a possible option in any country. Margaret Thatcher offered it to Britain. But in Italy the market is associated with the family and with the sense of community – the *paesi-fabbriche* (factory-villages) of the Veneto are an example, which explains why FI carried the Veneto.

Like all successful movements it embraced the past – in its emphasis on the post-war economic miracle – and the future – the assertion that the miracle could be repeated. Berlusconi's parable of Italy's four million entrepreneurs who would create one million jobs, was logically absurd. It conveys the unreality which is Forza Italia's weakness. But it fitted the myth of the creative industrialist, which is far stronger in Italy than in Britain. Berlusconi had declared to a group of Padua businessmen that 'the future is bright and all the brighter for us because Italian entre-preneurs are the best' (quoted in D'Anna and Moncalvo 1994: 110).

In a crisis caused by the political class's invasion of economic territory, a businessman won out by boldly invading the territory of politics. He used his company to form a party and he opposed managerial efficiency to the chaos of the public services. We must examine the language and themes of his campaign before passing to the structure of FI.

A NATION OF WEALTH-CREATORS

Berlusconi swiftly dispatched the old regime. Its discourse was the 'chat-ter' of a do-nothing political class, which hid its impotence behind incom-prehensible language. However his sharpest criticism was reserved for the Left, which lost itself in 'abstract principles' and 'complicated ideologies'.[1] This is the standard language of right-wing populism, which presents itself – deceptively – as simple and transparent, a mere vehicle for action.

However Berlusconi had to find a brand of populism that belonged to him alone. The PDS, which had abandoned its Gramscian heritage, offered no competition. Occhetto seemed determined to display economic competence and to demonstrate that the PDS could be trusted to govern. Alleanza Nazionale had a rich vein of populism, which Alessandra Musso-lini had tapped in the Naples mayoral race, but which Fini consciously spurned. Like Occhetto, he was seeking legitimacy so he deployed a language which was less turgid but equally solemn. Berlusconi's rival was Bossi, whose wilfully crude language had broken with DC incomprehensi-bility and undermined the old regime.

Bossi's was a language of protest, of 'us' and 'them'. In the mid-1980s he had used the Lombardy dialect and, when he switched to the vocabu-lary used in the bars of the Milan hinterland, he was still trying to define an 'us'. The 'them' could then be assaulted in an invective full of sexual allusions. Whereas 'we' were virile, a member of 'them' could be described as 'a pretty-faced gay' (Borcio 1992: 69).

The drawback of such language and of the Lega in general is that it is exclusionary, and hence cannot become a language of government. Berlusconi's partial success in absorbing the Lega's support, lay in using a language which was simple but courteous. He criticised *L'Unità* for its 'excessive tones' and denounced 'the howling piazzas'. By contrast he described a Forza Italia candidate as a man of 'moderation and balance'.

A violence is present in Berlusconi, even if it is usually masked. It erupts in this portrait of Massimo D'Alema: 'He wore an unpleasant, threatening grimace. His thin moustache trembled with a hideous joy. I understood that he cared nothing for this country... nothing for the Italian family' (*Panorama* 4 February 1994 p. 11). These lines are all the more important in that they supposedly depict the moment when Berlusconi decided to enter politics. They reveal that anti-communism is not a remnant of the past, but a key trait of Forza Italia. The communist is the incarnation of evil, necessary if 'the people' is to be good. The failures of communism contrast with the success of Fininvest.

Who is this mysterious entity called 'the people'? Like Thatcher, whose autobiography he studied, Berlusconi distinguishes between the very poor, for whom the charismatic leader will provide jobs, and the groups who are his helpers.[2] They are 'decent, sensible people who have demonstrated their competence in the workplace'. Skilled workers, technicians and small businessmen, they belong to the growing urban middle class, which has no ties to unions but is not part of the traditional bourgeoisie. They are prosperous but fear the present world recession.

Berlusconi, who once more follows Thatcher, speaks to them of the individual, the family, the small company and the nation. Conspicuously absent is the state, which is dismissed as 'over-regulated, politicised and corrupt'. When he discusses the nation, Berlusconi substitutes for the Falklands triumph the victories of AC Milan. A historian has written of Italy's success in the 1982 World Cup, that 'the sporting nation had outlived the nation proper' (Lepre 1993: 306). As if to prove this, Berlusconi chose the soccer chant Forza Italia ('Let's Go Italy') as the name of his movement.

He achieved a fusion of AC Milan with the national side. When he bought his club in 1986, he worried lest supporters of rival clubs Inter or Juventus might shun his TV networks (D'Anna and Moncalvo 1994: 131). During the election campaign he transferred Milan's victories to the Italian team by referring to his campaign staff as 'the blues'. He also ran as a candidate Mariella Scirea, the widow of the Juventus player Gaetano Scirea, who starred in the 1982 World Cup. Purged of such unpleasant elements as the violence on the terraces and the financial misdealing which accompanies transfer payments, soccer is an excellent vehicle of populist patriotism. Norberto Bobbio has objected – arguing that Dante inspires a better brand of patriotism than sportsmen (*La Voce* 20 May 1994). This view, while certainly correct, has found few adherents. On the night of his victory in the Senate and AC Milan's victory over Barcelona, Berlusconi did not forget to wish the national side good fortune in the upcoming World Cup (*La Voce* 19 May 1994).

The key protagonist of Berlusconi's discourse remains the entrepreneur. He was clever to invoke the economic miracle, because many Italians, while prone to *gattopardismo* (appearing to favour changing everything while in reality seeking to preserve positions of privilege) when discussing political change, believe in the post-war transformation which they experienced directly. In his speeches Berlusconi ran the gamut of the private sector: from the family firm, where the father is the boss, the mother the bookkeeper and children or relatives provide the labour, to the grand *condottieri* (entrepreneurs), at whose head he placed himself. With unashamed narcissism, he promised to relaunch the economy, adding that 'there is no-one in Italy who can make this promise with as much credibility as I who am making it before you'. To oversimplify, one might argue that the electorate was invited to choose between Occhetto's discourse of austerity in a reformed state and Berlusconi's flamboyant appeal to Italy's – and his own – ingenuity.

Forza Italia's programme pledged to sweep away the 'bureaucratic muddles and the innumerable obstacles which prevent the creation of wealth' (Forza Italia, *Programma*, p. 6). The state was to be massively pruned: it was to do 'the things which only the state can do and remain aloof from all activities which are better left to the spontaneous, voluntary, private initiative of its citizens'. The link with Thatcher's theory, if not her practice, is obvious.

Berlusconi promised to get rid of the 'parasitic-bureaucratic class' which ran the welfare state. Hospitals were to be organised like private firms and would compete for patients. People were to be given health coupons which they could spend as they chose. Similiarly they would receive education coupons to be used in state or private schools. Pensions were to be privatised where possible and rent controls would be removed. The South's backwardness was to be tackled by strengthening its private sector.

The economic recovery was entrusted to tax cuts for individuals to promote consumption and for business to promote investment. Berlusconi's understanding of his electoral base is revealed when the programme notes that the important interest rate is not the prime but the top – the rate paid by small business.

FI's programme was less a guide to what its policies might be, than a sketch of a utopia where the civil service (diagnosed as Italy's greatest problem) surrendered its power to the entrepreneur. How this would happen was unclear. Once more this myth not of technology, about which Forza Italia says little, but of management seemed unreal. Berlusconi called on the electorate to have faith in the charismatic leader, who was no longer a soldier or a priest but the owner of a company which specialised in various forms of consumption. Pier Paolo Pasolini's night-mare had come true.

A WINNING TEAM

Although Berlusconi did not officially begin his campaign until 26 January, he began organising nine months earlier. His followers claim that he saw immediately that the electoral system, set up by the April 1993 refer-endum, would split Italy into right-wing and left-wing coalitions; that there was scant place for centrist parties and that the Left began with an advantage, because the only well-organised force to survive the clean hands investigation was the PDS.[3] Berlusconi's hatred of the Left was sharpened by its hostility to his company and by Fininvest's vulnerability.

How weak its financial position was and how much this influenced his desire to enter politics are hard matters to assess. Berlusconi's debts have been estimated at 3,550 billion lire or $24 billion. Moreover they were worsening: whereas between 1987 and 1992 turnover increased by 400 per cent, debts went up by 1,300 per cent; in 1987 they were 14 per cent of turnover, in 1992 they were 43 per cent (*La Repubblica* 25 January 1994; *Espresso* 11 March 1994). Enrico Cuccia's estimate of Fininvest's debts was even higher, and by autumn 1993, in the aftermath of the Ferruzzi crash, the banks, led by Credito Italiano, were worried enough to impose on Berlusconi Franco Tatò, who was given a mandate to make cuts. He was also supposed to bring segments of Fininvest onto the stockmarket, although this would entail making public information which Berlusconi had hitherto kept to himself.

Much of the money was owed to public banks like Comit, Credito Italiano (not then privatised) and the Banca Nazionale del Lavoro, which had been in the Socialist Party's orbit. So the prospect of a government led by the PDS, which had fought against the number of Fininvest's channels as well as against the plethora of commercials they showed, was enough to prompt Berlusconi to act.

Moreover the clean hands investigation was drawing uncomfortably close. By the summer of 1993 there were allegations that Fininvest had paid consulting fees so high as to constitute retrospective bribes to Davide Giacalone, who had been Oscar Mammì's assistant on the 1990 television law. An unsavoury issue of bribes paid to the Minister of Health, De Lorenzo, to obtain a share of government-financed spots warning against AIDS, had also been raised (*Espresso*, 20 June 1993).

In Berlusconi's eyes there was no conflict between his own and the general interest. The Left would stifle that entrepreneurial ability which constituted Italy's strength. The solution was to make yet another inno-vation in a career full of new departures. Having lost his ability to influence the political class, Berlusconi decided to supplant it. That does not mean that in April 1993 his goal was to become Prime Minister, but he began to take political action.

Giuliano Urbani was a Bocconi University professor and an occasional collaborator of Fininvest. He drew up a document called 'In Search of Good Government', which was signed by others in Berlusconi's circle, such as Leonardo Mondadori and Antonio Martino, who was to become Berlusconi's Foreign Minister. The document, which would be fleshed out into the Forza Italia programme, outlined the principles which guided Berlusconi's action. Italy's ills were listed as corruption and occupation of the state by the parties, but also as remnants of communism. The solutions lay in the market economy, the assertion of civil society and the politics of efficiency. Urbani's most original statement went unnoticed: 'We believe that a European Union can and must be realized without conflicting with the political and cultural institutions of its nations'.[4] A tiny island of 'Gaullism' in the ocean of Italian federalism, this sentence offers a hint of Forza Italia's European policy.

The document's immediate purposes were to gather elite support and to serve as a breviary for the general campaign. This took two overlapping forms, but in each case the agent was the Fininvest group and especially Publitalia. Already Berlusconi had conducted market surveys to discover what sort of political product the electorate wanted and how he could supply it. From June onward Forza Italia clubs, modelled vaguely on the AC Milan supporters clubs, were set up first in Lombardy and then across Italy. Simultaneously Publitalia's troops fanned out across the country, using the Forza Italia recruits but also other contacts, in order to find candidates. Most segments of Berlusconi's empire helped: in Rome Standa formed clubs and suggested candidates.

But no company could have performed these tasks as well as Publitalia. It is dangerous to draw general conclusions from FI's victory about economic power discarding the mask of political power, or about the new role of companies in politics. In each town Publitalia dealt with the local businesspeople, to whom it sold TV time. It had access to such organisations as the Chamber of Commerce and the Rotary Clubs. Via them it was familiar with the local politicians, media – Fininvest controlled 51 small TV stations – and sports clubs. Berlusconi's collaborators were divided about his venture into politics: Fedele Confalonieri, who became head of Fininvest, opposed it, while Adriano Galliani, who was responsible for AC Milan, was in favour. The head of Publitalia, Marcello dell'Utri, was enthusiastic and he dispatched his lieutenants. Vincenzo Ghigo, who was scheduled to run Publitalia in Turin, organised there instead and became a Member of Parliament. Gianfranco Micciché, who had worked in Brescia and Milan, went to organise in Sicily.

By September there were 4,000 Forza Italia clubs. Lombardy had the greatest number, but they spread throughout the country and Sicily would eventually have more than 1,000.[5] All they needed was a minimum of five members, a place to meet and a fax machine. In accordance with his emphasis on civil society, Berlusconi wanted the clubs to propagate the themes of 'In Search of Good Government'; quite unlike the local party organisations of the old regime, they were to be the models of citizen participation. Forza Italia clubs were to resolve the crisis of politics by placing the needs of civil society on the agenda of their movement's leaders. The obvious danger was that the clubs would become powerless electoral machines.

Meanwhile Publitalia went ahead throughout the autumn with its quest for parliamentary candidates. It sought out new faces, people below the age of 40, preferably managers. These it screened and turned over to Diakron, Fininvest's public relations company. A tough selection process was introduced, which tested public speaking, motivation, ability to perform on TV and even competence. The failure rate was high: at one point some 2,000 prospective candidates had been tested, of whom only 200 were selected.[6]

Sometimes the clubs and company meshed and the clubs were active in the selection process. However there was an inevitable clash between the clubs, which perceived themselves as the democratic base of Forza Italia, and the Publitalia organisers. Publitalia had a strong sense of identity and it was hierarchical. Berlusconi had drilled its members: no beards, no moustaches, jackets and ties, unflagging optimism – they carried 'the sun in their pockets' (quoted in D'Anna and Moncalvo 1994: 86). Publitalia believed less in the penetration of civil society than in presenting good candidates backed by TV. Moreover it sought power for itself: its leaders took many of the proportional representation slots.

If the clubs protested against the domination of Fininvest, Berlusconi's men suspected that the club leaders were ex-DC and ex-PSI officials who were using Forza Italia to recycle themselves. In Caserta a club was formed by former Christian Democrats, one of whom, an ex-member of Forlani's faction, became a parliamentary candidate. In Sicily there were accusations of Mafia infiltration. Of course the clubs could counter by pointing out that the FI leadership had allied with politicians from the old regime: Pierferdinando Casini was hardly a new face.

A National Association of Forza Italia was set up, and Angelo Codignano, former director of Berlusconi's French TV station, la Cinq, was the coordinator. Applications to form clubs poured in to headquarters, which did not have the people and time to vet them. By February there were 12,000 clubs and as many as a million members. In the enthusiasm of the election campaign and in the quest for votes the lack of vetting was ignored, but the problem of the relationship between the two segments of Forza Italia would fester. FI still does not know whether it is a branch of Fininvest or a new kind of political movement. This is all the more regrettable because the question is crucial.

The speed with which the clubs grew demonstrated that the collapse of the old regime had left a vacuum on the Right. In the autumn Berlusconi began discussions with such leaders as Segni and Martinazzoli. His avowed aim was to help them put together a strong, centre-right movement capable of defeating the PDS-led Left. Segni would become the candidate for Prime Minister, while Berlusconi would place at his disposal the Forza Italia movement, along with Diakron's expertise and the Fininvest TV networks.

It is hard to know whether this was a pretence, designed to demonstrate that the established politicians were not equal to their task and that Berlusconi must run himself. Certainly this is Segni's retrospective interpretation (*La Voce* 12 May 1994), but one can sympathise with the Fininvest view that Segni manoeuvred like a man bent on destroying his chances. At all events the decisive moment was the mayoral elections of 21 November and 5 December 1993.

The Left swept the major cities, winning in Palermo, Naples, Rome, Genoa, Venice and Trieste. A closer look might have indicated that the triumph was less glorious than it seemed: in Trieste the new mayor, Riccardo Illy, was a centrist and an entrepreneur. However the results furthered Berlusconi's cause in several ways. They probably made the Left complacent and they certainly galvanised right-wing opinion. They demonstrated to the Lega that it needed an ally. They corroborated Berlusconi's low opinion of the centrist leaders because in Naples the DC's disarray was so great that it supported Togliatti's ex-secretary, Massimo Caprara. The good performance of the MSI posed a problem, which Berlusconi was willing to tackle.

After the first round Gianfranco Fini and Alessandra Mussolini were in second place in Rome and Naples and went into the run-off. While most centre-right leaders hesitated, Berlusconi stated that: 'If I were in Rome, I would certainly vote for Fini' (*La Repubblica* 24 November 1993). On the second round Mussolini gained 43 per cent and Fini 47 per cent. Moreover the MSI elected 19 mayors, including those of four provincial capitals, Benevento, Latina, Chieti and Caltanisseta. The DC had collapsed in the South and the MSI had replaced it as the dominant party. In Rome, 37 per cent of the first-round DC vote went to Fini, and in Naples 34 per cent went to Mussolini. As Fini reiterated, without the MSI no coalition could be formed to defeat the PDS.

Berlusconi was able to see that Fini's was not an idle boast and that the electorate – rightly or wrongly – would no longer punish a party that formed an alliance with the MSI. He made conflicting statements for a short while and then embraced Alleanza Nazionale, which Fini had launched the previous summer as a front organisation, but which had acquired fresh significance with the DC's southern misfortunes. Berlusconi had had dealings with the far-right during his years as a Milan builder, when one of his backers was Tito Tettamanti, a very anti-communist financier who was alleged to have ties with Opus Dei (Fracassi and

Gambino 1994: 13). Nor was Berlusconi's membership of the P2 irrelevant in this context.

Some of his dealings with Alleanza Nazionale were handled by Domenico Mennitti, who had formerly been in the MSI, but the strategy was Berlusconi's own. His view of the electoral system led him to conclude that Segni and Martinazzoli were wrong in clinging to the Centre. Just as Occhetto was allied with Rifondazione, so the Right needed Fini. AN would bring southern votes in return for the legitimacy that Berlusconi could confer. The price was a coalition partner who periodically exalted Mussolini and sought to rehabilitate Fascism.

With his southern ally in place Berlusconi looked to the North. In its December meeting the Lega was kind to him out of strict necessity. Despite its strength in the small and medium-sized Lombard cities like Varese or Como, the Lega needed an ally. Its free market philosophy and its core of small industrialists made it look towards Berlusconi, who had previously been a benefactor and whose TV networks could offer the Lega the publicity it had earlier lacked. However the Lega was likely to be a more difficult ally than AN, both because its protest component saw in Berlusconi another Craxi, and because Berlusconi's very appeal to the small industrial component threatened Bossi's position. Sixty-three per cent of delegates to the Lega congress named Berlusconi as their choice for Prime Minister (*La Repubblica* 24 November 1993).

The surest sign that he intended to stand in the elections came in January when Indro Montanelli resigned as editor of *Il Giornale*. Montanelli supported Segni, opposed Berlusconi's entry into politics and was ferociously independent. When Berlusconi, whose brother, Paolo, was the official owner of the paper, met the journalists and promised extra resources if the paper changed its editorial stance, Montanelli departed to found *La Voce*. He took with him the prestige he had accumulated as the spokesman of intelligent, critical conservatism. However the loss did not prove vital to Berlusconi, who replaced him with the less eminent but more reliable Vittorio Feltri.

Despite murmurs of rebellion from some *Panorama* journalists and from the TV anchorman, Enrico Mentana, Berlusconi's media empire rallied solidly behind him. Aware that TV commercials were banned for a month before the election, he bombarded viewers in January and February with spots – as many as 19 a day – depicting beautiful old cities and blaring out the jingle 'Let's Go Italy'.

The long-awaited announcement of Berlusconi's entry came in the shape of a TV video on 26 January, which was followed by a Forza Italia convention in Rome on 6 February. Delegates from all over Italy called on Berlusconi to enlighten them – to which he responded with humour – and the most obsequious of his newscasters turned the convention into a media event. The alliances fell into place, proving that the months of meetings with centrist and right-wing politicians had converted the many and isolated the few. The break-away DC group, the Centro Cristiano Democratico (CCD), and the surviving Liberals, the Unione del Centro, joined Berlusconi because they needed a protector. The agreement on division of seats in the South with AN worked everywhere except in the Abruzzo, which duly and unnaturally fell to the Left. Bossi, after a last flirt with Segni, opted for Forza Italia, but he refused any deal with 'the Fascist pigs', which weakened the right-wing alliance but strengthened Berlusconi's position within it.

Forza Italia's 276 candidates were young – 60 per cent under the age of 50 – and well-educated – 74 per cent had a BA. The largest social group was the entrepreneurs – 15.3 per cent – followed by managers – 14.5 per cent. Self-employed professionals were well represented with 13.7 per cent doctors, 12.9 per cent lawyers and 9.2 per cent others. By contrast only 12.9 per cent were employed in the state sector. There were no workers (*La Repubblica* 1 March 1994). Sport was represented, as well as by Mariella Scirea, by the oarsman Giuseppe Abbagnale and by the former centre-forward, Ciccio Graziani. Tiziana Parenti, whose favourite game had been uncovering PDS corruption, transferred herself from the Milan pool to the Rome Parliament, while the film director Franco Zeffirelli lent an operatic touch. The Fininvest contingent was large and successful: the company's lawyers, Cesare Previtti and Vittorio Dotti, Diakron's pollster, Gianni Pilo, and Publitalia's legions.

Candidates came equipped with a kit that consisted of the party programme, 'Berlusconi's Little Blue Book', a video of the 6 February meeting and a catalogue of Diakron's many services – including polling, direct mailing, videos tailored to suit the candidate and inspiring messages from the leader. Forza Italia seemed to have no financial problems, although creditors noted that Fininvest had increasing difficulty in paying its bills.

Among the campaign themes, anger at corruption which had destroyed the old regime, was neutralised since both the Left and Forza Italia were under fire. Paolo Berlusconi admitted bribing public officials to obtain favourable rulings in his property deals, while AC Milan was accused of paying 'black' money in the Gigi Lentini transfer. More serious were the accusations against Marcello dell'Utri of falsifying the Publitalia accounts in order to create funds that could be used for bribery. Dell'Utri was also accused of Mafia ties and Standa was alleged to have paid protection money to the Catania chieftain, Nitto Santapaola (*La Stampa* 21 March 1994). That the 'Ndrangheta family, Piromalli, called on people to vote for Berlusconi may have helped or hurt him. But an implausible preelection raid on the Forza Italia offices by magistrates investigating Masonic corruption almost certainly helped.

It is probably wrong to conclude that Italian public opinion was weary of the war on the Mafia or that it was ready to wind up the 'Clean Hands' investigation. However, economic issues were more important in the election. Asked what the priorities of the new government should be, 77 per cent of people put job creation at the head of their list and only 17 per cent led off with elimination of corruption (Censis 1994a: 8). The Fiat crisis and the attendant threat to employment in Turin, Milan and Naples ran parallel to the campaign. This would appear to confirm our view that FI's victory stemmed from its ability to speak to the economic – and deeper cultural – fears of the country.

This does not mean that the substance of Berlusconi's statements was correct. His opponent in his Rome constituency, Luigi Spaventa, the Minister of the Budget, ridiculed his plans for cuts in personal income tax. Yet the Left's campaign, while full of good sense, was uninspiring. Its spokesmen spent too much time attacking Berlusconi, thus giving him yet more free publicity. Far from being one of several leaders, he became the dominant figure in the campaign.

Bossi joined in the attacks because he was losing votes to his ally. On 21 January polls gave the Lega 13 per cent of the vote and Forza Italia 11 per cent. By 3 March the figures were 8 per cent and 27 per cent (*La Stampa* 21 March 1994). Bossi may have halted the Lega's slide in the polls with his reminders that Berlusconi had been in the P2, with his calls for anti-trust legislation and with his rejection of the Fascist alliance. But the election became a referendum on Berlusconi – to whom Forza Italia increasingly seemed a mere appendage.

So the outcome was not really unexpected. The Left won in the 'red centre' and in outposts like Naples, but it was trounced in the North and the South. In the Chamber vote the Right gained 42.2 per cent to the Left's 34.4 per cent and the Centre's 15.6 per cent. In the Senate vote the figures were 40.4 per cent, 32.9 per cent and 16.7 per cent. The translation of votes into seats gave the Right an absolute majority in the Chamber but not in the Senate. Forza Italia became the largest party with 21 per cent of the vote to the PDS's 20.4 per cent. In the Northwest, which is the most industrialised and supposedly the most modern region, it gained 25.7 per cent, which was more than the PDS and RC combined. It defeated the Lega in Milan by 28.6 per cent to 16 per cent, overcame the PDS candidate in Mirafiori, became the largest party in the Veneto and it swept Sicily.

Forza Italia drew votes primarily from the old parties of government: 25.8 per cent of people who voted DC in 1992 turned to Berlusconi, as did 15.1 per cent who voted PSI or PSDI and 10.2 per cent who voted PRI or PLI. However, FI also picked up protest voters: 18.6 per cent of 1992 Lega voters, 13.8 per cent of MSI voters, 3.3 per cent of Verdi voters (Censis 1994b: 16). This was a broad mandate. Whereas the Lega and AN did better among men than among women, 52.6 per cent of FI's votes came from women.

FORZA'S FUTURE

Berlusconi was fortunate that the European elections of 12 June came after his first policy moves were made and before their effect could be assessed. His economic package unblocked public works, halted by the clean hands investigation. It also released funds for 100,000 posts in local government. Most important, it offered tax cuts to young entrepreneurs, for hiring new workers and for profits reinvested. Small business was aided by the removal of some regulations on hiring and on information to be supplied to the government. Critics pointed out that nowhere did Berlusconi explain how these measures were to be paid for. However they were electorally popular, whereas the Left's attack on the government's hostile attitude to state television aroused little public concern.

FI's success in the European elections cannot, however, be explained merely by the economic package or by the generic notion of honeymoon or even by the role of the Fininvest TV networks. The size of the increase in its share of vote can only be interpreted as a second expression of confidence in FI. It gained 9.6 per cent overall, while in the Northwest the difference between its score and the combined PDS-RC score went from 5 per cent to 14 per cent. Moreover FI's rivals were punished: the PDS lost 1.2 per cent, but the Lega, which had been obstructing from within the government, lost 20 per cent of its vote, slipping from 8.3 per cent to 6.6 per cent. In Bossi's capital of Milan, the Lega ran 26 per cent behind FI. How lasting would this triumph be?

If we return to our initial assertion that Forza Italia was successful because it appeared to offer the most plausible solution to the two-year crisis of the Italian state, then we must conclude that its future depended on its ability to provide answers to the many questions which that crisis posed. They included not merely economic revival but finding a more correct balance between the state and the private sector as between the state and civil society.

Three difficulties lay in FI's path. The first, which the European vote temporarily removed, was that it was part of a governmental coalition which had no majority in the Senate, where it lost important votes to decide committee chairmen in early June, and which was internally divided. Umberto Bossi seemed to regard cooperation with Forza Italia as a step towards annihilation, but the European vote showed that obstruction provided no solution. Alleanza Nazionale was more reliable, but even if the embarrassment of 'fascist' ministers proved to be short-lived, there remained wide differences of policy. In particular AN with its southern base could hardly support FI's bid to prune state intervention.

The other difficulties were internal. Forza Italia's world-view was the utopia created by a private sector at last free of greedy politicians. But the world recession, the government deficit, the immobile bureaucracy and tenacious unemployment were real problems, not to mention the

Mafia and the ongoing investigation into corruption. How well would the Berlusconi government cope with them? Moreover the reality of the private sector was that it was all too ready to cooperate with the old state, and it might want nothing more than a change in the balance of power. Fininvest almost became the state, which was no better than having the destiny of the public-private chemical consortium Enimont controlled by Craxi and Forlani.

To the government Fininvest provided the Prime Minister, the Minister of Defence and four under-secretaries, by one count ten people in all (*Espresso* 27 May 1994). It was also the dominant segment of the party of government, but it remained a private company – supposedly in competition with other companies and subject to governmental decisions. This was an untenable situation – a real not merely symbolic separation between company and government was needed, as well as between both of them and FI. If we are right in arguing that there was a genuine constituency for Berlusconi's arguments and not merely a Baudrillard-style silent majority, then Forza Italia could have an independent existence. Indeed it could evolve into that centre-right, capitalist party, which Italy has never had and which could provide a better balance between the state and industry.

In this optimistic scenario Berlusconi's government would succeed not just in massively pruning the state, but in shaping a new, more modest but more efficient state. In this project Forza Italia would be very different from the mass parties of the old regime, but it would not be a satellite of Publitalia. Its links with professional organisations, especially if they included more non-business organisations, would enable it to be a transmission belt, provided it were allowed a share of power.

The pessimistic scenario saw Berlusconi exploit his position to further Fininvest's goals. His long-term economic policies would probably fail, since they depended on changing the state. Forza Italia would become the new dominant clan, armed with Fininvest's TV networks and Pilo's magic polls.[7]

In summer 1994 FI was rent by disputes between its generals and its footsoldiers, many of whom felt betrayed (*La Voce* 1 June 1994). A group of clubs banded together to form a rebel army. This was the first sign of the sharpening conflict between FI as clan and FI as agent of reform. The priority which Berlusconi gave to the purge of the state TV and to his war on the magistrates, and his neglect of the lira and the deficit, demonstrated that he was a clan chieftain rather than a reformer. His victory was not a freak of post-modern politics, but had deep roots in Italian life. Forza Italia's job was to tend the new plant, but despite the efforts of an increasingly independent group of Parliamentarians led by Vittorio Dotti, it was not allowed to succeed. This was at least one of the reasons for the fall of Berlusconi in December 1994.

NOTES

1 It does not seem necessary to give the source of each short quotation from Berlusconi's speeches. We have drawn on: his TV address of 26 January; his 6 February speech at the Forza Italia convention; an interview in *Panorama* 4 February 1994 pp. 9–14, and a letter written in support of the FI candidate in the Twelfth Electoral College of Emilia Romagna. We wish to thank the Press Office of Forza Italia for providing the first two documents, as well as other material. For a longer but still incomplete study of Berlusconi's language see our 'Il linguaggio di Berlusconi' in *Il Regno* 15 May 1994, pp. 276–278.
2 For the various kinds of populism see Canovan (1992/3: 54–57).
3 Interview with Massimo Ghedini and Luca Turchi of Publitalia, 30 May 1994.
4 *Alla ricerca del buon governo*, Milan 1993, p. 31. I wish to thank Roberto Lasagna for providing me with this booklet and much other campaign documentation.
5 I wish to thank Nicholas Lasagna for collecting information on the FI clubs.
6 Interview with Giorgio Dragotto, FI candidate in Electoral College 10 of Emilia-Romagna, 30 May 1994.
7 During the campaign one of Pilo's polls gave FI 36 per cent – an 'error' of 15 per cent!

REFERENCES

Borcio, R. (1992) 'La Lega come attore politico', in R. Mannheimer (ed.) *La Lega Lombarda*, Milan: Feltrinelli.
Canovan, M. (1993) 'Il populismo come l'ombra della democrazia', *Europa/ Europe* 1992/3.
Censis (1994a) *L'Italia in Politica 1*, Rome: Fondazione Censis.
—— (1994b) *L'Italia in Politica 3*, Rome: Fondazione Censis.
D'Anna, S. and Moncalvo, G. (1994) *Berlusconi in Concert*, London: Otzium.
Fracassi, C. and Gambino, M. (1994) *Berlusconi, una biografia non autorizzata*, Rome: Avvenimenti.
Lepre, A. (1993) *Storia della prima repubblica*, Bologna: Il Mulino.
Pansa, G. (1994) *I Bugiardi*, Rome: L'Unità–Sperling & Kupfer.
Salvati, M. (1986) *Economia e Politica in Italia dal dopoguerra a oggi*, Milan: Garzanti.
Scalfari, E. and Turani, G. (1974) *Razza padrona*, Milan: Feltrinelli.
Sylos Labini, P. (1986) 'Struttura sociale, sviluppo e classi sociali', in Carlo Carboni (ed.) *Classi e Movimenti in Italia 1970–1985*, Laterza and Rome: Bari.

9 Towards a modern Right
Alleanza Nazionale and the 'Italian Revolution'

Carlo Ruzza and Oliver Schmidtke

The Italian elections in April 1994 yielded two surprising and unexpected results: victory for Berlusconi's Forza Italia, and the strong performance of the right-wing coalition Alleanza Nazionale (AN). This right-conservative alliance, led by the Movimento Sociale Italiano (MSI), received nearly double the votes that neo-fascist parties previously had attracted in post-war Italy. With 13.4 per cent of the valid votes, the AN now constitutes the third strongest faction in the Italian Parliament, even superseding the declining Partito Popolare Italiano (formerly the Christian Democrats, who had once led government coalitions). The ascendancy of the extreme right, confirmed by comparable gains in the May 1994 European elections, marks a radical change in Italian politics. For the first time in the country's post-war history, the extreme right escaped the political ghetto and gained an influential voice in the national government.

The Italian extreme right's resurgence highlights many of the paradoxes of Italian political culture. On the one hand, the Right never entirely faded after the defeat of the Italian Fascists in World War II. Both extremist extra-parliamentary groups, such as Ordine Nuovo or Avanguardia Nazionale, and political parties like the MSI, retained sufficient political influence to attract the fourth largest voter endorsement. Pointing to reasons for this extraordinary resiliency, as seen from a European perspective, Franco Ferraresi states that the 'Fascist heritage, political blockage, and poor political performance appear as the main factors that have sustained radical right extremism in Italy since the war' (Ferraresi 1988: 73–74).

The power base of the Italian extreme right has persisted in spite of the generally more progressive orientation of the mainstream political parties, which have perceived the Right's agenda as illegitimate. The Italian political establishment, and, until recently, the public as well, have systematically excluded the MSI from government. The combination of public ambivalence towards the institutions of parliamentary democracy (shed by the Right only recently) and public revulsion with violent terrorist acts committed by right-wing extremists, had helped to sustain this isolation.

Extreme right-wing movements in Europe face a critical challenge of overcoming resistance to the core of their collective identities which results from disgust with the now defunct fascist regimes of the 1940s. Disassociation with this heritage has been particularly problematic for the extreme right in Germany and Italy. The MSI has attempted such disassociation, in spite of the links many of its founders had held with the Mussolini regime. In the course of post-war mobilisation, these historical roots created what has been termed the 'paradox of identity' (Chiarini 1991a). Chiarini had argued that the neo-fascist collective identity, along with the Italian Right's continuous reference to the nation's 'heroic past' (Mussolini's Fascism), can be seen as the two main reasons for the MSI's failed institutional integration into the political system. The traditional collective identity of the Right thus severely restricted its ability to mobilise the public and to cooperate with other political forces.

The resulting political isolation notwithstanding, the history of the Right in Italy is one of a gradual, albeit ambiguous rapprochement to the established political parties. Two key factors have determined the political identity of the institutionalised Right in Italy (Ignazi 1989). The first is the party's roots in the Fascist movement of the Mussolini era, with its links to the northern Italian Social Republic. In the course of its development, MSI representatives have come to distinguish between the specific Mussolini regime and Fascism as a 'movement'. They have defined the latter as a broader political-cultural movement only loosely connected with the Mussolini regime (and therefore not responsible for the crimes of that regime). MSI has attempted to sell its claim to represent a 'third way', or an alternative to the antagonistic system generated by the Cold War.

The second factor shaping the course of the Right's political mobilisation has been the MSI's shifting attitudes towards the Italian electoral system. The MSI has oscillated between the two most extreme possible attitudes – from periods of radical opposition to 'the system', to an aspiration for acceptance by the mainstream political institutions. This contradiction reflects the very core of the Right's political identity which has grown out of the fundamental opposition to parliamentary democracy, but which, with the stability of the Republic, has adopted a position of 'immanent critique' of the other parties. On the one hand, deradicalisation and rapprochement to other parties has been designed to attract support from the conservative middle class, and thereby to widen the base for right-wing mobilisation. On the other hand, however, the MSI has had to emphasise its radical roots to retain the support of its old political base. This latter need has historically limited the constituency of the Right, and limited its political influence.[1]

The degree of alienation from or integration into the political system has hence been the decisive yardstick for the MSI's strategic orientation. The fact that the MSI responded to newly emerging opportunities in Italian politics and society by massively restructuring its platform and strategies for mobilisation, indicates that the party has returned to a period of desire for integration. The process by which the originally terrorist-linked neo-fascist organisation became a partner in the Berlusconi government included four phases.

PHASE I: INSTALLATION IN THE 'FIRST REPUBLIC' (FROM WORLD WAR II TO THE MID-1960S)

In a climate of claustrophobic anti-communism, the MSI gradually gained some political credibility through assisting the DC in their struggle against the PCI during the formative years of the Italian Republic. The MSI visibly collaborated with DC administrations at the municipal level, and also more subtly and indirectly supported the DC in the national arena as well. By partially repressing its fascist roots, and projecting a moderate image, the MSI quietly conquered the fringes of the *centrismo*, the governing coalition of moderate-centre parties led by the DC. The MSI aided the election of a conservative President in 1962. Even so, the MSI never achieved more than a loose alliance with the DC, and the MSI had been the decisively subordinate partner. During this phase, the MSI itself never gained a substantial voice in government, nor did it score electoral success outside its isolated strongholds in the South of Italy. The MSI thus remained marginalised in the predominantly anti-fascist political climate following World War II.

Being the direct heir of the collapsed Fascist regime of Salò meant that the constituency and supporters were mainly composed of fascist nostalgists and admirers of Mussolini, and members of the petty bourgeoisie, who feared losing their privileges granted by the Fascist state bureaucracy.[2] Many lesser governmental employees under Mussolini, especially in the armed forces, judiciary, police, and the intelligence service, retained their posts in the post-war reconstruction of the Italian state, and these people likewise provided a natural constituency for the MSI in the national political structures. Popular support for the MSI, however, was more geographically confined. Given the strong anti-fascist sentiments in the North, the MSI could only build up an electoral base in the South where the Resistance had been decisively less strong. During this phase, two-thirds of the MSI's votes came from the South. This regional pattern of support for and hostility against the Right remained a feature of Italian politics until the 1994 elections.[3]

The Right's very modest electoral results during this phase can be explained by the structural composition of the MSI's traditional electorate. By establishing itself in the pre-modern South, the MSI has never been able to build up strong links to a particular social class. The MSI neither could challenge the PCI's claim to represent the working classes, nor could it challenge the DC appeal to the Catholic sub-culture and the petty bourgeoisie. Instead, the MSI found support from a peculiar combination of marginalised groups, of the 'Lumpenproletariat' at one end and components of the high bourgeoisie on the other. The former voted for the neo-fascists to express disenchantment with the entire political system. The latter group, in contrast, desired to reinstate the old clientelistic system in which they enjoyed many privileges. The MSI had difficulty developing an ideology encompassing both these political beliefs. Furthermore, the processes of social and economic modernisation continuously eroded this electoral base. Still, the anti-system sentiments of the sub-proletarian classes of southern Italy remained a constant factor in the mobilisation of the MSI.

PHASE II: RADICALISATION AND MARGINALISATION (FROM THE LATE 1960s TO THE 1970s)

After the Tambroni crisis in the early 1960s, the DC severed its connections with the Right, abandoned *centrismo*, and openly courted the Left. The resulting isolation of the MSI in the following years was characterised by a growing support for clandestine and terrorist acts. In this period, the MSI had to cope with the defection of its more radical factions from the parliamentary wing. Most prominently, Rauti's Ordine Nuovo (an organisation of left-oriented fascists), the Avanguardia Nazionale, and other extremist groups challenged the MSI's claim to represent a united Right. These dissident factions attacked the parliamentary system by all means available.

In these years of intensified clashes between the Right and Left, the MSI adopted the so-called 'strategy of tension'. The MSI hoped to destabilise the political system, and thereby to make its authoritarian 'right-wing alternative' to the DC and the militant Left publicly attractive. Under the leadership of Almirante, who replaced Michelini in 1969, the MSI redefined its relationship to the state by denouncing the existing institutions as the corrupt organs of the Left. The era of 'political appeasement' when the MSI had participated in the clientelistic system erected by the Christian Democrats had come to an end. During the years of the student revolts, a growing polarisation of political forces spurred the mobilisation of the radical Right. During these years, the MSI strove to reunite the parliamentary Right with the extra-parliamentary groups. According to Piergiorgio Corbetta, Almirante achieved some short-term success by capitalising on lingering feelings of nostalgia for the Fascist order, fear among some members of the social elite of threats to their status raised by the Left, anger among the marginalised sub-proletariat, and fear among some of the petty bourgeoisie of their loss of status through 'proletarianisation' (Corbetta *et al.* 1988: 242). Some prominent

Table 9.1 Vote for the MSI (and allies) in general elections

Year	%
1948	2.0
1953	5.8
1958	4.8
1963	5.1
1968	4.5
1972	8.7
1976	6.1
1979	5.3
1983	6.8
1987	5.9
1992	5.4
1994	13.4

figures, including General De Lorenzo, openly endorsed the MSI during this phase. In 1972, the MSI scored its best result in general elections, attracting 8.7 per cent of national valid votes.

Ultimately, however, Almirante's strategy failed. In spite of the polarisation of public protest, the desire of the DC leaders and many of its supporters to forge an alliance with the Left created a climate suited to compromise and conciliation in the political mainstream which averted the polarisation the MSI had hoped to foster. In the end Almirante had guided the MSI up a dead-end street, and the right-wing coalition fractured again. The openly terrorist organisations dedicated to overthrowing the political system paid little heed to the MSI, but the party was unable to shake public perceptions of its association with acts of violence. The terrorist right thus discredited the extreme right in Parliament, and undermined any prospect of the MSI playing a relevant role in the institutional life of the country. Accordingly, in the 1976 general elections, the MSI lost almost all of its gains from 1972 (see Table 9.1). Following these losses, dissatisfied Parliamentarians, who accused the MSI leadership of failing to establish respectability for the Right, founded the alternative *Democrazia Nazionale* (National Democracy) party. Disunity and lack of popular support forced the Right back into the political ghetto.

PHASE III: DERADICALISATION AND THE SEARCH FOR RESPECTABILITY (LATE 1970S THROUGH TO 1993)

After the end of the violent phase of Italian politics, the MSI sought to reestablish its image as a serious actor. Such a transformation required a substantial change in the political identity of the main Right party. Not all members of the Right supported change, and little consensus developed among those who did. Consequently, the MSI suffered an identity crisis and failed to integrate the legalist approach of the old

Almirante wing now led by Gianfranco Fini, with the more radical parts of its constituency.

In the period of transition, the New Right (Nuova Destra), a more culturally oriented Right, formed along the lines of the French *Nouvelle Droite*, introduced new issues into the political discourse of the Right in Italy (see Zucchinali 1986). The New Right indirectly influenced the struggle for transformation in the MSI by inspiring interest in post-materialist values. The MSI now included environmental questions, civil rights issues, a critique of consumerist mass society, and other cultural matters together with its more traditional ideological concerns with social order, discipline, and hierarchy (see Cheles 1991). This 'ideological modernisation' meant that concern for quality of life and political participation, traditionally alien values in this element of Italian politics, found their place in the political struggle of the Right.[4]

Reacting to the overall climate of depolarisation between the Left and Right, the MSI sought to downplay its entanglement in the activities of the terrorist right and to adopt the image of a respectable right-wing party. Nonetheless, the MSI never explicitly disassociated itself from its fascist heritage; no equivalent of a *Bad Godesberg*, for example, emerged from the Right. Survival in the Italian political climate of the time may have required such change, but the MSI paid a heavy price. Moves towards 'ideological modernisation' enraged members on the right, and infighting both fractured the party and weakened potential for public support. The MSI suffered a series of electoral defeats during the 1980s and early 1990s.

PHASE IV: BEYOND THE GHETTO (1993 TO DATE)

By the 1990s, the MSI's new leader, Gianfranco Fini, sought to enable his party to shed the burden of its past. Fini forged an alliance between the MSI and the Alleanza Nazionale (AN) in November 1993, hoping that the public would accept that the change of name also signified a change of heart. The real symbolic test of Fini's new image came on 25 April 1994, at the 50th anniversary celebration of Italy's liberation from Fascism. Fini himself marked this day by attending a mass held in memory of *all* Italian victims of World War II. While publicly paying homage to the past successes of the Italian Resistance, the MSI also subtly questioned the suitability of old Resistance values from the 1940s for the Italy of the 1990s. MSI leaders insisted that Mussolini's regime arose in a unique period of history whose circumstances could not now be repeated. Thus by dismissing Mussolini-style Fascism as a thing of the past (and implying that the Italian Left deserved similar relegation), the MSI sought to frame its new image in partnership with the AN as a party of the 'reformed, post-fascist, European movement'.[5]

Not all factions of the MSI-AN alliance appreciated this characteris-
ation of the Fascist past, which Fini apparently acknowledges when speaking of the burdens under which the 'neo-fascist right has been operating
for many years in Italy'.[6] Indeed, not only have many grumbles suggested
deep-seated opposition to Fini's deradicalising reforms, some prominent
leaders, including established extremists Pino Rauti, Teodoro Buontempo
and Alessandra Mussolini, have left open the possibility of challenging
for the leadership of the Right in the event of the breakdown of the
coalition with the government.[7] Piero Ignazi's study of the MSI's XVI
congress held in 1990 provides evidence of how deep the dissent to the
shift to conservative mainstream politics may be. He summarises his
results as follows:

> Basically, the MSI seems to be divided into two groups: one in which
> anti-system convictions are still dominant. This means an orientation
> in favour of an even violent protest, a total rejection of all other parties
> and a radical opposition against the system. Within the other group an
> attitude of openness and willingness to participate in the existing politi-
> cal system and to cooperate with its political agents dominates. In
> effect, we have two groups that represent the traditional split between
> radical and moderates.
>
> (Ignazi 1994: 186)

While the private sentiments of the MSI leadership may remain unclear,
publicly the party has employed a two-fold institutional strategy to escape
the political ghetto. The first layer of that strategy has been the construction of a new image, achieved in part by the alliance with the AN. Much
like the decision to ally with the monarchist Destra Nazionale in the
1970s, the MSI decision to link with the AN, another monarchist party,
primarily reflects a desire for electoral gains. Fini himself has emphasised
that his strategy is designed to overcome the Right's past political isolation, and to this end has banned from party functions expressions of
anti-system sentiment and nostalgic longing for the pre-war era. Nevertheless, as with the previous coalition with DN, while the MSI has claimed
that its new partnership reflects a broadening of views, it remains the
dominant partner. Second, and more significant, has been the willingness
of the MSI-AN to join the Berlusconi government coalition. By acting in
coalition, the MSI has demonstrated that it has at least the short-term
objective of acting as a serious player in the present Italian political
system. By prioritising this aspiration, the MSI has created a rhetorical
ground from which it can even negotiate with such fellow serious players
as Bossi's Lega Nord, a federalist party whose aspirations threaten the
core of the Right's concern with state integrity and national unity.

The new look of the MSI-AN alliance constitutes the culmination of
changes in the extreme right that began in the 1970s, rather than a sudden

ideological shift. The line of appealing for support from non-traditionally conservative constituencies, which has become dominant under Fini, has enabled the MSI-AN alliance to capitalise on the opportunities created during the deep legitimation crisis now plaguing Italian politics. A spectre of ideological conflict potentially haunts the future of the new look, as the Right may not be able to sustain its potentially incompatible concern for individual rights and state stability, but, at least for now, the MSI-AN has successfully shed its old-fashioned and intransigent image. Even if the new-look Right enjoys only a short political life, Fini's changes have at least extended the Right's political viability for, in the present period of rapidly shifting economic, social, and political tides in Italy, Chiarini explains, the Right's more traditional 'values (the defence of religion, love of country, attachment to the family and respect for authority) were drained of their potency' and did not provide the basis for a functional political agenda (Chiarini 1991b: 33).

In evaluating this last phase of the MSI-AN's mobilisation, however, it is important to bear in mind that the new ideological and strategic orientation could only become successful because of the deep political crisis of the old political establishment, particularly of the old Centre. The rapid decline of the PSI and the DC, along with the disorganisation of other moderate and progressive parties, left a political vacuum which the formerly disreputable extreme right parties have been able to fill, at least for the time being. Simply by offering an organised and coherent alternative agenda, the Right has attracted a portion (though Berlusconi's Forza Italia party appears to have attracted the majority) of the protest vote – which helped to raise their electoral results to the high levels of 1994. Even Berlusconi himself may have aided the MSI-AN cause by making statements indirectly supporting MSI candidates. At the time of the November 1993 mayoral elections he stated, 'if I had to vote in Rome, I would opt for Fini'. The two most prominent Right candidates, Fini and Mussolini, helped attract over 40 per cent of the final round votes in Rome and Naples. Progressive candidates only narrowly eclipsed the MSI leaders. In ten smaller cities with populations over 15,000, MSI candidates won their election bids.

THE 1994 GENERAL ELECTION

A closer examination of the statistics from the 1994 general election, in which the MSI-AN coalition won a total of 13.4 per cent of the votes, provides more insight into the nature of the resurgence of the extreme right. Support for the Right varies considerably over different regions. In the northern regions, Lombardy, Piemonte, Trentino-Alto-Adige, and Veneto, the AN alliance attracted between 5 and 9 per cent of the vote. The Right alliance enjoyed better success in the central regions and islands, where it secured between 9 and 15 per cent of the vote, and performed best in the South, where it averaged over 20 per cent of the vote. The Right garnered its highest percentages in Campagnia (20.3), Lazio (24.3), Puglia (26.5), and Rome (26.98). The MSI-AN won more votes than any other party in Rome. Electoral support for the Right followed a similar geographic distribution in the May 1994 European elections.

One might well have predicted that the extreme right would fare best in the continental South, which has weak leftist and anti-fascist traditions, deep-rooted clientelistic systems whose privileged groups feel threatened by the Centre and Left, and economically underdeveloped areas suffering high unemployment. These demographic and cultural characteristics have favoured the extreme right in the past. More surprising, however, was the Right's equally strong showing in the Catholic areas of the southern regions which had traditionally supported the DC. While Forza Italia absorbed the majority of the protest vote against the corruption of the old mainstream parties, the Right's appeal to the minority of Catholic protest voters was stronger in the South than in the northern *zone bianche* (Catholic white zones). In numeric terms, the Right's gains in the centre of the country were modest, but politically these gains are significant. The centre of Italy has traditionally been the stronghold of the Left: an improvement in this region suggests that, while the extreme right may not be popular, its parties also are no longer political pariahs in this region.

The southern Catholics were not the only demographic group with which the extreme right increased its appeal. Voters under the age of 25 also expressed relatively higher support for the Right than older age groups. Even in the North, the percentage of younger people who voted for the Right is nearly double the percentage of the total vote the Right received. Further evidence of the age gap emerges in the composition of the Senate, whose members are elected only by voters aged 25 and older, and the composition of the Chamber of Deputies, elected by all voters aged 18 and over. The Left won a higher percentage of seats in the Senate than in the Chamber of Deputies, while nearly all AN seats are in the Chamber of Deputies. The present government coalition thus holds a solid majority in the Chamber of Deputies whereas it has no overall majority in the Senate.

ROOTS OF THE SUCCESS OF ALLEANZA NAZIONALE

The Right's success is largely explained by reference to public reaction to the corruption scandals in Italian government. That a large majority of voters rejected the old political structure in favour of a new system of elections in 1994 indicates the depth of public disgust with Italian politics and politicians. The name-recognition, influence in the *sottogoverno* (network of public institutions and semi-political organs of state bureaucracy), and experience in political office which had once provided electoral advantages to the major parties now became electoral liabilities. As a traditional outlier with a history of rejecting the old political structures, the MSI-AN could more effectively sell itself as a genuine alternative party than could the repackaged versions of the old mainstream parties. It was also aided by the alliance with Berlusconi and the way Forza Italia focused all of its campaigning against the Left. A further answer may lie in the growing public interest in immigration and tax issues. The anti-immigrant, racist feelings growing in parts of the Italian public have coincided with the agenda of the extreme right, which has emphasised the importance of protecting the state against the incursion of 'others'. The political climate shaped by *Tangentopoli*, the protest against the tax burden, and the outcry over revelations of the widespread practice of bribery in the government, fuelled the distrust of the existing state bureaucracies. As a traditional defender of the petty and middle bourgeoisie, the Right likewise succeeded in tapping discontent with the institutions which had hurt the interests of these groups of voters. Finally, Fini himself may have played a significant role in the turn of fortune for the Right. In his seven years as the head of the MSI, he has become the uncontested leader of the reformed Right.[8] With his clever use of the mass media, his rhetorical skills and public presentation, and his professional image, Fini has augmented the respectability of the Right. Although originally perceived as the heir to the Almirante line, Fini has initiated a new quality of political mobilisation for the Italian Right.

PROSPECTS FOR AN

In conclusion let us offer some considerations on the future prospects of AN, as the MSI was formally dissolved in 1995. It is beyond dispute that the far right achieved spectacular successes in 1993–94. Even in 1992 there can scarcely have been a single member of the MSI leadership who would have expected his party to have become a force of government in so short a time. In Berlusconi's administration there were five AN ministers: Giuseppe Tatarella, Deputy Prime Minister and Minister for Posts and Telecommunications; Domenico Fisichella, Minister of Education; Publio Fiori (a former Christian Democrat), Minister of Transport, Adriana Poli Bertone, Minister of Agriculture, and Altero Matteoli, Minister for the Environment. Whether these successes prove transient or more lasting depends on a number of factors, several of which concern the pattern of electoral behaviour. Once outrage at the corruption of the old parties has subsided and the electoral system is shaped in a context in which a polarisation of the political system is encouraged, further change in the identities of the parties is inevitable.

The political development of AN in this respect critically depends on the capacity of the traditional political Centre to reconsolidate itself. The

dynamic of the radically restructured party system in Italy will determine
the margins for the political future of an established right-of-centre mass
party.

To minimise the risk deriving from instability and competition, and to
maximise the chances of attracting the electorate of former Christian
Democrats, Fini embarked on a campaign to rapidly and substantially
reduce the remaining legitimacy problems of the MSI-AN. At the extraordinary convention of the MSI in January/February 1995 he secured
approval to dissolve the MSI into the broader, less ideologically distinctive
AN. In this sense it was programmatically decisive that the new AN has
committed itself to the principles of liberal democracy, the condemnation
of any form of racism or anti-semitism and the (strongly contested)
declaration that anti-fascism constituted an important part of the democratic renewal of the post-war order. The new political line crafted by
Fini was explicitly directed towards turning AN into the dominant force
of the Centre Right, attempting to inherit the role once held by the DC.
The endemic instability of the old Catholic Centre and the apparently
declining star of Berlusconi, made a scenario possible in which a 'deradicalised' Fini acquired the role of leader of the conservative bloc in Italian
politics (surveys conducted after the convention indicated that AN could
already count on the electoral support of almost 20 per cent). Of decisive
importance in this drive towards a united Centre-Right would be the
dynamic initiated by the newly implemented majoritarian system and
the consequent bipolar regrouping of the party spectrum.

However, two elements rendered it difficult for AN to achieve this
goal. First, Fini's strategy of turning the old MSI into a 'post-fascist' party
of the conservative Right led in the short term to strong internal opposition within AN. After the formal dissolution of the MSI, Pino Rauti
decided to leave AN – possibly striving for some sort of 'Rifondazione
fascista'. Other hard-liners such as Teodoro Buontempo and Almirante's
widow were willing to stay, and announced that they would fight for the
survival of the fascist tradition. They accused Fini of turning AN into a
'bourgeois' party without any distinctive political identity. Second, AN
was likely to experience continuing difficulties in appealing to the commercial middle classes of the North, which supported the League and
Forza Italia, as it was bound to give priority to the interests of its existing
electorate in the disadvantaged areas of the country. As the least liberal
component of the coalition in economic as well as social policy, AN had
a strong interest in maintaining the very sort of assistance and inefficient
institutional structures that its ostensible allies pledged to abolish.

NOTES

1 The fact that Italian political culture was, and to a lesser extent still is, shaped
  by anti-fascism, made the rise of a 'respectable' right party difficult. As Renzo

De Felice stated, 'in Italy the political struggle is structured such that a right wing force of a traditional type, that is a respectable, law-abiding Right, is unthinkable because it would soon be labelled as fascist' (1975: 97).

2　In its formative years, the MSI maintained excellent relations with the Roman bourgeoisie and the Vatican.

3　The vote for the MSI is traditionally shaped by two factors: urbanisation and underdevelopment. The main centres of electoral strength for the *missini* have in fact been the urban centres in the South, such as Rome, Naples, Bari, Catania, Messina and Palermo. Regarding the capital as the typical socio-cultural environment responsive to the MSI's mobilising efforts, Mario Caciagli states that 'in Rome, the vote for the MSI-DN comes from the mass of minor civil servants who regret the loss of the modest privileges they enjoyed under the Fascist regime and who remain faithful to the idea of a strong, centralised state. But they also come from those sectors of the marginalised population which inhabit the poor and run-down areas in the suburbs' (Caciagli 1988: 22).

4　Even so, the MSI did not relegate its discourse about the family, religion or, to a lesser extent, the state. Instead it continued to emphasise these concerns.

5　See 'La tentazione di Alleanza Nazionale', *La Repubblica*, 17 May 1994. See also an interview with Fini in 'Sganciate il Carroccio!', *Panorama*, 16 April 1994.

6　See 'La vecchia guardia striglia Fini', *La Repubblica*, 12 May 1994.

7　At this point, even Fini's own relationship with the fascist past of the party remains ambivalent. The attempt to historicise the period of Italian Fascism and to give it a less important status in defining the contemporary Right's political identity is accompanied by statements by Fini expressing a potentially contradictory view. Fini has claimed, for example, that 'Mussolini is still my political master' and that 'for me, Mussolini is the greatest Italian politician'.

8　See C. Valentini, 'Dio, Patria e Santoro', *L'Espresso*, 8 April 1994.

REFERENCES

Caciagli, M. (1988) 'The movimento sociale Italiano-destra nazionale and neo-Fascism in Italy', *West European Politics*, XI(2): 19–33.

Cheles, L. (1991) 'Nostalgia dell'avvenire: The new propaganda of the MSI between tradition and innovation' in L. Cheles, R. Ferguson and M. Vaughan (eds), *Neo-Fascism in Europe*, London: Longman.

Chiarini, R. (1991a) 'La Destra italiana: il paradosso di un'identità illegitima', *Italia Contemporanea*, 185: 581–600.

—— (1991b) 'The movimento sociale Italiano: a historical profile' in L. Cheles, R. Ferguson and M. Vaughan (eds), *Neo-Fascism in Europe*, London: Longman.

Corbetta, P., Parisi, A. M. and Schadee, H. M. (1988) *Elezioni in Italia: struttura e tipologia delle consultazioni politiche*, Bologna: Il Mulino.

De Felice, R. (1975) *Intervista sul fascismo*, Bari: Laterza.

Ferraresi, F. (1988) 'The radical right in Italy', *Politics and Society*, XVI(1): 71–119.

Fini, G. (1994) 'Interview with Fini "Sganciate il Carroccio" ', *Panorama*, 16 April, p. 19.

Fini, G. (1994) 'La tentazione di Alleanza nazionale', *La Repubblica*, 17 May.

Ignazi, P. (1989) *Il Polo escluso: profilo del Movimento Sociale Italiano*, Bologna: Il Mulino.

—— (1994) *L'Estrema Destra in Europa*, Bologna: Il Mulino.

Zucchinali, M. (1986) *La Destra in Italia oggi*, Milan: SugarCo.

10 The great failure?

The Democratic Party of the Left in Italy's transition

Martin J. Bull

This chapter documents and explains the changing nature, strategy and fortunes of the PDS in the period between its birth and the 1994 elections, viewed in the broader perspective of its relationship to old and new parties and movements and the changes at work in Italian politics in this period. After commenting briefly on the significance of the PCI–PDS transformation, the chapter evaluates the PDS's role in the period between its official birth in 1991 and the achievement of electoral reform of the Chamber of Deputies in July 1993, which effectively set in motion the long campaign for the national elections in 1994. It then analyses the PDS's attempt to 'realign' the Left in the run-up to those elections, before finally assessing the causes and consequences of the left's electoral defeat, and its difficulties in opposition to the Berlusconi government. The chapter documents a political failure, but one which has to be viewed both in terms of the party's history (see the chapter by Stephen Hellman, Chapter 4), and the political context of the deep undercurrents of change at work in Italy in this period. Viewed from this perspective, Achille Occhetto can be seen as a party leader navigating, for the first time, completely uncharted waters, the tides of which were not only difficult to see but constantly undergoing change. His failure to prevent a right-wing outcome to the Italian transition therefore should not go unqualified.

THE LEGACY OF THE PCI–PDS TRANSFORMATION (1989–91)

Space does not permit a detailed treatment of the PCI–PDS transformation (see Ignazi 1992 and *Italian Politics. A Review* 1992–93 volumes). But two points should be made here. First, the PCI was an important contributor to the sea-change in Italian politics which occurred in the early 1990s. In transforming itself into a non-communist party of the left, it removed the primary cause of a 'blocked' party system. True, it was not solely this which accounted for the subsequent changes, and furthermore, the transformation can of course be seen simply as a product of the end of Communism in Eastern Europe. Yet the rapidity with which Occhetto responded to the collapse of the Berlin Wall (his proposal to dissolve the party was made only five days later) certainly made a crucial difference to the speed with which the changes occurred. More importantly, the subsequent crisis of the PCI-PDS during and immediately after its formal transition prompted a good degree of complacency on the part of the Christian Democrats (DC) and Socialists (PSI), who seemed content to sit back and observe their rival's problems, unaware of the wave about to engulf them (see Bull and Newell 1993: 206–15). Occhetto's decision, then, was a true watershed in the development of the Italian political system.

Second, however, this did not mean that the PDS was in a good position to exploit the situation it had (partly) created for itself. Specifically, to be – or stay – in the vanguard of the changes engulfing the system and thus inherit the fruits of them (in the form of entering government) the party needed to be strong, united, sufficiently 'new' and with a feasible alliance strategy. But these four qualities were undermined at the outset by the manner of the new party's birth, which had carried the old divisions of the PCI into the PDS (essentially between the 'Democratic Communists' on the left and the *riformisti* on the right), and were then exacerbated by the particular direction which events in Italy followed. This ensured that the PDS's attempt (already undermined by the emergence of the Northern Leagues and the referenda movement) to monopolise the reform movement – in the sense of providing alternatives to a collapsing regime – would prove to be a far more complicated operation than expected.

THE PDS ON THE EDGE OF THE VORTEX: AGENT OF CHANGE OR VESTIGE Of THE OLD REGIME? (1991–93)

In one sense, the situation in which the PDS found itself in the period between June 1991 (the referendum on preference voting and the Sicilian elections, which together marked the first rumblings of the imminent electoral earthquake) and the electoral reform of July 1993 (which set in motion all parties' tactics for the 1994 national elections) was quite favourable. The PDS was the only established party organisation to remain substantially intact. By mid–late 1993, the membership of the DC and PSI had effectively collapsed under the weight of exposed corruption, and it was clear by then that their electoral support would be wiped out at the next elections. The PDS had 800,000 members, 16.5 per cent of the national vote (in 1992), an infrastructural patrimony estimated in billions of lire, and a wide network of sponsored social and media activities: if there existed an established and natural pivot around which a genuine alternative to the collapsing regime could be constructed, the PDS seemed to be the obvious candidate. There were, however, several factors working against the PDS in this period. Not only was the party's strength declining[1] but Italy's transition threw up a number of issues which the party tackled poorly and which exposed the deep divisions which had been carried into the new party from the PCI. These issues concerned the PDS's participation in government, its political alliances, electoral reform and the consolidation of the party's new image. Their impact was to leave the PDS continually on the edge of the vortex which had already claimed the DC and the PSI, and therefore adopting a strategy which was less that of directing Italy's transition than of simply trying to ensure its own survival.

Participation in government

The first key issue was whether or not the PDS should assist in stabilising the Amato (1992–93) and Ciampi (1993–94) governments – either through supporting or participating in them. Were these governments fundamental to the transition which the Italian Republic was undergoing or were they simply the last gasps of the old regime? Divisions on this issue in the party became apparent during the Amato government, when the party's fierce opposition to it – partly designed to avoid alienating the left (Hellman 1993: 149–50) – caused discomfort to many of the 'reformists' who felt that the party was not participating positively in Italy's apparent transition to the new.

Ciampi's self-styled transitional government, which limited its life to the time needed to carry through electoral reform and the Finance Bill (both deemed essential by the PDS), exposed these divisions fully. Occhetto agreed to hold three ministries, even though he was also aware that there were many in the party, including his own deputy, Massimo D'Alema, who had deep reservations about the PDS participating in a government led by the epitome of the establishment (the ex-Governor of the Bank of Italy), alongside a number of faces from the old nomenclature. Consequently, when, the day after the birth of the government, Parliament refused to lift Craxi's parliamentary immunity for four of the six requests by the magistrates, Occhetto did not hesitate to pull his ministers out (the Greens and Republicans doing likewise). Although, as Ciampi pointed out, there was no formal connection between the formation of the government and the behaviour of the Parliament supporting it, Occhetto unmistakably saw the political implications of participating in a government whose Parliament was now openly discredited. Yet, the alternative to participation – outright opposition along the lines that the left of the party wanted – would be equally unrewarding. It would fail to achieve electoral reform and would be perceived by many as hindering Italy's transition. Consequently, the PDS abstained on the reformulated Ciampi government, and the party was left in complete disarray by the whole affair. The 'Democratic Communists' toed the party line, but as Tortorella noted, only out of respect for party discipline (Ingrao's daughter, in fact, voted against the government). The right of the party, and particularly Vincenzo Visco, who was Ciampi's Minister of Finance for about 11 hours, disagreed with the decision to pull out the Ministers and saw it as a further damaging compromise by Occhetto to avoid a rupture with the left.

The search for political allies

The divisions over the PDS's role in relation to government during the transition period were a reflection of a second issue: the broader problem of the party's alliance strategy. The PCI had long been divided over this question (see Hellman, Chapter 4). Paradoxically, at the moment when the right of the party could have hoped to have its way (because of the increasing marginalisation of the left in the PDS), its long-proposed strategy (of a political alliance with the PSI as the cornerstone of an alternative government) was becoming untenable. Indeed, a combination of the PSI's collapse, splits in the traditional parties and the emergence of new umbrella movements reopened the question of the PDS's future allies and threw the party into turmoil. Symptomatic of the confusion was the leadership's decision in early 1993 to flirt (temporarily) with the Lega, despite having, until then, presented the PDS as a bastion of protection against the movement. This brought a hostile reaction from Ingrao who reminded the leadership that he had not taken out life membership of the party (and in fact he left the party in May of that year).[2]

More importantly, the birth of the Democratic Alliance (Alleanza Democratica, AD) in early 1993, with Mario Segni at its head, openly divided the party. This question – as will be seen in the next section – would become critical after the passing of the Electoral Reform Bill in the summer of 1993.

Electoral reform

The third issue was more controversial than any other, and saw leading party members campaigning on opposite sides in the referendum campaign.[3] The essential problem for the PDS was that, from 1991 onwards, the main impetus to achieve electoral reform came from political forces which did not favour the PDS's proposed second ballot system. The leadership decided – against the reservations of the left – to sign Mario Segni's 'Referendum Pact' to achieve electoral reform, even though Segni favoured a plurality system which the PDS opposed because it might have had the effect of maintaining the DC's centrality in the system through emphasising its strength in the South. Consequently, when the referendum on the Senate's electoral system (which would introduce a 'mixed' plurality/proportional system) was eventually declared to be constitutionally admissible, the PDS's dilemma was complete: the leadership was strongly in favour of electoral reform in principle, but the referendum would create an electoral system the party did not, in fact, want, and which would in all likelihood lead to a similar reform being implemented in the Chamber of Deputies.

Losing control over the direction of the electoral reform movement resulted in a deep division inside the party, with the two wings openly campaigning against each other. Some members campaigned against the reform, some members were disingenuous (arguing as if the choice were between the *doppio turno* or no reform at all), and some were half-hearted, arguing that they wanted the 'yes' vote to succeed but with a substantial number of 'no' votes to justify the carrying through of a different type of reform for the Chamber of Deputies. Whether or not this last belief was held sincerely (Salvati 1993: 120 argues that it was), the paltry 17.3 per cent who voted against the reform was insufficient to harness cross-party support for the introduction of the second ballot in the Chamber of Deputies: the PDS's proposal was easily rejected by the Parliament and a 'mixed' system adopted in the summer of 1993.

New or old? The PDS's ambivalent identity

If the PCI's XX Congress represented the end of the old party's formal transition into the PDS, it represented only the beginning of the process which would shape the new party, and this process was fraught with problems which undermined the leadership's effort to present the PDS as the chief reformist party which could guide Italy in its transition. Three factors were particularly salient: organisational changes; the persistence of internal divisions; the exposure of corruption in the party's ranks.

Organisational changes were slow to materialise and hesitant in their direction, as was confirmed at the party's National Assembly held in March 1993.[4] Mauro Zani, the Emilian leader responsible for party organisation, stated that the party recognised that the era of the 'party apparatus' was over, and that the organisational practices of the post-war period had to be rethought. The PDS, he said, was prepared to call its traditional form of organisation into question but not in the way that was being demanded by AD (dissolving the party and merging it into a 'party-movement'). Yet the PDS's own organisational project was hardly convincing. Zani spoke of a 'confederal project' of the Left within which a new PDS might participate. The party, he said, was involved in a big organisational experiment which had begun with the abolition of democratic centralism and would now move towards the abolition of centralism itself. But the leadership was equally aware of the danger of acute factionalism if too much central control were relinquished. Occhetto spoke of his belief in a 'third way' between democratic centralism and factionalism which could be achieved through an organisation inspired by the principle of 'decentralised centralism' (*sic*), and he reminded the party of the necessity of internal discipline, baldly challenging (in his closing speech) those who were critical of him to state it openly if they wished him to resign.

In fact, the persistence of internal divisions (the dimensions of which were noted earlier), constituted a considerable hindrance to the new party's consolidation. In particular, the existence in a non-communist organisation of a self-proclaimed 'Democratic Communist' faction weakened the claim that there had been an irrevocable break with the past. Indeed, the PCI's *diversità* (its claim to be 'different' from other parties) which had once been an important source of cohesion in the party quickly became a source of conflict as party members who had opposed the change refused to renounce it, and even many supporting the change failed to adapt quickly to the need for a new culture inside the PDS (Bull 1994).

This failure was exacerbated by the exposure of corruption in the party's ranks. More than anything else, this factor always threatened to engulf the PDS and threw the leadership into a paradoxical dilemma. By the summer of 1993 over 70 members of the party were officially under investigation for corruption, and many of them had been arrested. This number was to increase considerably in the period after October 1993 when Craxi began cooperating with the magistrates and exposing a number of other apparently illicit PDS activities. The allegations – including illegal funding from the Soviet Union, participation in a KGB-run *Gladio* network in Italy, and sharing in many of the kickbacks in contracts for transport, construction and large industry – became progressively more serious in their import and in the personnel involved. May 1993 saw the arrest of the party's ex-treasurer, Renato Pollini (the existing treasurer, Stefanini, had long been under investigation) and the party's controller of the cooperatives responsible for construction activities, Fausto Bartolini. In the summer Massimo D'Alema was implicated in illicit funding activities and rumours abounded that Occhetto himself was next on the list.[5]

The details of this judicial march into the heart of *Botteghe oscure* (the PDS headquarters in Rome) are less relevant than its political effects, which were to spark off a big debate on the role of the PCI in the 'First Republic', and thus the credentials of the PDS for office. That the PCI had never been totally isolated from a share in state patronage had long been well known, but the extent to which it may have apparently participated in a network of illegal kickbacks was a shock to many and caused panic amongst party militants. *La questione morale* had, after all, been turned into a crusade for the PCI under Berlinguer against the ruling parties. The PDS's critics seized on the opportunity to portray the PCI-PDS as never having been different to any of the ruling parties in terms of its domestic activities. The allegations, they argued, confirmed that only genuinely new parties could claim to be above corruption.

The PDS leadership fought a continual rear-guard action to try and prevent these assertions sticking. Paradoxically, the thrust of this (evidently) coordinated action was to emphasise precisely that which the leadership had been, until then, attempting to *overcome*: the party's *diversità*, its distinctiveness from all other political forces. It was argued that there was a clear difference between the 'individual' or isolated instances of PDS corruption and the *system* of corruption which had been operated by the DC and PSI, and that there was a difference between what most PDS officials had been charged with – violating the law on the financing of parties by accepting undeclared (and therefore illegal) contributions to party funds – and that which most DC and PSI officials were charged with – corruption through operating a system of kickbacks for personal and party enrichment. The PDS, Occhetto was at pains to stress time and again, had a 'clean face'; the party had always been, and remained, 'different' to all the others. Many of the accusations, it was suggested, formed part of a plot to prevent the Left coming to power.

This position became increasingly unconvincing and difficult to sustain as the number of allegations and arrests climbed the party hierarchy. The absence of any real explanation, and the silence on the role of Soviet financing left many questions unanswered. More importantly, the use of the generic argument of *diversità* – which, for the leadership, justified the reticence – represented a backwards step with regard to the new party's objectives, which were to free the PDS from this type of association. This prompted ferocious criticism from various quarters and retarded the development of a new culture inside the party, unwittingly giving support to those inside the PDS who had opposed the party's transformation.[6] Indeed, the PDS found itself in a true dilemma: on the one hand, to respond to the criticism (which became more forceful the nearer the election came) that the party was still 'communist', the leadership had to argue that it was no longer 'different' to the other parties; on the other hand, to respond to the criticism of corruption the leadership argued the reverse. The danger was that it was losing both arguments and being perceived as still 'communist' but no 'different' to the other parties when it came to the moral issue. The situation was testing of even the most loyal militant and voter.

REALIGNING THE LEFT (1993–94)

The defeat, in June 1993, of the PDS's proposed electoral reform and the subsequent approval of a single ballot 'mixed' system, changed what were indirect pressures on the PDS to seek new allies into direct ones. The two-ballot method would have enabled the party to retain its independence fully and secure allies after the first ballot. Now all parties, in order to survive, had to forge alliances before the only ballot took place. The subsequent departure of Mario Segni from AD in September 1993, while disappointing for many, freed the PDS to pursue more vehemently an alliance strategy based on a projected bipolarisation of the party system with itself as natural leader of a 'left-of-centre' alliance.

In response to this situation, the party leadership increased the intensity of its campaign to establish the PDS's credentials with the electorate, particularly after the December local elections which confirmed that the party was a major contender for national office. The fight on the moral issue continued, and this was accompanied by a series of high-level meetings to reassure key economic and political elites that the PDS was a reliable political force which no longer presented a threat to the establishment. There can be little doubt that this campaign was partially successful and that the PDS recovered some of its standing in the run-up to the national elections. Local elections and opinion polls suggested that the corruption allegations were not having a detrimental impact on the party's existing level of support, and various public pronouncements confirmed that the 'veto' on the old PCI of the United States government, NATO, *Confindustria*, the international banking community, sectors of Italian industry and the old Centre parties, was a thing of the past. Using this nascent credibility to forge a governing alliance, however, proved more difficult than expected.

Forging the Progressive Alliance[7]

In the late autumn of 1993 Occhetto launched the idea of a grand alliance of progressive forces stretching from the Left to the Centre whose objective would be 'to determine progressively a bipolarisation of the Italian political struggle in which the forces which currently occupy the centre will have to make the decisive choice of whether to stay with the Left or the Right' (*La Repubblica* 4 November 1993). In such an alliance, he said, the PDS was willing to give equal dignity to both small and large forces, and was willing to renounce its own symbol for a common one in the single-member constituencies. For the forces to whom this appeal was addressed this represented an important step. It ended claims to ideological hegemony, and it seemed to bury any pretensions to a pure alliance of the Left which might then extend towards the Centre (in two stages), thus apparently ending the PDS's negativeness towards the so-called 'moderates'.

The problem, however, was what exactly 'progressive' meant, or, put another way, how far such an alliance should stretch to the Left on the one hand and to the centre on the other. Occhetto's response to this question (in an interview in December 1993) was conveniently abstract in content. The alliance, he said, would stop moving rightwards 'at the point where the need for efficiency and the market become enemies of the need for solidarity', and it would stop moving leftwards 'when the need for solidarity and "paradise on earth" clashes with the necessity of guaranteeing an orderly economic development which aspires to the European model' (*La Repubblica* 9 December 1993). This had the potential of including a wide range of forces: the PDS; PSI; *Rinascita Socialista* (both of which were products of the splitting of the old PSI into four groups); the *Rete*; the Greens; the Social-Christians (which had broken away from the old DC); AD and RC. Further, the PDS was insistent that there should be no a priori exclusions of one political force by another.

The formulation of the Progressive Alliance was painfully slow and characterised by intense conflict in which questions of policy and programme became necessarily rather submerged (see Rhodes 1994). The PDS played a primary role in overcoming the opposition of some parties to the inclusion of others, but it was two other factors which eventually forced the issue and pushed the prospective partners together. First, in local elections in December the flexible operation of tactical alliances by the Left led to resounding successes, with PDS-led coalitions gaining control of all six cities where polling took place, and 53 out of 129 local governments – thus confirming both the necessity of an alliance and the PDS as its most influential member. Secondly, the entry of Berlusconi's Forza Italia into the political fray, its search for an alliance with the forces of the Right and its consistent rise in the opinion polls made the need for a coalition around the PDS more pressing, even if this were to be only a 'stopping alliance'.

The Progressive Alliance's programmatic declaration of intent was launched by the eight parties in February 1994, and understandably focused more on intent than programme. Its main points included: an extension of political democracy; decentralisation of power; economic growth; reduction of the public debt; efforts to increase employment; combating abuses of the welfare state; limited privatisation; an increase in the drive against corruption, and improvements in education, training, health and social services.[8] The striking characteristic about this programme was its moderation, something confirmed when the PDS's own election manifesto, closely resembling the Progressives' declaration, was published shortly after. If there was a starting-point it was continuity with Ciampi and a recognition that choices were limited in the existing economic juncture. Indeed, the PDS constantly argued that Ciampi's was the first government which had made genuine progress in key policy areas and that the goal was to build on these achievements. Furthermore, the party was prepared, if necessary, to see Ciampi reappointed as Prime Minister at the head of the Progressive Alliance.

The programme was accompanied by a common symbol (a tri-coloured wave) and stand-down arrangements for single-member constituencies. The latter proved far more difficult to achieve than in the local elections in December, because each of the parties was determined to win as much parliamentary representation as possible. There were fierce accusations by the smaller parties of old-style *lottizzazione* (spoils-sharing), and the arrangements had to be renegotiated in February. The constant divisions which emerged in the Alliance right up to polling day betrayed the fact that the 'realignment' of the Left was primarily a cosmetic operation forced on it by the logic of the new electoral system, and that the election result would determine the Left's real future.

THE 1994 DEFEAT: CAUSES AND CONSEQUENCES

To most observers the defeat of the Left in 1994 was not unexpected, although its scale perhaps was. In relation to all previous elections in the post-war period the percentage obtained by the Progressives (34.6 per cent) was (probably) the lowest 'the Left' (a changing and unclear concept itself) had obtained since the historic 1948 defeat (31 per cent). True, the PDS's share of the vote in the proportional element of the election (which, due to stand-down arrangements in the single member constituencies, provides the most accurate comparison with the past) increased to 20.4 per cent (from 16.1 in 1992), but this figure has to be seen in the context of the complete transformation of the party system between the two elections, and the PDS's failure to exploit the collapse in the DC's and PSI's vote.[9] The strengthening of the PDS in some of its heartlands brought little comfort to a party which had missed its greatest opportunity to win office since the war.

To a large extent, the Left's defeat is best accounted for by explaining the Right's (and particularly Forza Italia's) victory (on which see other chapters in this volume). Nevertheless, several points can be made which start with the Left and which are essential to any overall explanation. First, because the Progressive Alliance was made up of several small parties, it suffered from the new 4 per cent threshold rule for the proportional element of the electoral system: all the parties but the PDS and RC failed to cross the threshold and obtain seats in the proportional allocation, these two providing the bulk of the Progressives' overall number of seats in the Chamber of Deputies. Second, because the Progressive Alliance was formed so late in the day and with such difficulty, the 'joyous war machine' (as Occhetto described it) never had the time to make the transition from tackling its internal problems to campaigning on the basis of a united front. Third, the Progressives were hardly credible as a *governing* alliance. The vast differences between RC and the other partners on various policies confirmed that the formation of a government based on the Alliance was unlikely. Fourth, the Progressives appeared leaderless. This situation contrasted strongly with the Right, where Berlusconi appeared as the leader of the Liberty Alliance and natural candidate for the premiership (despite protestations to the contrary from Bossi), as a consequence of which he proved able to personalise the election campaign. This factor might not have been so important had the party system not undergone so much change. But in a campaign where three – and primarily two – fixed alliances were campaigning as potential governments in waiting, the Progressives appeared to be rooted in the old politics with the direction of the Progressive Alliance dependent upon the negotiating power of the various party leaders.

This introduces the final reason for the Progressives' defeat, which is that the PDS was effectively outwitted in its attempt to be the chief beneficiary of the bipolarisation of the party system. The PDS began to pursue this idea in earnest while the centre and the far right were in disarray, and it was hoping that, once the Progressive Alliance was formed, the party would be able to present the electorate with a choice between a united and reforming Left on the one hand, and an old-style, reactionary and divided Right on the other, with the political forces of the Centre expected to split between the two. Berlusconi's entry into the political arena, however, challenged the PDS on its own chosen terrain, and the party's position, when placed in stark contrast to that of Forza Italia, was found wanting. Berlusconi was able to polarise the choice between several dichotomies – and the PDS's image was on the wrong side of each: first, 'old versus new' (with the PDS struggling to be something new); second, 'change versus no change' (with the PDS representing, by the eve of the election, continuity with Ciampi); third, 'the state versus the market' (with the PDS failing to deal sufficiently with Berlusconi's ferocious assault on the PDS and the Progressives as old-style *statalisti* ('state-lovers')).

The PDS's election defeat, however, should not go unqualified. The historical record suggests that the size of the potential left-wing electorate in Italy has rarely been above 40 per cent (1976 being the exception), so a successful left-wing alliance was always going to be a very difficult task. At the same time, forging a genuine alliance between the Centre and the Left was undermined by the deep-rooted tradition of 'exclusion politics' (of the Left at least). There were simply too many suspicions and reservations on the part of both sides (Segni, Martinazzoli, La Malfa, Amato *et al.* on the one hand; Occhetto, Bordon, Del Turco, Orlando *et al.* on the other) for a new democratic area of the Centre Left to be created in such a short period of time. Finally, many on the Left felt that, in their defeat, something significant had been achieved. For them, the 1989–94 transition period had created the conditions necessary to achieve alternation in government, conditions which had not existed prior to then. True, the Right had emerged victorious, but this, it was expected, would galvanise the forces of the Left and Centre, whose turn to govern would inevitably come.

This view, however, turned out to be premature. It quickly became apparent that Italy's transition was not complete and that the Berlusconi 'experiment' was simply another ephemeral product of Italy's continuing political turmoil. Berlusconi's 'conflict of interests', the judiciary's decision to place the Prime Minister under official investigation for corruption, and his subsequent interrogation by the magistrates, all confirmed for the PDS leadership that Berlusconi's right or legitimacy to govern should be questioned and the government removed as quickly as possible because it represented a threat to democracy. This stance ruled out any form of cooperation with the government, and shifted the emphasis away from a 'positive' type of opposition (along the 'Westminster model') based around the presentation of alternative policies. A combination of the November 1994 local election results (which suggested that Forza Italia's support was waning) and Umberto Bossi's decision to break with the government, assisted the Left in achieving its objective, and Berlusconi – confronted with three no confidence motions – was forced to resign in December 1994. Yet the political crisis which ensued, and the fact that the new government (formed in January 1995) was a technocratic one led by an ex-member of the Bank of Italy, confirmed that the Left's strategy in opposition had a price to pay: the failure to forge an alternative alliance for government by the time the Berlusconi experiment had been brought to an end. Indeed, the period of opposition to the Berlusconi government was marked by an exacerbation of the problems which had brought about the Left's electoral defeat rather than their resolution.

The election defeat's first impact was on the PDS's leadership, and the party became absorbed by a bitter leadership struggle in the spring and summer of 1994. This struggle developed in two stages. In the first stage, pressure was put on Occhetto to resign, particularly by his deputy and heir apparent, Massimo D'Alema. Occhetto resisted these pressures until the European elections in June 1994, the results of which sealed his fate. The PDS vote dropped to 19.5 per cent (from 27.6 per cent in 1989 and 20.3 per cent in the general election of March), and the Progressive parties overall dropped to 31.1 per cent (from 34.4 per cent in March). The second stage was characterised by a contest between Massimo D'Alema and the Occhetto-backed Walter Veltroni (the editor of *L'Unità*) for the leadership – in which the former was elected by 249 votes to 173 in the National Council.[10]

The new leader was then confronted with the critical issue of attempting to rebuild a left-of-centre alliance, because the election defeat's second impact was on the Progressives. After the defeat, the Socialists, RC and AD refused to join a united parliamentary group. Consequently the PDS, La Rete, the Greens and the Social Christians formed a four-party grouping called the Progressive Federation, but such a small group was too small to present itself as an alternative alliance. The PDS declared its new objective to be the forging of a 'coalition of democrats', consisting of all the progressive forces of the Left and Centre, which could present itself as a viable governing alternative when the Berlusconi government fell. In the period of the Berlusconi government this strategy failed not only because the political forces of the centre refused to commit themselves to any alliance of the Centre and Left, but also because the myriad of non-PDS forces on the Left (while not, in principle, against the idea of a 'coalition of democrats'), were not prepared to enter a coalition on the PDS's terms (see Bull 1995b).

Consequently, when Berlusconi resigned in December 1994, the PDS was unable to propose a political alternative to the outgoing coalition, but at the same time, was not prepared to countenance early elections while Berlusconi retained wide-ranging control of the media. The party could do no more than propose a *governo delle regole* (literally a 'government of the rules'), a non-party-based government which would have the task of carrying through fundamental reforms necessary to complete Italy's transition towards a more stable political order. Its subsequent support for Lamberto Dini's new government of technocrats was a reflection, therefore, not only of the failure of the Berlusconi experiment but also of the PDS's own alliance strategy since its election defeat the year before.

NOTES

1 Space does not permit a detailed analysis of the decline of the PDS's electorate and membership, except to note that the party's vote in the 1992 elections dropped by 10.5 per cent (part of this going to the breakaway *Rifondazione comunista*), and its membership plummeted by over 30,000 members during the PCI–PDS transformation (see Daniels and Bull 1994 for a complete analysis).
2 *L'Unità*, 11 January 1993 and 20 January 1993.
3 On the general issue of electoral reform see Simon Parker, Chapter 2.
4 See *L'Unità* and *La Repubblica* 26 March 1993.
5 D'Alema was placed officially under investigation by the magistrates in January 1994.
6 For good (critical) examples of the PDS's position see Anselmi 1993 and Colletti 1993.
7 For a broader treatment of the Progressive Alliance, see Bull 1995a.
8 See *L'Unità* 1 February 1994.
9 In fact, the percentage of seats the PDS gained in the Chamber of Deputies was only 18.25.
10 The leadership succession was unorthodox and controversial. For a detailed account see Bull 1995b.

REFERENCES

Anselmi, T. (1993) 'La diversità strappata', *La Repubblica*, 12 May.
Bull, M. J. (1994) 'Social Democracy's newest recruit? Conflict and cohesion in the Italian Democratic Party of the Left', in D. Bell and E. Shaw (eds), *Conflict and Cohesion in Contemporary Social Democracy*, London: Pinter.
Bull, M. J. (1995a) 'The reconstitution of the political left in Italy: demise, renewal, realignment and . . . defeat', in R. Gillespie (ed.), *Mediterranean Politics* Vol. 2, London: Pinter.
Bull, M. J. (1995b) 'A new nadir for the PDS and the Left', in R. Katz and P. Ignazi (eds), *Italian Politics 1994: The Year of the Tycoon*, Boulder: Westview.

Bull, M. J. and Newell, J. (1993) 'Italian politics and the 1992 elections: from "stable instability" to instability and change', *Parliamentary Affairs*, 46: 2.

Colletti, L. (1993) 'Botteghe Oscure: le prove e la fede', *La Repubblica*, 23 May.

Daniels, P. and Bull, M. J. (1994) 'Voluntary euthanasia: from the Italian Communist Party to the Democratic Party of the Left', in M. Bull and P. Heywood (eds), *West European Communist Parties After the Revolutions of 1989*, London: Macmillan.

Hellman, S. (1993) 'Politics almost as usual: the formation of the Amato government', in G. Pasquino and P. McCarthy (eds), *The End of Post-War Politics in Italy. The Landmark 1992 Elections*, Boulder, Col.: Westview Press.

Ignazi, P. (1992) *Dal PCI al PDS*, Bologna: Il Mulino.

Italian Politics. A Review (1992–93), various editors, London: Pinter.

Rhodes, M. (1994) 'Reinventing the left: the origins of Italy's Progressive Alliance', in C. Mershon and G. Pasquino (eds), *Italian Politics. A Review*, Vol. 9, London: Pinter.

Salvati, M. (1993) 'The travail of Italian Communism', *New Left Review*, 202, Nov.–Dec.

11 The 'Left Opposition' and the crisis
Rifondazione Comunista and La Rete

John M. Foot

The Italian Left did not provoke the economic and political crisis of 1989–94; nor did the Left benefit from that crisis politically, as the elections of 1994 revealed. Most ex-DC and PSI voters backed the Right. The Progressive Alliance failed to win over those who had supported previous governments for so long. But the crisis after 1989, and particularly after 1992 and the 'clean hands' investigations, did rupture for ever the way the Left is structured and organised in Italy. Most important of all was the transformation of the PCI into the PDS. Also the new electoral system forced the Left to unify itself for the first time since 1948, in the umbrella group called the Progressives. In addition the early 1990s saw the formation of two new political groupings on the far Left of the Italian political scene. The first, Rifondazione Comunista (RC), was initially seen as merely the 'Stalinist' rump of the old die-hard wing of the PCI. However, through a combination of opposition to the economic reforms imposed by the Amato and Ciampi governments and street-based activity, RC established itself as the second biggest force on the Left in Italy. Meanwhile, the second new grouping La Rete (the Network), a 'movement for democracy' formed in 1990, suffered such a serious defeat at the polls in 1994 that its political life as an independent force seemed in danger. Yet, throughout Italy's so-called 'democratic revolution', La Rete represented an important component of the Left's hopes for radical political and social change. Its prioritisation of the anti-Mafia struggle in both the North and South did much to weaken the old DC-PSI political machine in Palermo *and* Milan. This chapter will examine the role of these two political forces during the Italian crisis. Its focus will be both electoral and social, looking at the way that La Rete and Rifondazione Comunista have looked to influence events both at the polls and in terms of movements within civil society. I will begin with Rifondazione Comunista (RC).

KEEP THE RED FLAG FLYING! THE FORMATION OF RIFONDAZIONE COMUNISTA

A substantial minority within the PCI were opposed to Achille Occhetto's decision to transform the PCI into a social-democratic party in 1990. Nearly 35 per cent of the party's delegates failed to vote for Occhetto's motion – and among the opposition leaders were several important personalities. This represented one of the biggest 'revolts' against a leadership decision in the party's history. However, the great majority of these dissidents eventually opted to join the PDS, respecting the decision of the majority of the party to follow Occhetto. Only a tiny minority of delegates, led by Armando Cossutta, who had won a mere 3.3 per cent of the votes for his motion at the 1990 congress, actually decided to leave the party. The final, long-announced division took place at Rimini, at the founding conference of the PDS, in February 1991. At first, this split was judged to be virtually irrelevant. Yet over time, many tens of thousands left the PCI for what was to become Rifondazione Comunista. A number of those associated with the left wing within the PCI decided to break with Occhetto in 1990 and form a new political grouping – a party of social opposition and of pride in the Italian communist tradition, its symbols and its name, a party based on the struggles of the dwindling industrial proletariat. There may well have been the 'lack of a great exodus' (Hellman 1993: 127) from the PDS towards the RC, but the party still managed to attract around 150,000 members (organised in 600 circles) by May 1991 (Hellman 1993: 127). A more accurate figure of 129,000 members was given in October 1993.[1] Above all, many of those who left were the most active members of the PCI, those most involved in grassroots organisation and protest. The PCI lost, according to its own figures, 142,272 members (10.6 per cent) between 1989 and 1991, the biggest such loss in the party's history (Kertzer 1992: 92).

In fact, RC has been able to continue the traditions of the old PCI (with *feste* and local meetings) with almost as much success as the far larger PDS. This tradition of militancy was maintained partly through the use of the classic symbols of the PCI – the hammer and sickle and the red flag. In fact, RC and the PDS were involved in a near-farcical court case in 1991 over the use of the old symbol of the PCI and the buildings and resources of the old party. Although the PDS eventually won its case, the RC symbol presented at the elections was remarkably similar to that of the old PCI, and complaints from within the PDS rumbled on. Many PDS leaders really believed that a large number of RC voters had chosen Rifondazione just because of these similarities.

June 1991 was a crucial month for RC; Democrazia Proletaria (DP), the last remaining party from the far Left 'boom' of the 1960s and 1970s, decided to dissolve itself and merge with RC. DP was a mixed party, deeply divided between a northern-based workerist tendency and other groups of feminists, greens and libertarians. It had always been deeply opposed to the politics of the PCI and to any favourable view of the Soviet Union. The decision to dissolve itself with RC therefore signalled that the end of the Cold War had marginalised previously crucial differences of opinion about the East and 'real socialism'. Before the fall of the Berlin Wall, any alliance with a figure like Cossutta, renowned for his support for the Soviet regime (and opposition to Gorbachev), would have been unthinkable. In fact, RC's unity has been maintained above all around questions of Italian internal politics and struggle – and far more through opposition to various governments, the union leadership and reform proposals than through positive ideas for change. Nonetheless, Cossutta did show a certain capacity for self-criticism. In May 1991 he argued that 'those regimes [of the Eastern bloc] had no foundation at all in the consciousness of the workers, of the people, of the young' (*Il Manifesto* 3 May 1991).[2]

In December 1991, after a series of consultative provincial congresses, the Partito della Rifondazione Comunista was officially formed. Its structure was remarkably similar to that of the old PCI, with a 16-strong executive and 20 regional directorates.[3] Sergio Garavini, an ex-PCI and CGIL militant who favoured alliances with the PDS was elected party secretary. Although Rifondazione was able to count on the support of a large minority of journalists on the independent left-wing daily *Il Manifesto*, the new party decided to launch its own weekly paper, *Liberazione*, in 1991.

Paolo Natale and Roberto Borcio have engaged in wide-ranging research on the sources of the vote for Rifondazione Comunista in the 1992 general elections. This unpublished research provides us with the best analysis available of the geography and socio-political basis of RC's support (Borcio and Natale 1992). The 1992 elections saw the three major Italian parties (PCI/PDS, DC, PSI) lose around 25 per cent of their combined support: 5.6 per cent of this vote went to Rifondazione Comunista.[4] In the lower house, RC won 27 seats and 1,560,000 votes, and eight Rifondazione Senators were also elected (Di Virgilio January to June 1992). In terms of regional diversity, RC did best (in terms of absolute percentages) in the so-called 'red' regions of Italy, the Centre-North of the country. The party did better in terms of members and votes in Tuscany than in Emilia. Tuscan Communism is traditionally more radical and less reformist than its Emilian variant. RC obtained more than 10 per cent of the vote in the provinces of Arezzo, Perugia and Massa. Interestingly, in these areas the split had a beneficial effect on the PDS/ RC combined vote, which reached more than that of the PCI in 1990. On the other hand, Rifondazione did badly in parts of Sicily (especially around Palermo and Messina), in the Trentino and in the Veneto. These results were not necessarily translatable across, for example, the South as a whole. In Calabria and Basilicata the party performed creditably, a trend which was repeated in the 1994 elections. However, these results mask a trend which was to become clearer with the local elections in 1993. Rifondazione took more votes away (in terms of percentages *on the Left*) from the PDS (or the old PCI) *outside* its traditional 'red zones'. In central Italy, the classic attachment to the PDS (and deference to the PCI leadership) kept most of their votes intact. Thus in Emilia-Romagna, the Marche, Tuscany and Umbria, Rifondazione won 8.7 per cent to the PDS's 28.5 per cent (less than 30 per cent), whilst in the 'white' regions (Trentino, Veneto, Friuli) this proportion reached 40 per cent – and in the areas with high concentrations of heavy industry (Piedmont, Liguria and Lombardy) the same figure was closer to 44 per cent (Borcio and Natale 1992: 9).

In all, between 75 and 80 per cent of RC votes across Italy were drawn from former PCI electors (Borcio and Natale 1992: 22). Not surprisingly, 95 per cent of RC voters had not chosen governing parties in 1987, confirming the party's identity as one of firm opposition (Borcio and Natale 1992: 22). However, when Natale looked at the break-up of the PCI vote in 1992, when for the first time in the history of the Republic huge numbers of voters deserted the largest left party (its support fell from 26.6 per cent in 1987 to 16.1 per cent in 1992), he found a slightly different story. Over the whole of Italy, only 58 per cent of ex-PCI voters not choosing the PDS plumped for Rifondazione. This figure reached its maximum in the 'red' areas of the Centre-North (70 per cent) and its minimum in the North-East, Northern League territory (50 per cent). The diaspora of ex-communist voters had begun to spread their wings, and many chose to leave the Left altogether (or not even to vote) (Borcio and Natale 1992: 22–24). Natale concluded that 'the option to vote for RC... is therefore characterised... by a type of electorate decisively oriented towards a vote of opposition or protest' (Borcio and Natale 1992: 24). In the summer of 1992 this protest was to spread across Italy.

On 31 July 1992, on the eve of the August holidays and without consulting their memberships, the leaders of Italy's three biggest trade union confederations signed an agreement with the employers which effectively abolished the automatic price-wage indexer (the *scala mobile*) and opened the way to wage cuts for their members. This agreement sparked off a storm of protest, especially when added to the effects of the austerity package announced by the Amato government in September 1992. The three trade union federations called a series of protest demonstrations and general strikes against the Amato measures in September to October 1992, but these mass meetings only served to unleash a wave of anger against these very leaders. Nuts and bolts were thrown at CGIL leader Bruno Trentin during a huge demonstration in Florence, and Sergio D'Antoni of the CISL was hit by a missile in Milan. Although Garavini of Rifondazione condemned single acts of violence, RC took a tougher

opposition line than the PDS. This opposition intensified with the formation of the Ciampi government in April 1993. In Parliament the PDS lent
Ciampi's administration tacit support whilst RC voted against. And on
the crucial votes for the budget in December, which contained measures
for swingeing tax increases and public spending cuts, the PDS voted in
favour. Rifondazione, meanwhile, continued its protests both inside and
outside Parliament. A huge demonstration was organised in Rome by the
factory councils, workers' base committees and Rifondazione in February
1993, and links were strengthened with leading figures on the Left of the
PDS, including Pietro Ingrao (who left the party) as well as Leoluca
Orlando of La Rete and the left wing of the Green movement.

1993 also saw continuing initiatives towards the *polo dell'alternativa* –
a grouping of movements, parties and associations on the Left. A series
of meetings were held to discuss various areas of policy (without any
agreement on final motions or documents) and congresses were addressed
by Ingrao and Garavini. These meetings showed the possibility of a more
open Left, one which, as Galasso argued, 'respects differences whilst
seeking to establish a collective identity' (*Il Manifesto* 11 July 1993).[5] At
the same time a number of big demonstrations were organised without the
official auspices of either the PDS or the CGIL. Most impressive of all
was the huge march at Rome held on 25 September 1993, called by the
factory council movement and other independent unions, when 300,000
trade unionists and activists marched through the streets of the city.[6] This
demonstration was instrumental in the later defection of Fausto Bertinotti,
leader of the minority opposition movement within the CGIL, *Essere
Sindacato*, to the RC leadership (along with 30 trade unionists and
intellectuals) in the same month.

The continuing opposition to the policies of the Amato and Ciampi
governments bore fruit in the local elections of June 1993. Dissatisfaction
on the Left with the line followed by Occhetto saw Rifondazione overtake
the PDS (and become the biggest party on the Left) in two of the most
important cities for the traditional Left – Milan and Turin. This was a
remarkable result: in Milan RC won 11.4 per cent of the vote to the
PDS's 8.8 per cent, and in Turin the difference was even greater – 14.4
and 9.5 per cent respectively. June 1993 saw a confirmation of the trends
identified in the 1992 results – a tendency for Rifondazione to eat much
further into PDS support in the northern industrial cities. Hence, RC did
relatively badly in the areas where the PDS did best – Siena, Ravenna
and Ancona, winning only one council seat in the former two cities and
none at all in the latter. It is also clear that the domination of certain
factions of the old PCI in Milan and Turin (the so-called *miglioristi*, close
politically to Craxi's PSI), and the involvement of top PCI functionaries
in *Tangentopoli* had affected the PDS's support.

The key question Rifondazione has had to face throughout its short
existence as a party is that of 'left unity'. What is its relationship with

the other left groupings and the PDS in particular? In the initial period of growth and protest, Rifondazione chose to attack the PDS leadership (and that of the trade unions). The bitter leadership struggles of June to July 1993, which ended with the removal of Garavini as Secretary and the confirmation of Cossutta's more autonomous line, were based around the very question of links with the PDS and 'left unity'. Garavini was in favour of a 'rapprochement' with Occhetto, Cossutta firmly opposed. In the run-up to local elections in mid-1993, certain alliances were formed at a local level (nearly always unsuccessfully, as in Milan behind Nando Dalla Chiesa's candidature for mayor) but elsewhere there were bitter electoral battles with the PDS, most notably in Turin where a straight fight between two left candidates (Diego Novelli and Valentino Castellani) showed how difficult in practice it could be to unite the forces of the Left. However, tactically at least, all this was transformed by the crushing victory of the 'Yes' vote in Segni's 1993 referendums, which signalled the end of the PR voting system. Rifondazione was forced, without making any real political shift, into a tactical alliance with other left groupings for local elections. The alternative was the electoral wilderness. The November 1993 vote produced the illusion of success, with victories for candidates backed by RC, the PDS and other left groupings in Rome, Genoa, Venice and, most remarkably of all, Naples. Beneath the euphoria produced by these triumphs, the left alliance was in serious trouble, and the Right was beginning to unite at last.

BETWEEN PALERMO AND MILAN: THE DEVELOPMENT OF LA RETE

The Rete movement has its origins in two experiences at opposite ends of Italy. Both began in the mid-1980s. In Palermo, Leoluca Orlando's 'anti-Mafia' administration, the so-called 'Palermo spring', originated within the Christian Democratic Party. In Milan, the Società Civile pressure group, formed in 1985, was the first to denounce the system of corruption which later took the name *Tangentopoli* (Kickback City). Both these experiences concentrated their efforts on exposing the infiltration of organised crime and illegality into all levels of civic life – and particularly political life – through the DC in Sicily and the PSI in Milan. The leaders of the two movements – Orlando and, in Milan, Nando Dalla Chiesa – were acknowledged as 'front-line' fighters in the anti-Mafia struggle. They were both to be founding members of La Rete in 1991. But to fully understand La Rete we need first to examine these movements of the mid-1980s.

It is difficult to separate La Rete's origins in Palermo from the figure of Leoluca Orlando. A brilliant law student, Orlando was educated at Palermo's Jesuit school (where he came under the influence of the priest Ennio Pintacuda).[7] In 1975 he joined the Sicilian DC, linking himself to the 'left' faction led by Piersanti Matarella. He worked for the Sicilian regional government under Matarella's presidency. Matarella himself was killed by the Mafia in 1980, after beginning to investigate the allocation of building contracts. Orlando continued his career within the DC and, with (hesitant) support from the then party secretary Ciriaco De Mita, became Mayor of Palermo in 1985. 1986 was a crucial year for the anti-Mafia struggle, as it saw the first of a series of maxi-trials (the *maxi-processi*) of Mafia suspects. Orlando took the unprecedented step as Mayor (apart from using the word 'Mafia') of attending the trial, sitting with the families of Mafia victims and making the city of Palermo *parte civile* in the trial. The Mayor became the centre of national and international media attention. The 'Palermo spring' had begun.

In 1987, after a series of bitter debates in the press over Orlando's 'anti-Mafia' credentials,[8] the governing coalition in the council broke up under pressure from national party leaders. Orlando decided to form a new coalition without the PSI and with support from anti-Mafia movements on the council. After a series of clashes with national politicians, especially the socialist deputy leader Claudio Martelli and De Mita, in August a new council administration was sworn. The PCI's abstention was crucial. The council limped along with a tiny majority until 1989, when the PCI officially joined the council. But this short-lived experience was brought to a halt in 1990 when Orlando resigned as Mayor, having refused to bow to national pressures and form a 'new' *pentapartito* administration.

What did the 'Palermo spring' actually represent? A very clear distinction needs to be made between the symbolic value of the Palermo spring and its concrete achievements. At a symbolic level, internationally as well as nationally, Orlando's council represented the first example of an anti-Mafia political movement coming from within the Sicilian political system. Certain sections of civil society were given encouragement in their daily struggles against *Cosa Nostra* by this very fact alone. With the *maxi-processo* the Mafia suffered the arrest and conviction of many of its leaders for the first time. Orlando's support for these trials, on behalf of the Palermo council, was crucial. However, very little else was actually done by the council administration. Most of the initiatives that were taken were also purely symbolic – such as the appointment of eminent urban historians to a commission to examine plans for Palermo's redevelopment. At best, the 'Palermo spring' can be seen as a tentative (and incomplete) beginning to the battle against the Mafia.

Meanwhile, in Milan, an analogous movement was taking shape – Società Civile. Nando Dalla Chiesa, a university professor and son of General Dalla Chiesa, the Prefect of Palermo killed by the Mafia in 1982, began to dedicate his life to political activism. He founded, with the help of journalists such as Corrado Stajano and judges including Gherardo Colombo, later a key figure in the *mani pulite* investigations, the organisation's journal which became an important focus for opposition to Craxi's control of the city and its resources, and of investigation into political corruption and the infiltration of the Mafia into Northern business (Dalla Chiesa 1994: 65–85). Società Civile identified, at the height of Craxi's popularity, the system of *tangenti* and crime-linked corruption which was later to explode as *Tangentopoli* and the 'Duomo Connection'. The paper identified the key figures in the system – Ligresti, Pilliteri, the Craxi family – and named names. It linked up the experiences of Palermo and Milan, and Dalla Chiesa, who had first met Orlando in September 1985, was profoundly influenced by the 'spring'.[9] Nonetheless, Società Civile remained a small movement on the margins of organised politics, a voice in the dark until the explosion of the *mani pulite* investigations in 1992.

Orlando was re-elected to Palermo's local council in 1990 with a massive 71,000 personal preference votes. Yet, because he was unable to form an administration which was not that desired by national government leaders, he left the DC in November 1990. By then, the Rete had already begun to function. A meeting at Trento in August 1990 identified the principles of the movement, but the official announcement of the Rete's birth came on 21 March 1991, when Orlando claimed that 'La Rete is not born today, it already exists'. The founders of La Rete made many claims for their new political grouping: that it was not a party – but a 'network'; a 'new political subject'; a 'movement for democracy' (the Rete's subtitle); a link between Milan and Palermo, between the Church, dissident Catholics and the Left. Orlando argued that 'La Rete lives in society ... and will never transform itself into a party' (*L'Espresso* 4 November 1990).[10] Whilst there were undoubtably large elements of wishful thinking in these claims, La Rete did try to link up a series of groups working in civil society.

The founding documents of La Rete were a heady mix of Christian values, anti-Mafia ideals, puritanical morality and libertarianism, although in later documents the specifically Catholic aspects of the programme were toned down. Positive proposals included the abolition of parliamentary immunity, more protection and power to the judiciary to fight organised crime, and a reduction in the number of Parliamentarians. In April 1991 La Rete launched its symbol (a group of blue and white youthful figures against a red background) and welcomed into its fold the former Communist Mayor of Turin, Diego Novelli. Novelli was close to La Rete in terms of his stance on the 'moral question', having denounced corruption in Turin whilst Mayor in 1985, and resigned over scandals involving his administration.[11]

La Rete fielded candidates for the first time in Sicily's regional elections of June 1991. The movement won 7.3 per cent of the vote and five seats on the regional council. Nearly half of these votes came in Palermo (where La Rete reached 16.3 per cent), and were mainly at the cost of the Left and far Right (Di Virgilio 1992). Encouraged by these results,

Orlando and his followers decided to mount a serious campaign for the general election of April 1992. In the meantime, the system of *Tangentopoli* in Milan was starting to unravel. Mario Chiesa was arrested in February 1992 and all Società Civile's hard work of muckraking and agitation seemed to be bearing fruit, at last. The 1992 elections gave La Rete a national profile for the first time, and showed they were not just a Sicilian party. Despite standing candidates in only two-thirds of constituencies, the movement picked up 1.9 per cent of the national share and won 12 seats in the lower house and three in the Senate. Seats were won in eight cities and seven regions, with concentrations in Trento (13.3 per cent) and Turin (4.3 per cent). However, nobody had predicted the scale of the result in Sicily. La Rete won a massive 24.5 per cent of the vote in Palermo and over 9 per cent in Siracusa, Agrigento and Trapani. This was a triumph for such a new party and seriously threatened the DC's traditional hegemony in Sicily. Nonetheless, there was also a worrying tendency for the party to anchor itself to a few, charismatic leaders with their own power bases – Novelli in Turin, Dalla Chiesa in Milan (who won more than 36,000 preferences – a result he was to repeat in 1994) and, of course, Orlando (Di Virgilio 1992). A new group of deputies entered Parliament, and their influence was to be far greater than their numbers.

The *Tangentopoli* crisis and anti-Mafia investigations of 1992–94 seemed to vindicate completely La Rete's stance on public morality. In Milan, politicians and businessmen whom Società Civile had been denouncing, almost alone, for years, were brought down by the *mani pulite* judges. In Sicily, investigations were launched into links between Andreotti and Mafia bosses. Repentant mafiosi and corrupt politicians came forward in droves. La Rete, previously a voice in the wilderness, was thrust to the centre of Italian politics. Società Civile announced, 'It's all over' (April 1992).[12] Craxi accused Milan's judges (especially Colombo) of being inspired by Rete-type politics. Politically, however, Rete candidates did not benefit from the scandals. Nando Dalla Chiesa's campaign for Mayor of Milan ended in heavy defeat by an uninspiring Northern League candidate. Novelli, another prominent Rete member, lost in Turin. Claudio Fava was narrowly defeated in Catania. But in November 1993 Orlando stood again in Palermo, this time as Rete leader and not a DC politician. He obtained an extraordinary 75 per cent of the votes. La Rete (whose list won over 32 per cent) controlled the local council in the heart of Mafia territory. Local councillors included Capponetto, head of the Palermo anti-Mafia 'pool' of judges. A revolution appeared to have taken place in Sicily. As Ginsborg wrote in early 1994, 'to find another similar success of a "radical" at Palermo, we have to go back to Garibaldi. Seen from abroad the Sicilian situation seems a revolution or, at least, a cultural revolution' (Ginsborg 1994: 16). Yet, within four months this progress was to be brutally and unexpectedly reversed in the general elections of

March 1994. Before turning to this let us first consider the defects of La
Rete.

La Rete has been the subject of bitter and sometimes vicious criticism
during its short life. These attacks can be summarised into four main
points. First, La Rete has been accused of 'extremism', of being a 'Jacobin
party' (Dalla Chiesa 1994: 10, 28, 89 and 90). Whilst there are elements
of truth here, particularly with regard to the language of Orlando and
others, the extent of the corruption of the 'regime' in the 1980s certainly
did not encourage a moderate response. Second, La Rete has been seen
as lacking in its respect for individual rights within the criminal justice
system. The so-called 'culture of suspicion' backed by Rete leaders can
easily lead (and did lead) to false accusations, damaging rumours and
false arrest. For the Rete leadership, it was better that one innocent was
falsly accused than 100 guilty *mafiosi* or corrupt politicians be allowed to
escape punishment: hence La Rete's support for long terms of prevent-
ative imprisonment (widely used by the *mani pulite* judges), and above
all for the reliance on supergrasses and state's witnesses (*pentiti*). Whilst
the use of *pentiti* has clearly played a crucial role in exposing *Tangentopoli*
and in the battle against the Mafia, it also carried extreme dangers for
individual justice where no other proof was required. A large number of
people were imprisoned in the 1980s and 1990s without any 'objective'
proof being available. Although this criticism can occasionally come from
unexpected quarters, its validity in terms of the general workings of the
justice system is unquestionable. *Pentiti* are easily manoeuvred for political
ends, and even Orlando himself was named by one *pentito* in Sicily.[13] This
takes us neatly to the third and most serious criticism of La Rete. For
some commentators, from both the Left and the Right, it was inconceiv-
able that an 'anti-Mafia' movement could emerge from the DC in Sicily
in the 1980s. For these critics (who confined their attacks on La Rete to
the Sicilian experience), Orlando was in some way linked to the system
of organised crime, and the 'Palermo spring' was essentially a form of
'bluff' which changed little. The writer Leonardo Sciascia had made a
similar point in 1987 in his famous article denouncing 'anti-Mafia professionals' in the *Corriere della Sera*. This argument can neither be proved
nor disproved; it is either accepted or rejected largely on the basis of
political prejudice.

Certainly, the 'Palermo spring' achieved little concretely against the
Mafia. But even if we take only the support for the prosecution in
the *maxi-processo*, it did more than had been done over the previous 40
years. And its symbolic effect was as important as the real content of its
policies.[14] Perhaps it is fairer to criticise La Rete in Sicily for an excessively
political vision of the Mafia. Without changes in the economics and
culture of Sicily and the South as a whole, and without dealing with the
international drugs trade, very little can be done against organised crime
in the *Mezzogiorno*. Finally, the Rete has been called an opportunist

political movement, ready to shift its tactics and ideas in line with sudden political developments. This tendency was most evident in the 1993 referendum campaign, when La Rete leadership called, disastrously, for a 'No' vote – that is, to keep the proportional voting system. Orlando had been a strong backer of Segni's crusade for electoral reform and Dalla Chiesa was a declared supporter of a majoritarian voting system. The arguments given for this shift – that a Parliament made up of corrupt politicians would delay reform for years – proved to be unfounded, and the change to 'No' smacked of 'small-party self-preservation' on the part of La Rete.[15]

RIFONDAZIONE, LA RETE AND THE 1994 ELECTIONS

Both La Rete and Rifondazione joined the left-wing Progressive Alliance formed to fight the 1994 elections, but Orlando's movement was far more enthusiastic about the organisation than Bertinotti's. The very nature of the shift by RC towards the PDS – dictated as it was not by shared political ideals but by the changes in the electoral system – meant that the 1994 Progressive Alliance (and this is crystal clear in the very few combined documents that were produced – triumphs of vagueness and completely lacking in positive proposals) was a shaky one. Rifondazione refused to 'play the game' during the campaign, attacking Ciampi's record (Bertinotti called him 'a man of the Right' (*La Repubblica* 17 December 1993) and pushing its own, very different agenda.[16] This type of campaign, which served Rifondazione as a party very well in terms of results (the 4 per cent barrier in the PR section of the vote also helped, pushing other left voters towards RC), did great damage to the chances of victory of the Progressives.

Although RC went into the 1994 elections in alliance with the PDS, and even with centre groupings like Alleanza Democratica, it looked to maintain its own, separate identity within the Progressives. RC's 29-page programme, 'La forza dell'alternativa' (Rifondazione Comunista 1994) was based around three main principles: the defence of employment (through government intervention and the introduction of a 35-hour week); the 'Rebirth of the Mezzogiorno' (again through state spending and a more 'energetic' fight against the forces of organised crime), and fiscal reform (more taxes for the rich, less for the poor and working class). The programme also called for an extension of the welfare state, increases in pensions, and strongly opposed any privatisation of the health service, education, telephones, the banks and universities. Further spending was proposed for housing and there were elaborate proposals for the reform of the public administration 'which do not mean that employees can be sacked' (Rifondazione Comunista 1994). The state was also to double its investment in the justice system. In the international field, the party opposed military intervention in the former Yugoslavia, called for the '*superamento* of NATO', drastic reforms in the structure of the UN, and argued for the need to 'overturn the logic of the Treaty of Maastricht, dominated by the supremacy of finance capital'. Immigrant rights were to be defended and increased through public investment. For any opponent of RC the obvious question was – where was all the money to come from, in a country with a record public debt?

The programme only talked about further income for the state in terms of more taxes on the rich, confiscation of the wealth of the Mafia and corrupt politicians and cuts in defence spending. When Bertinotti attempted to offer a more specific proposal by calling for taxes on public bonds (the *Bot*) during the campaign, he caused an immediate storm of protest from within and outside the Progressive Alliance. In general, RC's programme represented the hard-line state-based politics which the PDS had been attempting to move away from through its support for the Ciampi government (and its privatisation programme). The RC's much-vaunted 'acceptance of privatisation' (explicit in the Progressives' programme) remained unclear given the vetoes put on the areas not to be privatised in the RC programme. Ideologically, the party placed itself well to the left of the PDS during the campaign, calling for 'democracy . . . in the factories, in the offices, in all of society'.

La Rete went into the 1994 general election as a crucial component of the Progressive Alliance. But the election saw Orlando's movement emerge as clear losers, and the aftermath of the election was marked by bitter debate, the departure of leading figures (most notably Dalla Chiesa) and calls for the dissolution of the party. Why did the Rete move from its greatest triumph to electoral disaster in a matter of a few months? Many of the answers to this question lay outside the power of the Rete or its leaders – the weaknesses in the Progressive Alliance, the problems of leadership and alliances and, most importantly, the formation of Forza Italia in early 1994. However, there were elements of the Rete campaign and political strategy which aided its undoubted defeat. First, the insistence on presenting a separate party list in the PR section of the vote was a mistake. La Rete's 2 per cent did not get near the 4 per cent barrier required to elect deputies in the PR section of the election, and these votes were, literally, thrown away. Pollsters had been saying for months that La Rete had no chance of achieving 4 per cent of the national vote. Before the election Dalla Chiesa, amongst others, had proposed an alliance with the Greens and AD to prevent just such a waste of votes. Orlando refused. Second, the Rete joined an alliance without being fully committed to its other members. This was clear from the attacks on the inclusion of the PSI list (as well as that of AD and Rifondazione) at La Rete's national assembly in January 1994 (and afterwards) (*La Repubblica* 17 January 1994).[17] Third, La Rete was over-confident about the stability of its success in Palermo, and the transmission of that success to a national stage. As things turned out, the party lost votes everywhere, and even in

Sicily, to Forza Italia and to the PDS. Orlando's undisputed leadership (he was reelected 'coordinator' at the January Congress, for a further two years, with 168 out of 173 votes – being the only candidate) over the movement made the identification Rete–Palermo unavoidable. For Giampaolo Pansa La Rete had built up a movement of 'extraordinary youth and energy' in many ways ignored by its leaders who were 'too proud of their own small strength and... arrogant'. There had been a 'record number of errors' following the victory in Palermo (*L'Espresso*, 22 April 1994).[18]

As for the results themselves, only two left parties actually gained votes in the 1994 election – the PDS and RC. Rifondazione increased its seats from 27 to 41 in the Camera and from 8 to 18 in the Senate. Overall, the party won 6 per cent of the vote, compared to 5.6 per cent in 1992. These results were substantially confirmed in the European elections of 12 June 1994, with 6.1 per cent nationally and five MEPs. But this was small compensation for the overall crushing defeat of the Left, and the victory of the Polo della Libertà even in traditional left strongholds such as Turin-Mirafiori and even Sesto San Giovanni. The new electoral system and political changes meant that RC candidates were concentrated in the left regions of central Italy and in parts of the South – Campania, Sardinia and Calabria in particular. The 1993 successes were repeated in Turin (where Bertinotti and Rizzo won their seats) and Genoa but not in Milan.

The vote for La Rete reflected the errors of the leadership and the vacuum in the centre filled by Forza Italia. La Rete gained roughly the same amount of votes nationally as it had in 1992, with far more candidates and a much more high-profile campaign. Dalla Chiesa was the most popular left candidate in Milan, but had little chance against a combination of Forza Italia and the Northern League. In Sicily, where the Progressives had conceded large numbers of candidates to La Rete during the carve-up negotiations, the results were an unexpected disaster. Anti-Mafia judge Caponetto was heavily defeated in Palermo by an unknown candidate, Claudio Fava lost by 20 per cent in Catania: La Rete had failed in its stronghold. Over the whole of Sicily, the progressives won a mere four of the 41 head-to-head battles. The Euro-elections which followed saw La Rete take a mere one per cent of the national vote – enough to elect an MEP (Orlando himself) under the PR system. Although the movement gained over 220,000 votes in the 'Islands' constituency, its percentage vote represented a further fall from the March result. The only compensation for Orlando was the strength of his personal vote at Palermo, where the Mayor was the only candidate in urban Italy to beat Berlusconi's preference vote – winning 91,000 as opposed to 76,000 for the leader of Forza Italia.

CONCLUSION: IS THERE A FUTURE FOR THE LEFT OPPOSITION?

In 1994 Rifondazione ran a campaign from within the Progressive Alliance without fully supporting that alliance. Bertinotti distanced himself from the PDS by arguing that 'you don't win over the workers by visiting the City of London or by promoting continuity with the Ciampi government' (*Liberazione* 1 April 1994).[19] This reasoning was very similar to that of left leaders such as Ken Livingstone and Tony Benn after the Labour Party's defeat in 1983. The formation of a separate RC parliamentary group after the election, and the separate campaign for the European elections only underlined this trend. RC remains a party with a deep-rooted sub-cultural base and a clear role on the far left of Italian politics. Rifondazione supporters expect their leaders to form short-term electoral alliances, but there is far more opposition to any long-term project involving left unity with the PDS.

The immediate aftermath of the election was characterised by bitter debate within La Rete. Carmine Mancuso and even Father Ennio Pintacuda attacked the politics of La Rete and the running of the campaign.[20] Caponnetto resigned as President of the Palermo council. At the National Assembly in April, Dalla Chiesa, a 'founding father' of La Rete, who had criticised Orlando's leadership in January 1994,[21] left the movement. Dalla Chiesa argued for more concentration on movements within civil society and against a big left party which would merely be 'a kind of enlarged PDS'. Orlando himself claimed he was ready to dissolve the movement into a larger Democratic Party, the 'real objective' of the Rete since its formation (*La Repubblica* 15 April 1994).[22] However, La Rete would continue to exist as long as it was 'useful' for the country. Orlando saw himself as a possible leader of such a party, despite his own party's heavy defeat.[23] Unlike Rifondazione, La Rete is not a relatively stable sub-cultural party with a mass membership and strong links to the trade unions. La Rete is a much more shifting public-opinion-oriented force, relying on media attention and a few charismatic leaders and with mass backing only in Palermo. Rete members are overwhelmingly young and middle class. Many have links with the Church. Politically, the limited nature of Rete support, both geographically and numerically, makes alliances essential. Hence the strong support from Rete leaders for more binding forms of left unity and the merging of Rete deputies and senators in the Progressives' parliamentary group. Emerging divisions between the Rete organisation in its two centres, Milan and Sicily, make it more likely that the movement will shift to more of a pressure group role than in the past. Nonetheless, La Rete remains an important force in the social and political make-up of the country, and any plans for a rebirth of the Italian Left must deal with and take into account the forces and ideas represented both by Orlando's party and by Rifondazione Comunista.

NOTES

1 *Liberazione* 21 January 1994.
2 'Rifondazione Comunista: chi sono, cosa vogliono', *Il Manifesto* 3 May 1991. In March 1991 the militants from the old New Left grouping, the PDUP, decided to leave the PDS for Rifondazione.
3 'Da Rifondazione a Partito', *Il Manifesto* 4 May 1991.
4 The DP vote should also be considered though (1.5% in 1987) (Borcio and Natale 1992: 2). In fact, Natale's figures put the national PCI–RC shift at only 3.6%, with 0.2% coming from the Radical Party, 0.5% from non-voters, 0.2% from DP and 0.2% from 'others' (pp. 17–18). For the destiny of the DP vote, only a small part of which finished with the RC, see ibid., pp. 23–24.
5 A. Garzia and P. Sullo, 'Ingrao: "Nasce il polo dell'alternativa" ', *Il Manifesto* 11 July 1993.
6 Rifondazione also supported the riots and strikes at Crotone, in Calabria, in early September 1993, which prevented the closure of a chemical factory.
7 Most of this information is taken from Leoluca Orlando's autobiographical *Palermo*, 1990.
8 These debates centered around a famous article by Sciascia in the *Corriere della Sera* (10 January 1987) which accused Borsellino and Orlando of being 'professionisti dell'antimafia'. (See also Orlando 1992: part 1, and Dalla Chiesa 1994: 98–101.)
9 See the articles collected in *Società Civile, 1986–1991. Cinque anni di libertà*, numero speciale, December 1991.
10 R. Di Rienzo, 'Tutti in rete', *L'Espresso* 4 November 1990. See also Dalla Chiesa 1993: 113–139.
11 'La Rete in un cerchio', *Il Manifesto* 1 April 1991.
12 'È finita', *Società Civile* April 1992, 7(4). See also Dalla Chiesa, 'Per chi suona la tangente', ibid., 7, 6, June-July 1992.
13 For a reply to these criticisms see *Società Civile* April 1992, 7(4), pp. 106–111.
14 For a positive analysis see the comments of Luigi Bobbio in Ginsborg (1994: 25).
15 For the referendum campaign see Abse (1993) and for Dalla Chiesa's support of electoral reform see Dalla Chiesa (1994: 138).
16 For the debates within the party over this alliance (30 per cent of delegates did not back the leadership) see 'Rifondazione al governo', *La Repubblica* 21 December 1994 for reports of the party's second National Congress at Rome (the same Congress with the famous 'Cuba, Cuba' chant from the delegates) and *L'Unità* 25 January 1994.
17 'No a Del Turco tra i progressisti', *La Repubblica* 17 January 1994 and see also ibid., 10 February 1994.
18 'E Orlando il Borioso fece un buco nella Rete', *L'Espresso* 22 April 1994.
19 'Possiamo ancora fermarli', *Liberazione* 1 April 1994.
20 'Anche Pintacuda "spara" su Orlando', *La Repubblica* 7 April 1994, where Pintacuda talked about 'massimalismo statalista' and criticised certain council decisions, 'Rete, scoppia la guerra fratricida', *Corriere della Sera* 1 April 1994 and *La Repubblica* 2 April 1994, but see also Pintacuda's denials in *La Repubblica* 8 April 1994. For more recent problems at Palermo, and further attacks by Mancuso, see 'Chi ha visto Leoluca?', *L'Espresso* 13 May 1994.
21 He attacked 'the beginnings of dangerous personal loyalties' and called for a complete renewal of the leadership, including the resignation of Orlando, after the election. At the same debate, a deputy, Laura Giuntella, argued that 'three years ago we had a project and the Rete did not exist. Now there is La Rete but I can no longer see the project', *La Repubblica* 17 January 1994. Dalla

Chiesa had already hinted at the transitory nature of the Rete in his *Milano–Palermo* (1994: 181). For his resignation see 'Un buco nella Rete' and 'Questa rete perdente', *La Repubblica* 15 April 1994.

22 'Si, sono pronto a sciogliere la Rete: la parabola di Orlando', *La Repubblica* 8 April 1994, see also for a more upbeat analysis, ibid., 31 March 1994 and 11 April 1994.

23 'Orlando vuole guidare il polo perdente', *Corriere della Sera* 31 March 1994.

REFERENCES

Abse, T. (1993) 'The triumph of the leopard', *New Left Review*, 199: 3–28.

Borcio, R. and Natale, P. (eds) (1992) 'Il voto per Rifondazione Comunista', Istituto Superiore di Sociologia, unpublished research paper, Milan.

Dalla Chiesa, N. (1994) *Milano–Palermo: La nuova Resistenza*, L'Unità: Rome.

Di Virgilio, A. (1992) 'Le elezioni in Italia', *Quaderni dell'Osservatorio Elettorale* 27, pp. 157–193 and 28, pp. 169–263.

Ginsborg, P. (ed.) *Le virtù della Repubblica*, Il Saggiatore: Milan.

Hellman, S. (1993) 'La difficile nascita del PDS' in S. Hellman and G. Pasquino (eds) *Politica in Italia 1992*, Bologna: Il Mulino.

Kertzer, D. (1992) 'The 19th congress of the PCI: the role of symbolism in the communist crisis' in R. Leonardi and F. Anderlini (eds) *Italian Politics a Review*, London: Pinter.

Orlando, L. (1990) *Palermo*, Milan: Mondadori.

Rifondazione Comunista (1994) *Difende il lavoro: Cambia l'Italia con la sinistra. Il programma di RC per le elezioni di marzo*, Rome.

Violante, L. (ed.) (1993) *I corleonesi: Mafia e sistema evasivo*, L'Unità: Rome.

Part IV
Politics and society

12 A legal revolution?

The judges and *Tangentopoli*

David Nelken

'God is on the side not of the heavy battalions but of the best shots'
(Voltaire notebooks, 1778)

In the two years following April 1992 all the parties of government in Italy were swept away in the course of judicial investigations which revealed centrally organised systems of illegal financing of political parties and corrupt agreements between politicians and businessmen. Some of these parties, founded as long as 100 years before, had played notable parts in the construction of the Italian Republic; but since World War II they had formed an apparently immovable bloc, which kept the opposition parties, and especially the Communists, from any hope of taking power. The judges' campaign to remoralise Italian public life came to be known as *mani pulite* (clean hands), a codename given by the policemen involved in the earliest investigations. Because these investigations radiated out from cases of corruption uncovered in Milan, where the 'pool' of most active judges was based, the whole process also came to be known by the collective term *Tangentopoli* (Kickback City).

In what sense can these events be seen as revolutionary? *Tangentopoli* was clearly not an attempt to overthrow the state in the cause of a new group or class or even in the name of a new ideal. Nor was it a case of a defeated regime, such as those after the end of Fascism or Communism, being tried by the victors after its collapse. Rather, what was remarkable, as Piercamillo Davigo, one of the Milan judges, put it early on, was the way the judges found themselves 'putting a regime on trial before its fall'. In some respects therefore *Tangentopoli* can indeed be described as a 'legal revolution'. It represented a determined exertion of their powers by some judges, using existing criminal laws approved by the politicians themselves, which led to the condemnation not just of individuals or factions but of a whole political class. Moreover, apart from some controversial distortions of criminal procedure, this was a revolution conducted within the law. There was no need to resort to 'revolutionary legality' – it was the renewed insistence on legality which itself had revolutionary consequences.

At the time of writing these investigations are still going on and it might be said that the full meaning of *Tangentopoli* does depend in part on when and how it actually comes to an end. But the impression is that the campaign to clean up politics has essentially run its course. Although judges in Milan and elsewhere are still active, the work of 'the pool' suffered a severe setback in the shock resignation of Antonio Di Pietro in December 1994 (in protest, he said, at the continual political controversies which accompanied his investigations). In retrospect we could probably say that *Tangentopoli* reached its climax at the end of 1993 when the case concerning the Milan financier, Sergio Cusani, was itself staged by the Milan judges as a sort of show trial, to explain to the television public the significance of the previous, seemingly unconnected enquiries, and lay bare the underlying system of political and business complicity (Andreoli 1994).[1] The remarkable consequences of these investigations were then felt in the April 1994 general election which saw a massive turnover of representatives and brought into government a new alliance of parties under the leadership of the communications magnate Silvio Berlusconi. This, in turn, after just seven months, has been replaced by the (interim) Dini 'government of technicians'. The one heated debate about how to bring *Tangentopoli* investigations to a formal conclusion has lost much of its urgency. Instead other priorities have been placed on the agenda by the experience of the Berlusconi government, such as the need to strengthen anti-trust laws and guarantee equal access to the media.

We can therefore offer a first attempt to answer some of the most basic descriptive questions which are raised by this episode in Italian politics. What was *Tangentopoli*? How could it take place? Why did it happen? (and why didn't it happen before?)

WHAT WAS *TANGENTOPOLI*?

When, in March 1992, Mario Chiesa, a middle-ranking figure in the Milan Socialist Party, was caught red-handed taking one of his regular bribes from a cleaning contractor, there was little reason to think that this would be the beginning of the end for the Christian Democratic–Socialist axis run by the powerful CAF triumvirate of Craxi, Andreotti and Forlani. The political parties put into action their normal technique of denying knowledge and involvement: in a country accustomed to an unending succession of major 'scandals' and unsolved mysteries this seemed a relatively minor case of corruption soon to be forgotten. Yet the careful preparation and determination of a number of prosecutors such as Antonio Di Pietro in Milan (and later elsewhere), eventually ensured that this case and others would come to demonstrate a complex web of political criminality. The trial of the financier Sergio Cusani, transmitted on prime-time television at the end of 1993, represented a sort of watershed between what was increasingly being described as the First and the Second Italian Republic. Cross-examined as leading witnesses to the way the government parties had exacted tribute from the business com-

munity, the now ex-Christian Democrat Secretary Arnaldo Forlani uncon-
vincingly took refuge in a 'Reaganite' loss of memory, while the ex-
Socialist leader Bettino Craxi defended the system of political financing
of which he had been a major architect, by lashing out right and left
(mainly left). In the meantime, Giulio Andreotti, the most enduring
politician of them all, had been put out of play with accusations of
collusion with the Mafia levelled by various ex-members of that organisation (the so-called *pentiti*).

The enquiries which led up to the Cusani trial ('the father of all trials'
as Di Pietro called it) saw a succession of charges, arrests and measures
of preventive custody concerning ministers, party leaders and treasurers,
Parliamentarians (at one time as many as a third of them were under
investigation), administrators, civil servants, businessmen, financial
journalists and members of the secret services.[2] The accused were charged
with crimes such as bribery, corruption, abuse of public office, receiving,
fraud, criminal bankruptcy, false accounting and illicit political funding.
Some of those caught up in *Tangentopoli* had collected bribes for the
sake of their party's finances. (This seems to be the case for Severino
Citaristi, the Christian Democrat Treasurer, who collected the record
number of criminal charges. He claimed that the party needed 85 thousand million lire in annual running expenses.) Others, including senior
Socialist party figures, had considerable sums stashed away in foreign
bank accounts for undisclosed purposes. Particular resentment was felt
towards those like Francesco De Lorenzo, Minister of Health (and a
leading figure in the small Liberal Party) or Duilio Poggiolini, the Head
Administrator of the Health Department with responsibility for deciding
which drugs were to be approved, who used their positions to amass
incredible personal fortunes. Many of these bribes or kickbacks were
levied by politicians and administrators as a matter of routine in return
for their good offices as 'intermediaries' in directing public-works contracts, such as that of the Milan and Rome underground systems, or
construction contracts for the road network, into the appropriate hands.
But the major bribes were connected with complicated financial deals
between politicians, businessmen and managers of the enormous state
holding companies, such as ENI and IRI (the unravelling of which also
led to a number of deaths, suicides and suspected murders). Despite his
lack of political importance Cusani played a central role in these trans-
actions and in particular in the Enimont affair in which Raul Gardini and
the Ferruzzi group was accused of disbursing bribes of 150 thousand
million lire in their effort to monopolise the chemical sector. Media and
public interest in *Tangentopoli* was maintained at a high level by dramatic
developments such as the flight abroad and unexpected return of those
under investigation, announcements that charges would be brought
against senior party administrators and political secretaries of the major
and minor coalition parties, and their reaction, the difficulty of obtaining

the necessary parliamentary permission to proceed against or arrest ministers or deputies, and the attempted fight back by politicians – such as the draft law putting an end to the investigations which President Scalfaro refused to sign.

Narration of the events of *Tangentopoli* can only take us so far towards an explanation. It can help us to see *Tangentopoli* as a process which developed its own momentum, that it was not necessarily the judges who insisted on drawing out the agonised death throes of the regime (within a few months from the start the Milan judges were already suggesting a moratorium on further enquiries in return for confessions, return of improper gains and withdrawal from public life), and that the outcome of particular investigations was not always predictable or anticipated. But it is necessary to take a more analytical approach if we want to examine the conditions which allowed *Tangentopoli* to take place and interpret their significance. I shall therefore now turn to consider how *Tangentopoli* was made possible by a combination of features special to judicial organisation in Italy as well as by the peculiarly systematic nature of political illegalities. Perhaps paradoxically, the conditions which it required were, on the one hand, the lack of central coordination of the judiciary and, on the other, the high level of central organisation of political corruption. Following this, however, we shall need to ask why the judges came to attack political corruption at this time.

HOW COULD *TANGENTOPOLI* HAPPEN?

To some extent puzzlement in seeing judges turning on their own government may only reflect the English ethnocentric assumption that the judiciary consists of a small group of middle-aged and middle-minded members of the establishment.[3] Our surprise diminishes once we recognise that there are 7,000 or so Italian judges, and that they are recruited by competitive examination straight after university (as in most civil law countries), a method which produces a wide cross-section of political sympathies and makes it more difficult to control for political 'reliability'.

But, even as compared to other civil law countries, the key to *Tangentopoli* lies in the particularly strong guarantees of independence from both the executive and Parliament which Italian judges now enjoy (Guarnieri 1993; 1994). A number of connected aspects of judicial organisation are relevant: in particular how judges are recruited and governed, the fact that prosecutors and judges are part of the same judicial profession, and the rule of mandatory prosecution. The current arrangements were slowly built up after World War II, and in part they represent the delayed implementation of constitutionally entrenched reactions to previous experience of over-subservience of judges to their political masters. Other features reflect a changing process of political evolution and struggle in the course of which judges have acted as an interest and status group in their own right.

Despite their shared emphasis on the principle that judges are responsible only to the law, modern democracies normally arrange for some political influence to be exercised over the courts. This is most noticeable either in the process of recruitment of judges (as in the United Kingdom or the United States), or else through bureaucratic controls over promotion, discipline and coordination (as in the civil law tradition).[4] In the Italian case it is the gradual dismantling of the bureaucratic structure typical of the civil law systems which is particularly significant. Both in theory and in practice the higher levels of the judicial hierarchy have lost most of their former power to control their subordinates, even if at a local level the heads of offices still continue to exercise some effective residual powers over the allocation of cases. Instead, as laid down by the new Constitution, promotion and discipline came to be the exclusive prerogative of the Supreme Council of Judges (known by its initials as the CSM), a sort of judicial Parliament, two-thirds of whose representatives are elected by the judges with one-third nominated by the political parties. (The Council actually started work in 1959 and in 1975 made the important move to proportional representation in electing its judicial membership.) Some questions, such as which judges should be put in charge of the important tribunals of the major cities, became highly political and are decided by the CSM according to votes which reflected the different judicial quasi-political groupings represented on its council.[5] But in many other matters the Council unites the judges in a corporate defence or even extension of their autonomy from external control. For example, the question of salary and status has come to be separated from the kind of work judges are actually performing – with automatic promotion guaranteed for all judges simply on the basis of years of service (ostensibly as a means of avoiding the danger that judges might allow their decisions to be conditioned by the implications for their career). Similarly, selection for higher judicial office came to be based principally on seniority rather than merit.

A second distinctive element of Italian judicial organisation lies in the fact that prosecutors and judges form part of the same profession and regularly interchange roles.[6] With the exception of recent efforts to coordinate the fight against organised crime, each prosecutor's office is autonomous. Each individual prosecutor therefore benefits from the same guarantee of independence as the judges, nor are prosecutors answerable to a Ministry of Justice (as they are, for example, in France). Despite the introduction in 1989 of a new code of criminal procedure modelled along accusatorial principles, the prosecutors continue to think of their role as being like that of the judge – as concerned with 'jurisdiction' and ensuring respect for the law, rather than that of being functionaries whose task is to act simply as the counterpart of the defence lawyer. The importance of the prosecutor's role can be easily seen if we remember that by the time *Tangentopoli* had done its political damage, few trials (and certainly none involving leading political figures) had actually been brought to a conclusion. Finally, it is important to note that Italy is one of the very few countries which refuses to recognise the need for or the existence of prosecution discretion, insisting formally on the rule of mandatory prosecution for all reported offences (failure to prosecute being itself a crime).

I am not concerned here with how far the existing form of judicial organisation in Italy can or should be defended, or with whether the rule of mandatory prosecution is respected in practice.[7] What is of interest for present purposes is the way the combination of these factors made it difficult for politicians to block the judges' investigations. The decentralised and unpredictable nature of prosecution decision-making, for instance, made it difficult to predict the pattern of prosecution. Similarly the doctrine of compulsory prosecution prevented the government from raising considerations of public interest even when the investigations came to involve leading government figures and the Minister of Justice himself. Added to these formal protections of their independence, judges also had informal margins for manoeuvre 'in the shadow of the rules' of criminal procedure. Judges (and not only lawyers, investigators or clerks) sometimes made strategic use of their ability to make public information about the bringing of criminal charges, sometimes (illegally) leaking the story to compliant journalists. This offered not only opportunities for increasing prestige but also possible advantages for the investigations they were pursuing. At crucial moments they also made open statements about the nature and importance of their enquiries directed both at the politicians and the public.

The lack of formal political control over the judges goes a long way to explaining why Italy may be an exception to the general rule that judges never get too far out of step with the values prevailing in the political system. But there are also many other factors which help explain the distance which exists between the judiciary and the political and economic system in Italy, as well as the particular prominence of the criminal law in seeking to bring these activities within the bounds of legality. For those used to Anglo-American conceptions of the role and rule of law, the approach of many Italian judges and academic commentators seems much less concerned with law as a guarantor of reasonable expectations and the predictability of social and business life. Instead law is taken to be a rational source of aspirations to be secured even in the face of entrenched powerful interests and illegal patterns of behaviour (this may also reflect a Catholic culture of continuing respect for ideals even if these can only infrequently be realised fully in practice). Moreover, to some extent, the government coalitions approved a series of legal rights and protections for weaker groups as a sop to placate the Communist Party and its voters for their permanent exclusion from government (without imagining that these laws would eventually be used against them). Where Anglo-American law-making against the interests of politicians or businessmen tends to rely on self-regulation (Halevy-Etzioni 1990), Italians tend often to rely on collusive non-application (Flick 1993).

The centrality and hyper-inflation of penal law in Italian life, on the other hand, is connected to a variety of special characteristics of civil society. The civil courts have enormous backlogs, administrative methods of formal control are weak, banks and accountants find ways round regulations, and civil servants tend to bend to the dictates of the politicians. In general, there are overwhelming pressures on people to conform to the internal norms of the various legal and illegal groups which effectively make up the fabric of Italian society (see further Nelken 1994). Had other types of controls operated more effectively *Tangentopoli* would not have been necessary. Instead it provided irrefutable evidence that, at least from the late 1970s, leading politicians, businessmen and civil servants had constructed a sort of administered illegality based on the use of the public sector for the allocation of spoils and profits.

Putting together these features of judicial organisation and legal culture makes it easier to understand how *Tangentopoli* could occur. But the puzzle of *Tangentopoli* is not solved simply by knowing more about its legal and social context. Even the most informed of Italian commentators were themselves shocked that judges managed to translate their theoretical independence into effective action against seemingly impregnable politicians. For the Italian observer therefore the question becomes what had changed in the effective relations of power which kept judges from conducting their investigations up until then.

WHY DID *TANGENTOPOLI* HAPPEN WHEN IT DID?

Perhaps politicians in Italy were so vulnerable because they had already lost their hold on power? It is difficult, perhaps impossible, to decide exactly how much importance attaches to the judges in bringing about what increasingly came to be called the Second Republic. The investigations coincided with and encouraged a ferment of political activity – such as the sudden rise of the Northern Leagues, and the crucial referenda votes on the direct election of local mayors and the 'first past the post' electoral system. These developments, together with the results in national and local elections, all demonstrated a steady loss of confidence in the majority parties. Another sure sign of the loss of credibility of the political parties in this period was the way the Amato and Ciampi governments stressed that they were composed of 'technicians' rather than politicians. Nor did the judges fight alone. They increasingly enjoyed the moral support of the public[8] – who were particularly incensed about cases of personal enrichment – and the strong sympathies of parts of the media. They also had supporters amongst the opposition parties. This was strong in the case of the ex-Communist Democratic Party of the Left (the PDS), continuing their alliance from the years before *Tangentopoli*, though there were some difficult moments when some of their high functionaries were caught up in the investigations. At first this was also the case for the Northern Leagues though their enthusiasm cooled once they also became a target. Nonetheless, for those experiencing these events at first hand, it certainly felt for a long time as if the judges were fighting a battle against considerable odds in which any serious mistake could easily have led to a change of climate and an end to their investigations.[9] That they prevailed was in part due to the skill with which they minimised the risks, for example by proceeding to trial against the lesser conspirators before tackling the major political figures. It was only in May 1994, after the general election, that former leaders such as Craxi, Forlani and Pomicino were finally committed for trial for corruption, by which time they were discovered to be abroad or 'ill' – or both.

Success was certainly not a given. But why did the judges only make a sustained attempt at this time? One answer is that individual judges had in fact tried before but that exposures of corruption in, say, Genoa or Turin had not managed to get much beyond the local level (Cazzola 1988; della Porta 1992). Those, such as Judge Carlo Palermo, who initiated investigations which brought them too close to centrally organised plots involving networks of politicians, masons and organised criminals met fierce resistance; the case would be taken from their hands to be given to a colleague or taken over by another court. Just as in the fight against organised crime, troublesome judges could find themselves moved by disciplinary proceedings to other parts of Italy (and the policemen working with them could be transferred even more easily at the will of their respective Ministries); they became targets for defamation or even assassination.

Despite the formal independence of the Italian judiciary, the politicians never abandoned their attempt to exert formal and informal influence. In the CSM, with its built-in majority of judges who were generally sympathetic to the political views of the government parties, special attention was devoted to placing the right people at the head of the main 20 to 25 courts. Thus despite its 20 to 30 per cent representation, members of the left-wing *Magistratura Democratica* found themselves regularly excluded from these sensitive posts. Particular care was reserved for the prosecutor's office in Rome, the infamous 'foggy port', where all the important political cases eventually arrived and were then lost from view (Calabrò 1993). Businessmen too might feel they would be entitled to some special consideration in return for the rich compensation earned by those judges who presided over the extra-judicial arbitrations which almost entirely replaced the use of the civil courts for inter-business disputes.

But even apart from these pressures, few judges were equipped with the financial, computing and other expertise to tackle difficult enquiries into political and business malpractice. Many would not have been enthusiastic about creating problems for themselves, in practice adapting their role to what was expected by the more powerful and respectable of the citizens in the areas where they worked. A small but important number, including some in high places in the courts of Milan, Rome, Naples and Palermo, were corrupted by businessmen, politicians or even by organised criminals.

So what had changed? With hindsight, we can point to a number of political and economic developments which were a precondition of *Tangentopoli*. The end of the Iron Curtain dividing West and Eastern Europe was crucial. More prosaically the explanation can be sought in the effects of the economic recession – businessmen were becoming less willing to keep paying bribes in the face of decreasing returns from their 'investments' and growing international competition.

Another relevant development was the beginning of international regulation of banking movements which may have forced politicians into recycling their bribes in illegal channels which were then easier for the judges to identify. The system of corruption was in any case inherently fragile (as compared to the bonds of loyalty amongst organised criminals). Once the silent collusion or *omertà* between bribe-givers and takers was broken, events took on their own momentum as politicians, administrators and, more often, businessmen, scrambled to explain or to 'confess' their account of the part they had played.

The conditions were there. But for what? Was *Tangentopoli* simply a fight against corruption or was it a deliberate strategy by the Milan judges to bring down the government? It is not easy to establish the answer to this heavily loaded question. At most we can draw some inferences by examining who were the targets (and who the beneficiaries). It seems fair to say that *Tangentopoli* was more about demonstrating the political ramifications of corruption than about the pursuit of corruption as such. It may have come about because demands on business had exceeded previously tolerated limits: *Tangentopoli* succeeded in uncovering large illegal payments[10] and, together with the influence of the recession, certainly helped to reduce the burden of these practices on the economy.[11] But the judges must have known they could have little overall impact on the diffuse activities of the submerged economy.[12] The enquiries therefore seem to have been directed in the first instance at the political system, and at political corruption as a way of undermining its credibility, rather than, for example, at business and its willingness to use bribes to rig or corner the market. Despite admitting their participation in the system of corruption, top managers of the calibre of Cesare Romiti, the managing director of Agnelli's Fiat, and Carlo De Benedetti, of Olivetti, were given only small starring roles in the drama of *Tangentopoli* – in which they claimed that they were compelled to pay tribute to the politicians so as to stay in business. Even in the Cusani trial the spotlight was on illegal methods of party financing rather than on what was to be learned about the methods of Italian capitalism.

But does it follow that the choice of politicians as (the primary) target is to be interpreted as a judicial vendetta? Arguably it was essential to start with the political parties, since, as controllers of public resources, they really were the prime movers of corruption. Crimes against public administration may also have been considered more serious than business misbehaviour because of the abuse of public trust. Possibly there were also practical calculations: it was relatively easy to obtain proof of the universal crime of illegal financing of parties and then to use that as a lever to uncover corruption. Investigations of politicians also had more immediate effects than charges against businessmen, especially once it came to be expected that accused politicians would resign from their government or party posts (and once Parliament stopped voting for the protection of immunity that had been used as a shield in the years before *Tangentopoli*).

It would thus be wrong to give much credence to the charge of 'government by the judges'. *Tangentopoli* was in no sense an officially or even unofficially coordinated project by the judges as a whole (even after a year the investigations involved only a small number),[13] and there is plenty of evidence of clashes of jurisdiction which could have had dangerous consequences for the investigations. On the other hand, it would also be naive to accept the judges' description of themselves as pursuing lawbreakers without regard to political consequences or public opinion (Colombo *et al.* 1993). Whether or not it was their intention, the opposition parties, and in particular the PDS, were bound to be the main beneficiaries of these investigations. The small Milan pool did contain two important members of *Magistratura Democratica*,[14] and it is significant that the only open division in their ranks came when one temporary member of the pool, Tiziana Parenti, insisted on proceeding against the PDS Treasurer (she went on to become a successful parliamentary candidate in Berlusconi's 'anti-communist' coalition). But, on the other hand, neither Saverio Borrelli, the authoritative head of the Milan prosecutor's office, nor Di Pietro, its leading member, had left-wing sympathies,[15] and there is anecdotal evidence that Di Pietro treated Craxi with kid gloves for a long time because he kept promising to provide him with hard evidence to use also against the PDS (Andreoli 1994).

Though some Parliamentarians and functionaries were charged,[16] PDS leaders remained relatively untouched by corruption accusations (even if not everyone was convinced of their innocence). This was probably because the blocked political system had allowed government parties to take the lion's share of the opportunities for corruption; the PDS had other sources of financing and a more disciplined party structure less disposed to shift blame to its leadership. Quite apart from any past alliance therefore, the interests of the PDS as the largest opposition party were bound to be furthered by the actions of the judges. Indeed, after the promising results in the mayoral elections in late 1993, it did seem as if the PDS would inevitably take over the government. From the point of view of vindicating the rule of law in Italy it was thus probably for the best that the party most in sympathy with the judges was not the one to win the general election. Tiring of the hunt for corruption, people voted for jobs (or the promise of them), not for more justice.

But what of the future? Is *Tangentopoli* over? What did it achieve? And – not least – could it happen again? Investigations connected to the earlier stages of *Tangentopoli* are still continuing and could have unexpected implications. Enquiries are now extending to PDS leaders as central figures in the influential league of cooperative businesses to which they are closely linked. On the other hand, Paolo Berlusconi, brother and business associate of the ex-Premier, has already confessed to financial irregularities and is still undergoing investigation. There are heated announcements of investigations either against Berlusconi himself,[17] or concerning companies he previously headed such as Fininvest or Publitalia, which allege corrupt payments to avoid tax, and false accounting so as to conceal undisclosed slush funds held at home and abroad. (At the end of 1994 an unexpected and controversial Supreme Court decision moved crucial court proceedings from the jurisdiction of the Milan pool to that of the judges in Brescia. The case involved senior officers of the Milan Financial Police who were accused of corruptly accepting – or demanding – bribes from companies such as Berlusconi's.) But unless the judges finally manage to provide conclusive evidence of financial wrongdoing against Silvio Berlusconi, it seems likely that *Tangentopoli* will end 'not with a bang but with a whimper'.[18] Corruption scandals of greater or lesser importance will continue to erupt periodically. But future political change in Italy is now tied less to judicial investigations than to the formations and alliances made necessary by the move to a majoritarian (rather than proportional) electoral voting system.

Will the predicted emergence of two competing coalitions bring an end to the well entrenched patterns of spoils-sharing which come to light regularly in spheres as different as the media, the banks, the health system or the universities? Unless this happens the long-term effects of *Tangentopoli* on Italian civil society, despite the not inconsiderable merit of having unblocked the political system, do not seem likely to be as revolutionary as it once might have appeared. Although its immediate deterrent effect, particularly on the public administration, was considerable, few of the collusive practices which bind administrators and the worlds of business or finance together have been dismantled. The intervention of the judges remains only a risk to be contained, as opposed to the 'living law' which governs the many closed worlds of public and social life in which the price for revealing illegal practices is exclusion from future participation.[19]

No legislation or (more important) administrative reorganisation has been implemented to deal with any of the underlying causes of the corrupt practices uncovered by *Tangentopoli*, whether these regard the illicit financing of political parties, kickbacks in the award of public contracts, or the systematic tax evasion which relies on official complaisance. Even the failure so far to agree on either a legal or a political 'solution' to ending *Tangentopoli* may be taken as a sign of unwillingness or inability to close the gap that exists between legal norms which enshrine formal, impersonal principles and customary practices which lay stress on sponsored participation. From a narrow criminological point of view (leaving other more significant political, legal and moral considerations to one side) *Tangentopoli* could thus be characterised as no more than a successful attempt to 'criminalise the mediators' – and in particular, to stigmatise one long-standing group of political mediators whose brokering activities reached an exploitative peak in the 1980s. But as long as there continues to be a role for 'mediators', in freeing and distributing public resources and in managing the long-identified gap between the official Italy and the 'real' Italy, those who perform this function – politicians, administrators or financiers (and in parts of the South also organised criminals and their allies) will claim monetary or other compensation for their services. Alternatively, as has been seen with the Berlusconi government, different – and not necessarily minor – problems arise if the role of mediators is cut out as a result of businessmen choosing to enter politics directly.

The central political role played by the judges throughout the *Tangentopoli* investigations could also rebound to their disadvantage. All sides of the political spectrum agree that when judges take on the role of an opposition this is not a sign of a well-functioning democracy (De Ponte 1993; Violante 1993). In their first administration Berlusconi and his Minister of Justice Alfredo Biondi did what they could to blunt what they saw as the political threat posed by the judges, for example by questioning the credibility of 'informers', or by sending in judicial inspectors to check the activities of the Milan pool. Should Berlusconi be reelected, a swing of the pendulum against the judges seems inevitable. Despite the positive press gained by the *Tangentopoli* judges, newspaper and television reports of the daily functioning of the legal system regularly reveal many serious failings: on the penal side, the large numbers of prisoners awaiting trial, in often shameful conditions; on the civil side, the incredible delays in arriving at a final verdict. Examples of such malfunctions can easily be used to put judges back on the defensive (it seems too much to hope that government energies and resources would actually be reallocated to tackle the problems themselves). Indeed it can even plausibly be argued that some of the same features of judicial organisation (such as the lack of overall coordination of prosecution priorities) which allowed the judges to succeed in their investigations of political corruption do to some extent make them less efficient in the performance of everyday justice. To avoid the spectre of future *Tangentopoli*, the politicians could choose either to reshape the prosecution system, using as their excuse the existence of everyday problems, or they could set out to tackle the general level of tolerated illegalities. The first course is certainly the easier of the two. Unfortunately, however, not all the steps that go in the direction of making another *Tangentopoli* investigation impossible are ones that would also make it unnecessary.

NOTES

1 Andreoli's book, a reportage of events by a journalist 'insider', is one of the first detailed accounts of *Tangentopoli*, but it has a tendency to read motives backwards in the light of the Cusani trial.
2 By the end of 1993 it was reported that 1456 businessmen, civil servants and national and local politicians had been charged, including 251 MPs and 4 former Prime Ministers. Ten suspects had killed themselves – or, in some cases perhaps, been killed (Sullivan 1993).
3 Amongst other differences in criminal procedure which are particularly relevant in a comparison with England are the proactive role of the prosecutor (or, more exactly, prosecuting judge) who directly organises the work of the police.
4 There is also the issue of how many or how few resources are provided to the courts – which is one area where the Italian political system has considerable powers of conditioning the work of the judges.
5 The major groupings, from left to right, are *Magistratura Democratica; Movimenti Riuniti; Unità per la Costituzione; Magistratura Indipendente.*
6 Considerable ambiguity was created by the fact that Di Pietro and other leading protagonists of *Tangentopoli* were widely described as judges even while carrying out the role of prosecutors.
7 Giuseppe di Federico (1991) has waged a steady campaign for the law to recognise the need to structure prosecution discretion in the light of the empirical realities of its exercise (since failure to acknowledge discretion may make its exercise all the more uncontrollable). But, as he is the first to admit, he has not managed to separate the reception of his research from the wider controversy over the alleged politicisation of the judges and the need to cut back their powers.
8 According to newspaper polls, reports of public protests against fallen politicians and administrators – and the vogue for 'we love Di Pietro' logos printed on the T-shirts worn to fashionable discotheques.
9 Both some judges and PDS spokesmen did make some bad moves at the time of the 1994 general election in attempting to smear Silvio Berlusconi's political campaign with Mafia and Masonic support, or to exploit bribery charges being brought against his brother Paolo.
10 Borrelli announced that by January 1993 his office alone had uncovered evidence of 300 thousand million lire's worth of bribes.
11 The costs of public works, such as building the Milan underground railway, were said to have halved following *Tangentopoli*. According to *Il Resto di Carlino* (10 February 1994) even in areas where public works were largely in the hands of the communist cooperative construction companies costs went

down in the period June to September 1993 by 20 per cent in Bologna, 30 per cent in Ferrara and 20 per cent in Ravenna.

12 In *Il Corriere della Sera* (17 October 1992) it was estimated that 100,000 people live directly or indirectly off political corruption. This was about one-tenth of the submerged illegal economy as a whole which employs up to a million people.

13 Just over 400 judges had been involved by December 1993, but this was still little more than 5 per cent of the judiciary.

14 From the 1970s on members of Magistratura Democratica were prone to use constitutional principles, and especially Article 3 with its explicit call for equality, as a legal justification for interpreting laws (many of which were left over from the fascist period) with a left-wing slant. More recent debates amongst influential intellectual figures (see e.g. Fassone 1987; Grassi 1991; Scarpari 1992) have begun to erode older certainties that 'the judge of the Left' was characterised by the pursuit of the crimes of the powerful and the defence of the weak, in favour of a new search for legitimation in terms of an ethic of impartial service to the citizenry. Given the mass of crime brought to the attention of judges, the choice of which crimes to proceed against, and when, does have political overtones but the rule of compulsory prosecution has so far made this issue impossible to debate.

15 Borrelli was the bourgeois scion of a judicial dynasty. Di Pietro, who was not identified with any of the judges' associations, became a judge after having emigrated to Germany and then studied at nights before first working as a policeman.

16 The *Resto del Carlino* of 10 February 1993 reported that the accused Parliamentarians in the previous year included 70 members of the Christian Democrats, 50 members of the Socialist Party, 10 Republicans, 6 PDS, 6 PSDI, 4 Liberals and 1 each from Rifondazione Comunista and the MSI.

17 One such supposedly confidential notice of investigation was presented to Silvio Berlusconi as the Premier was hosting the United Nations conference on organised crime in Naples.

18 The defence lawyer Giovanni Flick hailed a finding of acquittal of the Mayor of Genoa in early 1995 as a possible basis for distinguishing penal responsibility from administrative accountability.

19 Instead of finding himself a hero, Luca Magni, the owner of the small cleaning firm whose rebellion against paying a small bribe launched *Tangentopoli* on its way, finds himself excluded from the award of public cleaning contracts and (still) on the verge of bankruptcy (*Panorama*, 3 June 1994).

REFERENCES

Andreoli, M. (1994) *Processo all' Italia*, Sterling & Kupfer: Milan.

Calabrò, M. A. (1993) 'Il porto delle nebbie' *Micro Mega* 5(93): 89.

Cazzola, F. (1988) *Della corruzione*, Il Mulino: Bologna.

Colombo, G., Davigo, P. and Di Pietro, A. (1993) 'Noi obbediamo alla legge non alla piazza', *Micro Mega* 5(93): 7.

De Ponte, C. (1993) 'Se Di Pietro è un eroe qualcosa non funziona', *Micro Mega* 5(93): 63.

della Porta, D. (1992) *Lo scambio occulto: Casi di corruzione politica in Italia*, Il Mulino: Bologna.

di Federico, G. (1991) 'Obbligatorietà dell'azione penale, coordinamento delle attività del pubblico ministero e loro rispondenza alle aspettative della comunità', *La Giustizia Penale* XCVI: 147–171.

Fassone, E. (1987) 'Essere a sinistra oggi nella giurisdizione', *Questione Giustizia* 4: 835–847.

Flick, G. M. (1993) *Lettera à un procuratore della Repubblica*, Il Sole 24 Ore: Milan.

Grassi, L. (1991) 'Magistratura progressista negli anni '90', *Questione Giustizia*, 4: 951–959.

Guarnieri, C. (1993) *Magistratura e politica: pesi senza contrappesi*, Il Mulino: Bologna.

—— (1994) 'Justice and politics in a comparative perspective', *Indiana International and Comparative Law Review*, 2: 241–257.

Halevy-Etzioni, E. (1990) 'Comparing semi-corruption among parliamentarians in Britain and Australia' in E. Oyen (ed.), *Comparative Methodology*, London: Sage.

Nelken, D. (1994) 'Whom can you trust? The future of comparative criminology' in D. Nelken (ed.) *The Futures of Criminology*, London: Sage.

Scarpari, G. (1992) 'Crisi della sinistra e prospettive della giurisdizione', *Questione Giustizia*, 1: 177.

Sullivan, S. (1993) 'Shame without end', *Newsweek*, 13 December: 20.

Violante, L. (1993) 'Idee per una riforme del pianeta giustizia', *Micro Mega*, 5(93): 52.

13 The mass media and the political crisis

Stephen Gundle and Noëlleanne O'Sullivan

Under the old Italian regime the mass media were a central site of the exercise and negotiation of political power. They were also, as they had been throughout most of the history of the unified state, a terrain of interaction between political and economic elites. In consequence, the tremendous loss of credibility and collapse of the traditional parties following the outbreak of *Tangentopoli* and related corruption scandals had a dramatic impact on the mass media at all levels. First, the removal from the scene of powerful individuals and political forces that had acted as masters and gatekeepers of the system as a whole left a great gap. Second, both established professional practices and the legal framework introduced in 1990 – which legitimised the trends towards concentration in ownership of the previous decade – were called into question. Third, the crisis of traditional vehicles of representation resulted in the media themselves, and especially television, taking on a central role in furnishing new reference points, even though their having been closely bound up with the old order meant that they were not always well qualified to do this.

This chapter will analyse the Italian media in the transitional phase between the demise of the traditional parties and the struggle of the short-lived right-wing government elected in 1994 to consolidate its position in the state. It will examine how pre-existing anomalies and distortions shaped responses to events within and in relation to television and the press. It will be shown how the political rise of Berlusconi was a consequence both of Italian television and popular culture, and of the previous *laissez-faire* approach to concentration in media ownership. This development ensured that the tentative moves by media personnel towards a more detached relationship with political power that marked the period up to early 1994 were checked, and that questions concerning the ownership, regulation, management and functioning of the media would assume a place at the very centre of political debate. Their importance remained paramount after Berlusconi was constrained to resign in December 1994.

THE MASS MEDIA SYSTEM IN THE 1980S

In the course of the 1980s the press and television came to occupy a much more central place in Italian culture, society and politics than they had done previously. This occurred as a result of changes in collective values and behaviour, economic growth, technological innovations, the deregulation of broadcasting following rulings of the Constitutional Court in 1974 and 1976, and a process of concentration which saw the media come under the control of a small number of large firms: the Fiat-Rizzoli group, Mondadori, Rusconi and Berlusconi's Fininvest company (Forgacs 1990: 130–31; Giglioli and Mazzoleni 1990). For the political elite the process of expansion and concentration was disturbing because it meant that the traditional political and ideological motivations for media owner-ship were replaced by more strictly economic ones. This concern was compounded by the increasing difficulty the government parties encount-ered in controlling state broadcasting after passage of the 1975 reform of RAI, that shifted control from the hands of the executive to Parliament, that is to the party system as a whole. Overall the DC and the PSI conserved a predominant influence and shared common aims. Both aimed to condition news programmes and render them 'official' and 'tame', and preferred light-weight entertainment, which provided an atmosphere of optimism and escapism. This type of television was symbolised by the North and South American soap operas that proliferated on all channels. Yet in practice it proved very difficult to guarantee conformity and stab-ility in broadcasting policies. In the late 1980s the shoe-string cultural and regional channel, RAI-3, which had been entrusted to the Communists in order to gain their complicity in the broader share-out of posts and resources between the DC and the PSI, became an exciting, innovative channel, that with a series of tendentious current affairs programmes and highly unconventional entertainment shows, conquered an audience share of 10 per cent (Monteleone 1992: 463). Repeated censorious interventions failed to bring the network to heel.

Even more difficult for the government parties to swallow were the unpleasant surprises that their own networks occasionally reserved for them. March 1984 saw the inception on RAI-1 of the internationally successful coproduction series *La Piovra* (The Octopus). The broadcast of *La Piovra 5* in the autumn of 1990 provoked a political uproar that was ferocious enough to threaten the continuation of the series. Although earlier episodes had given rise to murmurings, *La Piovra 5* provided what in effect was a subversive critique of the corrupt 40-year-old political system that the DC headed. The explicit suggestion that there were links between the DC, and in particular Andreotti, and the Mafia, led to the series being accused of supplying a slanderous and unbalanced indictment of the political elite which misrepresented both the party and the state. Furthermore it was held to portray a misleading and nationally and internationally damaging image of southern Italy as a no-man's land dominated by *mafiosi* which would disconcert the public and reinforce in it an 'anti-state ethic': that of a powerless and ineffectual state system engaged in an unwinnable battle against an omnipotent criminal organisation. As tempers and viewing figures rose,[1] *La Piovra* became a substitute newspaper for a large slice of the audience, which through it became more aware and better informed about Mafia dealings and methods. It became a game of guessing which real-life figures had been the inspiration for the fictional screen characters.[2] RAI was put under a double pressure: politicians demanded self-censorship, adjustments or the abolition of the series, while the public clamoured for more of the same. The intervention of the all-party parliamentary watchdog committee meant that RAI was constrained to compromise. On the one hand it could not bear to lose either the record audience figures or the income from international sales of the series, whilst on the other it could not risk further incensing the DC right, which claimed that RAI was contradicting its role as a public service by depicting a defeated state. Political and top-level RAI attempts to bury *La Piovra* in the politically delicate period in the run-up to the 1992 election had limited success. Popular demand, financial rewards and contractual obligations meant that the green light was reluctantly given for one last *La Piovra* film, albeit in the disguised spin-off *L'ultimo segreto*, which would deal less controversially not with Italian internal affairs but with European drug-trafficking, and be set not in Palermo but in Turkey and Eastern Europe.[3]

The difficulty of governing tightly the state broadcasting system in the post-reform era induced a substantial segment of the political elite to alter its attitude towards concentration. Politicians who had initially been suspicious of powerful multi-media enterprises realised that in fact, because there were so few 'pure' media firms, most of these still had interests they wished to advance or protect in a range of other areas and for which they required political favours. Thus they had every interest in providing conformity in their output. This applied both to the press and to television. The unprecedented profitability of newspapers in the 1980s did not lead to them taking a more independent or critical role. If anything, it has been argued that less journalistic and editorial space was available than ever before to those who failed to join the chorus singing the praises of the establishment (Bocca 1989; Pansa 1990). News coverage remained for the most part stodgy and ideological, obsequious in tone and opinionated rather than investigative in style (Porter 1983; Giglioli and Mazzoleni 1990: 122). In the television sector political dependency was particularly pronounced. Berlusconi engaged in intensive lobbying across the political spectrum and simultaneously forged a special link with the PSI in order to stave off any possible anti-trust legislation that might have limited his business activities (Martini 1990).

It is not possible here to examine the many bonds of mutual interest that linked Berlusconi and the parties of government. Only two important episodes can be mentioned. The first is the battle for control of the publisher Mondadori which took place in 1989–90 after its merger with the *L'Espresso* group (see Pansa 1990; Ottone 1990). It would be wrong to see Berlusconi's raid on the group purely as a political operation performed on commission, for he already held a stake in Mondadori and in 1984 had taken over its ailing television station, Rete-4. But there can be no doubt that by taking on a powerful conglomerate that included anti-governmental publications such as *La Repubblica* and *L'Espresso*, and which was led by Carlo De Benedetti, the 'dissident' chairman of Olivetti, he acted in a way that won political approval. The final deal between De Benedetti and Berlusconi, under which the former retained control of the *L'Espresso* group while the latter kept Mondadori, was brokered by Giuseppe Ciarrapico, a businessman whose whole career had been conducted under the patronage of Giulio Andreotti.[4]

The second episode concerns the Mammì law, which represented the culmination of the parties' efforts to reassert their control through legitim-ation of the 'duopoly' of RAI and Fininvest. With this law 14 years of almost total deregulation were brought to an end; not however with a legislative and regulatory framework that would limit concentration and guarantee pluralism and competition in both broadcasting and advertising, but rather with an *escamotage* designed to confirm the existing situation and prevent the formation of any future 'third pole' in the broadcasting sector (Monteleone 1992: 469).The Mammì law bore all the hallmarks of the pact between Craxi and the DC right-wingers Forlani and Andreotti that so heavily conditioned Italian affairs in the late 1980s and early 1990s. Yet, far from leading to a pacific 'normalisation', it gave rise to immediate dissent on the part of the DC left, whose ministers resigned from government in protest. And, almost more than anything else, it was sharply called into question as one of the worst products of the old regime as public confidence in the parties dissolved in 1992–93.

RIDING THE TIGER: THE PRESS, TELEVISION AND THE COLLAPSE OF THE PARTIES

As the mass medium that was most important in social communication, television had the potential either to accelerate the process of disaffection and channel it towards constructive outlets, or in some way to divert or smother it. In fact different networks or, more frequently, different programmes and personalities responded in conflicting and variable ways, with the result that no univocal role was played and a process of segmen-tation set in. Only after Berlusconi entered the political fray did the main division come to be that between public and private channels.

As the nominees of the parties held control of RAI, and the style of the Fininvest news broadcasts, which began following the granting of the

right to transmit live entailed in the Mammì law, was scarcely less close
to officialdom, the general role prior to 1992 was one of smothering.
Virtually no attention was given by the most popular channels to the
referendum of June 1991 or to any other fact or event that was embarrass-
ing to the DC and the PSI. Only when the *Tangentopoli* scandal exploded
and the scale of events made them impossible to ignore did news programmes begin to free themselves of their long subordination. But even
then the situation was far from unambiguous as the most loyal sidekicks
of the powerful used RAI-2 and the Fininvest channels to go on the
counterattack. Loud and intemperate personalities such as the art critic
Vittorio Sgarbi and the ex-Communist turned journalist Giuliano Ferrara
played a confusing and mystificatory role by adopting a pseudo-oppo-
sitional stance and provoking verbal brawls in live broadcasts while
repeatedly attacking anti-corruption magistrates and the Left opposition.[5]

The network that went furthest in the opposite direction was RAI-3.
It was not afraid to tackle controversial issues and it created public heroes
out of a rebellious breed of politically and morally *engagé* presenters and
journalists such as Michele Santoro of *Samarcanda* and later *Il rosso e il
nero* (The Red and the Black) and Gad Lerner of *Milano, Italia*. On the
Fininvest channels only the populist Gianfranco Funari, whose polemical
Mezzogiorno italiano (Italian Midday) programme on Rete 4 was sum-
marily taken off the air following protests from Berlusconi's political
allies, and the late-night-talk show host Maurizio Costanzo played any
sort of free role. Santoro, Lerner and Funari were anti-conformist and
anti-establishment. They stirred up heated discussions and launched
deadly accusations in transmissions that often diacritically counterposed
an (innocent) studio audience to (guilty) political guests. In consequence
they regularly locked horns with the conservative editorial line favoured
by the broadcasting authorities, and in particular the RAI director general
from 1990 Gianni Pasquarelli, as well as politicians. Those who cried foul
most loudly were Sergio Bindi, Carlo Grazioli and Enzo Balocchi, who
all railed against what they perceived to be programmes predicated on
an anti-DC prejudice. Especial anger was caused by the 'unwarranted
attacks' to which President Cossiga was subjected on *Samarcanda* in
December 1990 (*La Repubblica* 1 December 1990). Their most vociferous
criticisms were directed towards the participating studio audience, which
symbolically represented a biased judicial tribunal taking part in a sort
of 'trial by television'.

Objections to *Samarcanda* were especially strong. These exploded after
an extraordinary episode of the show dedicated to the memory of the
anti-Mafia businessman Libero Grassi, who was murdered in Palermo in
September 1991. The resonance the programme had was all the greater
because, in an unprecedented link-up, Costanzo continued with the theme
later the same evening on Canale 5. The furore which resulted from the
explicit thesis that the DC was a party of the Mafia led to calls for

censure, interventions on the part of the parliamentary watchdog committee, disciplinary action against Santoro and even demands for the dis-
missal of Pasquarelli. On the other side, what was held to be at stake
was journalistic freedom and autonomy. In the battle royal that ensued,
the DC found itself counterposed to the PDS, some Socialists, the
Northern League, sections of the press, and the broadcast journalists'
union USIGRAI – with the evident back-up of the public.

During this period a range of measures was adopted to contain the
desires of some presenters and journalists to put themselves at the head
of public opinion and give television an active role almost as a party in
its own right. At Fininvest the offer to Santoro of a contract with the
youth-oriented network Italia 1 was withdrawn, Funari's midday show
was cancelled and even Ferrara was (temporarily) dropped (although
here audience rather than political considerations were paramount). At
RAI such action was much more difficult. The outcome of the wrangle
was a set of rules issued by the board of RAI in October 1991 that was
designed to ensure the impartiality and representative pluralism of TV
debates and studio audiences. The intention was to eradicate the possibility of any repetition of subversive, militant 'trials by television' on
RAI-3 which, according to Andreotti, 'poisoned Italy's youth' and
depicted some of the country's gravest problems as farcical entertainment.[6] However these rules were viewed as an authoritarian restriction
by journalists and in practice they had little or no effect. Faced with a
public outcry and unable to risk the loss of the six and a half million
viewers of *Samarcanda* and the two million plus of *Milano, Italia* had
he censured or axed these programmes (*La Repubblica* 30 May 1992),
Pasquarelli backtracked. Humiliatingly, he was even forced to renege on
his previous stance of suspending them in order to ensure a period of
calm in the run-up to the 1992 elections. In the subsequent period the
change in public opinion meant that even in networks and programmes
that had been close to the parties, journalists struggled to regain their
credibility by carrying out the sort of investigations – for example into
the South – that had never been contemplated previously. *Mixer* on RAI-
2 and *Spazio 5* on Canale 5 were two examples.

For some sections of the press, like *La Repubblica* and *L'Espresso*, the
exposure of corruption offered a vindication of everything they had been
saying through the 1980s. But the participation of Fiat-owned newspapers
like *La Stampa* and *Il Corriere della sera* in the vigorous reporting and
denunciation of the malfeasances of the political class was the fruit of late
conversions on the part of journalists keen to reassert their professional
credibility. Papers of record were also obliged to follow the 'agenda-
fixing' path opened by *La Repubblica* and the independent right-wing *Il
Giornale.* Nonetheless the influence of the parties was still powerful into
the autumn of 1992. Craxi, who considered *Il Corriere* to be an ally
of the PSI, not least because Ferrara and the philosopher Lucio Colletti

were among its columnists, used his influence to block the promotion of the acting editor, Giulio Anselmi, to the editorship to replace Ugo Stille, as he had been very aggressive in pursuing anti-corruption (*L'Espresso* 13 September 1992). Instead Paolo Mieli was appointed. Yet, much to Craxi's chagrin, this made scarcely any difference at all. The only comfort the elite could draw was from the local press, which was generally more cautious and conservative (see della Porta, Chapter 14). Especially in the South, where DC fiefs like *Il Mattino* and *La Gazzetta del Mezzogiorno* commanded large readerships, a polemical anti-northern, anti-magistrate line prevailed.

REFORMING RAI? THE YEAR OF 'THE PROFESSORS'

At RAI changes were introduced by the Ciampi government, which took office at the highpoint of disaffection from the traditional elite and which counted on the de facto support of the PDS. By the spring of 1993 the beleaguered public service company was demoralised, in turmoil, and propped up by government handouts. It was also in need of an ideological and normative overhaul. In order to break the spiral of *lottizzazione*, reform was introduced to the system of appointment of the board. Instead of the government making the appointments, through the holding company IRI which in fact owned RAI, the task was entrusted to the Presidents of the Chambers of Parliament, who customarily represented the opposition as well as the majority. Spadolini and Napolitano appointed four men (Claudio Demattè, Feliciano Benvenuti, Tullio Gregory, Paolo Murialdi) and one woman (Elvira Sellerio) who were given the unenviable job of making RAI economically viable and restoring its reputation as a national institution. Because of the academic connections of several members of the council, they were collectively dubbed 'the professors'.

The task they faced was formidable. RAI was the epitome of inefficiency. It wasted vast sums of money every year on running costs and in 1993 alone it amassed a deficit of 479 billion lire (*La Repubblica* 15 June 1994). Years of seemingly limitless spending, costly external productions (such as Raffaella Carrà's astronomically expensive broadcasts from New York in 1986), staff costs that bore little relation to need or efficiency, the maintenance of a large number of regional outposts and inefficient advertising administration reduced the coffers of the company to much the same state as those of the public sector generally. The internal structure was chaotic and was complicated by complex, self-serving bureaucratic procedures. Moreover as a cultural organisation with a public service mission RAI had lost its sense of direction. This was both because it had been fatefully and organically shaped by the discredited practice of *lottizzazione* and because almost nothing had been done to face the challenges of new technologies and the decline everywhere of the 'generalist' model of television.

Criticism of 'the professors' began even before they started work. They were deemed to be unsuitable for the job in hand, because although they had varied economic and cultural backgrounds, they had no previous practical experience of television or of RAI. Moreover doubts were raised about their supposed independence. Suspicion that old customs had not been entirely done away with was fuelled by the appointment of Gianni Locatelli to the post of Director General after the members of the council elected Demattè as their President. The selection of these two men perpetuated the dynastic tradition of a 'lay' President and a DC Director General. It was also feared that their overtly high cultural backgrounds would lead to RAI's output being transformed into an indigestible diet of 'serious' programmes that would attract few viewers. Finally disquiet was expressed by some over the dangers implicit in the reliance on expert outsiders after the long season of party-political control.

In July 1993 Demattè set out a clear plan for the renovation of RAI. First it was to be freed of political interference and control, and instead become a purveyor of pluralist information, not just between channels but on each channel. Second, RAI's role as a public service was to be redefined in the image of the British BBC – on the basis of a recuperation of the tripartite vocation to educate, inform and entertain. One consequence of this was that extremely popular variety shows such as *Saluti e baci* (Greetings and Kisses), which attracted ten million viewers, fell under the axe. A light-weight entertainment featuring minor comedians, lookalikes of politicians and scantily clad dancers, the show was out of favour as an example of 'inferior entertainment'. The fact that its costs were also extremely high provided the perfect excuse to cancel it on the grounds that it was out of line with the new climate of austerity at RAI. Third, severe cutbacks were to be implemented across the board in line with the harsh cost-cutting policy captained by the economist Demattè in order to bring RAI back into the black. Fourth, both production and executive functions within RAI were to be centralised and profligate regional headquarters drastically reduced in number.

How did all this impact practically? News and current affairs was obviously the most sensitive sphere and the predominant concern. A proposal to tackle the wasteful triplication of operations by suspending RAI-3's news output was probably naive rather than politically inspired, but the furore it provoked especially on the Left forced a retreat. The desire to return the third network to its original regional function remained a constant theme of the professors' actions. However these proposals did not become reality until after the victory of the Right because angry journalists threatened to strike; instead of a reduction of news programmes an increase was eventually agreed. The board was more successful in forcing changes of personnel. The directors of the first and second networks resigned, as did the heads of all the news staffs (although Sandro Curzi of RAI-3 only went after a spirited resistance).

They were replaced by men who, although they were drawn from existing politico-cultural alignments, were deemed to be competent enough to be granted operational autonomy.

These moves failed to lead to the desired objectivity. Within RAI – and more widely within the news media – the eclipse of the parties produced two main responses. There was on the one hand a noble attempt to establish new criteria of appointment and of professional conduct that amounted to an effort to import what was perceived to be a BBC model of impartiality. The commitment to this, for example on the part of 'the professors', was usually genuine but often abstract, and in any case it was extremely difficult to enact in a period of turbulent change in a country that had no history of detached journalism. The other response was less high-minded and more practical. It involved a concern to identify the alignment that was likely to emerge victorious from the political and moral confusion – and jump on the bandwagon. Following the success of the Left in the local elections of June and November 1993 there was a marked shift towards the PDS among news staffs, and, so it appeared to observers on all sides, in the editorial lines of current affairs programmes.

In terms of the cultural level of programmes, some changes were introduced but also 'the professors' were forced to come to terms with the reality of the star system and public tastes in order to ensure that ratings victories were not handed on a plate to Berlusconi. Despite the much publicised cancellation of *Saluti e baci*, the production company's resubmission of the proposal with costs reduced by a third from 810 to 500 million lire per episode was accepted, and it was reinstated under the new name of *Bucce di banana* (Banana Skins). It would be argued by the Right after their victory in 1994 that this was not the only area in which the impact of 'the professors' had failed to meet expectations. They offered a facade of reform that eliminated the worst excesses but fundamentally failed to address the basic issues of a disastrous economic situation and years of occupation by the parties. This charge was politically motivated but it was not entirely ill-founded. Without state intervention the accounts would still have been weighed down with 700 billion lire of debts in 1996. Demattè and his colleagues began a process of reform but they remained at least partly within the framework of existing RAI politics. Like Ciampi and those of his ministers who were drafted from the professions, they were obliged to coexist with the remnants of the old parties that conserved institutional power well after they lost public support. Moreover the purposes of some of the actions of 'the professors' remained highly ambiguous. In the name of a move from 'generalist' to diversified broadcasting, which was itself necessary, they dismantled the most innovative and anti-conformist aspects of the public service.[7] Virtually their last act in June 1994 was to impose the regionalisation of RAI-3's evening programmes – a decision which had the effect of quashing Santoro's plans for a *Newsnight*-style show and in effect putting an end to the third network as a stimulating national channel.

How did television interact with the processes in course in the country during this period? It should be noted that programmes like *Samarcanda* and related current affairs shows, which escaped enforced decline, underwent a natural one. By October 1993 it was clear that the viewing public was saturated with political debates. Plummeting audience figures (*Milano, Italia* suffered a loss of 17 per cent of its audience between the spring and autumn) signalled that a public weary of political crisis was switching back to the light-hearted entertainment that Fininvest and the two main RAI channels had continued to supply most of the time (*La Repubblica* 29 November 1993). The return in two special shows of the comic Beppe Grillo, for long banned from the screen on account of his ferocious satire, was an isolated moment. The real state of affairs was demonstrated by the success of the innocuous *Bucce di banana* and its blonde star Valeria Marini. Her vapid screen image, optimistic, unproblematic personality, communication of reassuring, infantile and restful platitudes and 'homemade Marilyn Monroe' appearance constituted a complete antidote to the atmosphere of gloom and crisis that abounded. The quite extraordinary success she enjoyed in this period offered a warning of the vulnerability of Italians to optimistic visions. In much the same mould was the Canale 5 programme *Non è la Rai* ('It's not the RAI') with its dancing and singing teenagers. Only briefly and memorably in the autumn did the issues bound up with the demise of the political class once more win mass audiences – with the broadcast of the first trials born of the *Tangentopoli* scandal. The trial of the financier Sergio Cusani, which was broadcast on prime-time television in late 1993 and early 1994 fascinated Italians to the extent that it won a 25 per cent audience share, and was considered to mark a watershed between the old order and the new Republic. Although Cusani himself was an insignificant figure, the appearance as witnesses of many of the disgraced politicians from Forlani to Craxi and Martelli, La Malfa, Citaristi and Altissimo, with the extremely popular magistrate Antonio Di Pietro conducting the questioning, transfixed audiences. The 'trial by television' phenomenon attracted its critics, although in this case all that was happening was that a regular trial was being broadcast. Some observers however saw the Cusani trial merely as a sort of Italian *Dallas* or *Beautiful*, rich with heroes and villains and *coups de théâtre* (*La Repubblica* 8 January 1994; 21 January 1994).

BERLUSCONI TAKES OVER (TEMPORARILY)

Berlusconi's decision to enter the political fray in January 1994 undermined assumptions about the likely course of events that had taken shape over the previous year. The unprecedented fact of a media magnate putting himself forward as a saviour of the nation removed any question about whether the relationship between politics and the media in Italy might be made to conform to the norms and standards of other advanced democratic societies. It also ensured that through the election of 1994 and in the battles that ensued television was not just a forum of campaigning but also a central issue of the contest.

Elsewhere in this volume Patrick McCarthy (Chapter 8) argues that the triumph of Berlusconi can only properly be explained by reference to his skilful mobilisation of lower-middle-class interests. Television however was a key precondition both to his acquiring mobilising potential and to his generalisation of it to a wider range of social strata with weak partisan ties or none at all, including women, youth, the unemployed and even some workers (see Diamanti 1994: 65–67). This could be achieved because over a period of 15 years, Fininvest networks had furnished Italians with a new set of values and aspirations. Through variety shows, quizzes, innumerable spot announcements, sponsored slots and imported soap operas, substitutes had been offered for the old reference points that were in decline: the Church, the parties of the Left, the organised labour movement, values of parsimony and sacrifice. The channels supplied models of living in terms of consumerism, change, efficiency, conformism and modernity that were reinforced by sport, films and family magazines. During the build-up to the election all the modern techniques of marketing that Berlusconi had deployed in the early 1980s to defeat his commercial rivals were geared to the battle against his political opponents. Seasoned entertainers like Mike Bongiorno and Raimondo Vianello lent their contributions while even Ambra Angiolini, the 16-year-old star of *Non è la Rai*, was drawn into the campaign of persuasion. The images that Forza Italia conveyed were largely pre-political. Turning to his advantage the fact that his channels were not tainted with the old order in the eyes of the public, Berlusconi merely lent a political hue to the advertiser's amalgam of seductive commonplaces that people already associated with Fininvest: stability, happiness, family, prosperity and faith in the future. In the climate of uncertainty and economic recession these proved to be very powerful.

From the moment Berlusconi 'took to the field', questions were raised more forcefully than ever about the distortions which his vast interests and resources would bring to political life and to the functioning of democracy. Berlusconi himself was not sensitive to these concerns. For 15 years he had lobbied the parties intensively to impede the passage of legislation, and it is clear that one of the factors which led him to enter politics was the mounting clamour for revision or replacement of the Mammì law, which, if it were to have occurred, would have drastically reduced the scale of the Fininvest empire. Despite his assurances that he would not allow his business interests to influence his political decisions, it soon became apparent that Berlusconi recognised no distinction between his private concerns and the good of the collectivity. Although there were some cosmetic concessions and he gave an undertaking that he would divest himself of Fininvest as soon as a workable solution could be found, his actions revealed that his aim was to conserve all his power, and wherever possible to extend it, overcoming counter-powers and eliminating dissident voices along the way.

The nature of the Berlusconi doctrine was illustrated in relation to RAI after the Right took office. As a long-time adversary of state television, the Prime Minister's view of RAI was hostile. He saw it as an inefficient and more or less unjustifiable branch of the state that illegitimately also cornered a part of the market in advertising revenues. Throughout the campaign Forza Italia attacked RAI as being 'in the hands of the communists'. It was joined in this assault by other components of the new majority which had long been excluded from RAI and therefore had axes of their own to grind. This attitude was understandable, for the news teams of RAI mirrored Fininvest's support for Forza Italia by favouring the Progressive Alliance. In fact this proved to be no advantage as the state broadcasting company was still widely perceived to be a cornerstone of the corrupt old regime.[8] It merely fuelled a desire for revenge within the Right that, after its victory, showed no interest in perpetuating the practice of power-sharing with the opposition.

The battle to create the premises for control over RAI was swift and brutal. A campaign of verbal intimidation against named journalists and managers was supplemented by a sharp attack on 'the professors'. The objections to them were fourfold. First they were not pliable appointees of the new majority. Second, they were broadly of a centre-left extraction and were out of sympathy with the Right. Third, it was argued that they had failed to overcome the legacy of *lottizzazione*. Fourth, their overall aim was to turn RAI into a more competitive and commercially dynamic company, something which, from the point of view of Fininvest and its allies, was to be avoided at all costs. Only the intervention of President Scalfaro prevented the new administration from granting itself the right to dismiss the board of RAI. But in the end the government obtained its desired goal as Demattè and his colleagues resigned in July 1994 after their economic plan for the recovery of RAI was rejected. They were replaced by a team of little-known business people (Letizia Moratti, Alfio Marchini, Mauro Miccio, Ennio Presutti), plus a medieval historian (Franco Cardini) who willingly implemented the government's plans for a domesticated and hamstrung RAI. Locatelli was dismissed, and in September all the network directors and news department directors appointed in 1993 were replaced by pliable figures of lesser standing. Some of these, including Carlo Rossella and Clemente Mimun, the new directors of RAI-1 and RAI-2 news, were products of the Fininvest-Mondadori stable while others were politically aligned with

Alleanza Nazionale. Much to its chagrin, the Northern League was excluded almost completely from the share-out.

Broadly speaking, the Right's appointees acted to render RAI's output compatible with the government's interests. Although some right-wingers made clear their continuing dissatisfaction, Rossella and Mimun introduced significant changes. They shifted the emphasis from hard news to human interest stories, reduced the coverage accorded to opposition parties and reintroduced an attitude of deference towards the holders of power. The influence of Fininvest on RAI was also evident in several new programmes launched in the autumn of 1994 that bore a marked resemblance to the sort of family and human interest broadcasts favoured by the private networks.

Yet by no means everything went Berlusconi's way. Despite a concerted campaign by the Right to ensure the subservience of the print media, most national newspapers proved unwilling to renounce the independence of judgement they had demonstrated since 1992. Moreover the pressure for reform of the broadcast media remained strong. In July 1994 the Court of Cassation gave the go-ahead for signatures to be collected in favour of the abrogation of specific clauses of the Mammì law, and in December the Constitutional Court ruled that the law violated the constitution because it legitimised existing positions of strength instead of guaranteeing the widest possible pluralism. This ruling returned the question to Parliament, where the opposition parties were already pushing for genuine anti-trust legislation. They were spurred on by President Scalfaro's call for equal treatment for all parties on television. In this sense the fall of his government at the end of 1994 occurred at a particularly dangerous time for Berlusconi. Although his successor, Lamberto Dini, did not include anti-trust legislation among his priorities, and appointed a former Fininvest lawyer as his Minister of Posts, he had no reason to act specifically to thwart efforts to reduce or check the influence of Fininvest. Thus, unless fresh elections were held in the short term as Forza Italia and Alleanza Nazionale insisted, there was a risk that despite continuing public sympathy, Berlusconi would ultimately fail in his determination to retain all his power in private television. Because of the immense resources he still controlled however, this was only a risk and not a certainty.[9]

CONCLUSION

The 'golden age' of RAI, it may be argued, came to an end in the mid-1970s. With the end of the state monopoly and the reform of 1975 a new era opened in which the old pedagogical model of public broadcasting was displaced by a more commercially oriented one. It was inevitable in this context that the axis of the media system would swing towards private television. The economic growth of the 1980s underpinned this trend, as did the 1975 reform which led the parties to seek to guarantee their hegemony by means of a mutually convenient relationship with media entrepreneurs. However, because RAI remained within the dominion of the parties, it was unavoidably compromised by their decline. Two broad attempts were made to regain public confidence and reassert RAI's public service vocation. First polemical, tendentious current affairs programmes and true-to-life dramas explored issues and gave voice to views that had been excluded hitherto. Second, a non-political board was given the task of restoring RAI's authority and tackling the legacy of wastage and mismanagement. Although some successes were achieved, both these attempts ultimately failed. The 'reality television' of *Samarcanda* and *Il rosso e il nero* spectacularised the crisis and helped arouse public opinion, but their very tendentiousness was in the end an obstacle – the mirror image of the obsequiousness that had previously been the most obvious proof of the lack of any sense of professional objectivity. 'The professors' played a role in liquidating the use of polemic but the custom of kowtowing to the authorities was only suspended for their period in office, and their broader impact was transient and superficial.

In the end all efforts to renovate RAI and reassert its pre-eminence were dashed by the rise of Berlusconi. It should be emphasised that it was not 'television' but rather the highly particular model of relations between political power and press and television owners as it developed in the 1980s that created the premises for the emergence of Berlusconi as a political player in his own right. Other conditions for his success were however internal to Italian television culture. In contrast to what many expected, it was not television news and current affairs, or even political fiction like *La Piovra*, that ultimately had the biggest influence on the aspirations of the population, but rather entertainment and commodification. After a brief interlude, the optimistic-escapist model revealed that it retained all its power. The arrogant desire of the Right to quash controversial programmes and oust awkward journalists and managers should not obscure this fundamental point. Although Berlusconi's opponents took hope from the rapid demise of his government, and appeared determined to use all the means that were institutionally available to them to reintroduce pluralism to the broadcasting sector, their problem ultimately was that they had no equivalent purchase on the collective imaginary.

NOTES

1 *La Piovra* attracted a regular audience of between 11 and 17 million viewers, taking an audience share of around 45 per cent. This made it one of the most successful television shows of recent years (*La Repubblica* 6 October 1990).
2 The homicide of the fictional commissioner Corrado Cattani (Michele Placido) was closely based on that of Nini Cassarà. The magistrate Francesca Morcelli

was said to have provided the model for the fictional character Silvia Conti; (*Panorama* 21 October 1990).

3 This 'last' *Piovra* film however continued to be marketed internationally under the original title of *La Piovra 6* (*La Stampa* 16 November 1991). In the summer of 1994 filming began on yet another episode in the series.

4 As part of the deal that Ciarrapico settled, both Berlusconi and De Benedetti received concessions from the state: the concession of more television frequencies in the case of the former, the granting to Olivetti of extraordinary lay-off funds (*cassa integrazione*) in the latter (*Panorama* 12 May 1991; *L'Unità* 26 May 1991).

5 It is significant that both men were elected to Parliament in the lists of Forza Italia in 1994. Ferrara subsequently became Minister for Relations with Parliament and Sgarbi President of the Culture Commission of the Chamber of Deputies.

6 The directives were reported in *L'Unità* 5 October 1991; Andreotti's outburst and the vigorous protests of the DC paper *Il Popolo* in *La Repubblica* 1 October 1991.

7 The only councillor to object to this was Sellerio (*L'Espresso* 8 July 1994).

8 In the aftermath of the election the social science department of the University of Turin revealed that television had been responsible for determining how six million people voted. Four million were influenced by Fininvest, two million by RAI (*La Repubblica* 1 June 1994).

9 Berlusconi's powers of persuasion were confirmed in June 1995 when he mobilised his three networks to ensure defeat of the referendum to abrogate parts of the Mammì law and of two other proposals that would have reduced his grip on television and advertising. The margin of his victory in each case was 57 to 43 per cent.

REFERENCES

Bocca, G. (1989) *Il padrone in redazione*, Milan: Sperling & Kupfer.

Diamanti, I. (1994) 'La politica come marketing', *Micro Mega*, 2: 60–77.

Forgacs, D. (1990) *Italian Culture in the Industrial Era 1880–1980*, Manchester: Manchester University Press

Giglioli, P. P. and Mazzoleni, G. (1990) 'Concentration trends in the media' in F. Sabetti and R. Catanzaro (eds), *Italian Politics*, vol. 5, London: Pinter.

Martini, P. (1990) 'Molti affari, molta politica. Nei rapporti con i partiti il lato forte di Berlusconi', *Problemi dell'informazione* 15(4): 513–527.

Monteleone, F. (1992) *Storia della radio e della televisione in Italia*, Venice: Marsilio.

Ottone, P. (1990) *La guerra della rosa*, Milan: Longanesi.

Pansa, G. (1990) *L'intrigo*, Milan: Sperling & Kupfer.

Porter, W. E. (1983) *The Italian Journalist*, Ann Arbor: University of Michigan Press.

14 The system of corrupt exchange in local government

Donatella della Porta

The aim of this chapter is to give a systematic description of the complex network of actors involved in corrupt exchange, and of the resources exchanged amongst them. In order to do so, I shall use, by way of illustration, the findings of research that I conducted in Italy on some cases of political corruption at local level.[1] The research, which was based on legal documents and backed up by interviews, concentrated on some political scandals that emerged in the 1980s in three Italian cities. The first case studied concerns the allocation of contracts and the granting of licences in the construction sector, administered by city council or provincial administrations and the organisation responsible for the construction of low-rent public housing – Istituto Autonomo Case Popolari (IACP) – in the province of Savona. The second case concerns the acquisition, on behalf of the city council of Florence, of two buildings: the Albergo Nazionale and Villa Favard. Finally, the third concerns the purchase of medicine and pharmaceutical products by a public organisation responsible for National Health in Catania – the Unità Sanitaria Locale (USL) 35.[2]

ASSOCIATIONS IN CORRUPT EXCHANGE

Where corruption is widespread it often involves groups of administrators and businessmen, who between themselves negotiate the size of the bribe and the public resolutions to be taken, either directly or through the intervention of middlemen. The structure of exchanges appears as that shown in Figure 14.1.

Cartels of businessmen reach agreements on a series of public decisions

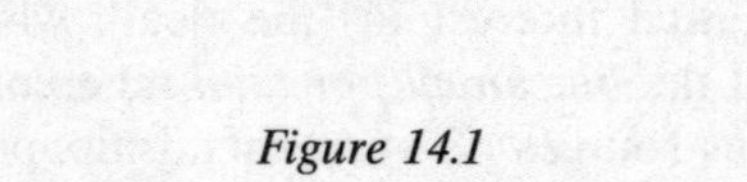

Figure 14.1

which they must demand from the politicians: they collect money and hand it over to political cartels, in turn these offer privileged access to public decisions, and they distribute the money between politicians. Often middlemen intervene to establish contacts between the two parties, to conduct the negotiations, and often to transfer the bribe money. In this complex web of exchanges, bases of loyalty and trust are established which allow the corrupt exchange to be brought to a conclusion. In what follows I propose to analyse in greater detail the structure of corrupt exchange, by examining both the characteristics of the actors who directly engage in it and the resources that are exchanged.

The politicians

If, looking at Figure 14.1, we begin the analysis from the standpoint of the associations of public actors, we can see immediately that the system of exchange is made more complex by the presence of figures with different roles, whose coordination in reaching administrative decisions that can be exchanged for bribes is indispensable. In fact in corrupt associations particularly, we find public administrators (both those in elected positions and those with party appointments), career administrators and party functionaries. In the case study we were able to identify some of the resources that are exchanged between different political actors. The structure of exchanges is shown in Figure 14.2.

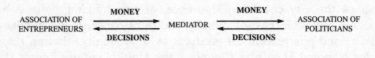

Figure 14.2

To begin with, the local administrator often adopts a 'central' role between party functionaries and civil servants. The most common figure, in this case, is that of 'politician as entrepreneur', that is, the person 'responsible for the broking of deals, both legal and illegal, and who generally takes a particular interest in the economic activity through traditional political intermediation' (Pizzorno 1992: 24; on the politician as entrepreneur, see also della Porta 1992b). To the bureaucrat, the public administrator can offer career stability, while in exchange he will obtain alliances which will favour the realisation of certain administrative decisions. On the other hand, the administrator can guarantee the party functionary certain political career advantages in exchange for the party's, or rather the party faction's, protection in his career. The alliance is cemented by the mutual interest in 'the deal', which is linked to the sharing of bribes and the *blackmail potential* inherent in the illicit act. To this are added various sources of trust: friendship, political bond, fidelity to the freemasons' association and mutual interest in entrepreneurial activity.

Comparing the three cases, I have been able to determine different forms of association which are distinguished by some notable characteristics, in particular: the prevalence of the political figure within the corrupt association; the degree of organisation; its decision-making mechanisms; the division of labour; the presence of an internal hierarchy; the terms of trust, and stability versus conflictuality within the association (see also della Porta 1990). I have, consequently, distinguished three forms of associations among political actors, using the term a 'clan' to describe the associative structure prevalent in the case of Savona, the 'business committee' that present in the USL of Catania, and the 'party faction' the one which prevails in Florence.

The clan is endowed with a well-structured organisation, with a sophisticated division of labour between public administration figures who plan the deals, consultants and functionaries who contribute to the decision-making process, 'collectors' who collect the kickbacks (without revealing the names of the corrupt politicians), and 'name-lenders' who recycle the money. The functions of intermediation between public and private actors are, therefore, assimilated by the group. The division of labour is complemented by a hierarchy with a 'leader', 'middle-level agents' and 'followers'. The clan always acts in solidarity, its funds always end up in the leader's account and are administered by a member of the group – even if individual contributions for single cases of corrupt exchanges are paid separately. The group forms around a party current, but it then allows for the development of transversal alliances. However, trust is based not only or even predominantly on common political membership, as on the affinities between 'instrumental friendships' which are secured by long-term contacts, and the development of members' common interests in various 'societies' with cross-member participation. For example, the judges who investigated the Savona case have written that:

> [The] detailed investigative activity has made possible the disclosure of the presence of a whole coterie of links of political militancy, friendships, masonic brotherhood and self-interested collaboration which have constituted the bedrock on which the criminal activity of the accused has been grafted.
>
> (Tribunale of Savona 1984: 122)

The group tends to stabilise, and its persistence over time 'normalises' and broadens the system of bribes. As long as new entries to the group are counterbalanced by the expansion of the potential range of the extortion of bribes, the level of internal conflict is kept low.

A second type of association in political corruption, among those that I have attempted to reconstruct, is the 'business committee'. The level of internal organisation between public administrators is rather low, its logic is purely based on dividing-up the 'booty' obtained through the management of a public body. What unites this association – which is entirely transversal with respect to parties – is the administrative participation in the same public entity and the possibility of reciprocal blackmail. The degree of labour division is minimal, and administrators directly solicit bribes from the private sector members. There is not even a hierarchy within the association – even if the Presidents of the administrative councils have greater administrative power which they can exploit to impose bigger bribes. The individual member is, therefore, free to use the bribe money obtained at his discretion – nevertheless, he will first have 'balanced' his gains according to those of others.

A third type of association is what we have termed the 'party faction'. The division of roles is very simple in this case: a party functionary who coordinates; public administrators who collaborate; bureaucrats who 'turn a blind eye'; middlemen who 'make things happen'. The cornerstone of trust is based on party affiliation, and the most important role is, in fact, that of the party functionary who 'keeps the queue moving'. Unlike other cases, however, the associations of corrupt members are not long-lasting but linked to a single event. The number of 'corruptees' is kept to a minimum and the bribe ends up predominantly in the party coffers – or, better still, in the account that the functionary manages for the faction that leads the federation – with a somewhat 'modest' recompense for the administrators involved. The terms of reciprocal trust in the group, which unites precisely on that single occasion, are extended principally by a common sense of belonging to a party current. The fortuitous nature of the corrupt exchange means that the role of mediators is particularly important – we shall deal with this in the next section.

The entrepreneurs

Let us now move across to the other side of Figure 14.1 and look at the associative structure involving private entrepreneurs.[3] In the greater part of the investigations dealing with episodes of political corruption we find a section dedicated to the description of the relations between public and private actors. It is not only in Italy that the offence is viewed differently if the private side of the exchange is the injured party, that is, if the entrepreneur was coerced into paying a bribe in exchange for something that he had a right to (extortion offences by public officials); or if the private actor was the accomplice of the administrators, that is, he also benefited from the corrupt deal (and in this case both sides were guilty of an offence dealing with corruption).

From the study of the three cases of political corruption in Italy, it has emerged that public actors possess blackmailing potential that is very influential in the course of the corrupt exchange. Among the coercive means employed are threats to entrepreneurs that they will not be included in the list of firms able to tender for public contracts, or the threat that the entrepreneur will no longer receive privileged information on the 'confidential estimates' which the firm's projected costs must come close to in order to win the contract, or the simple holding-up of payments. On the other hand it seems that private individuals hardly ever make an economic loss when they agree to take part in a corrupt exchange. Thanks to the backing of politicians the money involved in the bribe is in fact recuperated through fraud, which allows the private members to recover illicit gains at the expense of public administration (on such mechanisms see della Porta 1992c). Often, by grouping to form 'cartels', businessmen actually manage to manipulate the rules governing the issue of contracts, thus recovering a surplus in profit which can be 'reinvested' in bribes.

What are the conditions that favour the entrepreneurs' taking part in the corrupt exchange? We were able to observe, first, that the system of corrupt exchange seems simplified by the existence of *stable relations* between administrators and private members. In fact, the constancy of the relationship allows for the stabilisation of the size of the bribe, keeping it at a 'calculable' cost.

But this is not all. We can add that the constancy of the exchange encourages the diffusion, especially among a sub-group of businessmen who have frequent contacts with the state, of a system of rules and values condoning illicit behaviour. In these milieux, 'corrupt' administrators find their counterparts among entrepreneurs who consider the bribe as a 'fair game'.[4] The payment of bribes is, therefore, considered like a normal 'marketing' or advertising expense.

The mediators

As illustrated in Figure 14.2, contacts between public and private actors are at times kept by middlemen. In our cases of corruption, people who were not party members, and who were not directly interested in administrative measures, were involved – defendants who went by the description of 'Jacks of all trades', 'unlicensed property agents' (Tribunale di Firenze 1986: 24), officially unemployed people but with thousands in their bank accounts and in shares, or 'flags of convenience' (Tribunale di Firenze 1987: 38). Theirs was the role of mediators, or middlemen – an important function in the fulfilment of the corrupt form of exchange.[5] Thus, in the corrupt forms of exchange individuals participate whose official job as consultants, lawyers, or public employees acts as a cover for their real role which, as we have noted, is to create contacts and promote negotiation between the two or more parties interested in the dishonest exchange. In fact, the mediators are not quite entrepreneurs, nor politicians; they do not have direct political power, nor do they manage economic concerns – their main expedients are 'discreet acquaintances' which they accumulate and 'sell'.

Situations in which the presence of the mediator is more important in the conclusion of the corrupt exchange are, in the first place, those in which contacts between public administrators and the private party are more sporadic. In this case the task of the middleman is properly that of stage-managing the initial contact. The middleman can, nevertheless, play a significant role in the more 'complex' cases of corrupt exchanges, that is, those in which a function of mediation among the different parties which have to split the bribe is necessary. In addition, in the corrupt exchange the mediator can perform a further function which is to disguise the bribe as the cost of the intermediation.

Finally, through the creation of mixed societies of intermediation with cross-cutting participation of politicians and entrepreneurs, the mechanism of corrupt exchange is perfected, and becomes institutionalised to the point that it is no longer possible to distinguish between public and private actors, or between politician and entrepreneur. As an interviewee from Catania concluded, at this stage 'the bribe is no longer a briefcase full of cash that is concealed by illegal accountancy, it is the profit from an economic activity that in reality does not exist.'[6]

COMPLICITY, CONNIVANCE, CONSENSUS

The corrupt exchange is not just limited to people who have a direct interest in it. Rather, it involves other actors, who although they may not directly take part in the sharing out of the bribe, nevertheless obtain other favours in exchange for resources that are indispensable for the completion of the exchange. The actors in the corrupt exchange must, in effect, be guaranteed 'cover-ups'; in other words, they must minimise the likelihood of administrative illegalities occurring, being reported and investigated. With either threats or favours, the corrupt politicians must erect a wall of silence around their illicit dealings.

As Figure 14.3 indicates, they therefore make contact with some actors who can offer them resources of physical violence, but, above all, they

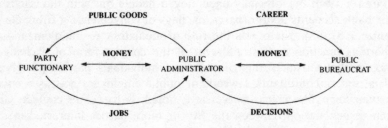

Figure 14.3

exchange favours with a series of actors who might otherwise jeopardise their illicit activities.

Corrupt politicians sometimes have at their disposal resources of violence with which they intimidate potential denouncers. These resources are drawn from a reciprocal exchange of protection with some of the representatives of organised crime. However, our research has indicated that silence is not obtained with the threat of violence, but through the complicity and consensus obtained using a vast distribution of votes and favours. In relations within the party system, corrupt politicians offer the votes they control, building alliances either within the party or inside the elected assemblies or within the local boards. At the level of civil society, they exchange political consensus in return for privileged access to public resources. In what follows I seek to reconstruct in greater detail the networks of relations that business politicians build outside the so-called ring of corrupt exchange, and which enable corruption to spread.

Consociationalism and party-linked connivance

An outer circle of connivance, which enables the widespread reproduction of corrupt exchange, forms within the party system, where a type of mutual protection is created which includes not simply the 'corrupt', but also the non-corrupt. In the course of the research, we were able to observe that not only were there few declarations of corruption presented by party representatives, but also that – with the emergence of scandals linked to cases of corruption – all parties of government as well as those in opposition, seemed to converge in expressing reciprocal solidarity and trust in each other. In the Italian case, as in others (see e.g. Frognier 1986), the hidden form of consociational democracy which prevailed in the 1970s and the 1980s in the management of public bodies is the main explanation for this widespread complicity.

Consensus in 'civil society'

The business politicians involved in the cases of political corruption examined in Italy were generally people highly endowed with networking capacities, in other words, they were able to cement relations, to create trusting relationships, to promote mutual needs and favours. Such flair allowed them not only to organise their illicit dealings, but also to organise a network based upon mutual agreement, made up of 'clients' and also 'friends' among the local elite. By running a generous and shrewd system of favours facilitated by the treatment of public office as a system of spoils, the corrupt politicians successfully obtained the complicity of civil society.

Corrupt politicians also succeeded in gaining approval and acquiescence from within one of the organs that is supposed to fight corruption –

namely the judiciary. Concerning the role of the magistrates, our research has uncovered two different types of judges. On the one hand, there are those magistrates who – as Pizzorno has noted (1992: 63) – with respect to political parties have an almost vicarious function in fighting corruption. On the other hand, some of the corrupt seem to have found protection among the magistrature.[7] In both Savona and Sicily, those whom we interviewed cited the 'good relations' that existed between several politicians under investigation and some judges at the head of the magistrature in the two cities as the reason for the initial pardoning of their misdemeanours.

Once again, thanks to the shrewd management of favours, the corrupt politicians ultimately succeed in gaining the support of the local media. Research on the treatment of corruption on news programmes has revealed that because the ownership of newspaper titles is also the subject of *lottizzazione* between the parties, this has resulted in the non-reporting of political scandals (Cazzola 1988). We were able to conclude in our research that the local press rarely led an action campaign to emphasise political scandals (see della Porta 1992a: 272–280; Sherman 1978). On the contrary, it often seemed to relinquish professional ethics and sales promotion if it could protect the local administrators involved in cases of corruption.

The resources of violence

Returning to Figure 14.2, we can observe that in the cases of political corruption there are sometimes episodes of intimidation – attacks on the property of those who refuse to pay bribes or who try to negotiate their size; threats of violence against potential accusers or against those who oppose the bosses. Generally the business-oriented politician obtains resources of violence by means of exchanges with organised crime. Naturally, from our research we cannot determine how widespread the exchanges between politicians and organised criminal groups are. However, we can see that a number of different types of relationships between politicians and organised crime emerge. There is, in the first case, a political class that is organically linked to criminal organisations. For example, in the case of Catania, there is a political staff that is either a direct expression of this criminality or which depends on it, or which, ultimately, is 'created' by it (Tribunale di Catania 1988). Nor are these political staff of little importance within local society. Second, there are politicians who sustain privileged relationships with some criminal groups, that is, they weave a network of persisting exchanges, which constitutes a basis for long-term mutual trust (see Chapter 15 for an analysis of this phenomenon in the case of Naples). Finally, there are politicians who have infrequent exchange relations with a few common criminals – in other words, they offer services from time to time – be it votes or attacks on building sites. The real or potential use of violence resources seems to depend to a great extent on the degree of illegality in some zones. Where organised crime is stronger, the contacts with the political class are more frequent, as the Mezzogiorno of Italy shows. However, it seems that in general, a widespread level of corruption and threats of violence go hand in hand.

The locations of secret exchange

Up to this point we have observed that in highly corrupt systems, the perpetual reproduction of vitiated exchange is possible thanks to a complex network of relations and associations which link together public actors, private actors and mediators, consolidating the base of mutual trust which allows for the continuation of exchanges. Thanks to the private management of public office, through 'a strategy of favours' or 'corruption power', the corrupt politicians are able to extend the circle of connivance beyond the group of those who directly take part in corruption. Moreover, privileged relations with representatives of organised crime often supply the local politicians with a consistent reserve of violence which can be used against those who put the system of corruption at risk.

An observation that has frequently emerged in the course of this research is that political corruption requires special outlets wherein to mediate interests, or organise business, other than the institutional ones. It is no coincidence that a common feature of corrupt administrators is their contempt for representative institutions – a clear example of this contempt is provided by the image of the President of the Regional Council of Liguria, who sent in his stead a tape-recorder containing a cassette with the decisions to be approved, to a sitting of the regional council. One of the conditions that facilitates corrupt exchange seems to be the extraction of decisions from institutional forums where the opposition exercises a scrutinising control. With elected assemblies that have neither the time nor the ability to control an ever-more complex government, an unusual type of association between local political and non-political elites becomes widespread.

In effect, the system of corruption seems to be interwoven with the creation – or the solidification – of secret associations, where decisions are taken far from prying eyes. It seems to be more than a coincidence that in our research the 'corrupt' administrators showed a high propensity to participate in masonic lodges which, as is well known, insist on the secrecy of their members. Regarding the Savona group, the permeation of the masonry seems to have been a planned strategy – with the concentration of some corrupt politicians in certain lodges – but also with a differentiated presence in more than one lodge. The membership of masonic lodges was also common among many of the individuals involved in the Florentine investigations. In all three cities that formed the subject of our research, we came across 'exceptional' numbers of active free-masons. Freemasonry's greater than average concentration of power, especially in the health and construction sectors, provoked complaints of degeneracy even from within the associations themselves. In the secrecy of some lodges, the 'corrupt' and the 'corruptors' could meet and organise their deals.

FINAL OBSERVATIONS

Throughout the course of this chapter I have attempted to make a systematic reconstruction of the networks of actors involved in clandestine exchange. In conclusion it should be noted that in the long run, the system of corruption has also shown its own inherent weakness. Its expansion dynamics in fact imply a constant waste of both material resources and legitimacy (della Porta 1995). At the beginning of the 1990s, three factors were responsible for the crisis in the corrupt exchange network. The difficult international economic conjuncture reduced the available resources for ambiguous earnings at the very moment when the Maastricht agreements were increasing expectations for efficiency. Simultaneously, the chronic shortage of extended consensus produced the most dramatic effects at the moment when – with the collapse of the Eastern socialist regimes – there was a lack of legitimacy for those party systems which (and not only in the Italian case) were born out of the division of the world into two blocs. If the traditional political parties seem to be in difficulty in different European countries, it is in Italy – because of the limited consensus we have spoken of – that the crisis of the traditional parties took the most exasperated forms and dimensions. Thus a type of 'virtuous circle' was begun. The dissatisfactions with the increasing inefficiencies of public services led to the delegitimation of the political class. This led in turn to the investigations into political corruption, the results of which further discredited the political class when the consequent rapid spread of the legal investigations into crimes against the public administration also brought to light the buying and selling of votes, as well as the organic relationship between some politicians and organised crime. The very loss of political protection then seemed to weaken some of the organised crime-based groups, which lost power at the same time as their political allies. Their difficulties, in turn, resulted in a further loss of power for the politicians they supported.

Even if it is still too early to make forecasts, we can note that the altered political climate might halt the widespread reproduction of corruption, in two ways at least. To begin with, it alters the conditions which made the calculation of individual participation in the corrupt exchange valid, to the extent that it jeopardises a system of values where corruption appeared as an almost 'respectable' way of behaving. In other words, the string of arrests – and the support for the judges by the general public –

began to question a deeply entrenched system of values which allowed for self-justification and self-absolution. As far as the overall system is concerned, the work of the judges has, furthermore, attacked the delicate balance of reciprocal trust between the corrupt and the corruptors which allowed for the widespread reproduction of corrupt exchanges.

NOTES

This chapter was translated by Maria La Falce.

1 My research on political corruption took place in the ambit of a broader project on 'Illegal Systems', directed by Alessandro Pizzorno of the European University Institute, Florence. For the complete results of the research, see della Porta 1992a; for a summary, see della Porta 1991.

2 In the case of Savona, the criminal proceedings, which involved cases of extortion, corruption and – initially – Mafia activities, gained common currency on 14 June 1983, when the Socialist President of the Region of Liguria was arrested. Thirteen local administrators, members of the PSI, two administrators of the PCI, and the President of the Province of Savona (DC) were involved. In the Florentine case, during the course of two criminal proceedings, three city council administrators of the PSI and the administrative secretary of the same party were found guilty of corruption and extortion. As for Catania, in the criminal proceedings for corruption and extortion, begun at the end of 1987, five politically nominated functionaries and three administrators of a Local Health Unit, USL 35, were involved – two from the Christian Democratic Party and a member of the Republican Party (PRI). All criminal proceedings ended with the conviction of most of the accused. For more information refer to della Porta 1992a, chapter 2 and chapter 9.

3 Cases involving 'private' entrepreneurs are more frequent, but a recent scandal in Milan has shown that even managers of public enterprises paid bribes, often to their party colleagues. On the Milanese case refer to della Porta 1993.

4 The bribe was described in such a way by some business constructors interviewed in the United States and in France (Becquart-Leclercq 1984). As far as Italy is concerned, in an opinion poll 24 per cent of a sample of 400 businessmen, company managers and freelance workers confirmed that the application of bribes can be considered 'acceptable' (*Il Mondo* 1987: 38–39).

5 On the role of middlemen in corruption, see Oldenburg 1987.

6 A similar mechanism was observed by Mény in the French case, where politicians pushed businessmen to turn to societies of intermediation and consultancy which were controlled by political parties, in turn guaranteeing them a privileged access to public contracts (Mény 1992: 254 ff.).

7 In particular, concerning the magistrature in Italy, it has been noted that – in stark contrast to an organisational structure which should assure a high degree of independence to the judges – 'a notable inclination in the development of contacts and connections between the magistrature and the political environment, between magistrates and politicians, between currents of the magistrature and parties or party currents has emerged' (Guarnieri 1991: 25–26). The flourishing of highly rewarded 'extra-judicial assignments', together with the relevance of the attachments to parties or currents in career promotion could explain 'the long and tormented course of penal investigations involving politicians or public administrators' (ibid.: 26).

REFERENCES AND FURTHER READING

Becquart-Leclercq, J. (1984) 'Paradoxes de la corruption politique', *Pouvoirs* 2: 19–36.

Ben-Dor, G. (1974) 'Corruption, industrialization and political development, revisionist theses revisited', *Comparative Political Studies* 7: 63–83.

Bocca, G. (1983) 'Ruba compagno ruba ordinò la banda Teardo', *La Repubblica*, 8 September.

Caciagli, M. *et al.* (1977) *Democrazia cristiana e potere nel Mezzogiorno. Il sistema democristiano a Catania*, Florence: Guaraldi.

Cazzola, F. (1988) *Della corruzione. Fisiologia e patologia di un sistema politico*, Bologna: Il Mulino.

Chubb, J. and Vannicelli, M. (1988) 'Italy: a web of scandals in a flawed democracy', in A. Markovits and M. Silverstein (eds), *The Politics of Scandals. Power and Processes in Liberal Democracies*, New York: Holmes & Meier.

della Porta, D. (1988) 'Il denaro corrompe chi non lo ha?', *Politica ed economia*, 18: 65–68.

—— (1990) 'Risorse e attori nella corruzione politica. Appunti su tre casi di governo locale in Italia', *Polis* 4: 499–532.

—— (1991) 'La logica della corruzione in Italia', *Il Mulino* 40: 902–915.

—— (ed.) (1992a) *Lo scambio occulto. Casi di corruzione politica in Italia*, Bologna: Il Mulino.

—— (1992b) 'Corruzione e carriere politiche: immagini dei "politici d'affari" ', *Stato e mercato* 34.

—— (1992c) 'Meccanismi amministrativi e corruzione nel governo locale', *Rivista trimestrale di scienza dell'amministrazione* 2: 57–77.

—— (1993) 'Milano: capitale immorale', in S. Hellman and G. Pasquino (eds), *La politica in Italia*, Bologna: Il Mulino.

—— (1995) 'The Vicious Circle of Political Corruption in Italy', in D. della Porta and Y. Mény (eds), *Political Corruption and Democracy*, London: Pinter.

Eisenstadt, S. N. and Roniger, L. (1984) *Patrons, Clients and Friends. Interpersonal Relations and Structure of Trust in Society*, Cambridge: Cambridge University Press.

Frognier, A. P. (1986) 'Corruption and consociational democracy: first thoughts on the Belgian case', *Corruption and Reform* 1: 143–148.

Gardiner, J. A. and Lyman, T. R. (1978) *Decisions for Sale. Corruption and Reform in Land Use and Building Regulations*, New York: Praeger.

Guarnieri, C. (1991) 'Magistratura e politica: il caso italiano', *Rivista italiana di scienza politica* 21: 3–32.

Key, V. O. (1936) *The Technique of Political Graft in the United States*, Chicago: University of Chicago Press.

Klaveren, J. van (1970) 'The concept of corruption', in A. J. Heidenheimer (ed.), *Political Corruption: Readings in Comparative Analysis*, New Brunswick: Transaction.

Landesco, J. (1968) *Organised Crime in Chicago*, Chicago: University of Chicago Press.

Mény, Y. (1992) *La corruption de la République*, Paris: Fayard.

Nye, J. S. (1967) 'Corruption and political development. A costs–benefits analysis', *American Political Science Review* 61: 417–427.

Oldenburg, P. (1987) 'Middlemen in third-world corruption: implication of an Indian case', *World Politics*, 39: 508–535.

Padiolau, J. (1975) 'De la corruption dans les oligarchies pluralistes', *Revue français de sociologie* 14: 33–58.

Peters, J. G. and Welch, S. (1978) 'Political corruption in America. A search for definition and theory', *American Political Science Review*, 72: 974–984.

Pizzorno, A. (1978) 'Political exchange and collective identity in industrial conflict', in C. Crouch and A. Pizzorno (eds), *The Resurgence of Class Conflict in Western Europe since 1968*, New York: Holmes & Meier.

Pizzorno, A. (1992) 'Introduzione: la corruzione nel sistema politico', in D. della Porta (ed.), *Lo scambio occulto. Casi di corruzione politica in Italia*, Bologna: Il Mulino.

Rose-Ackerman, S. (1978) *Corruption. A Study in Political Economy*, New York: Academic Press.

Sherman, L. W. (1978) *Scandal and Reform: Controlling Police Corruption*, Berkeley: University of California Press.

Tilman, R. O. (1968) 'Emergence of black market bureaucracy: administrative corruption in the new states', *Public Administration Review* 28: 437–444.

Tribunale di Catania (1988) *Sentenza istruttoria di rinvio a giudizio in procedimento n. 3755/87* (Rapporti giudiziari 1196/88 E).

Tribunale di Firenze (1984) *Sentenza-ordinaria di rinvio a giudizio in procedimento n. 380/83A*.

Tribunale di Firenze (1986) *Sentenza in prima istanza del tribunale penale, n. 407 RS*.

Tribunale di Firenze (1987) *Sentenza-ordinanza di rinvio a giudizio in procedimento n. 212/84A*.

Tribunale di Savona (1984) *Sentenza-ordinanza di rinvio a giudizio in procedimento n.141/81 ARGGI*.

15 The resistible rise of the new Neapolitan Camorra

Percy Allum and Felia Allum

'If there is a place, a town, where vultures can satisfy their appetites, then that place is Naples...'

(Tahar Ben Jelloun, *L'Ange aveugle*, 1992)

'Naples is the capital of corruption'

(Chief Prosecutor Agostino Cordova, 1994)

The 'Kickback City' scandal (*Tangentopoli*) was late in breaking in Naples – and this despite the city's reputation for corruption and political clientelism (Allum 1973). Indeed, it was more than a year after the arrest of Milan Socialist administrator Mario Chiesa, on 17 February 1992 – which set in motion the city prosecutor, Antonio Di Pietro's 'clean-hands' criminal investigation (*Inchiesta 'mani pulite'*) (della Porta 1993) – when Christian Democrat MP, Alfredo Vito, better known as 'Mister Hundred-Thousand Votes', decided to collaborate with investigating magistrates and confessed to buying votes and accepting bribes on 19 March 1993.[1] However the immediate effects were devastating: permission was requested to lift the parliamentary immunity of eight Neapolitan MPs (Cirino Pomicino, Conte, Del Mese, Gava, Mastrantonio, Meo, Raffaele Russo, Alfredo Vito) accused of Mafia-style conspiracy (*Camorra e Politica* 1993). Almost contemporaneously, the former Socialist Mayor of Naples, Nello Polese and 16 city councillors were arrested together with a former provincial legislator, a former President of the Campania region, six regional legislators and five regional councillors for 'corruption or Mafia connections' (Commissione Antimafia 1993: 4).

CAMORRA AND POLITICS IN NAPLES

The Camorra domination of Neapolitan politics is a relatively recent phenomenon of the 1980s and 1990s. It was not that relations did not exist earlier; indeed they did, but they were casual not systematic. In the 1950s to 1960s, bands of American-style gangsters (variously called *camorristi* or *guappi*) organised a series of 'rackets' in three sectors: black market in smuggled cigarettes, petrol and narcotics; control of the fruit and vegetable markets (*Pasacalone 'e Nola* and *Totonmno 'e Pomigliano*) in addition to the rag trade; and finally the control of credit and instalment payments (the *magliari*) (Ricci 1989: 116).

The link with politics at the time was very simple: the *camorrista* furnished the politician with votes (usually preference votes), obtaining in exchange protection for his various illicit activities. The writer Carlo Bernari noted at the beginning of the 1960s that:

> the exercise of *guappa* legality finds its expression in the ranks of illustrious university professors, eminent lawyers, respectable Right Honourables or Excellencies, who come to terms with the *guapperia* to ensure their election or reelection, whether it be to the local municipal council or that of the provincial capital or again to the provincial council, as well as to Parliament or the Senate . . .
>
> (quoted in Allum 1973: 62)

The point to stress here is the subordination of the *camorristi* to the politicians and to the established authorities.

The situation is qualitatively very different today: 'The Camorra is all pervasive' – the President of the Parliamentary Anti-Mafia Commission, Luciano Violante, has written in the Commission's recent report, *Relazione sulla camorra*:

> Its characteristics enable it to be present wherever there is profit. Ruthlessness, opportunism and cynicism are the principles common to all Camorra gangs. There is no lucrative activity that they cannot undertake, no political relation that they cannot set up; no service that they cannot render.
>
> (Commissione Antimafia 1993: 16–17)

Corresponding to this pervasiveness is a spontaneous readiness to accept Camorra support by politicians, civil servants, business and professional men for economic, professional and electoral self-interest or for reasons of pure power or through a lack of a civic sense. Pervasiveness on the one hand and readiness on the other have created in Campania a widespread phenomenon of integration and connivance between the Camorra and the social and institutional spheres. The Commission came across several serious cases of incredible tolerance towards the Camorra – the result certainly of this integration between Camorra, society and institutions. A good illustration of the latter is to be found in an instructing magistrate's case against Camorra boss, Carmine Alfieri, where one reads that 'in reality, political dynamics and electoral success are directly connected to the consciously demanded and encouraged action of criminal organizations aimed at hegemonic control of the area and the activities carried on there', and where named politicians 'are the primary authors of such connections, contemptuously availing themselves of the intimidatory power of Mafia organizations identified as a pillar of their own political power.' (Tribunale di Napoli 1993: 274–275). In other words, we are talking about the immediate participation of politicians as members, associates and partners in serious criminal activity.

THE GREAT LEAP FORWARD: THE ECONOMICO-POLITICAL CONTEXT

If there is systematic interpenetration between Camorra and the institutions, both economico-financial and political, as suggested, and in consequence, the domination of organised crime over Neapolitan social and political life today, it is important to understand how the Camorra was able to make this great leap forward. The crucial period was the decade between the early 1970s and the early 1980s. Indeed, two events in 1973, one local and the other international, were particularly significant in creating the context for what was to follow: they were the cholera epidemic and the first oil crisis. The former, thanks to the mobilisation of civil society organised as an act of solidarity by the local PCI (which formed part of the post-1968 social struggles), revealed the total incompetence of the local DC-dominated municipal, provincial and regional authorities – provoking a serious crisis in the Gavas' political machine: the result in Naples was the great progressive electoral victories of the years 1974–76 (in the divorce referendum of 1974, the local elections of 15 June 1975 and the General Election of 1976[2]).

The latter was responsible for the reversing of economic growth, both nationally and in the South particularly. Indeed, it effectively marked the end of the post-war 'economic boom', and gave rise to a cycle of world economic crises, in which each was more severe than its predecessor. National economic policies were switched to give top priority to the restructuring of northern industry to ensure its international competitiveness. This resulted in the cessation of industrial investment in the South and, hence, to the suspension of the policy of industrialisation. In compensation, it was decided to maintain consumer spending in the South through the traditional policy of family income support and public works' programmes, using it to replace a policy of real development (Trigilia 1992: 71–72). This policy was adopted quite simply because the needs of northern industry required the enlargement of the national consumer market. The result was, as Sales (1993: 54) has claimed, to render the South dependent twice over: on public transfers as well as on the prosperity of the northern economy, with consequences that have only been felt 20 years on in the anti-southern polemic of Bossi and the autonomous Northern League.

The loss of the control of the Naples municipality, following on his defeat in the battle for the Campania regional Presidency and national splits in the *Doroteo* faction, seriously weakened the Gavas' hold on local power in the mid-1970s. This was all the more so since their methods (false membership cards to control the party machine, political clientelism to secure election to local and national office, etc.) came under violent attack in the national press as emblematic of a certain system of government. To survive politically, the young Antonio Gava was forced to call on all his links with the DC national leadership. Fortunately, for him, he had already made the leap to a national position (elected a Deputy in 1972, and appointed to a post in the National Secretariat in 1973) before his father Silvio, Senator and former Minister, retired. Thus, he was able to effect a strategic personal withdrawal from local politics. In the meantime, the strength of the DC in the Neapolitan hinterland (the party was always electorally stronger in the provinces than it was in the city (D'Agostino 1992: 170–171)) enabled Antonio Gava to survive politically the years of 'flight' from Naples.

On the other hand, the precarious political position of the left-wing administration under Communist Mayor, Maurizio Valenzi – a heterogeneous alliance without an established majority and, hence, under the Christian Democrat sword of Damocles for the annual approval of the city budget[3] – left its mark on the whole experience. The PCI was, in fact, taken by surprise at its electoral success in 1975 and totally unprepared to administer the city, so lacked any specific programme of projects. Moreover, it assumed responsibility for the city at a very difficult moment in the midst of a serious social crisis, provoked on the one hand by the economic recession, and on the other, by the disengagement of the state-holdings' economic sector which, in laying off the organised working class, began to undermine the party's social base. Moreover, these were also the 'years of the bullet' (*anni di piombo*), which in Naples meant not only 'political terrorism', but also 'mass Camorra'.

In addition to the social problems, the administration faced grave political problems due to its lack of projects combined with the hostility of the state apparatus and the para-state agencies. The first meant resort to the personnel (i.e., the same Socialist legislators who had administered the city for the previous ten years with the Gavas' DC, as a warranty of technical capacity) as well as to the projects (e.g., the underground and the new commercial centre) of the previous administration, which had been violently attacked by the PCI when in opposition. The second meant being blackmailed by a local bureaucracy inflexible in defence of its privileges and a local economic state-holding sector largely subjected to the DC. Thus, not by chance, an experience that was understood at the time as a generous effort at renewal and modernisation, remained trapped in a politics of emergency. At the end of the day, however, the 'red administration' was unable to withstand the pressure of the socio-criminal tensions – of which those caused by the 1980 earthquake were only the greatest and most intractable.

THE GREAT LEAP FORWARD: THE MAFIA-ISATION OF THE CAMORRA

At this point, it is necessary to examine the transformation of the Camorra that took place in the second half of the 1970s with Raffaele Cutolo's (known as *'o prufessore*) attempt to create a structured and hierarchical criminal organisation, the so-called *Nuova camorra organizzata* (NCO: New Organised Camorra). Traditionally, the Camorra, in marked contrast to the Mafia, does not have a vertical and hierarchical structure. It consists of a series of clans and gangs that form, split and reform at will – usually as a result of bloody clashes. The Parliamentary Anti-Mafia Commission's report (1993: 28–29) lists a number of events, in which the Sicilian Mafia played a key role, in the transformation of the 1950s-style *camorristi-guappi* into the *Nuova Mafia campana* (New Campanian Mafia) of Carmine Alfieri (known as *'o 'ntufato*):

(1) The closing of the free port of Tangiers which necessitated the transfer of organised smuggling to a new destination and the port of Naples offered a favoured site in the centre of the Mediterranean.
(2) The difficulties created for the Mafia in Sicily by the reaction of the forces of order to the Ciaculli massacre of 1963 that suggested that it would be wiser to move its business centre temporarily to a safer location.
(3) The compulsory residence (*soggiorno obbligato*) of a large number of *mafiosi* in Campania, and above all in the provinces of Naples and Caserta, during the 1960s.
(4) The Sicilian Mafia's need of allies in its struggle against the better organised *marsigliese* (French connection) to win monopoly control of the drug traffic.

Thus, the more aggressive and better equipped local Camorra gangs slowly became the Neapolitan 'leading associates' of the Sicilian Mafia.

Cutolo opposed the monopoly pretensions of the Sicilians and raised the flag of emancipation of the Campanian groups from the Mafia, claiming his cut of the illicit trade, above all of the drug traffic which afforded huge sums of capital. He embarked on a ruthless campaign against the Sicilians: the years of his domination, from 1979 to 1983, saw the highest number of homicides (over 900 in Campania alone). At the same time, Cutolo was responsible for introducing two novelties: first a sense of identity, and second organisation. He offered to the criminal classes (expanded from the ranks of the 'Organised Unemployed movement' frustrated at not being able to enter the legal labour market, as well as from disbanded sub-proletarian youths) 'ceremonial rituals, criminal careers, wages and protection in prison and outside' (Tribunale di Napoli 1993: 30), and a job for everybody: from bag-snatcher (*scippatore*) to dope peddler, from extortioner to criminal lawyer, from swindler (*pataccaro*) to businessman. A mass organisation, then (the police calculated that the NCO has some 7,000 armed associates in 1980), that Cutolo was able to unite around his charismatic personality: centralised and complex, but with an 'open structure' in which there was a place for the thousands of violent and disbanded youths in Naples and in Campania. Not surprisingly, Sales has defined the NCO as 'the expression of a kind of collective mass movement of the violent and disbanded youth of Campania' (Sales 1987: 23). It represented, in a certain sense, together with the terrorist groups – *Nucleari autonomi proletari* (NAP), Neapolitan column of the Red Brigades (BR) – the degeneration of the 'new social movements' in Naples (Melucci 1989).

At all events, a part of the success of the NCO has been attributed to its organisational strength – that is, the capacity of Cutolo to overcome the family structure of clans and gangs, even if he was unsuccessful in unifying all criminal activity in Campania as he aspired to do – and also to the undoubted complicity of the public authorities. Thus, Cutolo's strategy was aimed, as the *Relazione sulla camorra* commented, 'at enrichment and impunity through ruthless violence against enemies and solidarity with the poorest strata of the population' (Commissione Antimafia 1993: 31). *'O prufessore* saw himself as a Robin Hood of crime, and always boasted that he actively promoted a redistribution of wealth to the advantage of the poorest strata of the population!

Such intrusive actvity could not but provoke the reaction of the anti-Cutolo gangs, which is precisely what happened: to defend themselves but also to be able to attack the NCO, these gangs copied the centralized organisational structure of the NCO, creating a sort of federation in the three-year period, 1979 to 1981, and adopting the name *Nuova Famiglia* (NF). However, once they had defeated the NCO with the help of the Sicilian Mafia, the NF split up once again into so many different gangs that fought each other for individual supremacy. This Hobbesian struggle of 'all against all' ended in the mid-1980s with the triumph of the Alfieri clan. 'In all of Campania today, the strongest Camorra group', according to the Parliamentary Anti-Mafia Commission (Commissione Antimafia 1993: 37), 'is that of Carmine Alfieri...'[4]

THE 1980 EARTHQUAKE AND THE CIRILLO AFFAIR

Both the Parliamentary Anti-Mafia Commission and the Neapolitan magistrates are agreed that the Cirillo case represents the decisive moment in the establishment of the power system that governed Naples and the Campania region in the era of the national CAF (Craxi–Andreotti–Forlani) iron pact, that is 1983 to 1992. To appreciate the significance of the kidnapping of Cirillo, it is necessary to recall that it occurred in the middle of the post-earthquake[5] emergency, just at the very moment (spring–summer 1981) when the 'reconstruction' funds to be used under the special emergency powers were becoming available. Cirillo, moreover, was at the time a key figure in the Campanian regional DC hierarchy: he was Gava's (by now one of the national leaders of the *Doroteo* faction) right-hand man, responsible for appointments and public works contracts, and so someone who knew a great deal about all the 'behind the scenes' deals of local Neapolitan politics. He was, therefore, a natural target for the Neapolitan column of the Red Brigades. Furthermore, his kidnapping ended happily, unlike that of former Prime Minister Aldo Moro three years earlier: he was not killed, but released after three months captivity against the payment of a ransom of one and half billion lire (circa £700,000), thanks above all to the decisive intervention of Cutolo's NCO.

It is now more or less confirmed by the various judicial investigations[6] that during the sequestration of Cirillo, Gava and his party associates contacted both the NCO and the NF with a view to their using their good offices with the BR to secure his release. It appears that the NF, in the person of Carmine Alfieri, refused to act, preferring to have nothing to do with the whole affair because he did not want to be used by the politicians. However, Cirillo's release, as a result of the good offices of Cutolo and the NCO, raised the spectre for Alfieri and the NF that Cutolo and the NCO had reinforced their association with Gava and his faction by this action. A little while later, Cutolo began to blackmail Gava, demanding that he respect the deal made, and threatening, in the event of non-compliance, to create a public scandal by revelations that would have invested the state institutions (that is the secret services) which had plotted[7] with him to secure the hostage's release.

It was for this reason that the Gavas, feeling themselves threatened by Cutolo, contacted the only person capable of opposing Cutolo and his NCO effectively, that is Carmine Alfieri. The request was backed by adequate compensation in the form of participation in the post-earthquake reconstruction public works' programme. It appears, in fact, that Alfieri had already decided to eliminate the NCO's general staff in revenge for the killing of his brothers carried out by the NCO in the mean time. The murder of Rosanova (the NCO's financier) in April 1982, followed by the even more important homicide of Casillo (Cutolo's deputy and the NCO's military chief, whose car mysteriously exploded with him in it in January 1983) were intended to signal to Cutolo that the game was up, and that he should quite simply forget all about blackmailing the politicians over the Cirillo affair. It was also intended to demonstrate to the criminal world at large that Alfieri was now the new 'contact' with Gava and his political faction. In point of fact, the elimination of the NCO's general staff not only marked the NCO's defeat as a criminal and political force, but also the rise of Alfieri and his henchmen who, by now virtually unopposed, became the main contact for businessmen and politicians in Campania as well as for other criminal organisations. This position enabled them to obtain very large cuts of the earthquake reconstruction public works' contracts. Indeed, according to the Parliamentary Anti-Mafia Commission, they constituted, for a long time, 'the effective government of large areas of the region' (Commissione Antimafia 1993: 129).

Today the Camorra has assumed the name *Nuova Mafia Campana* (New Campanian Mafia), and this refers to what has been called the 'enterprise Camorra'. Amato Lamberti, Director of the *Osservatorio della Camorra* in Naples, claims that its configuration is that of a system of economic enterprises whose goal is capital accumulation (Lamberti 1987). Its peculiarity, moreover, is that it operates contemporaneously in two markets, the illegal and the legal, indifferently promoting the constant circulation of capital between the two. The earnings of the criminal enterprises serve to control and extend monopolistically the criminal market. Finally, the resulting financial profits are invested in the legal market to make the individual *camorrista* appear a genuine businessman. In consequence it becomes virtually impossible to distinguish between criminal and legal economic activity.

This was a direct result of the mafioso-political management of the earthquake reconstruction. It is crucial to understand that it dealt with enormous sums of money (50 thousand billion lire – about £20 billion) in a period of economic recession – hence, was seen by many businessmen, not only as a great opportunity to get rich, but probably the last such opportunity – money that was covered by special legislation characterised by emergency and exceptional procedures, and so subject to the minimum financial control. In this situation, the mayors and administrators of the communes struck by the earthquake (i.e., almost all of the communes in Campania) enjoyed the greatest discretionary power in the distribution of public funds, thus all that was required to secure a cut was to control the election of local mayors and administrators. This could quite easily be done by a judicious use of the carrot (various favours) and the stick (violence and intimidation). It is no surprise, therefore, that Alfieri and his henchmen demanded to control the political situation directly, forcing their men onto party lists and securing their election both as mayors and administrators as well as simple communal councillors. This explains why 32 communes in the Campania region were dissolved for Mafia connections in 1993, and why more than 60 mayors and administrators were removed from office for the same reason.

Such tactics were easier to implement in the provinces than in the big city and this was also due to the fact that major Camorra bosses, businessmen like Alfieri[8] and Nuvoletta, were active in the provinces. In the city of Naples, in fact, the new-style Camorra was late in becoming established not only because the programme of major funding had suffered delays – indeed, the funds only began arriving in 1983 – but for two further reasons. The first was the lack of a business mentality among the numerous city Camorra gangs, which were still bound to the traditional activities of extortion and building-site protection. Moreover, the reconstruction funds were too large a meal for them and so the New Campanian Mafia of Alfieri and his henchmen moved in. The second was the presence of Naples city Communist Mayor Valenzi and his 'red' administration. However, the Neapolitan Socialists, strengthened by the appointment of PSI National Secretary Craxi to the Prime Ministership in 1983, did not hesitate to abandon Valenzi in order to force new local government elections and reassume control of the city once again in alliance with the DC.

THE LOCAL POLITICIANS: THE RISE OF THE THIRD REPUBLICAN GENERATION

The significance of the way in which the reconstruction public works' programme and funds were administered is that it encouraged, according to a recent study, the emergence in Naples of a new DC-PSI class of local politicians: the so-called third Republican generation.

> Having lost the sense of the independent contribution of politics and of its policy dimension the role of the administrator in the 1980s – increasingly a professional politician seeking the basic political resource, that is electoral support – has been reduced to that of simple receiver of demands and pressures and their mediation in the political market, 'floating' as it were on the stratification of demands and social interests, supporting the strongest, the most organised or, at least, those most rewarding in electoral terms . . .
>
> (Minolfi and Soverino 1993: 247)

The second characteristic of these new Neapolitan politicians, reared in local politics and without a real political project, if not that of strengthening their own local power, is their rapid rise to the role of national leadership. Typical of the so-called Neapolitan 'band of four' (Cirino Pomicino, Vito, DC; Di Donato, PSI; De Lorenzo, PLI) was the hyperactivity of Cirino Pomicino, who in the four years (1983–87) in which he was President of the Chamber of Deputies' Budgetary Commission, succeeded in directing 3,000 billion lire (circa £1.5 million) to the Campanian region – to which must be added the sums that he destined to the same area subsequently between 1988 and 1992, first as Minister of the Civil Service and later as Minister of the Budget – and which placed him at the centre of vast sectors of Neapolitan business activity. With this kind of national political leadership,[9] the politico-institutional crisis of the country in the early 1990s should come as no surprise to us. Indeed, as the Parliamentary Anti-Mafia Commission has spelt out, Campania is the region with the highest number of dissolved communes and administrators for Mafia connections; and within the Campania region, the provinces with the highest number are those of Naples and Caserta (Commissione Antimafia 1993: 5–6).

CONCLUSION

Racketeering and clientelism, Camorra and corruption have been staple ingredients of Neapolitan life ever since unification. Traditionally, they have been separate activities, although they have come into contact from time to time, because carried on by different social classes. Before World War II, clientelism was limited to the middle classes because suffrage was restricted. It became extended in the post-war period as a result of universal suffrage. Initially, clientelism was practised in a casual manner, but with the stabilisation of the party vote in the 1960s, and the growing importance of the preference vote to the individual politician, the practice was systematised.[10] Contemporaneously, but separately, the Camorra developed from a very individualistic, uncoordinated and apolitical group of racketeers into a vast network of organised, commercially active and politically well-connected clans as vast resources came within its purveyance. The crisis of the hegemonic political forces round the Gava power bloc in the 1970s led to an objective alliance of interest between them and the Camorra. This was sealed by a conjunction of events culminating in the 1980 earthquake to which the Cirillo affair provides the key.

Such relations as existed between the Camorra and politics in the 1950s were largely casual and had an individual basis – that is the links were between individual *guappi* and individual politicians. Moreover, as noted, the Camorra was always subordinate to the established authorities. In the 1990s, this was no longer the case as an 'iron pact' was sealed between the criminal and political worlds in which they were equal partners. As the Neapolitan magistrates have noted, 'the criminal organisations would not be able to pursue their own business goals without the collusion of public administrators' (*Camorra e politica*, 1993: 8). In Milan, the *Tangentopoli* scandal broke, in the end, because the pressures the politicians placed on business reached a point where they became untenable, with the result that businessmen were prepared to collaborate with the magistrates (della Porta 1993: 113). In Naples, it took the turning state witness (*pentitismo*) of leading *camorristi*, and in particular Alfieri's chief lieutenant, Pasquale Galasso, to convince the magistrates to investigate and open somewhat tardily the 'exchange vote inquiry' (*Inchiesta voto di scambio*) that was the immediate cause of Alfredo Vito's confession, and the revelations, arrests and accusations that followed. The fall of the First Republic and the apparent birth of the Second under the auspices of Berlusconi's 'Freedom and Good Government Alliance' raised the question whether the judiciary would be free to pursue its campaign against the association of Camorra and politicians to its normal conclusion now that it had won power.[11] This was all the more problematical as some in Berlusconi's entourage and commercial empire have been accused of Mafia association.

> 'If the Mafia is so powerful and if it scoffs at us today it is because it is both outside the institutions and at the heart of the institutions. . . . There are too many politicians who, in one way or another, have had at some time to ask a favour of the Mafia. As a result they were ensnared because the Mafia does not have a short memory . . .'
>
> (*L'amour à Palerme*: Jelloun 1992)

NOTES

1 In his confession, Vito declared:

> 'What I am about to do is a life choice that comes following a very profound crisis in my relations with politics and with the system in which for years I have been involved. I want to resign as a Deputy and put at the disposal of the judiciary three-quarters of my savings. I intend to change my life. I shall do what I am about to do above all for my daughter but also to help dismantle a bad system and to guarantee a better future for my daughter's generation.'
>
> (quoted in Marino 1993: 125)

One can compare Vito's declaration with that of Carmine Alfieri at his recent trial:

> 'I have repented in order to obtain justice, I am a tranquil *pentito* . . . because we are inadequate (or similar) before certain divine perfections . . . but also to contribute, so to speak, to a better tomorrow . . .'
>
> (Tribunale di Napoli 1994: 14–15)

2 It is worth noting that in the elections of 20 June 1976, the PCI had its greatest post-war electoral success in Naples, polling its highest vote in the former capital of the Kingdom of the Two Sicilies: 40 per cent. See Allum (1978: 556–557); and Galasso (1978: 270–285).

3 The approval of the city budget requires an absolute majority, and the left-wing coalition could only count on 40 votes out of 80. See Wanderlingh (1988: 53) and Valenzi (1978).

4 Alfieri was finally arrested in 1993, after having been in hiding for a long period. He has subsequently decided to turn state witness.

5 The earthquake occurred on 23 November 1980; its effects were felt in large areas of Campania as well as the city of Naples itself.

6 See Vasile (1989), *Camorra e politica* (1993). For the most recent account, see Sales in Tranfaglia (1994: 33–97).

7 It should perhaps be pointed out that throughout this whole episode (and indeed for most of the time that Cutolo was the acknowledged boss of the NCO), he was in prison serving long-term sentences, and directed the NCO from there.

8 In a recent statement in court in Rome, Alfieri has confirmed that 'I was a tradesman', and that he was only involved in the Camorra because of Cutolo's iniquity (Tribunale di Napoli 1993: 17).

9 Many observers have emphasised the 'meridionalisation' of the national political class – see Sales (1993), Trigilia (1992), also Minolfi and Soverina (1993) – against which Bossi's Northern League has led the revolt – culminating in

the fall of the First Republic and the Freedom Pole's victory in the 1994 general election.

10 In her decision to arrest ex-Health Minister, Francesco de Lorenzo, the investigating magistrate Laura Triassi wrote that de Lorenzo had 'put the system of bribe collection on an industrial footing, by means of an organisation of which he is the creator and promoter and to which the members of the medicines committee appointed by him and arrested in the course of the inquiry belonged...' (Tribunale di Napoli, quoted in *Il Manifesto*, 13 May 1994).

11 In the meantime the judicial action continued. A second series of arrests included four former MPs (Salvatore Varriale, Camillo Federico, Raffaele Russo (DC) and Bernardo Impegni (PDS)), eight communal councillors, two party functionaries, a former regional councillor and an MEP (Antonio Fantini of the PPI). More importantly, five top policemen (Matteo Cinque, former Naples Police Chief; Ciro del Duca, his deputy; Paolo Manzi, head of security; Umberto Vecchione, head of Criminalpol, and Carmine Espositio, his deputy) were also arrested for favouritism and corruption in concealing the relations between Camorra and politicians (see *Il Manifesto* 20 and 21 April 1994). There was still no judicial let-up in the autumn – witness the arrest of Antonio Gava, former MPs Enzo Meo, Raffaele Russo, Francesco Patriarca and Raffaelle Mastrantonio, and 91 others (including businessmen – e.g. Bruno Brancaccio, former President of the *costruttori napoletani* – and leading *camorristi*, Carmine Alfieri, Mario Fabbrocino and Giuseppe Autorino) on charges of *associazione camorristica* on 20 September 1994 (for details, see *La Repubblica* 21 September 1994 and subsequent days). The fall of the Berlusconi government in December 1994 and its replacement by the Dini government supported by the Progressive Pole and the Northern League did not dramatically alter the situation: the judicial processes continued, despite the Justice Minister's pressure on Prosecutors' offices (including Naples.)

REFERENCES

Allum, P. A. (1973) *Politics and Society in Postwar Naples*, Cambridge: Cambridge University Press.

—— (1978) 'La Campania: politica e potere: 1945–1975' in F. Barbagallo (ed.), *Storia della Campania*, vol. 2, Naples: Guida.

Camorra e politica (1993) *Richiesta di autorizzazione a procedere nei confronti di Gava ed altri*, 7 April, supplement to *La Repubblica*, 15 April.

Commissione Antimafia (1993) *Relazione sulla Camorra*, Rome: Camera dei Deputati.

D'Agostino, G. (1992) *Il posto in gioco. Politica ed elezioni a Napoli dal 1987 al 1992*, Naples: Athena.

della Porta, D. (1993) 'Milan: immoral capital' in S. Hellman and G. Pasquino (eds), *Italian Politics: A Review, vol. 8*, London: Pinter.

Galasso, G. (1978) *Intervista sulla storia di Napoli*, Bari: Laterza.

Jelloun, T. B. (1992) *L'Ange aveugle*, Paris: Editions du Seuil.

Lamberti, A. (1987) 'Dalla camorra "massa" alla camorra impresa: le trasformazioni della criminalità organizzata in Campania', in F. Barbagallo *et al.*, *La Camorra imprenditrice. Analisi, legislazione e proposte per combatterla*, Naples: Sintesi.

Marino, G. (1993) *Bella e mala Napoli*, Bari: Laterza.

Melucci, A. (1989) *Nomads of the Present*, Philadelphia: Temple University Press.

Minolfi, S. and Soverino, F. (1993) *L'incerta frontiera. Saggio sui consiglieri comunal a Napoli, 1946–1992*, Naples: ESI.

Ricci, P. (1989) *Le origini della camorra. 150 anni di malavita napoletana*, Naples: Sintesi.

Sales, I. (1987) 'La camorra massa e la camorra impresa' in various authors, *La camorra imprenditrice. Analisi, legislazione e proposte per combatterla*, Naples: Sintesi.

—— (1993) *Leghisti e sudisti*, Bari: Laterza.

Tranfaglia, N. (ed.) (1994) *Cirillo, Ligato e Lima. Tre storie di Mafia e politica*, Bari: Laterza.

Tribunale di Napoli (1993) *Ordinanza custodia cautelare in carcere contro Alfieri Carmine e 22 altri*, sentenza n. 638/93, 3 November.

—— (1994) *Processo penale n. 3952/RG contro Carmine Alfieri + 9*, Udienza 22 April.

Trigilia, C. (1992) *Sviluppo senza autonomia. Effetti perversi della politica nel Mezzogiorno*, Bologna: Il Mulino.

Valenzi, M. (1978) *Sindaco a Napoli. Intervista di M. Ghiara*, Rome: Riuniti.

Vasile, V. (ed.) (1993) *L'affare Cirillo. L'atto di accusa del giudice Carlo Alemi* (2nd edn), Rome: Riuniti.

Wanderlingh, A. (1988) *Maurizio Valenzi. Un romanzo civile*, Naples: Sintesi.

16 The changing Mezzogiorno
Between representations and reality

Salvatore Lupo

Italy has been united for 130 years. United, that is, in its legal and institutional form, but nonetheless marked throughout that period by the general perception of a difference, a dichotomy, between North and South. This 'southern question' has often been posed in terms of the Mezzogiorno's anomalous or deviant status when compared to a norm which is always modelled either on northern Italy or, more often, on some vague European standard. In the way that it has been elaborated in the culture, as in the practical measures to which it has given rise, the southern question tells us a great deal about Italy's path to modernity. More than that, it tells us about the very idea of modernity in a country that has come to be numbered amongst the industrialized and 'modern' nations during the same nineteenth- and twentieth-century period in which the southern question has been debated.

NORTH AND SOUTH: A FALSE DICHOTOMY

One of the striking aspects of the southern question is its persistence through time. The liberal-oligarchic period (1861 to 1882) had its southern question; as did the liberal-democratic period (1882 to 1922). Under Fascism (1922 to 1945), for all the regime's repeated declarations that it had 'solved' the problem, and during the half century of the Republic, there was nevertheless a southern question. It is all too apparent that we are not dealing with something that is merely the effect of the far-off events of national unification – despite the fact that, at the time, Piedmontese hegemony and the defeat of the Kingdom of the Two Sicilies did create a political imbalance between the component parts of the new realm. In the more or less recent past, there has been a greatly exaggerated emphasis on this *incipit* to the history of the united Italy: people have even talked in terms of a 'colonial model'. In reality, by the 1870s, the situation was already changing with the formation of a national power bloc of which the southern ruling class came to form a legitimate part.

As far as the profile of the ruling classes and the field of 'high' political and institutional history is concerned therefore, the absolute dichotomisation of North and South does not seem justifiable. Nevertheless, just this type of analysis is still widely practised. Indeed, many observers have followed this line of inquiry into the deep structures of southern society, where they have sought out the roots of its supposedly anomalous status. It is claimed, for example, that the southern family takes a particularly compact and restrictive form, which tends to cut the individual off from a fruitful, modern relationship with the social community and history. Interpretations of this kind, which have made their presence felt in debates in Italy as far back as the last century, reached a canonical form in Banfield's category of 'amoral familism' (Banfield 1958). Studies of clientelism display the same insistence on the absolute prevalence of personal ties in the South. At least in their early formulations, such studies maintained that the relations of patronage typical of traditional, agrarian society, had been preserved in the Mezzogiorno beyond the first half of this century. In the North over the same period, collective and impersonal political structures were established on the basis of ideology and/or class (Graziano 1974). Most recently, Robert Putnam has introduced the notion of *civicness*, a quality which he sees as having been part of the social climate of northern and central Italy since the age of the city-states (i.e. from the eleventh century). By contrast, 'civicness' was as absent from the Mezzogiorno in the middle ages as it is today (Putnam 1993). The millennium between these two historical moments has, it would seem, only served to confirm the initial, underlying datum.

Putnam's argument, which forces the entire history of Italy to fit a dichotomous model, seems untenable for a series of reasons which I have tried to explain elsewhere (Lupo 1993). For now, I intend only to point out that if Putnam were to be believed, it would be the city-state traditions of northern Italy which would have to be identified as anomalous, whereas the history of the South would be one of the very many instances in Europe in which feudalism, absolutism, moderate liberalism and democracy succeeded one another without creating a kind of trans-historical vicious circle. The supposed distinctiveness of the South is not even clearly visible in the area of clientelism. One of the main routes to representative democracy in Europe was a system managed by notables who would form groupings by deploying a reserve of personal relationships in the political market-place. Even if we limit the search for examples to the history of Italy – North and South – it is clear that the political and parliamentary system in the liberal era functioned in this way. It is certainly true that, in some areas of the North and Centre, the twentieth century has seen the establishment of a type of political mobilisation based on horizontal relations of solidarity around the Socialist (later Communist) and Catholic 'mass' parties. In general, in these parties, the southern regions play a lesser role. However, it is important to point out that ideological support for and involvement in a political movement often does not preclude the persistence or even development of clientelistic networks: this is the case with the Catholic movement of north-eastern Italy – and with the party which is its epigone, the DC. The Socialism and then Communism of central Italy is the most successful instance of political mobilisation based on horizontal class links. But that socialist culture has rural origins, in the day-labourers (*braccianti*) and the sharecroppers of the *mezzadria*, which make it the only case of its kind in Europe. What these reflections go to show is that Italy's variegated political geography cannot easily be understood by using a binaristic model, or by treating the Mezzogiorno as a historical anomaly. The 'amoral familism' thesis has turned out to be even more tenuous: no-one has managed empirically to demonstrate the existence, now or in the past, of a specific model of southern family; and no one has proved that in the South the family supplants the functions of associations, parties and the market in a way more significant than other cases within Italy or beyond it.

What remains to be considered is the kernel of Italy's dualism, and the aspect of it which is least open to discussion: the economic difference between North and South. Today as in the past, the Mezzogiorno is much less developed than the North. But Italy as a whole has developed a great deal over the last century, and not only has the Mezzogiorno not missed the bus, it has taken the motorway which has placed Italy amongst the most advanced countries thanks to extremely large increases in income and gross domestic product. In the South, as elsewhere in the last 40 years, there has been a gigantic transformation in the availability of individual and collective resources, in lifestyles, in the relations between the sexes, and in the opportunities available to men and women. The parallel, which is still repeatedly invoked, between the problems of the South and those of the 'third world' is completely inappropriate. Only if we move beyond the 'southern question', the dualistic model, the eternal and often sterile contrast between North and South, can we perceive the great transformations which have traversed one part of the country as much as the other. This change of perspective is necessary if we want to avoid the optical illusion which seems to affect so many observers, and which makes the difference between North and South appear to be a question of stagnation, of the total failure of the state and the market.

THE POST-WAR PERIOD: ECONOMY AND SOCIETY

Today southern Italy has nothing in common with agrarian or traditional societies. But just after World War II, after two decades in which fascist rhetoric had relegated the South to an exclusively rural role, things seemed very different. It was then an area which had been shut off from vital links to the international market by the impersonal forces of the crisis of the 1930s, along with the policy of Italian economic 'autarky' and foreign trade restrictions: this applied to both its goods (quality agricultural products) and its labour-force (the great flow of migration across the Atlantic). Before the war, the South had had to carry the burden of 700,000 more workers than in the period after World War I; in the late 1940s the situation was even worse.

Everything conspired to turn attention back on the old problem of the great estates based on extensive agriculture, the *latifundia* of the nobility or bourgeoisie. Generations of *meridionalisti* had asserted that the *latifundium* constituted a residue of feudalism (and the fact that in Sicily, even recently, the *latifundia* were commonly called 'feuds' (*feudi*) chimed with their assertions). After World War II, the Left – both Socialist and Communist – took up this tradition. With a resolve that was lacking in their forerunners, they placed themselves at the head of the peasant struggles which had already reached high levels of intensity after World War I. The Christian Democrats, the new barometer of conservatism across the country, ended up by adopting proposals for agrarian reform as the best response to popular pressure. At the same time, in contrast to the Left, they reassured the ruling class that the expropriated *latifundists* would be adequately compensated, and that state regulation would be restricted to clearly delimited cases.

The agrarian reform laws of 1950 produced one result of great importance: the expropriation and redistribution of 700,000 hectares of land. The two aspects of the policy, the redistribution of land and the work of drainage and irrigation, would have needed to be better integrated to obtain better results. The effects of the redistribution in particular were not those hoped for. But it is open to question whether things could have turned out differently. Famous agrarian economists such as Manlio Rossi-Doria demonstrated the existence of a kind of peasant *'minifundium'*, with a very low level of productivity, which was analogous to the *latifundium* of the nobility and bourgeoisie. On the other hand, there were also peasant (and bourgeois) enterprises able to get access to rich markets and high incomes. What these facts demonstrated was that the notion of the Mezzogiorno as a uniform peasant society excluded from the ownership of land, immobile in its folkloric and near archaic culture, and cut off from history, was useless both as a picture of reality and as a guide to action. (This was a notion of the South which had prospered in the 1950s in the work of anthropologists like Ernesto De Martino and writers like Carlo Levi.) In addition, the theories put forward by both the Left and the moderates, whilst being different in many respects, rested on the common assumption that there would be a long-term stagnation of industrial capitalism, and that the problem of employment would therefore have to be tackled on the terrain of agriculture. The idea on which the reforms were premised – of a democracy based on peasant smallholders – was already off the historical agenda: it was simply no longer compatible with the reality of a South formed of a diversity of towns and villages, of types of trade and agriculture which were not all organised around subsistence. The 'relative over-population' from which the South suffered was a problem directly related to, if not totally explained by, the unfavourable conditions under Fascism. It was therefore destined to disappear when industry, against all the pessimistic predictions of stagnation, began to build up a head of steam.

But in a country where industry was located almost exclusively in the North, the movement of the labour force from the primary to the secondary sector inevitably took the form of migration. Italy had already been a country of emigration in the nineteenth century. In the post-war period the flow of migrants began again. Between 1946 and 1976 around four million Southerners left their homes. Although the traffic across the Atlantic started up again, the main destinations were now Switzerland, Germany, Belgium, and in a completely new development, northern Italy.

The migrants arrived in the North to find inadequate housing and structures of social support: there was a wide margin for scandalous forms of profiteering on the housing and sleeping berths rented out in the crumbling buildings of the historic centres of northern cities. The barbarians arriving in ever greater numbers on the trains 'of hope' received a rather surly welcome. Prejudice and discrimination against Southerners began to spread. At the same time that FIAT, owned by the Agnelli family, used the newly available labour to carry through a massive expansion in its production of cars, *La Stampa*, the newspaper also owned by the Agnellis, demanded from the immigrants 'a full adaptation to the rules of life in the metropolis'. It declared that public opinion could not tolerate the contagious spread of archaic habits such as the crime of honour (*delitto d'onore* – a classic and greatly exaggerated example of the socio-cultural difference between North and South) (1960, quoted in Levi 1993: 136). To give credence to the stereotype of the dirty and barbaric alien, a pseudo-humorous story spread: emigrants were so incapable of understanding civilization that they set about growing parsley in the washing facilities of the modern apartments generously supplied to them by locals.

What intolerance of this kind evinced was the anxiety experienced by a nation whose mechanisms of collective identification were suddenly revealed in all their fragility. Paradoxically, however, emigration, rather than confirming an irremediable alienation of Northerners and Southerners from each other, ended up by revealing the exact opposite. The migrant ghetto areas only lasted as such for a fairly short period. Quickly, with the second generation, the sense of diversity disappeared, along with the association between southern extraction and a subordinate role in the social hierarchy. The growing proportion of the various waves of migrants which comprised white-collar workers and the petty bourgeoisie gave rise to even faster integration. Let us, for a moment, take a brief step forward in time, and examine the new wave of anti-southern feeling which has run through a substantial part of northern Italian public opinion since the 1980s, contributing to the electoral successes of the various more or less separatist leagues. The target of these feelings has been the southern teachers or bureaucrats of various levels working in the North – the argument being that they are competing with locals for jobs. But these disputes seem very mild when compared to the ferocious struggles between unskilled workers which have occurred at various points in American and European history.

In short, there have been no significant instances of segregation or self-segregation: racist or segregationist political movements have not been created; neither have lasting vertical divisions on social and ethno-cultural grounds (as has been the case elsewhere and as would presumably have happened if Turkish or North African workers had been brought in to work at FIAT: Cafagna (1994)). The point is as obvious as it seems: we are dealing with a single people, united by the same language and culture. For this reason, the effects of the cultural shock of emigration, albeit substantial at the time, have proved to be moderate and easily remedied in the medium term: the learning process has been smooth, and social mobility relatively rapid. For all that it is obvious, this fact merits underlining because it demonstrates something which is often denied in the teeth of the facts: the existence of an Italian nation.

We could add that the 'modernisation' experienced by the Southerners who migrated to the North is the same process, undergone (at a slower rate in some respects) by those who remained in the South: the majority of Southerners know how to read and write; the *delitto d'onore* has died out; women are no longer segregated; Southerners consult fortune-tellers, but not in greater numbers than other Italians; they read only a little less than their co-nationals; they are careful not to have more than two children per couple. If a clearly defined southern cultural identity based on these characteristics did ever exist in the past, it has gradually melted away under the influence of state education and the mass media, as well as because of the extraordinary growth in income levels achieved in the last half-century.

THE ROLE OF THE CHRISTIAN DEMOCRATS

In the field of politics, as in the economy and society, the South of the immediate post-war period looked very different from the North. Part of that difference can be traced to the macroeconomic and macrosocial variables associated with backwardness. Another factor owes more to immediate circumstances – namely the fact that Italy was invaded from the South where the allies helped to restore a government based on the army and the monarchy, the foundations of pre-fascist power. By contrast, the long period between 1944 and 1945 in which military operations were held up in the central band of the peninsula caused in the North the rapid spread of the partisan campaign, the radicalisation of political struggle, the dissolution of the liberal forces which had been hegemonic in pre-fascist

Italy, and the strengthening both of the Left parties (the Socialists, Communists and Party of Action) and of the Christian Democrats.

The Socialists and Communists managed to influence a substantial segment of the popular classes of the southern countryside during the season of peasant activism. The bourgeois and moderates of the Mezzogiorno could obviously not turn to the Left; but then neither was it easy for them to turn to the Christian Democrats. Apart from the odd important individual, such as the Sicilian Luigi Sturzo, the strength of the Catholic movement had never been in the South: not in 1919, the year of the foundation of the Popular Party, and not in the aftermath of World War II, at the foundation of the DC. In the first 25 years of the century, the various groups which could be classified as the southern Left, including the peasant movements, belonged to radical and liberal-democratic groupings. These were precisely the movements which tended to be marginalised after the war by the logic of the 'mass' parties. The South therefore only contributed politically to developments in that it formed a brake, a counter-current to Italy's movement towards a Republic 'of the parties'. In the 1946 referendum, the Mezzogiorno supported the monarchy, and up until the beginning of the 1950s it voted for a plurality of right-wing groups which identified themselves as local or localist, and which tended to be personalised, demagogic, clientelistic and suspicious of the national parties.

It was the Christian Democrats who took the situation in hand. In the first instance, they absorbed the riotous forces of the Right by confronting Communism head on after 1948. But it was state intervention, identified with the majority party, which gave the South the chance to participate in national government and overcome the sense of alienation which had taken root in a substantial part of the Mezzogiorno in the aftermath of the war. If agrarian reform created splits in the ruling groups, it also gave them the chance to modernize themselves. It necessarily involved the distribution of resources in the form of land and finance for the creation of peasant smallholdings. The Christian Democrats managed these resources in a clientelistic manner through bodies and associations closely tied to the party. We are one step away from the theory and practice of state intervention aimed at industrialising the Mezzogiorno, and from the accompanying promise of growth and modernity, of jobs created locally and not in some far-off, foreign place.

The Mezzogiorno Development Fund (*Cassa per il Mezzogiorno*) had begun by investing not only in agriculture, but also in the infrastructure, which was considered a prerequisite for industrialization. The results were fairly good, notably from projects which were fundamental to raising the level of civilization, such as the elimination of malaria, and the construction of sewers, housing and communications. However, intervention of this kind, spread thinly over a wide area, came to be considered insufficient to break the vicious circle whereby industrial investment tended to be concentrated in areas which are already developed, where companies can make savings on external costs. The attempt was made to escape from this trap by concentrating state intervention in restricted, carefully defined areas which were called 'growth poles'.

During the 1960s, as part of this policy, the large state-controlled companies, and with them private-sector firms from Italy and abroad, carried through important industrial initiatives, particularly in the steel, chemical and petrochemical industries. A significant proportion of government orders was guaranteed to firms located in the South. At the beginning of the 1970s, the proportion of industrial investment in the South, as a percentage of the national total, had gone up from 20 per cent to 30 per cent. Between 1960 and 1975, the number of people in the Mezzogiorno employed in companies with over 20 workers had risen from 240,000 to 343,000: 194,000 new jobs had been created in the South as compared to 148,000 in the North and 156,000 in the Centre.

However, many of the results immediately proved to be less satisfying than these figures would seem to indicate. The problem of the disproportion between costs and benefits began to be posed. It was pointed out that large companies installed 'from outside' had not managed to create a fertile terrain around them for small and medium enterprises: as a result they came to acquire the sarcastic nickname of 'cathedrals in the desert'. In fact it was rather misplaced to talk about the failure of the theory of the 'growth poles' when, in practice, the fundamental premises of the policy were turned upside down. The objective had been carefully targeted intensive intervention, but instead there was an unstoppable process whereby the number of 'poles' was multiplied and the policy slipped back into the much maligned one of scattering investment over a wide area.

This distortion of the theory was due to the way different aims were superimposed on it. The Christian Democrats had to give some kind of return to the groups in the Mezzogiorno which had supported them: the result was that the river of investment was dispersed into a thousand tiny streams in order to allow local groups to manage the redistribution of jobs and finance, and thus build support for the majority party.

The example of the construction of Christian Democrat power in Sicily is particularly significant. A central factor in it is the DC's alliance with an old political and criminal structure, the Mafia or Cosa Nostra, which had initially lined up behind the Separatists after the war. The DC–Mafia alliance formed around the management of public affairs, but also around the redistribution of important resources such as the land that had once belonged to the *latifundia*. In many cases, this land was bought and redistributed by Mafia intermediaries, such as Calogero Vizzini and Giuseppe Genco Russo, with the support of Christian Democrat cooperatives and public bodies controlled by the DC. In addition, numerous local groups coalesced around the aim of obtaining finance and diffuse forms of state intervention through the chain linking national government, regional government and the political class. Although the government initiatives solicited were often not economically rational, they allowed the political class to reinforce its power.

There was, in this way, a movement to bond local society into a kind of Union Sacrée, setting social and political differences aside in the pursuit of growth. Just as, in the past, the state had denied Sicily its fair share of growth (or so the argument went), it would now have to provide it. After 1947, Sicily was one of the few autonomous regions with a special constitutional status, whereas in the rest of the Mezzogiorno, excluding Sardinia, the centralised system inherited from the liberal period was in force. But despite this institutional difference, the Sicilian example can help us grasp the characteristic ways in which the southern political class coalesced. It did so by projecting conflict outwards, towards the state, and by making demands for external intervention which became the central prop of the debate on the South. In this context, the opposition parties themselves united with the governing parties in their demands for state intervention, and therefore did not always maintain the commitment to keeping alive some form of conflict within southern society. After 1970, the model of regional autonomy was applied to the whole of Italy, thus allowing what has been called 'the united party of public spending' to consolidate its hold.

After 1975, southern industry found itself in increasing difficulty, whilst state policy progressively lost sight of the goal of industrialisation. Today, the South, with 36 per cent of the population, accounts for only 18 per cent of Italian industrial production. In recent years, the whole concept of special intervention in the Mezzogiorno has been called into question by neo-liberals for whom the South is a parasitic region which contributes only 18 per cent of the state's tax revenue whilst absorbing 35 per cent of public spending.

From the above it should be obvious that it is simplistic polemically to wipe the slate clean of 40 years of special state intervention in the South: for a long time that intervention produced results which are not to be despised. For another thing, over the last two decades only a small percentage of the funds transferred to the South by the state has gone through the channel of special intervention. Ordinary forms of spending, such as on health, pensions and salaries, all of which could not be paid at different rates between regions for reasons of fairness, have accounted for the great majority of funds going to the South. To a certain extent at least, the gap between revenue and expenditure is due to the progressive nature of taxation which inherently favours the South where income from wages is much greater than that from capital. In general, public spending has centred on supporting the spending power of families – a practice which is very useful for Italian industry at a time when the South has begun to represent a substantial proportion of the domestic market. The freeze on all incentives on the production side has brought about an industrial crisis in the South, with a return to high levels of unemployment – now at 18 per cent. But this is a set of problems very different to those traditionally associated with the South. The lack of a renewed flow of migrants from South to North, the presence in the South of migrants from the 'third world', and the fact that the excess labour supply is predominantly of an intellectual kind, all demonstrate that the South's problem is no longer one of poverty.

THE SOUTH AND THE CRISIS OF THE REPUBLIC

During the 1980s the southern question predominantly appeared in the guise of the criminal question. The signals could not be more clear: the hundreds of people murdered in the street during ferocious bouts of account-settling between rival bands; the boom in illegal trade and the spread of rackets; the evidence of complicity within the political, economic and administrative establishment; the murders of honest magistrates and police officers which have long gone unpunished, above all in the area where the Mafia has been established for longest, Western Sicily. Worthy of note in this regard is the DC faction whose regional head was Salvo Lima and which was defined by the prefect Carlo Alberto Dalla Chiesa (one of Cosa Nostra's most eminent victims) as 'the island's most corrupt political family'. At a national level, Lima's faction constituted one of the cornerstones of the power of Giulio Andreotti, the leading politician of the last 20 years. The fact that Andreotti has subsequently been directly involved in investigations by Palermo judges gives credence to the grimmest theories about the relationship between the Mafia and the political sphere. There are many other examples from Sicily, Campania and Calabria which justify such theories. As press reports have shown, organised crime and corrupt elements in politics and business have benefited together from the management of government contracts, public works, easy finance for parasitic companies and the system of bribery. In the last two decades in particular, the Christian Democrat regime, with its own version of the welfare state, has produced political stasis by creating a clientelistic system in which support is exchanged for the redistribution of resources. The fact that the southern economy is to some extent based on finance from outside has aided the worst elements in the political sphere by creating the ideal conditions for the spread of crime of all sorts, and in particular for the activities of the Mafia and Camorra.

The conclusions which have been drawn from this state of affairs have perhaps tended to be too radical: the Mezzogiorno has been seen as corrupt right down to the roots of civil society, as being a kind of one-dimensional world destined to support the government under any circumstances. This line of interpretation owes something to the historical memory of the years at the turn of the century when parliamentary majorities were constructed within a rampart of conservative southern members. More recent evidence to support it has tended to be drawn from the 1980s, when the governing parties dominated elections in the South. In the early 1990s it was all too easy to predict that the Italian revolution led by the Lega Nord would run up against its Vendée in the Mezzogiorno.

But things did not quite turn out that way. As far as corruption is concerned, the North too has been shown to be seriously infected: even in the North, the perverse intertwining of politics, corrupt business and civil society has caused profound damage. The political parties, both in the South and in the North, have not been immune to infection. Indeed the resistance and counter-attack have come from the magistracy, as is clearly demonstrated by the two symbolic figures of Giovanni Falcone and Antonio Di Pietro. In addition, cracks have appeared in the myths of progress and modernity which bolstered the almost universal idea of the North's moral superiority. (Amongst these myths, it ought to be pointed out, was the idea that the working class and the bourgeoisie had a common progressive agenda.) The would-be Lega revolution seems to have receded. It has been channelled into the right-wing front which, beginning in Milan, conquered the whole country in the elections held on 27–28 March 1994. As I write, there are many indications that the Right are trying to save as much as possible of the inheritance of the old regime.

The fear (or hope?) that the traditional power bloc would manage to hold out in the South has proved groundless in circumstances in which it was morally and economically impossible to carry on along the same path of corrupt and corrupting welfarism. The fact that everything is now politically 'up for grabs' demonstrates that the great power of the political machinery was not due to some unbridgeable cultural gap between the two halves of the country.

Palermo is an emblematic case. Over the last few years an anti-Mafia movement has grown up which is not limited to La Rete and its leader Leoluca Orlando, the outright winner of the local elections in November 1993; rather it is based on a dense network of some 100 associations which are leading a battle for renewal entirely independently of the parties and institutions. The murderous challenge of Cosa Nostra seems to have provoked a response which is just as strong. Nor, it seems to me, does the surprising success of Forza Italia in Palermo and across Sicily in the general election mean that these results have to be called into question. The voters are clearly disoriented: electoral demand has not been met with a convincing political supply. The situation is still a very open one in which a number of factors are in play. The need for a clean new start is combined with the need for protection and security. An impatience with the sluggishness and failings of the democratic process is finding charismatic outlets. There have also been some demands for a summary, punitive response to corruption. If a majority of Sicilians have backed Forza Italia and Alleanza Nazionale, other regions such as Campania, Basilicata, Calabria and Abruzzo have turned to the Progressives so that, to judge from the variegated electoral map, the 'southern question today is an equation with many degrees of freedom' (Diamanti 1994: 134).

It would seem that the time has finally come to abandon the binaristic model which presumes to explain everything – whether it be the economy, politics, culture or society. The model is an old one which to some extent corresponds to conditions at the start of Italy's history as a united country. Although it was used by many different people in a variety of conjunctures, such as during the great migrations of the post-war period, the binaristic model was never a great theme for political mobilisation; it had, until recently, never given rise to parties like the Northern League, based on the idea of 'defending territory'. Today, educated commentators in the press and elsewhere have unexpectedly discovered a relationship of irremediable alterity between Italy's component parts. Their observations are based not on the characteristics of specific localities, but on the contrast between North and South. This 'discovery' has been made just when the historical processes which have had the effect of homologising the two halves of Italy have reached their culminating moment: from a political and moral point of view, both halves now seem to suffer from the same ills, albeit in a more serious form in the weaker area, the Mezzogiorno.

The Mezzogiorno has become the symbol of, and pretext for, the torrent of abuse now heaped upon the welfare state, the intervening state, the taxing state which takes much more than it gives out. But, at the same time, anti-southern polemic can be read as a sign of the way in which collective identities crumbled in the last few years of the DC regime under the pressure of particularized political demands. In this sense, the League's federalism is the offspring of a regime which worked to fragment and devalue unifying factors: it exacerbated the sectional interests of groups and factions, whether based in a given locality or not, by promoting the formation of lobbies, clienteles and Mafia groups around the political machinery; it indulged in sham forms of political representation by dividing up and sharing out jobs in public, semi-public and (sometimes only apparently) private bodies on the basis of party affiliation; it devalued bureaucratic mediation; it cohabited with the unions; it deployed the forces of party domination in the occupation of the health system. The old Christian Democratic system was very, very decentralised. Indeed it always abdicated its responsibility to govern from the centre in favour of the continuous drive to find new channels and niches where it could install its own political personnel, make them independent from general rules and swell their ranks even more. The institution of the regions has all too often been reduced to these practices: the start of the degeneration of policies such as the special state intervention in the Mezzogiorno coincides with the regional reforms of 1970.

The League has tended to follow the bargaining methods used by the southern political class across more than a century of Italian history. It stresses the distinctiveness of local society and waves the banner of a 'northern question' as people used to do for the 'southern question'. Like southern politicians, the *leghisti* speak a language which is two-sided: it strikes polemical and radical attitudes towards the outside (the centralising state); yet it tends to create a moderate, centrist bloc on the inside. Hence the way in which, particularly in Northeastern Italy, the League has occupied the areas which used to be Christian Democrat strongholds.

This is the context which has seen the emergence of what could be called the 'decentralising prejudice' which has overrun Italian culture both on the Right and on the Left. It is my contention that in fact Italy is in need of centralisation: it needs comprehensive government plans and agencies to put them into operation which are isolated from purely electoral pressures; it needs clear principles of legality which are clearly respected. Italy needs a state, but not so much (or not only) the Keynesian welfare state; rather it needs a state which makes rules, conceives those rules as applying across the board, and ensures that they are observed in the same way by everyone. This notion is one which has become especially clouded over the last decade. If the Mezzogiorno has a particular need for this kind of state, it is not because it is made from radically different stuff from the rest of Italy, but because it feels more strongly the demands, problems and defects of the nation as a whole. It is in the South that the divide between public consent and legality has been most apparent: the former has been pursued to the detriment of the latter. The Mezzogiorno as the place of special economic intervention, of secret dealings between centres of power, of the scattering of investment funds, of cyclical law and order emergencies requiring exceptional legal powers, of the chaotic and, in the end, futile redistribution of resources, of the magistrates who have been assassinated and those who have colluded, is nothing but a gigantic metaphor for the failings of a democracy deprived of a state; a metaphor for a risk which concerns Italy in its entirety.

NOTE

This chapter was translated by John Dickie.

REFERENCES

Banfield, E. (1958) *The Moral Basis of a Backward Society*, Glencoe, Ill: Free Press.
Cafagna, L. (1994) *Nord e Sud: non fare a pezzi l'unità d'Italia*, Venezia: Marsilio.
Diamanti, I. (1994) 'I Mezzogiorni', in I. Diamanti and R. Mannheimer (eds) *Milano a Roma: guida all'Italia elettorale del 1994*, Rome: Donzelli.

Levi, F. (1993) 'Torino oh cara. . . . Dove va la città della FIAT', *Meridiana*, 16, 135–58.

Graziano, L. (ed.) (1974) *Clientelismo e mutamento politico*, Milan: Franco Angeli.

Lupo, S. (1993) 'Usi e abusi del passato: le radici dell'Italia di Putnam', *Meridiana*, 18, 151–68.

Putnam, R. (1993) *Making Democracy Work. Civic Traditions in Modern Italy*, Princeton: Princeton University Press.

Part V
Economic aspects of the crisis

17 The economic elites and the political system

Alan Friedman

The phenomenon of Silvio Berlusconi's rise to power in early 1994 ranks, without a doubt, as the seminal political event following the 'revolution' triggered two years earlier by Antonio Di Pietro and his team of anti-corruption judges of Milan. That a business tycoon who grew his multi-billion dollar media empire in the 1980s with the patronage of former Prime Minister Bettino Craxi and other discredited members of the country's old *partitocrazia* should be elected as the man to put Italy's corrupt past behind it and begin a new era in Italian politics is, of course, not without irony. But the novelty of Mr Berlusconi and his Forza Italia is striking for other reasons as well, not the least of them being that it marked the first time in post-war Italian history that a leading member of the country's economic elite had undertaken a direct, personal, and explicitly partisan role in national politics. In the past, relations between Rome and the financial and industrial elites of Milan and Turin had been more nebulous, more concealed, and more generally a question of trading favours – as often as not in the form of bribes from the businessmen in exchange for tailor-made legislation from the politicians.

'We industrialists', observed Giovanni Agnelli, the founder of Fiat and Gianni Agnelli's grandfather, 'are ministerial by definition'. And indeed, for much of this century the politicians of Rome had a symbiotic, even incestuous relationship with economic elites from the industrialised North, starting with the Agnellis of FIAT fame. Gianni Agnelli was made a life senator during the dying days of the corrupt old *partitocrazia*, symbolised by Bettino Craxi and Giulio Andreotti, but that was not surprising for a man who embodied financial, industrial, media and political power as leader of the country's most influential corporate entity; in fact one could look back nearly 70 years and recall that Gianni's grandfather Giovanni had, in 1923, been honoured with the same title by Benito Mussolini.

The splashy political debut of Silvio Berlusconi in 1994, however, was genuinely without precedent, and his ascendancy to the premiership raised several important questions which this essay will attempt to address. First, what was the make-up of the economic elite at the time of Berlusconi's daring move? And how well did Berlusconi fit, or not fit into the elite from whence he came? Next, how tainted by their relations with the discredited political class were some of Berlusconi's top advisers, aides and ministers? And how legitimate were concerns about a possible conflict of interest between Berlusconi the Entrepreneur and Berlusconi the Prime Minister? Then, what is the nature of the economic elite at mid-decade, a mere five years away from the new millennium? And finally, somewhat speculatively, is Berlusconi most likely to be seen by historians of the future as a transition figure, born of and consumed by the tumultuous, non-violent 'revolution' of the early 1990s in Italy, or, rather, as a leader who was able to pilot the very same transition with a positive impact upon his troubled country?

These are profound, difficult issues, each of them. But Italy is by no means the only country to have experienced a political revolution toward the end of the twentieth century. Its nearest parallel is, perhaps surprisingly, Japan, another advanced, industrial democracy whose corrupt political system imploded messily after nearly 50 years of virtual one-party rule. Another, obviously less similar example, is the end of Communism in Russia. At the time of writing, Silvio Berlusconi appeared to have squandered the chance of becoming an Italian-style Mikhail Gorbachev – meaning a revolutionary leader who had grown up as an *apparatchik* in a corrupt former system and who none the less was able to throw off the old and champion the new, desperately needed reforms, albeit at the cost of his own political survival. At the same time, Berlusconi also ran the risk of confirming the suspicions of his political enemies – namely that he was of the old system, unable or unwilling to change sufficiently to do good for his country, and thus ultimately a figure of transition rather than its leader.

BERLUSCONI AND ITALY'S ECONOMIC ELITE

Toward the closing months of 1993, as Silvio Berlusconi laid the groundwork for his entry into the political arena, his position as a member of Italy's economic elite was anomalous, to say the least. A de facto member by virtue of his control of Fininvest, a media, publishing, retailing and financial services empire that employed 40,000 people and had an annual turnover of nearly 12,000 billion lire, Berlusconi was unusual in that he had consistently maintained a discreet but noticeable distance from Gianni Agnelli, Leopoldo Pirelli and other members of the Old Guard business establishment. Moreover, he was even more of a self-made man than his arch-rival Carlo De Benedetti, the Olivetti chief who had challenged the Agnelli-led establishment during the 1980s but who also maintained a fairly orthodox presence within the clubby world of Italian capitalism by virtue of his ties to Mediobanca, the powerful Milan-based merchant bank that controlled a spider's web of cross-shareholdings in nearly every large financial and industrial company in the private sector.

Berlusconi was the single leading business tycoon in Italy who, at least until 1994, had not gone cap in hand to seek the assistance or blessing of 86-year-old Enrico Cuccia, the Mediobanca honorary chairman. Cuccia's influence was such that he could make or break stockmarket operations, mergers and financial rescues. 'I don't need to be a member of any special club', Berlusconi remarked during a dinner gathering in the late 1980s, speaking with pride and reflecting the insular nature of Fininvest.

What Berlusconi most certainly did have in common with his peers was a firm belief in family-structured capitalism. The difference with Agnelli, De Benedetti and even the late Raul Gardini of the Ferruzzi-Montedison agro-chemicals group was that Berlusconi steadfastly refused to float his business empire on the Milan bourse. His family held 100 per cent control of Fininvest, of its three commercial television networks, of the Standa department store chain, of the Mediolanum insurance group and, until 1994, of the Mondadori newspapers, magazines and book publishing group. Financial analysts complained that it was almost impossible to understand Fininvest because so little information was made public. The profit disclosed for the Fininvest group was negligible, but by the autumn of 1993 it was well known that Fininvest had substantial debts with state-owned banks, and was in need of a tougher management structure. This was undertaken under the leadership of Franco Tatò, a manager appointed to restructure Fininvest in October 1993, and who aimed, ultimately, to bring the company to the bourse. Mr Tatò did float 53 per cent of Mondadori on the Milan bourse in 1994, but he was later to become frustrated at his inability to push through radical measures at Fininvest, and eventually gave up the job to return to a senior post at Mondadori.

By the time Berlusconi entered politics in early 1994 the fortunes of several members of Italy's economic elite were already waning, and a slow-motion generational change was already under way. The FIAT group, in particular, had been affected severely by the Europe-wide recession of 1992 to 1993, and Gianni Agnelli was grappling with financial losses and the fact that there was no obvious successor for his family dynasty. Raul Gardini had committed suicide in the summer of 1993 in one of the more dramatic responses to the anti-corruption drive by Milan magistrates, and the Ferruzzi-Montedison group was technically insolvent – later to be rescued by Mediobanca, restructured and downsized. Gardini left behind the legacy of the Enimont scandal, an investigation by the judges that concerned huge bribes allegedly paid to politicians in exchange for extremely favourable tax breaks and asset valuations in connection with the aborted merger of Montedison and Enichem, the state chemicals company. Pirelli had been hobbled by a failed takeover bid for Continental Tyres in Germany, and in 1993 De Benedetti's Olivetti was searching for a new strategy as world competition in the personal computer market threatened the company's margins, and briefly, even its survival.

With the political demise of Craxi, Andreotti and Arnaldo Forlani, the trio of discredited political leaders known as the 'CAF', Italy's leading industrialists, ever dependent upon relations with the state and state industry for a substantial portion of their business, found themselves scrambling to identify new interlocutors in Rome. Amid the chaos of Italy's political earthquake, it was hard for business leaders to know who to turn to.

Given this environment it was striking that Berlusconi chose, during his campaign in the run-up to the general election of 27–28 March 1994, to attack Confindustria, the employers' confederation which had traditionally looked to FIAT for leadership. Why did he do so? In electoral terms the answer may have been that criticising Confindustria was a low-cost piece of populist demagogy. But it is probable that Berlusconi actually meant to take issue with the stodgy, business elite, which he resented for having given too much support to the government of Prime Minister Carlo Azeglio Ciampi, the former Bank of Italy governor who steered Italy through its most dramatic period of judicial and political turmoil in 1993. In Ciampi Berlusconi perceived a left-leaning technocrat who was far too close to the Old Guard establishment. That may have been unfair, but it was and is his belief.

Thus Berlusconi did not feel comfortable with his peers in the economic elite of which he was a de facto member. And his alliance with the neo-fascist Alleanza Nazionale led by Gianfranco Fini did not sit well with the centrist political sentiments of men like Agnelli and De Benedetti. Berlusconi is fervently anti-communist, and can become quite emotional when discussing the political Left. 'Look', he said during a conversation with the author in August 1994, 'this country is divided into two parts, a moderate 65 per cent and an extreme Left that represents 35 per cent. The opposition are the orphans of a political faith that has been condemned definitively by history, and they are thus condemned as well to remain in opposition forever'. Agnelli, by contrast, had been traditionally close to the tiny Republican Party led by Giorgio La Malfa, while De Benedetti was known to harbour sympathies for the more centrist elements of the former communist PDS (his brother was even elected a Member of Parliament in an alliance with the progressive PDS). Thus the single most apposite description of Berlusconi's relations with the business establishment was contained in a remark made during the 1994 campaign by Gianni Agnelli: If Berlusconi were to win, said Agnelli, 'we all win'. If Berlusconi failed to be elected, 'he loses alone'.

THE CONFLICT OF INTEREST ISSUE

In the event, Berlusconi did win, and decisively. But his resentment of Agnelli, De Benedetti and other leading entrepreneurs only increased once he took office. In part this reflected the normal rivalry among Italy's latter-day *condottieri*, and in particular a bitter rivalry with De Benedetti, with whom he had sparred on many occasions.

Berlusconi's critics, both on the Left and among the economic elite, made much in 1994 of the ties between several of his key aides and the discredited political class that had been symbolised by Bettino Craxi's Socialist Party. They also worried, and quite loudly in the media and in Parliament, about the dangers of a conflict of interest between Berlusconi the Entrepreneur and Berlusconi the Prime Minister. With half of the national television market, magazine and newspaper publishing, one of the two leading retail groups, interests in financial services, property and sport, Berlusconi would find that government decisions could have direct consequences on his personal business interests.

Berlusconi's kitchen cabinet comprised his personal lawyer, Cesare Previti, whom he named Defence Minister after an uproar halted his attempt to appoint him Minister of Justice. Gianni Letta, the Vice-President of Fininvest and Berlusconi's Rome-based political lobbyist in the 1980s, was named the junior minister at Palazzo Chigi. Giuliano Ferrara, a former Craxi-era Socialist and television polemicist, became Berlusconi's government spokesman. And several other Fininvest executives became Members of Parliament and top advisers to Prime Minister Berlusconi.

On taking office Berlusconi promised to seek a solution to the possible conflict of interest problem. His proposal was to form an Italian version of the model of a 'blind trust' under which American Presidents place their shareholdings into a trust managed by an outsider, and thus avoid the possibility of a conflict of interest. No law existed in Italy to permit blind trusts and in any case the Italian version – involving continued control of Fininvest by the Berlusconi family – had little to do with the American model and so generated immediate scepticism on the part of critics. By July 1994 the conflict of interest issue exploded into a major political controversy for two reasons: the Berlusconi government was accused of trying to emasculate the RAI state television network by way of changes in the board and management of RAI, Fininvest's traditional rival, and Mr Berlusconi held a meeting at his home that included both Fininvest lawyers and executives and ministers of the government, namely Messrs Previti and Letta, both former Fininvest executives.

The debate over RAI was destined to feature as a constant controversy for the duration of Mr Berlusconi's seven months in office (see Gundle and O'Sullivan, chapter 13). But the meeting at Mr Berlusconi's villa in Arcore, on the outskirts of Milan, on 24 July 1994, triggered an avalanche of criticism that forced the Prime Minister to make a renewed public commitment to resolve the conflict of interest issue. It is worth dwelling upon that meeting because it spoke volumes about the difficulties Mr Berlusconi faced in serving as head of government while simultaneously maintaining control of his business empire. As such, it embodied the unique and unprecedented circumstances whereby a member of the economic elite had become the political leader of Italy.

The meeting at Arcore came on the eve of the arrest of Mr Berlusconi's brother Paolo, a Fininvest executive who was later said to admit to magistrates having organised and managed a slush fund used to make payments to officials of the Guardia di Finanza (the fiscal police) in order to avoid tax inspections. Present at Arcore were the Prime Minister, his brother Paolo, two Fininvest lawyers, Mr Letta, Mr Previti, and Salvatore Sciascia, a Fininvest executive who was accused of paying bribes with Paolo Berlusconi's authorisation. Opposition politicians and much of the Italian and international media perceived the meeting as an overt conflict of interest – a kind of council of war in which plans were made to deal with the judges' investigation of Fininvest. Prime Minister Berlusconi responded by deriding critics, and told the author during a subsequent interview that 'there was no impropriety because it was a private dinner in a private house on a holiday'. He added, 'I will not permit anyone to enter into my private life'.

The fact that Mr Previti, as Defence Minister, had nominal control of the para-military carabinieri was dismissed by Mr Berlusconi as irrelevant. The Prime Minister pointed out that President John F. Kennedy had named his brother Bobby the Attorney-General of the United States, and explained that the presence of Fininvest lawyers was 'necessary' because they brought information about his brother Paolo's legal problems. When asked whether he received the lawyers in his role as the Prime Minister or as the owner of Fininvest Mr Berlusconi said he received them simply 'as the brother of my brother'.

Critics continued to argue, long after the event, that it was Mr Berlusconi's nature to surround himself with old friends, advisers and cronies from Fininvest, and that blind trust or not, this would never change. Mr Berlusconi responded by saying again that he would present legislation aimed at creating a blind trust, and noted that 'the Italians knew who I was when they elected me'. Yet Mr Berlusconi subsequently failed to address the conflict of interest problem during his time as Prime Minister.

In fairness to both Mr Berlusconi and his critics, there was simply no precedent for a member of the economic elite taking control of the government, and each of these half-dozen or so leading members of the economic elite controlled financial, industrial, media and other interests that might well have raised anti-trust concerns in Anglo-Saxon countries because of the concentration of power these holdings engendered. The challenge, therefore, for Italy's Parliament, was to address issues that went beyond Mr Berlusconi's personal circumstances, and which reflected the need for more fundamental reforms in Italy's under-regulated and oligopolistic economy.

POLITICS, THE ECONOMIC ELITE, AND THE REFORM OF ITALIAN CAPITALISM

Mr Berlusconi's electoral rhetoric included numerous references to the need to provide fiscal incentives and other aid to the millions of tiny, small and medium-sized businesses which form the backbone of Italy's dynamic and flexible economy. And his government did offer a series of incentives, although less than had been expected by the bulk of Italy's small businessmen. The rhetoric of the Northern League was meanwhile virulently critical of the lopsided structure of Italian capitalism, and especially of the big groups and their ties to Mediobanca.

By the time the Berlusconi government took office in 1994 it was virtually an article of faith among Italians and among foreign investors and banks doing business in Italy, that Mediobanca and its chairman Cuccia posed a threat to those who wished to encourage a more democratic form of capitalism. Mediobanca was committed to a status quo that stifled competition and restricted the ability of companies to raise equity capital. Its credo was oligopoly; its clients the oligarchy of Italy's economic elite.

Confirmation of Mediobanca's continuing resistance to the reform of Italian capitalism came just as Mr Berlusconi was taking office. Mr Cuccia and his allies hobbled two of the biggest privatisations ever launched in Italy – the sale of shares in Banca Commerciale Italiana and Credito Italiano, two of the four big state banks. Professor Romano Prodi, the chairman of IRI, the big state holding group that controlled the banks, had wanted a British-style privatisation programme that would allow many small investors to own shares in the banks, through a transparent market operation. But Mediobanca formed concert parties with a handful of Old Guard companies and stymied the bank privatisations by buying up blocks of shares that individually totalled less than the maximum allowed, and by then taking effective joint control, finally forcing out the banks' executives and boards and packing them with cronies and allies. The internationally respected Professor Prodi was livid, and went public with his concerns. He was promptly forced out of IRI, in the first sign that the Berlusconi government was not prepared to take on the clout of Mr Cuccia. Then, Mediobanca was given the mandate to restructure Mr Berlusconi's Fininvest – hardly a sign that the new Prime Minister was determined to reduce the clout of the Old Guard. Professor Prodi was later to emerge, in early 1995, as the standard-bearer of an emerging centre-left coalition that offered the first hope of Italy's developing a genuine bipolar political system similar to that of other Western democracies.

By the autumn of 1994 the issue of anti-trust legislation became another battleground between reformers and the Old Guard. Here too, there were few signs that Mr Berlusconi was prepared to undertake radical change in the structure of Italian capitalism. Little was accomplished also when it came to reinforcing the powers of Consob, the Italian stockmarket regulatory authority.

The difficulty of modernising Italian capitalism was further compounded by a series of astonishingly paranoid statements by leading members of the neo-fascist Alleanza Nazionale, who warned of the 'strong powers' of big business as a distorting factor in the economy, but who at the same time included the Bank of Italy, Opus Dei, and masonic lodges among their targets. Clear campaign rhetoric and the overwhelming desire for reform in Italian capitalism was replaced by a confusing and politically damaging free-for-all. The Alleanza Nazionale had also returned to the bad old ways of *lottizzazione* (carving up state jobs via political patronage), the Northern League was pushed into a corner, and Mr Berlusconi affected to be above the fray while actually doing little to clarify matters.

A generational change was undoubtedly underway in Italian business during the mid-1990s; as noted before, the Agnelli dynasty was facing a succession problem, and Carlo De Benedetti, probably the most internationally minded of Italian business leaders, found himself preoccupied with rebuilding Olivetti for the next decade. But even newcomers such as Luciano Benetton, or reform-minded tycoons such as Pietro Marzotto, the textiles and clothing magnate, were unable to achieve much in the way of change. To make matters still worse, Italian industry and finance suffered from a serious lack of talented younger managers, meaning that those older managers who retired, died, or were prosecuted as a result of the *Tangentopoli* scandal were not being replaced.

The only factor strong enough to force the recognition that reform in Italian capitalism was needed, and in everyone's interest, was international competition. Ultimately the foreign merchant banks and manufacturers would make inroads into Italian capitalism, but their salutary impact on the business scene was diluted by demagogic rhetoric from those politicians and entrepreneurs who played the card of nationalism and protectionism. The outlook at mid-decade was thus still not very auspicious – change in Italian capitalism would come, but over a period of many years, and almost certainly stretching into the first decade of the twenty-first century.

THE ENTREPRENEUR-TURNED-POLITICIAN AS A TRANSITION FIGURE

Silvio Berlusconi said during an interview with the author in August 1994 that he had been 'obliged to take the field and enter politics' because of the threat of a left-leaning government being elected had he not taken action. His critics contended that he had entered politics solely in order to defend and advance his personal business interests.

Neither of the above, altogether too absolute statements is likely to be completely true. Those who know Mr Berlusconi well maintain that he believed his own rhetoric, and honestly wished to steer his country through a transition phase that he acknowledged would be long and difficult. But even close friends noted that as a politician he had problems learning the art of compromise, of mediation. 'He is used to commanding, as chairman of a board of directors. Politics is different', said one of his closest aides a few months after he took office in May 1994.

With the collapse of communism, the onslaught of *Tangentopoli* and the rise of Berlusconi, as a political force Italy was clearly embarked upon a period of tumultuous change. But Italy's economic elite was simultaneously facing unprecedented challenges from the increasingly globalised marketplace. And the old nexus between economic elites and the political system had meanwhile been broken. The result was a general state of confusion that characterised much of Mr Berlusconi's period in office. What is more, some members of the economic elite were leaning toward a centre-left coalition that they believed would eventually follow the Berlusconi-led transition.

This became a real possibility with the arrival on the political scene of Professor Romano Prodi as the self-styled leader of a broad centre-left coalition. Mr Berlusconi, in turn, became increasingly bitter, and occasionally even hysterical in public, after his government collapsed in December 1994 following the withdrawal of the Northern League from his coalition. Although the new caretaker Prime Minister, Lamberto Dini, had served as Treasury Minister in the Berlusconi government during 1994, Mr Berlusconi turned on his former minister and was able to wreak havoc in financial markets in the opening months of 1995 by constantly insisting on a new general election and by demagogically attacking the mini-budget Mr Dini presented in February 1995.

The fact that Mr Berlusconi – who was facing multiple judicial investigations because of alleged irregularities at Fininvest – should have been able to carry on as a political leader in 1995 was a testimony to the confused state of Italian politics in 1995. At the time of writing, the transition between the previous system of rampant corruption and fragmented politics and the future prospect of a more stable bipolar system seemed destined to be long and painful, and likely to take until 1996 or 1997.

If, at mid-decade, Mr Berlusconi appeared destined to remain a figure of transition rather than its ultimate leader this may have been partly because of the disorder inside his initial governing coalition, and especially because of the corporatist tradition of his neo-fascist allies. The presence of too many Craxi-era and Andreotti-era aides and ministers inside the cabinet also hindered efforts by the Berlusconi government to make a decisive break with the past.

Mr Berlusconi's own place in history is guaranteed by virtue of his remarkable transformation from business tycoon to political leader. That, in itself, is a fascinating phenomenon. It is, however, one thing to achieve electoral consensus, and quite another to make use of it subsequently to effect sweeping change.

18 Excesses and limits of the public sector in the Italian economy

The ongoing reform

Fiorella Padoa Schioppa Kostoris

This chapter examines the substantial degree of public intervention in the Italian economy, and considers the internal contradictions and weaknesses of public action in this sphere. New policy initiatives directed at resolving the country's long-term structural problems are then discussed, including the privatisation programme which was launched in 1992 together with the major budgetary cuts aimed at curbing public debt in order to maintain sustainability. Finally, the chapter tries to explain why, despite all the excesses and limits of the policy-making process, the performance of the Italian economy is none the less quite impressive. The conclusions follow from those developed in an earlier study of the contemporary Italian economy (Padoa Schioppa Kostoris 1993).

THE SIZE OF THE PUBLIC SECTOR

We can gain an impression of the significant presence of the public sector in the Italian economy by looking at the budget of the so-called general government.[1] This aggregate is defined in homogeneous terms across different countries and is economically relevant because it produces non-marketed services, namely services for which no price is paid by the users (e.g., forests, roads, defence, justice, public order and internal security). If we then look at the budget of the general government, we see that in Italy in the 1990s the public expenditure of the general government represented more than 50 per cent of GDP (Table 18.1). This is a fraction larger than in the average of EU countries and much larger than that prevailing in Japan and the United States (Table 18.2), mainly due to interest payments which in Italy constitute 11.5 per cent of GDP versus 5.3 in the EU, 2.2 per cent in the United States and 3.8 per cent in Japan.

Moreover, it should be stressed that the general government is only a small part of a broader concept of the public sector, because the majority of public utilities provided by public enterprises are excluded – for example postal services, railways and local transport, electricity, gas, water, waste disposal and other minor local services.[2]

Table 18.1 Revenue and expenditure account of general government in Italy (ratio to GDP)

Expenditure	1980	1985	1990	1991	1992
Gross wages and salaries[a]	10.9	11.7	12.7	12.7	12.7
Collective consumption	14.7	16.3	17.4	17.5	17.2
Production subsidies	2.8	2.8	2.2	2.4	2.0
Social security benefits	14.0	17.1	18.2	18.3	19.1
Transfer to private social institutions	0.2	0.2	0.3	0.2	0.3
International aid	0.1	0.2	0.2	0.3	0.3
Other transfer payments	0.4	0.3	0.5	0.5	0.5
Current expenditure net of interest payments	32.4	36.9	38.8	39.2	39.2
Interest payments	5.3	8.0	9.6	10.2	11.5
Total current expenditure	37.7	44.9	48.4	49.4	50.7
Gross fixed investment	3.1	3.7	3.4	3.3	2.9
Net purchase of land	–	–	–	–	–
Investment grants	0.9	1.5	1.3	1.1	1.2
Other transfer payments on capital account	0.2	0.7	0.3	0.1	0.1
Total capital expenditure	4.3	5.9	5.0	4.5	4.2
Total expenditure net of interest payments	36.4	42.8	43.8	43.7	44.1
Total expenditure	41.7	50.9	53.4	53.9	55.5
Revenue					
Gross operating surplus	0.3	0.4	0.6	0.6	0.7
Interest received	0.6	0.6	0.5	0.5	0.5
Income from land	0.1	0.1	0.1	0.1	0.1
Indirect taxes	8.6	8.9	10.6	11.1	11.0
Direct taxes	9.6	12.9	14.4	14.5	14.7
Actual social security contributions	11.4	11.9	12.9	13.1	13.3
Imputed social security contributions	1.3	1.6	1.6	1.6	1.7
International aid	–	0.1	–	–	–
Other transfer payments	1.1	1.5	1.5	1.8	1.7
Total current revenue	33.0	38.1	42.2	43.3	43.7
Investment grants	0.1	0.1	0.1	0.1	0.1
Capital taxes	0.1	0.1	0.1	0.2	2.0
Other transfer payments on capital account	0.1	0.1	0.1	0.1	0.1
Total capital revenue	0.3	0.3	0.3	0.4	2.2
Total revenue	33.2	38.4	42.5	43.7	46.0

Table 18.1 Continued

Expenditure	1980	1985	1990	1991	1992
Current balance net of interest payments	0.8	1.2	3.4	4.1	3.9
Saving or dissaving	−4.4	−6.8	−6.2	−6.1	−7.5
Overall balance net of interest payments	−3.2	−4.4	−1.3	−	1.9
Deficit (−) or surplus (+)	−8.5	−12.5	−10.9	−10.2	−9.5

Sources: Malizia and Pedullà 1988, for data concerning 1980 and 1985; ISTAT 1993, for 1990; elaboration on data from Senato della Repubblica 1993, for 1992.

Note: [a] including social security contributions

Table 18.2 Expenditure account of general government in six major countries (ratio to GDP)

Country	1980	1989	1990	1991	1992
Collective consumption					
United States	18.7	18.5	18.9	19.1	18.6
Japan	9.8	9.1	9.0	9.1	9.2
EEC	18.5	17.9	18.0	18.7	18.7
Germany	20.2	18.9	18.4	22.1	22.6
France	18.1	18.0	18.0	18.2	18.2
United Kingdom	21.2	19.4	20.0	21.2	21.9
Italy	14.7	16.6	17.4	17.5	17.2
Transfers to households					
United States	11.7	11.7	12.2	12.3	13.8
Japan	10.1	11.0	11.1	11.1	11.2
EEC	16.2	17.0	17.0	n.d.	n.d
Germany	17.2	16.4	15.9	17.6	18.3
France	19.0	21.0	21.2	21.6	21.9
United Kingdom	11.0	11.1	11.3	12.5	13.2
Italy	14.1	17.6	18.2	18.3	18.6
Interest payments					
United States	1.2	2.0	2.1	2.2	2.2
Japan	3.2	4.0	3.9	3.8	3.8
EEC	3.1	4.7	5.0	5.0	5.3
Germany	1.9	2.7	2.6	2.8	3.5
France	1.5	2.8	3.1	3.2	3.3
United Kingdom	4.7	3.7	3.4	3.0	2.9
Italy	5.3	8.9	9.6	10.2	11.5
Total current expenditure net of interest payments					
United States	30.6	30.4	31.2	31.4	32.5
Japan	21.8	21.4	21.3	21.1	21.5
EEC	38.4	38.6	39.0	40.2	40.6
Germany	41.3	39.4	40.0	42.2	42.4
France	41.3	43.7	43.7	44.1	44.3
United Kingdom	35.5	32.5	33.2	34.9	36.9
Italy	32.4	38.0	38.8	39.2	39.2

Table 18.2 Continued

Expenditure	1980	1989	1990	1991	1992
Total current expenditure					
United States	31.8	32.4	33.3	33.6	34.7
Japan	25.0	25.4	25.2	24.9	25.3
EEC	41.5	43.3	44.0	45.2	45.9
Germany	43.2	42.1	42.6	45.0	45.9
France	42.8	46.5	46.8	47.3	47.6
United Kingdom	40.2	36.2	36.6	37.9	39.8
Italy	37.7	46.9	48.4	49.4	50.7
Total expenditure					
United States	31.8	32.4	33.3	34.1	35.1
Japan	32.0	30.9	31.7	31.4	32.2
Germany	47.9	44.8	45.1	48.5	49.0
France	46.1	49.1	49.8	50.6	51.8
United Kingdom	43.0	37.6	39.9	40.8	43.2
Italy	41.9	51.3	53.2	53.6	53.2

Sources: Ministero del Bilancio 1993; Senato della Repubblica 1993; for data on total expenditure OECD 1993

If we include all these public enterprises in the public sector we obtain the so-called enlarged public sector. This is an important aggregate from a financial point of view because the public borrowing requirement refers to it. To give an impression of the under-estimate of public sector activity that we make by only looking at the general government in the case of Italy, it should be noted that on average in the last decade the investment of the general government has been only 70 per cent of that of the enlarged public sector.

Finally, in Italy there is a third relevant concept of public sector (in an even wider perspective) which includes state-controlled companies: some of these provide essential public utilities such as telecommunications and air transport. These state-controlled companies operating in the industrial sector have always been considered in the national accounts as part of the private sector, but up until recently they have usually[3] behaved as public enterprises, because they were controlled by state holdings totally owned by the state, namely IRI, ENI, EFIM. Now the last-named is being liquidated, and following a 1992 law (n.359), the other two state holdings have been transformed into joint-stock companies owned by the Treasury. The two financial holdings, IRI and ENI, control a number of sub-holdings which in turn control a number of subsidiaries: the control of the joint-stock companies IRI and ENI is ensured by majority stakes in the equity of the state-controlled joint-stock companies (OECD 1993).

This legal change was the prerequisite for privatisation, but the latter process is far from completed. Among state-controlled companies working in the industrial sector, those producing foodstuffs were completely sold off by 1993, thereby eliminating the well-known paradox of the 'state *panettone*' (a Christmas cake produced by a state-owned company). Moreover, few minor state-controlled companies operating in the mining and mechanical sectors have been sold during 1993, while the major state-controlled steel company (ILVA) will be sold in the near future. Finally, all state-controlled companies working in the telephone sector are being merged and restructured in preparation for privatisation in the short term.[4]

Given that the privatisation of state-controlled companies supplying public utilities is still a policy proposal rather than a policy action,[5] it is not insignificant that during the decade which ended in 1992 the investment of the general government was only 52 per cent of the investment in the public sector in its broadest sense (which includes all the general government, the public enterprises and the state-controlled companies). If the same percentage was applied to public expenditure as a whole, public expenditure in this larger perspective would be almost as big as current GDP in Italy. This is not as surprising as it may seem at first sight, because part of the public budget is not included in the GDP, as it does not produce but simply redistributes value added.

The considerations set out so far relate only to budgetary interventions. Perhaps an even more widespread phenomenon in Italy is indirect state intervention via the regulation of the private economy. This is aimed at giving rights and duties, obligations or prohibitions, barriers to market entry (shopkeepers, taxi drivers, doctors or lawyers) or inhibitions from exit (credit or primary education). For example, in the labour market, a strong regulation exists on hiring and firing, on length of working hours, on holidays, on conditions for permanent or transitory employment, on wages etc.. Economists usually divide these regulations into economic and social. The former concern prices and quantities, while the latter regard standards and qualities.

THE INTERNAL CONTRADICTIONS OF PUBLIC ACTION

How can one say whether this massive intervention of the public sector – both in the form of budgetary interventions and in the form of the regulation of the private economy – is excessive or not in Italy? To make this evaluation one has to make use of a standard paradigm or benchmark. Economists tend to agree that the public sector in its largest sense should intervene only when the private economy is unable to get the best output results from existing resources or when the results are overall optimal but not enough consideration is given to the redistribution of resources between different individuals or to commodities of a special social interest (so-called merit goods).

Of course there are cases of market failures where the public sector has to intervene: for example in producing public goods like defence, justice, internal security and public order;[6] or commodities with large

Table 18.3 General government expenditure in Italy by purpose (percentage composition)

Purposes	1980	1985	1990	1991	1992
Traditional area	15.4	15.9	14.9	15.1	14.7
National defence	4.0	4.1	3.6	3.4	3.4
General services[a]	11.4	11.9	11.3	11.7	11.3
Welfare state	60.4	56.5	56.6	56.3	56.3
Education	11.4	10.0	10.0	9.6	9.6
Health	13.3	10.6	11.8	12.0	11.6
Housing[b]	3.3	3.6	2.6	2.6	2.3
Leisure, cultural and religious services	1.1	1.1	1.1	1.1	1.0
Pensions and other social benefits	31.4	31.2	31.1	31.0	31.8
Mixed economy	24.2	27.6	28.5	28.5	29.0
Economic services[c]	15.2	13.5	11.6	10.8	9.9
Expenditure not specified elsewhere[d]	9.0	14.1	16.9	17.7	19.1
Total	100.0	100.0	100.0	100.0	100.0

Sources: For 1980, 1985, 1990 and 1991 see Table 18.1; ISTAT, unpublished data (kindly supplied by Raffaele Malizia) for 1992

Notes:
[a] Including expenditure for justice, public order and internal security
[b] Including expenditure for environment
[c] Including expenditure for agriculture, industry, water, gas, electricity, roads, transport and communications
[d] Including interest payments

externalities such as an adequate environment;[7] or public utilities where the presence of ever-increasing returns to scale and economies of scope would lead to non-contestable natural monopolies;[8] or, finally, strategic services,[9] like those necessary to promote the development of some backward regions (e.g. the Mezzogiorno of Italy).

Using this paradigm, it is clear that on the one hand the public sector intervenes in Italy too little where there are obvious market failures, but on the other hand it intervenes too much where there are no compelling reasons to do so. In essential goods like defence, justice, public order or internal security, public expenditure in Italy seems to be insufficient and it is decreasing over time in relation to total expenditure – only 15 per cent of the budget of the general government is devoted to the production of essential public goods (Table 18.3), and the quality of the functions performed is consequently low and possibly declining.[10] On the other hand, the Italian public sector produces or distributes commodities that do not have any of the characteristics outlined in the paradigm above, for example supermarket foods and meals in motorway restaurants that are provided by state-controlled companies.

Our general point is that public intervention in Italy is not only disproportionate but is also self-contradictory. There are four main reasons why public intervention in Italy is simultaneously excessive and inadequate. First, because the volume of budgetary resources allocated to (or drawn from) certain activities is too large while too little is devoted to (or derived from) others. Second, because even within one and the same budget item, public measures are excessive in some respects and inadequate in others. Third, because some instruments of economic policy are over-worked while others are under-utilised. Fourth, because the quantitative input is large but the qualitative output in terms of social wellbeing is often poor.

The examples of public ownership of supermarkets and restaurants, on the one hand, and public goods, on the other, fall into the first category. Looking at revenues rather than public expenditures, various inconsistencies of the first and the second kind appear in relation to taxation. In terms of percentage of GDP, direct taxes are heavier in Italy than in the average of EU countries, in the United States and in Japan. Indirect taxation is, on the contrary, abnormally low by European standards (11 per cent of GDP versus 13.5 per cent in the EU in 1992; although the percentages are 8.4 and 8.0 in the United States and in Japan), and there exist possibly too many general exemptions from social security contributions which are seen to be ineffective largely because trade unions adjust to these exemptions by raising the long-term wage target by an almost proportional amount. Altogether, the tax wedge which was approximately identical in Italy and in the United States in 1980, has now become 10 percentage points higher in Italy than in the United States (where it remained static), while in Italy it has remained a little below the EU average (Table 18.4).

With regard to the second form of contradiction mentioned above – expenditures that can be identified within one and the same budgetary item – the most illuminating example concerns the welfare state, that is public expenditures for pensions, health, education and housing which constitute approximately 56 per cent of the budget of the general government. The size of expenditures is obviously very large but the system leaves most Italians dissatisfied.

We can explain why by taking as an example state old-age pensions for private employees. First, the retirement age is among the lowest in the world – 56 for women, and 61 for men after 1 January 1993 (legislative decree n.503, 1992).[11] On average the old-age pension is paid for almost 20 years to men and for more than 25 years to women, given their long life-expectancy when they retire. Second, the general benefit formula for calculating the pension is by far the most generous in the world, although it is true that there is a ceiling. There is a floor for those who would not reach a minimum pension according to the general formula. Old-age pensions paid to private employees are generally calculated as follows:

Table 18.4 Tax revenue of general government in six major countries (ratio to GDP)

Country	1980	1989	1990	1991	1992
Direct taxes					
United States	14.7	13.9	13.7	13.0	12.3
Japan	10.8	13.5	13.5	13.1	12.7
EEC	11.6	12.9	12.6	12.7	12.7
Germany	12.8	12.7	11.3	11.9	12.1
France	8.4	9.0	9.0	8.9	8.8
United Kingdom	13.4	13.8	14.0	13.1	12.1
Italy	9.6	14.3	14.4	14.5	14.7
Indirect taxes					
United States	7.8	7.8	8.0	8.3	8.4
Japan	7.4	8.1	8.1	7.9	8.0
EEC	13.0	13.4	13.3	13.4	13.5
Germany	13.1	12.5	12.6	12.8	13.0
France	15.3	15.2	15.0	14.7	14.4
United Kingdom	15.8	16.0	15.9	15.6	15.6
Italy	8.6	10.4	10.6	11.1	11.0
Social security contributions					
United States	8.0	9.0	9.1	9.3	9.4
Japan	7.3	8.3	8.7	8.7	8.8
EEC	14.1	14.7	14.7	15.2	15.2
Germany	16.9	17.3	17.1	18.3	18.6
France	19.6	21.0	21.1	21.1	21.2
United Kingdom	6.0	6.5	6.3	6.4	6.2
Italy	12.8	14.0	14.4	14.7	15.0
Tax wedge[a]					
United States	30.5	30.7	30.8	30.6	30.1
Japan	25.5	29.9	30.0	29.7	29.5
EEC	38.7	41.0	40.6	41.3	41.4
Germany	42.8	42.5	41.0	43.0	43.7
France	43.3	45.2	45.1	44.7	44.4
United Kingdom	35.2	36.3	36.2	35.1	33.9
Italy	31.0	38.3	39.4	40.3	40.7

Sources: Ministero del Bilancio 1993, Senato della Repubblica 1993.

Note: [a] This is approximated by the sum of the direct tax rate, the indirect tax rate and the social security tax rate

the pension is equal to the average wage of the last 5–10[12] years of the active life, multiplied by a coefficient equal to 2 per cent times each year of contribution to social security. The maximum is reached after 40 years of contribution, so at the top the retiree gets 80 per cent of his last 5–10 years average wage. The multiplicative coefficient in the rest of Europe is not 2 per cent but approximately 1.3 per cent, while in Japan it is 0.75 per cent. Moreover, in most countries the pensionable income is not the average of the last 5–10 years – the years in which the wage rate is usually higher in Italy – but it is often proportioned to the life-cycle income.

Despite the apparent generosity of this system almost everybody is dissatisfied: those at the top level because of the imposition of the ceiling, and those at the bottom level because the minimum pension is inadequate, although the benefit formula for those at the bottom of the scale is more generous since they receive more than 2 per cent times the number of years of contribution times the last 5–10 years average wage. Moreover, all retirees are dissatisfied because the average ratio of old-age pensions relative to wages in the Italian private sector does not even reach 50 per cent (46 per cent in 1991) – due to the small number of years of effective contributions (though higher than the minimum requirement of 16 years). Finally, workers as much as retirees are dissatisfied because the social security deficit as a whole amounts to approximately 3–4 per cent of GDP. For this reason, and because of the rise in the proportion of older people combined with an expected net decline in the population as a whole, the currently active Italian population forecasts that its pension will be considerably reduced by the time it reaches retirement age.

From a more general viewpoint, a very basic reason for the simul-taneous expansion and degeneration of the Italian welfare state lies in the attempt to provide the same service to everybody without concentrat-ing on those who are in most need of a transfer of public resources. Although the intention behind this system is to avoid stigmatising the recipients and to win the consensus of the median voter, the consequence is that the needy receive too little while overall expenditure is enormous.

In regard to the third aspect of the internal contradictions of the public intervention that we mentioned above – the excessive use of some instruments of intervention and the under-utilisation or absence of others – it may be interesting to look at the case of the indirect regulation of the private economy. On the one hand, there is an excess of dirigistic regulation aimed at protecting the weak by means of legal and adminis-trative procedures that take no account of market reactions – and hence are evaded, with negative consequences for those the law wanted to protect. Rather than over-protecting the weak it would certainly be better to strengthen them instead. On the other hand, there is a marked lack of regulation through incentives and tradeoffs, aimed at guiding agents towards forms of behaviour which are both optimal for themselves and consistent with social welfare: for example tax-based incomes policies for wages, or progressive tax allowances on profits from actual investments.

Some examples of excess of dirigistic regulation in Italy may clarify my point. Let me first refer to the so-called Maternity Law of 1971. This law does not simply allow but compels a pregnant woman to take paid leave from two months before the birth to three months after the birth of the child, and further gives many possibilities for partly paid absences in the first three years of the child's life. The law is designed to protect women without 'discriminating' against those with health problems (thus even healthy women are forbidden to work for three full months after delivery). But in fact the law weakened the entire female labour force by increasing its expected costs while reducing its expected employment duration, thus raising its average fixed costs.

The law aimed to inhibit gender-discrimination in the labour market by imposing equality of opportunity for women who were assumed to be weak. But in fact while the legislation strengthened those who already had a job it diminished opportunities for all those who were still outside the labour market. Indeed, in the first years of implementation of the law, there was a decline of female employment in Italy – unique in the OECD countries in the early 1970s. Different policy measures, like better and more extensive social services (kindergarten, homes for the elderly etc.) would have strengthened rather than over-protected the female labour force. In the United States, in the name of the same equal opportunities principle, at about the same time a law (title VII of the 1964 American Civil Rights Act and its 1972 amendments) abolished all specific protections for women (inhibition of heavy or night jobs etc.). In Italy the trend was in the opposite direction and the relative over-protection of women subsequently diminished only because a new law providing for paternity leave introduced some over-protection for men as well.

Other examples of dirigistic regulation aimed at increasing the equality of opportunity, which in fact turned out to be harmful for those it wanted to protect, are given by a series of public actions concerning the South of Italy.[13] What I have in mind here regards various forms of dirigistic regulation, for example the abolition of the so-called 'wage cages', namely the wage differentials between regions, decided in 1969 by an inter-union agreement, later transformed in law and thus made valid 'erga omnes'. According to this law, there should not be any regional difference in base wages and in automatic wage increases, the only possible source of differentials being wage drift. The intention was again to increase equality of opportunity – this time for southern workers.

But again as an equal opportunities policy it was ill-conceived because it did not correspond either to the equality of needs or to the equality of worth. It transpires that needs are not the same in the South as in the North and Centre of Italy because price levels are lower in the former area due to public interventions (on rents, tolls for motorways etc.), and because of market forces; worth is not the same because the level of labour productivity in the South is approximately equal to 70 per cent of that of the North-Centre – mainly due to poor infrastructure and insufficient vocational training which the state has been slow to improve. This kind of action would have strengthened rather than over-protected Southern workers.

The result of the dirigistic regulation was very negative for the Mezzogiorno. First of all, in order to lower the labour cost in the South which

was becoming too high after the abolition of the 'wage cages', the government had to introduce some special relief from social security contributions, to reduce the labour cost per worker in the South relative to the
North-Centre. This action was expensive for the public budget but it did
not give sufficient incentives to northern and central firms to invest in
the South for several reasons, including the fact that southern productivity
was also lower. As a result, the labour cost per unit of output, which in
1969 was substantially lower in the Mezzogiorno than in the rest of Italy,
by the end of the 1970s became (and still remains) higher in the South
relative to the Centre or North.

At the same time, given that what is relevant for workers is not the
labour cost but the wage rate net of taxes in real terms, and given that
the net real wage started growing in the South much more than in the
rest of Italy, the incentive to migrate from the Mezzogiorno first declined
and then stopped around 1973. While demographic and economic factors
led (and still lead) to a broadening of the labour supply in the South
relative to the North or Centre, labour demand was (and still is) smaller
in the Mezzogiorno, so that the disequilibrium in the southern labour
market kept growing. Clearly a reduction of this labour market disequilibrium requires, among other things, greater wage and price flexibility –
itself possible only if dirigistic public regulation diminishes and the real
wage rate again becomes a market signal of relative insufficiency or excess
of labour demand and supply.

With regard to the fourth form of internal contradiction in public action
– that of the lack of quality associated with the size and number of
interventions[14] – the major causes seem to be excess regulation, mismanagement of resources and waste or kickbacks. Quality is particularly low
when dirigistic regulation is particularly heavy, the latter consisting in
imposing constraints on the behaviour of civil servants to limit their
discretion but also their operational responsibility, in order to ensure a
formally correct decision-making process rather than an effective and
useful result.

In addition, quality is certainly lowered by the mismanagement of
resources, as for example even the Ministry of Posts and Telecommunications itself confessed (see Direzione Centrale dei Servizi Postali 1988;
Onofri *et al.* 1987). In 1987 a letter posted in Milan to an address in Italy
took an average of 8 days to be delivered; a letter addressed to Rome took
just as long if it was posted in a provincial capital, but 9.3 days if it was
posted in a smaller town. All the quality indicators for the Italian postal
service have deteriorated over recent years and are worse than those for
many other countries, such as the United Kingdom and Germany, where
three-quarters of all letters are delivered within one day.

This degradation in services has occurred in spite of the fact that the
budget assigned to mail delivery is huge. In the judgement of the Ministry
of Posts and Telecommunications, the combination of poor service and

low productivity, in both absolute and comparative terms, and the deterioration over time are attributable to three factors. First, the poor professional standard of the staff, which is comprehensively too large and irrationally deployed owing to internal rigidities and the absence of sufficient wage incentives. Second, the virtual absence of managerial skills, computerisation, and personnel-management techniques appropriate to the size and importance of the postal service. Third, institutional constraints imposed from outside the Ministry that ultimately cause internal difficulties (e.g. the refusal of public transport firms to carry mailbags following the regionalisation of public transportation).

The postal service also provides an example of the waste of resources – to the extent that the hiring and promotion of employees is not always determined according to efficiency or performance criteria, but rather to political influence or union pressure. These are, loosely speaking, weak forms of corruption, but sometimes civil servants and high public officials engage in corruption and kickbacks of a more direct kind as recent trials are beginning to reveal. As a consequence, the public sector pays for goods and services it buys, or for public works it builds through a procurement system, at a price which is higher than the quality and the quantity of output obtained justifies. Indeed, not only does the price include the cost of kickbacks, but competition is also distorted to the detriment of the most fair and possibly best-performing enterprises (see also della Porta, Chapter 14, for an account of this phenomenon in local government).

PRIVATISATION AND PUBLIC DEBT

In summary, the example of the Italian postal service shows that government failures may be larger than the market failures which originally required public intervention. More generally, public utilities are always supplied in Italy by public enterprises or by state-controlled companies, irrespective of the fact that the performance of public enterprises is more expensive and less effective than the market would produce by itself (e.g. telephones).

In principle, the policy decision to deregulate these markets and privatise these firms should depend precisely on these issues, with the aim of increasing efficiency through resource reallocation (possibly including the development of a well-functioning stock exchange market). In practice, in Italy the privatisation process has thus far followed a different path, essentially directed towards relieving some of the liquidity constraints of the public sector. The decision to sell state-controlled companies was determined more by financial reasons than by strategic supply considerations within a consistent industrial policy.

This is why privatisation has been advocated in Italy as an instrument to reduce public debt and even to tackle the public deficit (Commissione

Scognamiglio 1990). However, it is clear that privatisation does not affect the flow account of the public sector, as it concerns its stock account. In the initial phase, privatisation affects the stock holdings of the seller (the state) only by changing the structure of the company's assets – reducing its wealth in real capital while raising its liquid wealth. Whether the latter is higher or lower than the former only depends on the market value of the company that is to be sold, relative to its book value (Giavazzi and Noera 1991). In a second phase, the seller can transform the acquired liquidity into a reduction of debt,[15] matched by an identical reduction of assets. If (and only if) the seller is the Treasury, the latter action is compulsory, following a 1993 law (n.432). A reduction in public debt can also be obtained indirectly if a joint-stock company (and not the Treasury) is the proprietor-vendor, because once a holding sells or restructures a sub-holding or a subsidiary, it becomes less dependent on public funds.

The central role that public deficit and debt play in the Italian economic policy debate is due to the fact that they are both much larger than the EU average and in countries like the United States and Japan (Table 18.5). Moreover, public debt is steadily increasing and is well beyond 100 per cent of GDP. The effort recently made by policy-makers (in 1992 by the government led by Prime Minister Amato, and in 1993 under Prime Minister Ciampi) is, however, noticeable: indeed, the primary deficit has been turned into a primary surplus of 2 per cent in 1992–93, thanks to a restrictive fiscal policy, particularly severe in the cyclical downturn experienced in that period by all Western countries. It is no accident that at the same time these other countries have generally broadened their public deficit.

Whether such a restrictive budgetary policy is or is not a must in the Italian situation remains, however, an open question for various reasons. To those who recall (Blanchard *et al.* 1990: 12) that 'for a fiscal policy to be sustainable, a Government which has debt outstanding must anticipate sooner or later to run primary budget surpluses' if the real interest rate is (as it is in Italy) higher than the growth rate, others oppose that sustainability only implies that the ratio of debt to GDP *eventually* converges back to its initial level. This being no more than a transversality condition over an infinite horizon period, it does not offer any prescription for the short run.

As a consequence, explanations of the kind 'post hoc ergo propter hoc' become widespread: therefore, the debt is considered sustainable (ex post) if it continues to be financed, while it appears to be unsustainable (ex post) if the 'animal spirits' of the financial community fail to keep their confidence level high.

To those who observe that by continuing to buy government securities, the Italian and the international financial communities reveal a large degree of trust in Italian economic policy, others counter that episodes

Table 18.5 General government budget deficit and net public debt in the USA, Japan and the EEC countries (ratio to GDP)

Country	1980	1989	1990	1991	1992	1993[a]
General government deficit (−) or surplus (+)[b]						
United States	−1.3	−1.5	−2.5	−3.4	−4.7	−4.2
Japan	−4.4	2.5	2.9	3.0	1.8	0.1
EEC	−3.8	−2.7	−4.0	−4.6	−5.1	−6.3
Germany	−2.9	0.1	−2.0	−3.2	−2.8	−4.6
France	0.0	−1.3	−1.5	−2.1	−3.9	−5.9
United Kingdom	−3.4	0.9	−1.3	−2.8	−6.2	−7.7
Belgium	−9.2	−6.4	−5.7	−6.5	−6.8	−7.0
Denmark	−3.3	−0.5	−1.5	−2.2	−2.5	−4.3
Greece	−2.9	−16.6	−18.1	−14.4	−11.1	−14.8
Ireland	−11.4	−1.0	−1.5	−1.4	−2.6	−3.2
Netherlands	−3.9	−4.7	−5.1	−2.6	−3.5	−4.1
Portugal	5.5	−3.1	−5.3	−6.0	−4.6	−8.2
Spain	−2.2	5.4	4.2	−1.2	−7.1	−14.7
Italy	−8.5	−9.9	−10.9	−10.2	−9.5	−9.8
General government deficit or surplus net of interest payments						
United States	−0.1	−0.5	−0.4	−1.1	−2.5	−1.7
Japan	−1.2	6.6	6.9	6.8	5.6	4.0
EEC	−0.5	2.0	0.9	0.4	0.3	−0.7
Germany	−1.0	2.8	0.6	−0.5	0.5	−1.1
France	1.5	1.4	1.4	1.0	−0.5	−2.0
United Kingdom	1.3	4.6	2.1	0.1	−3.4	−4.6
Belgium	−4.0	3.1	4.1	2.8	3.0	3.0
Denmark	−2.8	3.3	1.9	1.2	0.1	−1.3
Greece	−0.5	−8.5	−6.4	−3.3	0.1	−1.3
Ireland	−7.8	5.1	4.7	4.3	3.1	2.6
Netherlands	−1.2	−0.3	−0.8	2.0	1.3	0.7
Portugal	8.6	4.1	2.8	2.3	4.3	−0.5
Spain	−1.9	0.3	−0.8	−1.4	−0.6	−2.5
Italy	−3.2	−1.0	−1.3	0.0	1.9	2.0
Gross public debt[c]						
United States	37.7	53.2	55.4	58.9	61.7	63.4
Japan	52.0	70.6	69.8	68.2	67.3	68.3
Germany	32.8	43.2	43.5	41.8	42.8	46.2
France	37.3	47.5	46.6	48.6	51.6	57.1
United Kingdom	54.1	36.8	34.7	35.4	40.5	47.3
Belgium	79.9	130.2	130.7	133.9	136.0	141.6
Denmark	33.5	58.9	59.5	60.7	62.4	66.2
Greece	27.7	76.0	89.0	96.3	94.6	98.4
Ireland	72.5	105.4	98.7	96.7	93.8	92.1
Netherlands	44.8	76.3	76.5	76.6	78.0	80.6
Portugal	37.5	71.7	66.6	67.5	62.6	67.6
Spain	18.3	46.9	46.8	49.3	51.4	57.4
Italy	59.0	97.9	100.5	104.0	108.0	114.0

Table 18.5 Continued

Country	1980	1989	1990	1991	1992	1993[a]
	Net public debt[d]					
United States	18.8	30.4	32.8	34.0	37.4	39.1
Japan	17.3	14.9	9.1	5.9	5.0	6.0
Germany	12.8	22.7	22.8	23.1	24.1	27.5
France	14.3	24.8	25.0	27.1	30.0	35.6
United Kingdom	47.0	30.1	28.5	30.0	35.1	41.9
Belgium	69.3	119.7	119.4	121.3	123.4	129.0
Denmark	7.3	26.1	26.5	27.7	29.4	33.3
Netherlands	24.4	54.9	55.9	55.9	57.2	59.8
Spain	6.1	30.8	31.6	33.9	36.0	42.0
Italy	53.9	96.1	99.0	102.7	106.7	112.6

Sources: Ministero del Bilancio 1993. For data on public debt, OECD 1993.

Notes:
[a] Forecast
[b] General government deficit, or surplus, is the difference between total revenue and total expenditure, net of financial operations
[c] Gross public debt equals total financial liabilities of the general government, including those generated by financial operations and including financial liabilities of the Central Bank
[d] Net public debt equals gross public debt less financial assets, evaluated in nominal value

of serious financial instability have already emerged, for example in the 'Black Wednesday' crash of 1992 which caused the exit of the lira (as well as sterling) from the EMS.

Those who believe that tying the Italian social system to European standards is the most solid basis for a sound economic and political development of the country therefore stress the importance of Italy's adaptation to the criteria defined by the Maastricht Treaty in December 1991. Others argue that Italian economic policy-making should not lose all its degrees of freedom in trying to reach a stable economic and monetary union at the European level.

At the moment Italy does not meet *any* of Maastricht's four convergence criteria. Namely that the average inflation rate should not exceed that of the three best performing member states in terms of price stability (measured by the consumer price index) by more than 1.5 percentage points; that the exchange rate should not be devalued against any other member state's currency at least in the two years prior to convergence; that the average nominal long-term interest rate on government bonds or comparable securities should not exceed that of at most the three best performing member states in terms of price stability by more than two percentage points; that the reference value of 3 per cent for the ratio of the government deficit to GDP at market prices, and of 60 per cent for the ratio of the government debt to GDP at market prices should be a prerequisite for convergence.

While it is true that at the end of 1993 only Luxembourg would have

Table 18.6 Nominal long-term interest rates and inflation rates (percentage)

Nominal long-term interest rate	1980	1985	1989	1990	1991	1992	1993[a]
United States	11.5	10.6	8.5	8.6	7.9	7.0	5.9
Japan	8.9	6.5	5.2	7.0	6.4	5.3	4.4
Germany	8.5	7.0	7.0	8.8	8.5	7.9	6.5
France	13.8	11.9	9.2	10.4	9.5	9.0	7.0
United Kingdom	13.9	11.1	10.2	11.8	10.1	9.1	7.6
Belgium	11.9	11.0	8.6	10.1	9.3	8.7	7.2
Denmark	20.0	11.6	9.7	10.6	9.3	9.0	7.2
Ireland	15.4	12.6	8.9	10.1	9.2	9.1	8.1
Netherlands	10.2	7.3	7.2	9.0	8.8	8.1	6.5
Spain	16.0	13.4	13.8	14.6	12.8	12.6	10.5
Greece	17.1	15.8	n.a.	n.a.	n.a.	n.a.	n.a.
Luxembourg	7.4	9.5	7.7	8.6	8.2	7.9	6.6
Portugal	22.2	25.4	14.9	16.8	17.1	15.4	11.3
Italy	15.3	13.7	12.8	13.5	13.1	13.7	11.3

Inflation rate							
United States	10.4	3.9	4.9	5.1	4.3	3.3	2.7
Japan	7.5	2.2	1.8	2.6	2.5	2.0	0.9
EEC	13.3	5.7	4.8	4.5	5.2	4.6	3.8
Germany	5.8	1.8	2.9	2.7	3.7	4.7	4.1
France	13.3	5.7	3.4	2.9	3.0	2.4	2.3
United Kingdom	16.3	5.3	5.9	5.3	7.1	5.0	3.5
Belgium	6.2	6.0	3.2	2.9	2.7	2.4	2.7
Denmark	10.7	4.3	4.3	2.6	2.5	1.9	1.1
Ireland	18.6	5.0	3.6	1.6	2.2	2.6	2.2
Netherlands	6.9	2.2	1.2	2.2	3.4	3.0	2.0
Spain	15.7	7.1	6.7	6.3	6.4	6.5	4.8
Greece	21.9	18.2	14.7	19.3	18.6	14.6	14.1
Luxembourg	7.5	4.3	3.6	3.6	2.9	2.8	3.5
Portugal	21.6	19.4	12.1	12.6	11.1	9.4	6.3
Italy	20.4	9.0	6.4	6.2	6.8	5.4	4.5

Sources: OECD 1993; Commission of the European Communities 1986, 1993a, 1993b.

Note: [a] Forecast

satisfied all the conditions of the Maastricht Treaty, the empirical evidence illustrated in Tables 18.5 and 18.6 clearly shows that no other country, with the possible exception of Greece, is as far from meeting the convergence criteria.

For those that stress net rather than gross public debt – because they believe that insolvency rather than unsustainability (Buiter 1985) might cause financial instability in Italy, the OECD data on the general government debt net of liquid assets (Table 18.5) should confirm that the ranking of Italy relative to other Western countries is even worse on such a net public debt criterion.

To critics who argue that this data is misleading because only financial assets in nominal value directly owned by the general government (liquidity and credit) are used to transform the gross into the net public debt, one should object that better data on the general government stock account, based on cross-country comparable criteria, simply do not exist. As far as the Italian case is concerned, Table 18.7 provides some tentative estimates of all assets and liabilities of the public sector in 1990. According to this empirical evidence, the net worth of the Italian public sector is barely negative (approximately by 87,752 billion lire) provided roads, bridges, and railway tracks are included, while excluding some goods of state demesne (seas, rivers, commodities for military use) and all archaeological, historical and cultural commodities – from the Colosseum to the Botticellis and the other heritage assets of the country.

One should not be too reassured by this information: figures on public debt reported in Tables 18.5 and 18.7 do not take into account the huge hidden debt of the social security system, which in Italy was calculated in the mid-1980s (Castellino 1985) to be about four times the size of the then-known public debt, while in 1990 the present value of public pension future liabilities was estimated to be about twice as large as the conventional debt (Van den Noord and Herd 1993). More recent estimations (Ministero del Bilancio e della Programmazione Economica – Consiglio Tecnico Scientifico 1994) criticise the value given by Van den Noord and Herd as inadequate and too optimistic, and fix the 1992 value of the social security debt at equal to two and a half times the public sector debt.

IS THERE AN ITALIAN 'ECONOMIC MIRACLE'?

The sketchy conclusion that one can make from these analyses is that Italy not only needs more market and less state, but it needs a very different kind of public intervention altogether. Why then, one might ask, does Italy continue to rank among the seven most industrialised nations, and to enjoy an enviable rate of growth, notwithstanding obvious and large mistakes in economic policy?[16]

The answer is that Italy is a heterogeneous, fragmented country, and it is much more divided than the conventional concept of economic dualism would imply, although admittedly the regional schism is probably the most painful. The latter is epitomised by the fact that per-capita GDP in certain northern and central regions of Italy (Piedmont, Lombardy, and Emilia Romagna) is the same (in terms of purchasing power parity) as in the richest areas of Europe (Luxembourg, Ile-de-France and the wealthiest German Länder), while the Mezzogiorno has a standard of living similar to that of the weakest areas of the EEC (Greece, Portugal, Ireland, and parts of Spain). Both the North-Centre and the South, however, have enjoyed approximately the same, high rate of growth in the last 40 years.

Table 18.7 The public sector[a] stock account in Italy (billions of lire, 1990)

Own net[b] real capital of the general government[c]	1,044,783
OWN REPRODUCIBLE CAPITAL[d]	805,730
Construction	772,610
Machines and equipment	31,488
Means of transport	1,632
OWN IRREPRODUCIBLE CAPITAL[e]	
Estates[f]	239,053
Own net[b] real capital of public enterprises included in the public sector[a]	51,209
Liquidity and net[g] credit to other sectors of the general government[c]	53,872
Liquidity and net[g] credit to other sectors of public enterprises included in the public sector[a]	31,348
Equity stock evaluated as net worth[h] of the general government:[c]	49,010
IRI	16,914
ENI	14,743
EFIM	281
ENEL	11,583
Local public services (1987)	5,489
Equity stock evaluated as net worth[h] of public enterprises included in the public sector[a]	270
TOTAL DEBT	1,318,244
TOTAL ASSETS	1,230,492

Notes:
[a] The public sector is defined as the general government consolidated with some of the public enterprises (railways, state monopolies, mail services and state telephone services). It differs both from the general government and from the enlarged public sector defined above. The gross public debt of the public sector does not include the debt for commodities already supplied by the private sector still unpaid and the debt for taxes to be reimbursed. Assets do not include taxes computed for 1990 and yet to be paid by the private sector. Data on debt do not include the 'hidden public debt', that is the present value of pensions to be paid by social security, because it can be 'repudiated' in the future by a change in the pay-as-you-go mechanism.
[b] Net of depreciation.
[c] See note 1 in the text.
[d] Reproducible capital is evaluated according to the Perpetual Inventory Method at current prices. Construction includes infrastructure and public works made by private enterprises through franchise bidding.
[e] Data do not include public property of artistic, cultural and historical interest.
[f] Elaboration on *Commissione di indagine sul patrimonio immobiliare pubblico* (1988). Estates are agricultural land and rural and extra-urban areas. Some goods belonging to the state demesne are not included (internal waterways and seas – including shores, beaches, roadsteads, and lagoons connected with the sea). Other capital goods belonging to the state demesne not considered in this table are those concerning artistic, cultural and archaeological commodities because they cannot be evaluated at the present level of information together with goods for military use because expenditure in this sector are never considered investments by the national accounts.
[g] Net of earmarking funds.
[h] Net worth equals total assets less total liabilities.

Sources: unpublished ISTAT data (kindly supplied by Susanna Mantegazza) for own reproducible capital; elaboration on Commissione di indagine sul patrimonio immobiliare pubblico 1988, for data on own irreproducible and scarse capital; Banca d'Italia 1993, for liquidity and credit data; IRI 1991; EFIM 1991; Ente Ferrovie dello Stato 1991; Ministero del Tesoro 1991; CISPEL 1990, for equity stock data.

One could point to other forms of dualism that have equally far-reaching economic consequences: for example, small and medium-sized enterprises, and the private sector in general, are strong and have growth potential, but large firms and the public sector in the broad sense (the enlarged public sector plus state-controlled companies) exhibit structural weaknesses and their role may be declining.

In other words, some parts of Italy work well, keep abreast of technical progress and are therefore capable of placing the country in the league of the richest seven nations of the world. This side of the economy is so strong that it offsets the problems of the rest of Italy, including those generated by public intervention.

Italian society displays almost unique imagination, as well as an ability to maintain its equilibrium and to operate outside the rules of the game: Italian prosperity therefore appears to be an 'economic miracle' because it has been achieved in spite of Italy's apparent dominant values, and thus this success seems totally unexpected. In reality, however, it is the logical result of a collective propensity to ignore general principles and dominant ideas and to circumvent laws, affirmative actions, and economic policy rules.

In other words Italian society is already doing what I have argued that the government should allow it to do – primarily by introducing deregulation and flexibility into its economic activity. Italy is achieving these goals through the informal economy by evading taxes and union rules in small private enterprises, but it is largely failing to do so in larger companies and in the public sector. In short, the country is developing thanks to what the Italians call 'l'arte d'arrangiarsi' (their generalised talent for improvisation) – thus providing living proof that deregulation and flexibility, at least in the Italian context, seem to work.

NOTES

1 The general government is constituted by the state and other central government bodies, by one autonomous company (forestry), by local governments, by hospitals and social security institutions, and by other central or local agencies. The former autonomous company ANAS (roads) is now a public agency called ENAS.

2 These public enterprises are currently of two kinds: public agencies with an autonomous balance sheet (the post office, which used to be an autonomous company without an autonomous budget, local public services such as gas, water, waste disposal, local transports, etc.) and joint-stock companies (electricity, railways, salt and tobacco).

3 This is less true for state-controlled financial intermediaries. Indeed, in 1993 and 1994 the state had already divested itself of the shares of two banks (CREDIT and COMIT). More recently, other banks and an insurance company, which were public agencies, have been turned into joint-stock companies ready for privatisation. The privatisation process is ongoing for only one of

them (Istituto Mobiliare Italiano-IMI), but the public quota (approximately 20 per cent of the shares) still leaves the state with substantial control.

4 Whether restructuring is or is not a prerequisite for privatisation remains an open question and indeed it is a highly debated issue in Italy.

5 The outcome of the privatisations has thus far been minimal in financial terms (around 5,000 billion lire), corresponding to a rounding error if compared with the public deficit or public debt.

6 The non-rivalry and non-excludability existing in public goods implies that there will be free-rider private behaviour.

7 This is a case of externalities where social costs and social benefits are not internalised in private costs and private benefits.

8 Natural monopolies are monopolies with ever-decreasing marginal and average costs, where a first best solution with price equal to marginal cost is never profitable and therefore never possible. A second best solution can be obtained without public intervention if the natural monopoly is contestable, that is if there exist potential competitors and investment costs are not heavy and sunk. Public intervention is necessary if the natural monopoly is non-contestable. It could then take the form of a public enterprise or of a regulated private enterprise.

9 Strategic sectors may be those where merit goods are produced or where there exists a clear incompleteness of the market.

10 The most recent evidence on the quality of public goods in Italy is potentially encouraging: in the field of public order, for example, important successes have been recently obtained against organised crime, while in the last years Italian judges have become world famous for their courageous activity. At the time of writing, however, few trials have been completed, and slowness is certainly one of a number of problems that the Italian judicial system faces. As for public order, despite the advances made by the police and the judicial authorities it would be hard to deny that the Mafia remains a major threat to law and order in Italy.

11 The retirement age was 55 for women and 60 for men and will be 60 for women and 65 for men after 1 January 2002 through progressive adjustments.

12 It was 5 years until January 1993; it will be 10 years in 2002. Between 1993 and 2001 the pensionable income is calculated as an average of wages earned since 1988.

13 The most noticeable public intervention in the Mezzogiorno however concerns various budget transfers particularly to support the households' disposable income.

14 It should be said however that the poor quality of public intervention is sometimes due to the insufficient resources that are devoted to them (as in the case of public services).

15 If the vendor is not the Treasury, but a joint-stock company owned by the Treasury, the reduction of its debt is not computed as a reduction of public debt.

16 Between 1976 and 1990 Italian GDP grew by 50 per cent, at an annual average rate of 2.8 per cent. This was 6 percentage points above the EEC average over this period.

REFERENCES

Banca d'Italia (1993) *Assemblea generale ordinaria dei partecipanti anno 1992*, Rome: Banca d'Italia.

Blanchard, O., Chouraqui, J., Hagemann, R.P. and Sartor, N. (1990) 'The sustainability of fiscal policy: new answers to an old question', *OECD, Economic Studies* 15: 77–117.

Buiter, W. H. (1985) 'A guide to public sector debt and deficit', *Economic Policy* 1: 13–79.

Castellino, O. (1985) 'C'è un secondo debito pubblico (più grande del primo)?', *Moneta e Credito* 38 (149): 21–30.

CISPEL (1990) *Compendio dati 1987–1986*, Rome: CISPEL.

Commissione di indagine sul patrimonio immobiliare pubblico (1988) 'Relazione conclusiva', *Rivista Trimestrale di Diritto Pubblico*, 1.

Commission of the European Communities (1986) 'Annual economic review, 1986–1987', *European Economy*, 29.

Commission of the European Communities (1993a) 'Annual Economic Report for 1993', *European Economy*, 54.

Commission of the European Communities (1993b) 'Reports on the borrowing and lending activities of the community', *European Economy Supplement A*, 10.

Commissione Scognamiglio (Commissione per il riassetto del patrimonio mobiliare e per le privatizzazioni) (1990) *Rapporto al Ministro del Tesoro*, Rome.

Direzione Centrale dei Servizi Postali (1988) 'Indagine sui tempi di recapito delle corrispondenze', Rome: *mimeo*.

ENI (1991) *Bilancio consolidato del Gruppo ENI al 31 dicembre 1990*, Rome: ENI.

EFIM (1991) *Bilancio consolidato 1990*, Rome: EFIM.

ENEL (1991) *Bilancio al 31 dicembre 1990*, Rome: ENEL.

Ente Ferrovie dello Stato (1991) *Relazione al bilancio 1990*, Rome: Ente Ferrovie dello Stato.

Giavazzi, F. and Noera, M. (1991) 'Una nota su privatizzazioni e sostenibilità del debito pubblico', pp. 29–39 in Euromobiliare (ed.), *Privatizzazioni: scelte, implicazioni, miraggi*, Milano: Euromobiliare.

IRI (1991) *Bilancio consolidato 1990*, Rome: IRI.

ISTAT (1993) *Conti delle amministrazioni pubbliche e della protezione sociale anni 1986–1991*, Rome: ISTAT.

Malizia, R. and Pedulla, G. (1988) 'L'attività delle amministrazioni pubbliche nel sistema economico con particolare riguardo al Welfare State', working paper, Consiglio Nazionale delle Ricerche.

Ministero del Bilancio e della Programmazione Economica (1993) *L'economia italiana nel 1992*, Rome: Ministero del Bilancio e della Programmazione Economica.

Ministero del Bilancio e della Programmazione Economica – Consiglio Tecnico Scientifico (1994), *Il debito pubblico previdenziale: definizione, significato, entità e sostenibilità*, 13 July, Rome.

Ministero del Tesoro (1991) *Rendiconto generale dello Stato 1990*, Rome: Tipografia del Senato.

OECD (1993) *OECD Economic Surveys 1992–1993. Italy*, Paris: OECD.

Onofri, R., Patrizii, V. and Zangheri, P. (eds) (1987) *Analisi della gestione e del funzionamento dei servizi della amministrazione delle Poste e delle Telecomunicazioni*, Rome: Commissione Tecnica per la Spesa Pubblica.

Padoa Schioppa Kostoris, F. (1993) *Italy, The Sheltered Economy*, Oxford: Clarendon.

Senato della Repubblica (1993) *Relazione generale sulla situazione economica del Paese 1992*, Rome: Senato della Repubblica.

Van den Noord, P. and Herd, R. (1993) 'Pension liabilities in the seven major economies', *OECD Working Papers*, 1 (15).

19 Industrial relations and the labour movement

Mimmo Carrieri

AFTER THE 'GREAT SETTLEMENT' AND THE END OF THE UNIFIED CONFEDERATION

There is widespread agreement in Italy among scholars and observers over the 'trade union parabola' coined by the sociologist Aris Accornero (1992). This suggests that after the great reinforcement of the three trade union confederations CGIL, CISL and UIL in the 1970s (unionisation increased at a tremendous rate from 27 per cent in 1967 to 51 per cent in 1977), a downturn occurred. This was associated with the cycle of industrial reorganisation between 1980 and 1985, which reshaped many large firms (beginning with FIAT), and reduced employment in industry (while it increased in small, less unionised firms). In these conditions the three confederal unions faced increasing difficulties in representing the interests of employees as these appeared to become more and more differentiated. This divergence was resoundingly demonstrated at FIAT in 1980 when a sharp split occurred between assembly-line workers and the majority of employees, led by front-line managers (Baldissera 1988).

The down-curve of the trade union parabola was apparent above all in its troubled relationships with the parties and the political system (Regini 1985). Every time the CGIL, CISL and UIL approached the government to discuss economic and social measures, conflict resulted. Dissatisfaction was voiced by the rank and file of the trade unions who judged agreed measures to be too restrictive, and criticism arose over the excessive 'centralisation' of union activity which was considered to be too geared towards the institutions. However there were also differences in position between the three organisations, due to their diverse political leanings. In 1984 these tensions exploded. The reduction of the wage indexing system (the *scala mobile*) had been in the pipeline for some time, as a cut was deemed necessary to lower inflation. Yet the CGIL had many reservations because it was concerned with defending workers on lower incomes (who benefited most from the sliding scale). But besides questions of fairness, there was also political disagreement. The Prime Minister in the period from 1983 to 1987, the Socialist leader Bettino Craxi, engaged in a policy of 'competitiveness within the left wing' (Amato and Cafagna 1982). The main point of this policy was to reduce the popularity and influence of the PCI, the largest left-wing party and the sworn adversary of the PSI. It is for this reason that the majority in the CGIL (which was linked to the PCI) doubly distrusted the propositions of the government and in the end decided not to subscribe to them.

These events marked a new phase in union history. For the first time in more than 20 years a dramatic split occurred between the three unions. The Federazione Unitaria (the unified federation of CGIL, CISL and UIL) which had been formed in 1972 and was never free of tension, collapsed. When the PCI decided to sponsor a referendum in order to repeal the government's decisions on the *scala mobile*, relations between the three organisations became even more bitter. The defeat of the PCI's move in the 1985 referendum created a scenario in which the unions were forced into changing their strategy. Yet they did not manage to come up with any convincing ideas. It became clear that the unions had entered the down-side of the parabola. Half way through the decade unionisation was calculated to have fallen to 42 per cent, and the unions were evidently failing to recruit the new private-sector workers. Room for pay negotiation in the more competitive sectors of the economy was in fact limited, and some employers manifested a 'Thatcherite' anti-union aggressiveness (e.g. in the engineering industries: Mortillaro 1984). For some years the unions attempted to bring about the 'great settlement' with employers and government. But the break-up in 1984 rendered impracticable such a 'political exchange' (in which the union offered support for modernisation and industrial peace in return for social and economic benefits). The drama for organised labour lay in the fact that they now had a greater need for the support of the government and the institutions than the latter did for the unions. In these circumstances negotiations remained at a standstill. The unions' difficulties were compounded by the emergence of new problems of social representation. From 1986 onwards various categories of civil servants demanded substantial pay rises, either to reassert differentials reduced by 'egalitarian' contractual demands in the 1970s, or to keep up with other groups who had made progress in the last few years – for example judges, university professors and doctors.

In such conditions the incomes policies mooted by the Craxi government in reality had a limited impact. A real control of salary dynamics was accomplished only in industrial export firms which were bound by international prices. In the public and State participation sectors, the government – which also operated as employer – was much more lax. There were political reasons for this: the public sector was traditionally the electoral reserve of the DC and of the other parties of government and in this period the Socialists were looking to expand their influence in this area.

In this context two phenomena took shape and became intertwined. On the one hand, increasing conflict occurred within the service sector, while there was a substantial reduction of conflict in industry (after reaching record figures ten years previously). This is why the concept of 'tertiary conflict' (Accornero 1985) was developed. This alluded not only to the sector in which the conflicts took place, but above all to its victims: the 'third parties' – the public comprised of citizens and users, taken hostage by the strikers in order to increase the damage and their contractual power. On the other hand this unruly and unpopular type of dispute was directed against the values and the behaviour of the trade union confederations who tried to counter it with self-regulatory controls. In reality, during the period 1986 to 1990 the unions were systematically outflanked by conflictual actions conducted by the semi-organised rank and file representatives. Assertive rank and file committees (COBAS) sprang up which were in conflict with the confederations. For example, there were end-of-year test strikes by teachers (who left students in a state of uncertainty about their results), and strikes by engine-drivers, who managed to block most of the circulation of the railway network (even though they represented a tiny proportion of the total percentage of railway employees). The birth of these organisms and the decline of rank and file structures in industry – that is the factory councils, which were launched in the 1970s – symbolised the crisis of the social representation of trade union confederations.

Everywhere in Europe in this period trade unions faced similar problems: great technological innovations and a contraction in industrial employment; the demand for maximum corporate flexibility; the growth in tertiary employment; reduced discipline among the trade unions in the public sector. But in Italy these assumed particular forms. Above all the trade unions seemed more exposed to the effects of change in the relations of power between social forces than in other countries. In this sense they have paid the price for policies adopted in more prosperous years when they refused to agree to the establishment of too precise or definite legal procedures or agreements between the different sides of industry.

After the passage of the Workers' Charter in 1970, the trade unions preferred to maintain a high degree of informality and they continued to look with disfavour at certain articles of the Constitution which concerned them, but which had never been activated (article 39 on trade union association and article 40 on the right to strike). As a consequence, in a period of weakness they found themselves exposed on various fronts. Bargaining periods tended to become prolonged, and in the absence of clear rules the outcome often depended either on industrial muscle or good working relations in single sectors and firms. Whether or not the government intervened was similarly not dependent on specific rules and conditions but on purely informal and conjunctural considerations.

Consultation declined, as did rank and file representation, while in the field of labour policies no new legislation was introduced, in accordance with the demand for deregulation that was put forward by Confindustria.

YEARS OF STAGNATION

In the years after 1987, the power of the parties and the weakness of the unions was confirmed. There probably has never been a period in the history of Italy in which so many important decisions were taken by so few politicians as that between 1983 and 1991. The pact of steel between the top leadership of the DC and the PSI seemed destined to last a long time, not least because the PCI was in sharp decline. Even the internal life of the trade unions, in spite of declarations of autonomy, depended to a great extent on the balance of power between the parties. Even the PSI, which had a centrist role in the political system, conditioned the trade unions in these years, because senior figures in all three confederations belonged to that party and identified with Craxi's leadership. In the UIL as well as in the Communist-dominated CGIL, internal currents were organised on party political lines. That these links were still very close became clear in successive years. The former UIL secretary Giorgio Benvenuto became Craxi's successor in 1993 and his place was taken by Ottaviano Del Turco, assistant secretary of the CGIL. Two CGIL trade unionists, Sergio Garavini and Fausto Bertinotti, consecutively became secretaries of Rifondazione Comunista, the neo-communist party founded after the birth of the PDS in 1991. The secretary of CISL, Marini, resigned from his position in order to become Employment Minister in 1991 as a Christian Democratic nominee.

But the fact that trade unionists would be called upon to try and save the leading parties from crisis (especially the PSI) tells us little about the situation at the end of the 1980s when it was the parties who were controlling the game. For the trade unions these were years of stagnation within a political framework that appeared to be immobile. The CGIL was the most troubled of the three trade unions, both because its old identity founded on conflict was in crisis and because it was most exposed to the fallout from disputes between the PCI and the PSI (both parties having organised their supporters as factions inside the union). This trouble was also reflected at the level of the leadership. For the first time in its history a secretary general, Pizzinato, was forced to resign in 1988 before the end of his term because he no longer had majority support.

After this incident, the post of Secretary General fell to Bruno Trentin, historic leader of the metal workers and architect of such 1970s innovations as the concept of the union as a 'political subject'. Trentin tried to direct this large and complex organisation (which still counted five million members) towards a new identity. At the 1991 CGIL congress, notions of solidarity were combined with a policy of promoting workers' rights, even of individual workers. And in place of the traditional emphasis on conflict (which continued to be propounded by the extreme left minority faction *Essere Sindacato*) the new watchword was that of 'co-determination', which implied the participation of the trade unions in significant choices in the ambit of firms.

The Catholic union CISL did not need to change its line as it had anticipated the problems of the 1980s by distancing itself from the labourism and industrialism of the previous decade. In this period the CISL sought to reconnect itself to its original pre-1968 identity. Its main concern was with public employees and the Mezzogiorno – sectors where the union was powerful due to its old links with the governing Christian Democratic party. The process of southernisation, and the extension of the public tertiary sector continued apace at this time, due to the decline in industrial unionisation (in this sector CISL lost a third of its members at the end of the 1970s). The effects of this evolution in representation were felt at the most senior level. The successors as secretary to Pierre Carniti, an ex-secretary of the metal workers, were Marini and D'Antoni who were associated with the civil service and the Christian Democratic core of the confederation. In this context even the objective of 'political exchange' lost some of its meaning as it was concerned with maintaining a more advantageous status for public employees.

Thus both the two largest confederations sought to modify their identities in some way. The CGIL maintained and revised its perception of itself as the 'general' trade union by seeking to represent all workers even if they were not enrolled in the trade union. For its part, CISL renewed its identity as a 'trade union club' stressing as a priority the organisation and its responsibility towards its members (and not all workers). The third confederation, UIL, historically occupied a residual space as it did not have a clear identity and was also the weakest trade union organisationally. For this reason in the period 1987–91 it tried to develop an identity through strong leadership (the able Benvenuto), privileged relations with the PSI, the attempt to find new constituencies (such as managers, or professional workers in the private service sector). From this sprang the UIL's attempt to present itself as a trade union sui generis, capable of offering protection beyond the working environment – the 'citizens' trade union' – as in fact UIL defined itself.

As far as unionisation and representation were concerned, there was substantial stability until 1991–92. The rate of unionisation settled at about 40 per cent, with a slight fall in the CGIL (which remained the largest trade union) and modest increases in the number of active members in CISL and UIL. The confederations in the public sector (especially CISL and UIL) maintained their positions with greater success (with a rate of unionisation of nearly 48 per cent) in spite of the challenge of the rank and file committees and of the other associations outside the confederations. The number of pensioner members grew significantly in all three confederations, and this produced an overall increase in the total number of members (which exceeded 10 million), even with a decrease in active working members. This phenomenon was particularly relevant for the CGIL, where the non-active workers made up nearly 50 per cent of all members. In 1993 this barrier was broken. It should also be noted that decay occurred at the level of rank and file structures. Delegates often remained in office even for many years because of the delay in renewing these organisms.

Of all the representation strategies adopted by the diverse organis-ations, the most effective (but also the most traditional) was that of the CISL, which was concerned with winning support among public employees. And, in effect, between 1987 and 1991 the salaries of public workers increased at an average annual rate of 15 per cent as compared with 3 per cent for workers in the competitive sector. This was due in part to 'tertiary' forms of conflict adopted by the autonomous unions. Despite serious problems in the national economy resulting from the government's loss of control over the budget (leading to the spiralling increase in the public debt), the political elite favoured the growth of the divide between the privileges and salaries of the public sector and those of the private-competitive sector.

In this period there were no initiatives towards meta-agreements with employers and government. Any such moves were practically impossible after the traumatic outcome in 1984. For this reason it was necessary in 1986 for the government to intervene in order to extend the modified *scala mobile* from the public to the private sector, thereby confirming the wage-leadership of the former. By acting more cohesively the trade unions obtained some significant results. Various unitary strikes led to a bilateral agreement with the government in 1988 which established the periodic return of fiscal drag and confirmed the role of the unions in public and general themes. Overall what this showed, was that even in a period of difficulties and stagnation, the confederate trade unions did not lose the right of access to the political system, even though this was on a more precarious and inconsistent basis than a few years previously.

Even in the case of the negotiating process, attempts by firms and employers' organisations to exclude the unions were slightly hampered, and this produced effects that were anything but coherent. National cate-gory bargaining in fact declined and a great divide opened up between the public and private sectors. In the latter, negotiation was mainly defen-sive and was concerned with the preservation of rights which in some cases were actually reinforced; there was less action on salaries which were in line with the lower inflation rates of foreign competitors. In spite of the loss of dynamism in industry and in private services the national contract remains the epicentre of the Italian wage system, because it still covers the great majority of workers.

Firm-level negotiation was highly differentiated – on the whole there was more negotiation in medium- to large-sized firms, which accounted for 40 per cent of industrial enterprises (Baglioni and Milani 1992). A very interesting trend highlighted by several studies was the growth of 'micro-agreement' settlements between the social parties, based on their willingness to cooperate (and therefore to come to a general agreement) in order to resolve common problems (Regini and Sabel 1989). From 1988–89 participatory types of agreements increased in a few firms such as Zanussi, Parmalat and several public firms which set up mixed commissions in order to deal with various subjects (from job organisation to training and refectories etc.) – but this was not a general pattern. In other firms mechanisms were established which related a part of the salary to the performance of the firm.

This process became more pronounced only in successive years (particularly in 1992–93). But what is important to note here is that a type of schizophrenia was to be found in Italian industrial relations: at a national level the two sides of industry argued frequently and sometimes did not speak to each other; on the ground by contrast there was a pragmatic willingness to put aside rhetorical contrasts and to cooperate in looking for solutions to problems.

The legislative innovations of these years should not be overlooked. In 1970 a law was passed to regulate strikes within fundamental public services. This arrived after a long phase of incubation, which forced the confederate trade unions to face the reality of the situation (the increase in tertiary conflict) and to abandon the idea that self-discipline was sufficient in this area. The confederations contributed to the framing of the law, subjected the trade unions to rules, constraints and sanctions, because the majority of conflicts were promoted by the 'extra confederalists' who did not accept or respect the self-regulation code. The law therefore existed to protect citizens from excessive disruption and to guarantee a minimum level of services in all circumstances. That this was the first phase of a legislative reform of industrial relations demonstrated the importance of the intervention of the law, but also the difficulty, in the Italian case, of designing and accomplishing it.

Within this static framework, modified only by some ambitious aspiration to change, an important external factor intervened which opened up the boundaries of innovation: Occhetto's *svolta* (turn-around) at the end of 1989, in the wake of the democratic revolution in Eastern Europe, laid the foundations for the constitution of a post-communist party. The potential repercussions for the trade unions were considerable. Every residual ideological difference which could supply an alibi for the separation between the three confederations was overcome. The CGIL was the union most likely to be affected as it had for too long been hamstrung by a division of responsibilities between Socialists and Communists (respectively one-third and two-thirds) which was based on political leanings and not on leadership quality.

In response, the CGIL – with Trentin as Secretary – chose a far-sighted course. Rather than becoming involved in the complicated internal disputes within the old PCI (between the majority of reformists and the minority of neo-communists), they opted for a more radical innovation: the dissolution of the Communist current in the CGIL and the overcoming of the logic of these currents in the union's internal management. This sparked a series of reactions. On the one hand, it forced the Socialist component also to dissolve itself (even if this only became properly effective after the collapse of the PSI in 1992). On the other hand, a 'maximalist' minority faction took shape which mixed nostalgia for conflictual behaviour and communism. At the same time, the CGIL's decision to break its political allegiance prompted other trade unions to do likewise.

The elections in 1992 did not reward Occhetto's efforts or introduce any wide-ranging innovations from the trade union point of view. The new party maintained its lead over the PSI, Rifondazione Comunista emerged as a force, the Left became even more fragmented; the only change was produced by the success of the Lega Nord. Occhetto's operation did not produce any advantages for the trade unions as it did not give rise to a great party of Labourite inspiration which could unify the diverse fractions of the Left and act as a political voice for the trade unions. Thus no move occurred towards the northern European model of perfect interdependence between the political Left and the trade unions, and instead the Mediterranean model of pluralism and fragmentation, which in the past had often produced powerlessness, was confirmed.

NEW OPPORTUNITIES FOR THE TRADE UNIONS FOLLOWING THE COLLAPSE OF THE PARTY SYSTEM

Attempts at innovation and self-innovation carried out by the trade unions and the PCI did not produce significant results, and sometimes – as with the first steps of the PDS – had undesirable and negative effects. In addition several external events broke up old stabilities and therefore put the capacities of the trade unions for adaptation and renewal to the test. The first of these was the Maastricht Treaty for the European Union (1991), which introduced rigorous and binding parameters for all national economies. This struck at the 'open tap' public spending which every Italian government had used in order to boost electoral support. Instead a more realistic stance was adopted on the state of the economy, which in fact was aggravated by the crisis in the industrial system generally and in particular in a few large firms. Emergency measures to control salary dynamics replaced unrealistic and problematic incomes policies.

The second was produced by the judicial inquiries which revealed the depth of the moral crisis of the Republic and the degeneration of the ruling classes. The result was a true political earthquake – unimaginable until a few months previously – which engulfed and overwhelmed the two main governing parties. The PSI risked disappearing completely from the political scene as public opinion identified it as the main party responsible for the corruption. Therefore Socialist unionists were placed in a quandary, which the UIL resolved by opting to sever its links with the PSI and by establishing a preferential relationship with the new progressive movement – Alleanza Democratica (the Democratic Alliance). The trade unions were brushed by the scandals but were not actually involved. The main endeavours of the three leaders were directed to separating the image of the unions from that of the parties concerned.

The third event was the electoral victory of the Right in the March 1994 elections, an event which inevitably had consequences for industrial relations and social policies.

These combinations of events exposed the trade unions to stress and unexpected challenges which threatened the security and public protection the confederations had enjoyed for the previous quarter of the century.

RECENT TRENDS

Let us now focus on a few key tendencies to have emerged since 1992. The first of these concerns regulations for industrial relations. After many years of instability and uncertainty, an important protocol establishing an agreement between the government and the negotiating parties was reached on 3 July 1993, at the end of a tripartite negotiation begun in 1990 with the objective of defining the structure of the contractual system and of controlling the dynamics of labour costs. Under emergency conditions a first step was taken by Amato's government in July 1992. However the contractual structure was not dealt with, although decentralised negotiation was suspended until the end of 1993 and in fact the *scala mobile* was completely abolished (except for a modest equilibrating mechanism). This outcome gave rise to great protest, especially among working women and among employees in the North. Economic austerity, even though it was necessary, was not tempered by innovations and reforms. The agreement of the following year was wider and more significant. In fact the regulatory framework which emerged was innovative and substantial.

The end of indexation was confirmed but compensations of a contractual nature were offered to the workers, in such a way as to guarantee real incomes. Important measures concerning the management of the labour market and interim work were introduced, and even industrial policy intervention was foreshadowed. But above all two annual income policy sessions were established which institutionalised the consultative participation of the negotiating parties on macro-economic themes. The presence of two levels of negotiation was established – one national and compulsory, the other decentralised and optional. The sections of national contracts concerning salary were to be renewed every two years, while the sections concerning 'regulations' (rights, information, hours, arrangements etc.) were to last for a period of four years. Negotiation at plant level was to take place every four years and pay-rises linked to productivity and profit levels. In every work-place the establishment of new organisms of rank and file representation (called RSU) was to be agreed and these were to be elected periodically by all employees.

This protocol had the merit of regulating – in a solid though not legally binding way – goals which for a long time were dependent on informal arrangements and on the balance in the power relations between the parties. Agreements were now to be defined within thematic limits and procedures precisely linked to fixed periods of income policies. Agreements achieved in this way were expected to have a more stable character and a coherent structure. Confindustria's request to reduce everything to only one contractual level was rejected, but at the same time the optional nature of decentralised negotiation made it unlikely that an expansion would occur. The institution of the RSU gave trade unions the opportunity to inject new life into their organisations. At the same time, for the first time in 25 years, rank and file representation was organised in a manner that was formally agreed between the trade unions and employers' associations.

Yet the immediate effects of the protocol should not be over-estimated since much of its content referred to future industrial-relations procedures. However, this provision could nevertheless be regarded as a basis for negotiation – allowing the details to be collectively worked out by the parties at a later stage. Here it is important to underline that for the first time in Italy this agreement brought about the sort of 'social pact' or 'social settlement' model that a few people had been arguing was necessary for some time. This outcome was possible thanks to a fortuitous political conjuncture. The Ciampi government emerged from outside the logic of the old parties, and thanks also to the presence of ministers of recognised competence, it behaved in a more even-handed manner towards the interests involved. It was not a pro-labour government, but a government which maintained a proper distance and was able to win the confidence of both sides of industry in its efforts to find a solution to the long-running struggle between trade unions and employers.

A second key variable concerns trade union relations with the political system. From the mid-1970s, this complex question continuously posed dilemmas for the three confederations. The political allegiance of each federation prevented them from collectively using pressure in moments of strength, or fixing a common line of defence in periods of weakness. After the open conflict in 1984, CGIL, CISL and UIL established a pact of non-belligerence, in order to minimise the points of difference which derived from their political affiliations.

However it remained difficult to define the notion of a pro-labour government in Italy, given that a part of the trade union movement (a considerable section of the CISL) regarded itself as being represented by the DC – which was often incorrectly defined as 'a conservative party' but which in reality represented a good many 'popular' interests. Faced with the difficulty of defining a political framework that they could all approve, the trade unions simply proclaimed their autonomy. But in practice the indifference or false neutrality which they assumed passed over an essential fact – not all governments are or were equally well-disposed to trade unions.

The move towards diplomacy was practised above all in the 1980s by the CGIL, which found itself to be walking a tight-rope, given the conflictual relationship between the PSI, which was still in power, and the PCI, the main opposition. This showed that despite all the discussions of autonomy, the trade unions were still very dependent on the parties. It also showed that trade unions, which in the 1970s had entertained political ambitions, had in reality stopped exercising an influence on the political sphere. For example, they were not able to express clear positions in the debate on institutional reforms, and sometimes a virtue was even made of this, as if the rules of the democratic game did not also condition industrial relations and collective action.

This timidness was understandable before the collapse of the PSI and the DC, but it became less easy to comprehend in the period 1992–94 when the trade unions remained the only mass organisational structure in Italian society. Even the PDS was shown to have social roots and an organisational structure that were much more limited than those of the old PCI. To support or refound the parties became necessary in this context. This was the case for the Socialist trade unionists who tried in vain to revive their party after Craxi (see Gundle, Chapter 5). It was feared that the collapse of the mass parties, if not replaced by new mass organisations, could open the way to an American style of politics, with weak representative organisations and a great reliance on the use of image. On the other hand, the UIL, which became more involved on the political front and explicitly supported Alleanza Democratica, did not receive reassuring results. In the 1994 election less than 20 per cent of its members voted for AD, which itself obtained a derisory percentage of the overall vote.

It is difficult to say if a 'confederate' party model like that of the British Labour Party could be feasible in Italy as this system would probably involve the stable insertion of several trade unionists in the party arena. Yet the conflict that developed with the right-wing government that emerged victorious from the 1994 election compelled the confederations to deal once more with political themes. To maintain wide representation among workers, the confederate trade unions had no choice but to take up such issues of general importance as pensions, health and tax.

Many trade unionists discovered for the first time in 1994 the cost of under-estimating the importance of supporting legislation on essential subjects such as representation and participation. But it is also true, that thanks to the July 1993 agreement, there was a set of quite well-structured regulations. In many cases these regulations, as we have already noted, require ordered and predictable behaviour on the part of the negotiating partners. Therefore future arrangements in industrial relations depend, to a certain extent, on the willingness of the governments to avail themselves of bargaining mechanisms such as standing forums for deciding incomes policy which were envisaged by the protocol of 1993.

Also important will be the willingness of business to maintain and extend the practice of compromise and cooperation between both sides at the micro-economic level. In the presence of a hostile, or at any rate unfavourable government, it becomes vital for the trade unions to keep open any opportunities for dialogue and agreement with employers and managers. It goes without saying that the new framework does not auto-matically favour such efforts, indeed it encourages different responses from more conservative and more open employers.

The last issue that needs to be highlighted is the question of trade union unity. This too is connected to political factors. If unity was hardly in evidence even after the 'Hot Autumn' of 1969, this was never purely due to ideological differences. Differences in the strategies and interests of the organisations were crucial. But in 1992–94 the objective of unity regained momentum among the trade union leaders. Above all the sec-retary of the CISL, D'Antoni, insisted that this long sought-after goal was now ripe and attainable. At root, there was a conviction that the relaunching of confederate unionism had to pass through an operation of restyling capable of supplying the trade unions with a new image as well as a new role. Besides, a more united and authoritative trade union could count for a lot more in a political system which was no longer dominated by the classical mass parties (to which only the PDS is close to an ideal).

In the second half of 1994 'defensive' arguments were added to support pro-unity theories. There was anxiety over the accession of the Right to government because it could limit the privileges of the trade unions. A referendum was already in the pipe-line that proposed preventing the collection and automatic payment by employers of the quota paid by the members (the check-off system). The financial difficulties of the CGIL, and above all of UIL, also acted as an incentive to the reorganisation of the organisational apparatuses of the unions, which were enormous, and also to the reduction of costs, which were increasing because of the declining number of unionised public employees. Therefore the advan-tages of the unitary approach seemed to be increasing in a situation marked by new political and organisational difficulties. The desire to present the government with a strong trade union interlocutor also accelerated the unifying process.

In the event, and contrary to widespread expectations, the Berlusconi government did not produce a period of stability. Despite the brevity of its existence however, it had important consequences for the unions. First, the assumption of office, for the first time since 1945, of a government that was not sympathetic to organised trade unionism (even if the right-wing government was not avowedly anti-union) rendered relations between the confederations easier, and further accelerated the drive towards unity. This was also helped by the fact that the government granted recognition (for the first time) to the autonomous unions and attempted to weaken the standing of the confederations. Second, the protocol of 23 July 1993 was respected only formally. The government met with union representatives but tried to adopt policies – on the 1995 Finance Bill and pensions – that contrasted with union concerns. This however was a sign of its arrogance and incompetence because CGIL, CSIL and UIL found themselves united as they had not been for a decade – and emerged at the head of a wide social coalition that was opposed to the economic measures of the government. The result was a sort of boomerang effect since the confederate unions were able to regain a degree of influence over public opinion that they had not exercised for years. The autumn of 1994 witnessed a massive and unexpected upsurge of collective mobilisations, culminating in a national demonstration in mid-November that saw over one and a half million people parade through Rome. This was judged by some to have been the largest single demonstration of the post-war period.

There were several signs that the trade union movement was experiencing a phase of surprising vitality. In addition to successfully mobilising the social protest and articulating the concerns of a significant part of waged labour, the three confederations triumphed in RSU elections held up to February 1995. In a turn-out of above 70 per cent, they won a virtual monopoly of representation, scoring over 95 per cent of votes cast. Furthermore, the 1993 protocol, while it did not function as desired in its political and programmatic aspects, worked well in industrial relations. Due to more positive relations between the two sides of industry than at any time since 1947, excellent national agreements were reached in the chemical and engineering sectors. The problems that for so long had afflicted confederate unionism could not be said to have been overcome, and others were emerging on the horizon (such as the referendum on the check-off system). Although, in the event, the confederations were unsuccessful in their attempt to prevent abrogation of this, it seemed likely that the 'trade union parabola' had moved off the bottom, and was beginning once more to rise.

REFERENCES

Accornero, A. (1985) 'La terziarizzazione del conflitto e i suoi effetti', in G. P. Cella and M. Regini (eds) *Il conflitto industriale in Italia*, Bologna: Il Mulino.
—— (1992) *La parabola del sindacato*, Bologna: Il Mulino.
Amato, G. and Cafagna, L. (1982) *Duello a sinistra*, Bologna: Il Mulino.
Baglioni, G. (1986) *Il sindacato nel capitalismo che cambia*, Bari: Laterza.
Baglioni, G. and Miliani, R. (1992) *La contrattazione nelle aziende industriali italiane*, Milano: Franco Angeli.
Baldissera, R. (1988) *La svolta dei quarantamila*, Milano: Comunità.
Mortillaro, F. (1984) *Sindacati e noi*, Milano: Edizioni del Sole 24 Ore.
Regalia, I. (1984) *Eletti e abbandonati*, Bologna: Il Mulino.
Regini, M. (1985) 'Sindacato e sistema politico 1978–85', in M. Carrieri and F. Perulli (eds), *Il teorema sindacale*, Bologna: Il Mulino.
Regini, M. and Sabel, C. (1989) *Strategie di riaggiustamento industriale*, Bologna: Il Mulino.

Part VI
Conclusion

20 Italian political reform in comparative perspective

David Hine

This chapter considers the implications of the events of the early 1990s for reform of Italy's political institutions. It analyses the difficulties likely to be encountered in changing the relationship between voters, representatives, and governments. By comparing the Italian case with fundamental reform in other European states – most notably France – it asks whether the sequence of events culminating in the 1994 election can rework that relationship. It argues that the changes brought about during the life of the 1992–94 Parliament were unplanned, and uncontrolled. They were the result of immediate and often emotional responses to dramatic events, and they suggest that despite fundamental electoral reform, despite the resulting changes in the party system in the 1994 general election, and despite widespread assumptions that recent events constitute the watershed between the 'First' and the 'Second' Republics, the true extent and nature of political and institutional reform are still uncertain.

THE SPECIFIC AND THE GENERAL: ITALY'S CRISIS IN THE WIDER EUROPEAN CONTEXT

The crisis as a problem of distributional conflict

At first sight Italy's political crisis appears to be a specifically national one. Effective political leadership of the type said to have been lacking in Italy has also seemed in short supply in some other European states in the early 1990s, but the problems faced by governments in France, Germany, Britain, or Spain have not generated the same systemic crisis as in Italy. Political difficulties have to date modified the party systems of these countries only at the edges. Electoral volatility, though high, has not reached the recent Italian levels. There has been no collapse in the authority and prestige of an entire ruling class. Emergency governments of technicians governing, as in the case of the Amato and Ciampi governments, against Parliament as much as through it, have not been necessary. Nowhere else has an entrepreneur gone into the business of politics selling himself as a national saviour in the style of Silvio Berlusconi. And, developments in France and Spain notwithstanding, the linkage between business, politics, and the administrative system has not been exposed as quite so systematically corrupt elsewhere as it has in Italy.

Nevertheless, the underlying causes of the multi-dimensional crisis the political system faces have parallels elsewhere in Europe, and it is important to note them because they have a bearing on what problems need to be overcome to change the basis of political aggregation in the contemporary Italian party system. Just as, in the mid-1970s, the wider European political and economic problems that followed the first oil shock and the great increase in labour militancy were most profoundly felt in Italy, so in the 1990s Italy's problems are at least in part the outcome of wider difficulties. In both periods, the crises have provoked sharp distributional conflict. In the 1990s that conflict has been less overt and confrontational, because it has been centred more on budgetary politics and public expenditure than on the labour market – the overall slackness of which has largely tamed the former power of the union movement. This is especially so in a European Union of liberalised capital flows, managed exchange rates, and fixed convergence targets, where the scope for variations in overall budgetary policy between different governments is being progressively reduced. Distributional conflict is now diffused across a range of competing claims, and prevents parties developing distinct and clearly differentiated party programmes. All parties have to preach the same message of budgetary restraint, and differences over the detailed content of budgetary formulae are matters of nuance rather than fundamental dispute.

Inevitably, therefore, and particularly in a period of extended recession, European governments have difficulty in retaining popular support. But equally electorates are sceptical about putting their trust in alternatives offered by mainstream political oppositions when they suspect that their policies will prove little different from existing ones. Voters become less strongly identified with their traditional parties, more instrumental in attitude, and more willing to turn to various exotic alternatives, or to stop voting altogether. European democracies in the 1990s are passing through a phase of convergence in public policy solutions between major parties – rather as, in the 1950s, there was convergence, at least in northern Europe, on the Keynesian full-employment approach to the management of the mixed economy and the welfare state. At that time the absence of major differences between competing parties did not lead to serious problems of political management. Voters were locked into stable partisan attachments that reflected well-rooted social cleavages, and were backed up by strong party organisations. High growth and low inflationary pressures left a healthy surplus for budgetary redistribution. In the 1990s, in contrast, voters' partisan identities, and parties as organisations, are both weaker, while growth rates are lower, and, with deficit-spending more costly, and taxpayer resistance higher, budgetary pressures are much greater.

The Italian political crisis of the 1990s has some of its roots in these wider European developments. Budgetary matters lay at the heart of most of the more intractable political problems throughout the 1980s. Constrained by the damage that would have been done to their own socially diffuse bases of electoral support, the ruling parties were unable to introduce much needed reform, especially to the public sector, despite recognising its necessity, and despite the fact that much of the reform programme, however painful in the short term, would have eventually contributed to an easing of longer-term budgetary pressures.

At the end of the decade the distributional conflict at the heart of the politics of Italian public expenditure grew even harder to manage, for it became entangled in the increasingly important territorial dimension of political life. Southern voters had always proved fickle supporters of the ruling parties, but now Northerners started to act in the same way. The politics of territorial self-righteousness (Northerners believing they subsidised a 'parasitic' South) became a surrogate for the politics of public-sector reform. For significant numbers of Northerners, the argument that the state was inefficient, over-extended, and corrosive of market-based efficiency because it existed to redistribute resources from the productive North to the dependent South, became a beguilingly simple alternative to serious analysis.

The existence of a serious territorial imbalance has therefore exacerbated the distributional problem. The catch-all, centre-oriented nature of the governing parties, once a source of political strength, eventually became a source of weakness when a backlog of difficult distributional decisions needed to be faced. With an accumulated stock of public debt to service that exceeded 100 per cent of GDP by the start of the 1990s, with long-established patterns of inter-territorial transfer under attack, with firmly entrenched public-sector clienteles to sustain, and with the pressures of a more integrated European economy to face, the Italian government was destined to face trouble however good the performance of the private sector. Economists and some far-sighted politicians had already foreseen this crisis looming in the late 1980s, when Italy committed itself to eventual narrow-band membership of the ERM, and to the renunciation of the use of exchange rates as an instrument of macro-economic management. Such moves tightened the budgetary pressures on government enormously, and restricted its room for manoeuvre. When parties in power are overloaded by incompatible demands, few of which they can satisfy properly, and when other more stable bases of political aggregation are eroded, problems of government cohesion and effectiveness are certain to increase.

The crisis as an institutional problem

The Italian political crisis is not just a problem of distributional conflict within a tight budgetary straitjacket however. By the early 1990s, it had become an institutional as well as a policy crisis, because most observers had come to the conclusion that greater selectivity and the taking of difficult decisions could not be achieved under the old rules of political aggregation. This – more than the intensity of the distributional conflict per se – was what distinguished the Italian political crisis from its less serious equivalents elsewhere. Italians lost confidence in the capacity of the Italian state and Italian parties to cope with a set of policy problems that face all European governments. Institutional reform came to be seen, far more than elsewhere in Europe, as an essential *precursor* to policy reform. Having been debated inconclusively by party leaders for over a decade, it became a major political issue, and the two great referendums of 1991 (abolition of the preference vote in the Chamber elections) and 1993 (restriction of PR for Senate) took it out of the hands of party leaders and placed it with the electorate. In the process, however, the debate got out of control. There was no consensus on what new institutional structure should replace the old and discredited one. There was not even a majority and a minority view. Most attitudes focused on what was wrong with the old system, but there was little public understanding of, let alone agreement on, how the system was to be reformed.

Probably the major reason why public opinion remained in such a raw state was that just as the institutional reform debate was intensifying, political life was swamped by the exposure of political corruption on an unprecedented scale. Corruption emerged not in the modest quantities that might be expected to force the governing parties to reform themselves, but in massive quantities that not only destroyed voters' confidence that the existing party order was reformable at all, and made it impossible for the parties to make progress on a new institutional consensus.

This was so even though 1992 and 1993 were years of considerable innovation both in public policy and institutional reform. More progress was made towards budgetary rationalisation, administrative reorganisation, and electoral reform than for many years. The government managed to run a *primary* (i.e. net-of-interest) budget *surplus* – a comparatively good performance in European terms. That the *gross* deficit was inevitably pushed up to around 10 per cent of GDP was a reflection of past budgetary profligacy, and of an accumulated stock of public debt running back to the late 1970s, rather than of recent or current mismanagement. Likewise, important changes were introduced to the electoral system and to the structure of local government. However the circumstances under which these achievements occurred were not conducive to the long-term goal of stable and cohesive government. Changes were introduced by ephemeral reform movements, and able but essentially technocratic governments whose authority rested on uncertain psychological foundations. Rarely did Parliament itself take the lead. The extensive exposure of corruption which dominated political life in the 1992 Parliament thus focused attention squarely on the accumulated failures of the past rather than the modest possibilities of reform in the present. And, as in the debate on institutional reform, it fundamentally divided parties and coalitions, making the working out of a new institutional consensus much more difficult.

The Italian political crisis therefore combines various strands. It is a crisis over distributional demands (though by no means unbargainable ones), over the way the party system aggregates demands, over the probity of political leadership, and over the functioning of institutions. It looks like a *systemic* crisis, so widely has it spread. Yet it is difficult to argue – the reemergence of neo-fascism notwithstanding – that it presages the imminent collapse of liberal democracy. There is rather little fundamental disagreement on key features of the socio-economic system, and basic standards of material well-being and social welfare continue to be met quite well by European standards. The crisis does not therefore look like a rejection of liberal democracy but rather a search for more effective liberal-democratic government, and especially for a more stable relationship between government and parliamentary majority.

This is important because it makes the current crisis rather different from most other liberal democratic 'regenerations' in post-war Europe. Despite the potential threat posed by the crisis of public morality, liberal democracy in Italy does not have to be *consolidated* – in conditions of severe material shortage – in the way that was necessary in early post-war Germany or Italy, or after the collapse of authoritarianism in Mediterranean democracies in the 1970s, or after the collapse of Communism in central Europe in the late 1980s. The problems of reestablishing democratic institutions, rooting democratic values, and seeing-off disgruntled supporters of the old regime, are far less serious in contemporary Italy – if they can be said to exist at all.

As we shall see below, the best parallel is none of the above cases, but rather France in the transition from the Fourth to the Fifth Republics. This is so not because the eventual outcome is necessarily likely to be the same as in France (if anything, the contrary), but because the French example is the only other recent major case of the reform and modification, as opposed to the introduction or reestablishment, of liberal democracy. In the French case, as in the Italian one, the problem was to achieve the transition from one, unsatisfactory, form of liberal democracy, to a more effective and coherent one. But in some respects reforming liberal democracy is a harder task than building it from scratch, since the shocks and discontinuities likely to provoke it are less profound. Today, Italy does not stand defeated, occupied, or – corruption notwithstanding – disgraced by its recent past. Its economy has not collapsed. To under-

stand the more subtle psychological adjustment required, we need to look
in more detail at the problem of political aggregation Italy faces.

REPRESENTATION, AGGREGATION, AND PARTY REALIGNMENT

The root of the problem lies, as we have suggested, with inadequacies in
the mechanism which links voters, through elections, to representatives
in Parliament (and lower elected bodies), and hence to the government
and policy output. In a democracy, voters need to feel that the election
of representatives is meaningful in that the choices offered to them correspond to clear and understandable differences in policy outcomes. Given
the range of policy combinations available to governments in modern
democracies – and the attendant combinations of winners and losers from
public policy – that goal might seem unattainable. However the key
element is clarity not completeness. No democracy can offer more than
a few highly simplified and broadly dichotomous choices: but it should
be able to provide those few, and they should not be so sharp in their
contrasting consequences as to make it impossible for those who normally
opt for one set of outcomes ever to contemplate opting for a different
set.

Italy seems not to have done this adequately. The belief held by voters
that collectively they can affect the policy choices of those who govern
them, and the efficiency and probity with which government is conducted,
appears to be lacking. To sustain such a belief, the party system needs a
thorough overhaul – generating alignments that are simpler, more stable
and more enduring. Coalitions need to be based on more than electoral
convenience. Parties need mechanisms for formulating and articulating
policy, linking with the electorate and with interest groups, selecting
candidates for office, and most importantly of all in the Italian context,
maintaining internal discipline to ensure that policy, once established, is
implemented. Effective reform also requires that voters, interest groups,
and elected party representatives all see the act of electing a party or
coalition into office as choosing a clear-cut programme, and implementing
it over the life of a Parliament, rather than choosing representatives
whose task is to bargain out alliances and individual decisions on a case-
by-case basis.

To reach this virtuous state, the proposals which have been advanced
to date have focused on electoral reform, coalition reform, and the identification of voters with coalitions and parties that stand for new institutional arrangements. In the following sub-headings we consider how far
recent developments under each heading have advanced the cause of
party system reform.

Electoral reform

The commonest prescription for overhauling the party system has for many years been to reform the electoral system. The argument has been a simple one: a less complex and less proportional system will reduce the number of parties – perhaps right down to a broad dichotomous choice – or at least aggregate party alliances into clear programmatic alternatives. At first sight this was what was achieved by the electoral reforms of the years 1991–93. The 1994 election did help simplify the party system, by dividing it into three broadly competing groups of parties. More importantly, it produced a 'winner', and, because that winner consisted of parties which had not previously been in power, it produced the 'alternation' so long unattainable. However, while a form of alternation had occurred, subsequent events suggested that the realignment into two competing blocs might need further development to be effective. The 1994 outcome – a three-party coalition, lacking a majority in one chamber of the legislature – was certainly not, as it stood, a *sufficient* rationalisation of the party system, as the brief and tortured history of Berlusconi's first (and at the time of writing in early 1995, only) government demonstrated. Although parties aggregated themselves into blocs, the party system as a whole remained quite fragmented, with 10–12 parties present in Parliament.

Furthermore, it began to look rather doubtful, in the light of the 1994 outcome, whether additional reform, to remove the 25 per cent of the seats allocated by proportional representation in each House of Parliament, would produce greater reduction in the numbers of parties, and greater cohesion in the governing coalition. In the 1994 election, in the simple-plurality, single-member constituencies which were supposed to be the source of party system simplification, parties actually cooperated through stand-down agreements to *counteract* the rationalising effects the mechanism had been intended to bring. As a result, the formation of pre-electoral pacts contributed to the preservation of multi-partyism. It was not the lack of a majoritarian electoral system in 25 per cent of the seats in each chamber that led to inter-party cooperation and stand-down agreements. On the contrary, it was the absence of any party large enough to be sure of winning single-member seats unaided that did so. Parties on both sides of the main political divide feared that without stand-down agreements with selected allies, they would lose out to opponents that had established such agreements more effectively.

To overcome this problem in the future parties need to emerge on one or both sides of the political spectrum that are confident that they can afford to run candidates in single-member seats without allies. The abolition of the quarter of the seats in each house allocated on the basis of proportional representation seems a secondary matter, though admittedly in 1994 it would have significantly reduced the size of the centrist Catholic rump of the old DC.[1] With hindsight, the only parties which had a level of popular support great enough to risk going it alone were Forza Italia and the PDS. Had they done so, or should they do so in future, electoral consolidation might take place incrementally, with voters in the same general area of the political spectrum concluding that the only way to defeat the opposition in the absence of stand-down agreements is to focus their support on a single party. Getting this process going is a risky business however, and might only work if there really is a natural affinity between voters right across a particular wing of the spectrum. It looks unlikely to occur on the Left, given the gap between voters for Rifondazione Comunista, the PDS, and the progressive lay and religious Left. Whether it is any more likely in the Centre and on the Right, especially among the main parties is uncertain. Voters for the Lega Nord and the Partito Popolare on one side, and Alleanza Nazionale on the other, seem unlikely to have enough natural affinity to make one the eventual destination of the other's voters. Forza Italia might be a plausible destination for voters from all these parties, but given how territorially concentrated support for these parties is, even Forza Italia would need to be very confident of its national lead before it could contemplate taking them on directly in an election, rather than contracting stand-down agreements.

As for other types of electoral reform, the most likely continues to be the second ballot. This was supported by Forza Italia in its early months of existence – though it later seemed to veer towards 'first-past-the-post' – and it is firmly supported by the two main parties of the old system – the PDS and the PPI. It should have significant aggregative effects, but as long as the strength of parties is distributed unevenly across the country, it is likely to result in coalitions rather than single-party rule. If this is correct, the key question to ask is what effect the second ballot would have on the cohesion of such coalitions in office. Do first- or second-round stand-down agreements force parties into a greater obligation to work out tight programmes committing them, in voters' eyes, to holding together in government thereafter, than the stand-down agreements negotiated, as in 1994, under 'first-past-the-post' rules? On the face of it, there is no particular reason to think so.

Coalition reform

If the party system proves resistant to further simplification, then the key issue becomes coalition cohesion, rather than the prospect of single-party government. We need to examine the sequence of events culminating in the 1994 general election for evidence that it has brought, or will bring, coalitions that hang together better than those of the past. Certainly, there are grounds for thinking it may do. The party system appears to have moved towards a degree of *bipolarity*. The existence of two apparently clear-cut blocs makes government from the Centre much less likely.

In the past, governing coalitions lacked cohesion because they governed from the Centre, their component parties were pulled in opposite directions by competition from oppositions on Left and Right, and yet as governing centre-oriented parties they could never be replaced. The penalties of disarray were never sufficient to force them into a more coherent alliance.

However, there seem to be two conditions necessary before the new bipolar system produces more coherent coalitions. The first is that bipolarity forces competing coalitions to concentrate their efforts on winning voters in the centre of the spectrum, and that requires a uni-dimensional spectrum, and a relatively narrow one. If one party within the coalition appeals to voters on some other ground than a broad, Left–Right distributional one, or if one party benefits electorally from taking up a position well out to one end of the spectrum, the coalition may be no more cohesive than a centre-located one. The second condition is that *alternation* remains a viable possibility. Unless there is an opposition ready to come to power, the incentives to govern effectively and maintain a high degree of internal coalition cohesion are, as all critics of the First Republic lamented, drastically curtailed.

It remains unclear whether either of these two conditions will be fulfilled. The Lega Nord and Alleanza Nazionale seem to appeal to voters on bases that refute the logic of centre-directed competition along a narrow uni-dimensional spectrum, as suggested by our first condition. Equally, as regards the second, both the extreme fragility and diversity of the progressive coalition assembled around the PDS in the 1994 general election, and its disappointingly poor performance, might suggest that alternation between Left and Right in Italy remains as far away as ever. The irony of the alternation Italy finally established was that it was between an old centre-right elite and a new apparently more right-wing one, but that in sweeping away the former it left the more radical political alternative on the Left as far from power as ever.

This might seem too schematic and pessimistic a conclusion. The very fact that one elite has been swept away because of its style of government may be a sufficient incentive for the new elite to govern in a different manner. Despite coming from an area of the electoral spectrum overlapping with its predecessor, the new coalition was at least in principle committed to reforming the state, ending corruption, and injecting a more decisive and cohesive style into government. But almost from the outset, it was clear that for many observers these qualities of 'newness' needed closer scrutiny than they had received in a confused election campaign. The coalition contained numerous 'recycled' leaders from the old parties, not to mention a Prime Minister whose past business fortunes were intimately linked with the old regime. Moreover in its first real test – the 1995 budget cycle – the coalition faced formidable difficulties in aggregating a wide range of demands from its supporters. Its response closely resembled that of most previous governments, and it was a combination of budgetary failure (supplementary measures were needed even before the 1995 budget came into operation) and the smell of corruption, that allowed Berlusconi's chief rival to bring him down after only eight months in office. In short, claims merely to represent the 'New' against the 'Old' may not be a sufficient basis on which to appeal to voters dissatisfied with the old regime, and many voters who voted for the 'New' out of distaste for the 'Old' may subsequently have discovered – or may discover in future – that had they examined more closely the policy proposals put forward by the 'New', they would have seen that their natural electoral home lay elsewhere. This problem was, and remains, evident on several fronts, but is probably clearest on the issue of territorial politics. The territorial split between North and South ran right through Berlusconi's coalition, dividing voters every bit as sharply as did the split between the New and the Old. The implication was that to have northern and southern interests represented directly in government by *territorially differentiated* parties might prove no easier to manage than aggregating them in advance through nationwide parties.

Forging a new institutional blueprint

Arguably contradictions in a coalition of the new Italian Right would not matter if the electoral coalition could be held together by something other – perhaps 'higher' – than sectoral or territorial self-interest. If the desire for a new beginning is deeply rooted in Italian voters, and if they can be persuaded to accept sacrifices in the interests of a political system which in the long run will work much more effectively, then short-term policy dilemmas can be coped with.

As we have already observed however, while there is probably a genuine aspiration on the part of voters for a new institutional blueprint, it is vague and imprecise, and it is difficult to turn it into a lasting source of political loyalty running across, rather than congruent with, the immediate interests of competing groups of voters. It probably requires something equivalent to a 'party of national renewal' which elsewhere has occasionally, but rather rarely, emerged out of a fundamental reshaping of national political life. (Kemal Atatürk's Republican People's Party, the Mexican Institutional Revolutionary Party, or the French Gaullist Party are possible examples.) However, bringing about a process of psychological identification with a new party based on this quality seems to require a quite fundamental break with the past. The events of the last few years in Italy – dramatic as they have sometimes been – hardly seem to constitute this type of heroic renewal.

The task facing the new Italian Right in this connection is considerable. To use the aspiration for a new institutional blueprint to consolidate its electoral base, it has first to devise such a blueprint, and second to get it endorsed by an electoral majority in a way that would lock its identity, in voters' minds, with the new style of government such a blueprint produced. On this matter the comparison with recent French experience in the transition from the Fourth to the Fifth Republic is especially instructive. In France what proved vital to the success of party system realignment was that the reformers, the Gaullists, had a clear-cut institutional project which was sufficiently distinct in its fundamental features from what had gone before to be readily understandable to voters. They also had an effective strategy for implementing this project in the shape of opportunities to put it to voters for a clear endorsement (in the 1958 referendum, and again in 1962). Once the reform was understood, it realigned the party system *even before* the first direct Presidential election was held. Voters opted for a system in which a parliamentary majority accepted that it had been elected to support a strong executive. They made this clear by their support for Gaullist proposals in the 1962 referendum on direct election, and for Gaullist and allied candidates in the ensuing general election.

One major problem in Italy preventing the new Right from assembling a similar majority on the constitutional front is that there is no procedure equivalent to the French referendum. The Italian referendum is an abrogative one which has to be targeted at a specific item of legislation. It cannot propose new law, and cannot touch the constitution or constitutional law, either to delete items from it, or to amend it.[2] More seriously still, on the political front, there is little agreement on the sort of constitutional blueprint which might form the basis of a referendum.

This is particularly evident in connection with a move towards a more personalised form of government, and perhaps to the direct election of the chief executive. A reform of this type was much discussed in the 1980s, and was revived in the 1992 Parliament first by Mario Segni's campaign for the direct election of the Prime Minister, and second by the personality and leadership of Silvio Berlusconi in the 1994 general election. The parallel with the French case has always loomed large. In France realignment and the injection of discipline and cohesion on both sides of the main political divide was greatly assisted by the direct election of the President of the Republic. The personal leadership generated by a directly elected head of the executive transformed the institutional balance between legislature and executive, and under normal circumstances, made political reality of the head of state's ultimate constitutional weapon of the dissolution of Parliament.

The attention paid to personalised leadership had by 1993 already prompted an experiment along these lines in Italy at local government level in the larger cities, via the introduction of the direct election of the mayor. The procedure automatically guarantees the mayor a majority for parties supporting him, and if the coalition collapses, there are fresh elections. To date, however, the implications for coalition cohesion and electoral accountability at *national* level are unclear. The ultimate test of the effectiveness of the mechanism of direct election is not just survival in office, which for a mayor at local level may be a more simple matter than for a Prime Minister. It is also the ability to carry out a programme – the absence of which will be far more easily exposed at national level than locally. It is precisely because survival in office is not enough that the head of the executive must, in the case of policy deadlock, be able to use the threat of dissolution to force his will on a divided party or coalition. That capacity was at issue in the bitter argument between Berlusconi and President Scalfaro over whether the fall of the Berlusconi government in December 1994 should entail the automatic dissolution of the 1994 Parliament.

The question of direct election has been much debated in Italy, but there is uncertainty even over which office – President of the Republic or Prime Minister – should be elected. In the early years of the institutional debate, attention focused on the former. More recently, especially in Mario Segni's campaign for institutional and electoral reform, the focus has been the direct election of the Prime Minister. At first sight, such a move might seem an anomaly in a parliamentary system, and less radical than a directly elected Presidency. It could nevertheless be a bolder move if it addressed the principal weakness of the plan for a directly elected Presidency – namely that in Italian conditions the Presidency of the Republic might be won by an 'above-party' or a minor-party figure, lacking a parliamentary majority, and therefore enjoying little institutional leverage vis-à-vis Parliament, and little chance of creating a 'Presidential majority'.

In contrast, the direct election of the Prime Minister – if accompanied by rules allowing him to seek an automatic dissolution if he loses his majority – would provide a potentially very strong form of executive leadership, as long as voters chose to line up behind the Prime Minister in the event of a conflict with Parliament. On the other hand, if they did not support him, Italy would be saddled with an inflexible and possibly brittle institutional arrangement. It would not easily permit changes of leadership reflecting political adjustments inside a coalition. Moreover, if the state of coalition politics was complex and confused, it might be difficult for voters to identify exactly who was responsible for the policy deadlock which generated the dissolution of Parliament. In this case, the threat of dissolution might be insufficient to break the deadlock.

It is uncertainty of this type which has prevented any consensus emerging on the desirability of the direct election of an executive Prime Minister, or President of the Republic. Two related worries have always counselled caution. The first is that the Italian political class lacks political leaders with the stature to create a strong and enduring personal support base that would be a convincing weapon against a divided majority. The second – deployed against the direct election of the presidency – is that for this very reason, and also because of the weak institutionalisation and ambiguity surrounding many constitutional norms and values, Italy needs a constitutional umpire above party politics. In short, if introduced before a sufficiently cohesive majority existed, or before any obvious candidate for party or coalition leadership emerged, direct election might be counter-productive.

It is unclear whether the events of recent years have resolved these uncertainties – bringing leaders of greater stature, and improving the underlying state of party and coalition cohesion which might make a directly elected executive less of a constitutional gamble. Mario Segni at one stage seemed to be the sort of leader who, both through his personal popularity and the force of his ideas for reform, might provide a focus for such changes; but the party basis of his campaign was never clear to voters. Berlusconi's success (and its obverse – the Left's lack of a credible Prime Ministerial candidate) suggested that voters were attracted to stronger personal leadership. Certainly he had a more solid party basis from which to consolidate his leadership than Segni. However, in office his ideas for institutional reform were unclear, and the issue of reform had a fairly low initial priority. At times Berlusconi seems to have favoured a directly elected executive – recently of the Prime-Ministerial variety. At other times he appears to have believed that if Forza Italia could domi-nate its two coalition partners (a strong condition), then he himself could exercise effective personal leadership under a normal form of parliamen-tary government, by mechanisms which are more similar to those of a British Prime Minister than a French President of the Republic.

CONCLUSION

Beyond decisions about the future of formal institutional arrangements, there are several other issues surrounding the future exercise of political power in informal terms which it has not been possible to discuss here in detail, but which are quite fundamental to the nature of any new regime that establishes itself. The most important is to define the bound-ary between political parties and the state. The First Republic was a state colonised by political parties – the machinery of which was never just considered the neutral, quasi-technical, instrument of a government. It was a series of territories to be occupied – the judiciary, the public media, the (public-domain) financial sector, state enterprises, the range of public services – and a series of potentially hostile counter-powers to be con-trolled and tamed. In this sense political power was seen as highly divis-ible, and the more that a governing coalition attempted to occupy such territories, the more it was itself susceptible to internal divisions. Even-tually, the fragmentation of coalition power became so great that the boundary between government and opposition itself became blurred, and the quasi-consociational practices characteristic of the last two decades of the First Republic became entrenched.

The attitude of the new governing elite to these questions remains ambiguous. In its early months in office, it appeared to be firmly against any form of broad inter-party power-sharing arrangements, and to the chagrin of the older parties declined even to share out 'institutional' powers within Parliament on the cross-party lines of the past. However, its suspicion of those who occupy the state it inherited was so deeply engrained that there was a serious risk, before it was side-tracked by the complexities of budgetary politics, and collapsed, that it would itself become embroiled in the practices of placemanship and occupation it had hitherto criticised so heavily. Indeed, its apparent attempts in the early months of office to control senior appointments not just in RAI-TV and IRI, but also even in the hitherto untouchable Bank of Italy, and its unashamed comments on the need to control the judiciary, suggest a government every bit as alert to the need to occupy power as its predecessors.

All these questions are important to the fundamental theme of government cohesion and discipline that has been the concern of this chapter. A government – especially a coalition government – that embroils itself in battles to occupy the extensive range of public institutions and activities in Italy may end up spending more time arguing about sharing out state power than rolling it back.

There are, therefore, habits of mind as well as institutional rules which need revision before the real nature of the Second Republic emerges. These are often deeply engrained, and not always well understood, and could do much to deflect the impetus for reform. None of this is to deny the extent of the change which has already been wrought by the last five years, and especially by the last two. Despite the rapid collapse of his first government, there is no doubt that Berlusconi represented something new in Italian politics, and that, as other chapters in this volume argue, his capacity for effective political communication, and his shrewd understanding and exploitation of popular values, gave him formidable advantages. Certainly, the realignment of the Right did not, as of early 1995, seem to have come to a complete halt even with Bossi's dramatic defection from the coalition. But the ability of the new Right to survive in office in the future, and even to become a new hegemonic political elite to replace Christian Democracy, did not necessarily mean that its style of government, its cohesion and even its freedom from corruption, were guaranteed to be different from what had gone before.

NOTES

1 The paradox of the 1994 general election was that smaller parties obtained representation in Parliament not because of the allocation of seats to them

through the proportional mechanism, because most did not overcome the 4 per cent hurdle for qualification for the PR-based distribution of seats in the Chamber, let alone the higher hurdle in the Senate. In fact only six parties overcame this hurdle, and four of these won most of their seats in single-seat contests. The small parties won seats because they participated in stand-down alliances. Only the centre parties, the PPI and Segni's Patto were significant beneficiaries from the PR system.

2 It should be noted, however, that although a *consultative* referendum is not provided for in the constitution, a piece of ordinary legislation, similar in type to that which allowed a consultative referendum on a European Community issue in 1989, could be passed by Parliament without any prior change to the constitution, and would allow voters to express themselves informally on proposed constitutional changes, though this would not obviate the need for the full constitutional procedure for constitutional amendment to be followed. Once such an opinion had been expressed – assuming it amounted to unequivocal support for change – it would be difficult for Parliament to block enabling legislation leading to constitutional amendment.

Such a course of action would have significant parallels with the means by which Charles de Gaulle overcame opposition to the constitutional change leading to the direct election of the President of the Republic in France in 1962. A contested constitutional change, opposed by the National Assembly, was put to voters by a dubious constitutional procedure, after which, given the massive popular support the change enjoyed, it was impossible for the Assembly to block the reform. (The Assembly was in any case dissolved, and this led to the return of a pro-reform majority.)

However, the difficulties of passing legislation to allow a consultative referendum in a multi-party coalition might prove considerable. The greatest would be that different parties might demand the presentation of different proposals. This might necessitate putting a range of packages to voters, including some from the opposition. In such circumstances, the impact of a consultative referendum could be watered down drastically if the outcome was that a series of minorities lined up behind different proposals, with none obtaining majority backing. Ensuring that such a consultative procedure was restricted to a plebiscite on a single proposal – which is vital to the psychological identification of voters with a new regime – could therefore prove very difficult.

Index

Page references in bold denote major section/chapter devoted to subject; t stands for table; n stands for note.